THE
NATIONAL INCOME AND ITS PURCHASING POWER

By

WILLFORD ISBELL KING

OF THE STAFF OF THE

NATIONAL BUREAU OF ECONOMIC RESEARCH

INCORPORATED

Assisted by

LILLIAN EPSTEIN

NEW YORK

NATIONAL BUREAU OF ECONOMIC

RESEARCH, Inc.

1930

National Bureau of Economic Research, Inc.

Incorporated under the Membership Corporation Laws of the State of New York, January 29, 1920

ITS ORGANIZATION AND PURPOSES

THE National Bureau of Economic Research was organized in 1920 i
response to a growing demand for exact and impartial determinatio
of facts bearing on economic, social, and industrial problems.

It seeks not only to find facts and make them known, but to determir
them in such manner and under such supervision as to make its findings carr
conviction to Liberal and Conservative alike.

Entire control of the Bureau is vested in a Board of Directors, represen
ing universities, learned and scientific societies, financial, industrial, agricu
tural, commercial, labor, and technical organizations.

Rigid provisions in the Charter and By-Laws guard the Bureau fro
becoming a source of profit to its members, directors, or officers and fro
becoming an agency for propaganda. No report of the Research Staff ma
be published without the approval of the Directors, and any Director wh
dissents from any finding approved by a majority of the Board may hav
such dissent published with the majority report.

The members of the Board of Directors are as follows:

National Bureau of Economic Research, Inc.

Publications in the order of their issue

INCOME IN THE UNITED STATES
By Wesley C. Mitchell, Willford I. King, Frederick R. Macaulay and Oswald W. Knauth

Volume I. A summary of an Investigation of the Amount and Distribution of Income in the United States, 1909-1919. 152 pages, (Fifth printing) $1.58.

Volume II. A report giving in full the methods and estimates on which the results shown in Volume I are based. 440 pages, (Second printing) $5.15.

DISTRIBUTION OF INCOME BY STATES IN 1919
By Oswald W. Knauth

The share of each state in the national income. 32 pages.(Out of print.)

BUSINESS CYCLES AND UNEMPLOYMENT
By the staff of the Bureau with 16 collaborators.

Results of an investigation made for the President's Conference on Unemployment. 405 pages, $4.10.

EMPLOYMENT, HOURS, AND EARNINGS
IN PROSPERITY AND DEPRESSION
By Willford I. King

Gives details of investigation summarized in *Business Cycles and Unemployment* to which it is a companion volume. 147 pages. (Out of print.)

THE GROWTH OF AMERICAN TRADE UNIONS, 1880-1923
By Leo Wolman

Membership year by year; fluctuations with business cycles; women in trade unions; working population. 170 pages. $3.

INCOME IN THE VARIOUS STATES
By Maurice Leven and Willford I. King

Gives total and per capita inome for each state, in 1919, 1920 and 1921 with special tables showing the income of farmers, wage earners, and persons of large means. 306 pages, $5.

BUSINESS ANNALS
By Willard I. Thorp and Wesley C. Mitchell

A descriptive summary of business condititions in United States, England, and 15 other countries, for periods of 36 to 136 years. 384 pages. (Second printing). $4.

MIGRATION AND BUSINESS CYCLES
By Harry Jerome

A statistical study of the shortage and surplus of labor in the United States in relation to immigration and emigration. 256 pages, $3.50.

BUSINESS CYCLES: THE PROBLEM AND ITS SETTING
By Wesley C. Mitchell

Here Dr. Mitchell explains the numerous processes involved in business cycles; shows how our present economic organization was evolved; describes how to use statistics in the study of business cycles and how to use business annuals; and concludes with a working concept of business cycles. 512 pages, $6.50.

THE BEHAVIOR OF PRICES
By Frederick C. Mills

First results of an investigation of the movements of commodity prices, individually and by groups 598 pages, $7.

TRENDS IN PHILANTHROPY
By Willford I. King

A study of a typical American city. 78 pages, $1 75.

RECENT ECONOMIC CHANGES
By Edwin F. Gay, Wesley C. Mitchell, and others

A report of conditions in the United States, 1922-1928, made by a special staff of the National Bureau of Economic Research, Inc. for the Committee on Recent Economic Changes, Herbert Hoover, Chairman, 2 volumes, $7.50 per set.

INTERNATIONAL MIGRATIONS, VOL. I, STATISTICS
Compiled by Imre Ferenczi of the International Labour Office, Geneva, and edited by Walter F. Willcox for the National Bureau of Economic Research. Fifty-one countries represented, 1,112 pages, $10.

Copies of available reports may be obtained upon application accompanied by remittance to

NATIONAL BUREAU OF ECONOMIC RESEARCH, Inc.

51 Madison Avenue, New York

PUBLICATIONS OF THE NATIONAL BUREAU OF ECONOMIC RESEARCH, INCORPORATED

No. 15

THE NATIONAL INCOME AND ITS PURCHASING POWER

PUBLICATIONS OF THE NATIONAL BUREAU OF
ECONOMIC RESEARCH, INCORPORATED

No. 15

THE NATIONAL INCOME AND ITS
PURCHASING POWER

PRINTED IN THE UNITED STATES OF AMERICA BY
THE MESSENGER PRESS, ST. ALBANS, VT.

RESOLUTION

ON THE RELATION OF THE DIRECTORS TO THE ECONOMIC WORK OF THE BUREAU

1—The object of the Bureau is to ascertain and to present to the public important economic facts and the interpretation thereof in a scientific and impartial manner, free from bias and propaganda. The Board of Directors is charged with the responsibility of ensuring and guaranteeing to the public that the work of the Bureau is carried out in strict conformity with this object.

2—The Directors shall appoint one or more directors of research chosen upon considerations of integrity, ability, character, and freedom from prejudice, who shall undertake to conduct economic researches in conformity with the principles of the Bureau.

3—The director or directors of research shall submit to the members of the Board, or to its executive committee when such is constituted and to which authority has been delegated by the Board, proposals in respect to researches to be instituted; and no research shall be instituted without the approval of the Board, or of its executive committee.

4—Following approval by the Board, or its executive committee, of a research proposed, the director or directors of research shall as soon as possible submit to the members of the Board, by written communication, a statement of the principles to be pursued in the study of the problem and the methods to be employed; and the director or directors of research shall not proceed to investigate, study, and report in detail, until the plan so outlined has been approved by the board or the executive committee thereof.

5—Before the publication of the results of an inquiry the director or directors of research shall submit to the Board a synopsis of such results, drawing attention to the main conclusions reached, the major problems encountered and the solutions adopted, the nature of the sources from which the basic facts have been derived, and such other information as in their opinion shall have a material bearing on the validity of the conclusions and their suitability for publication in accordance with the principles of the Bureau.

6—A copy of any manuscript proposed to be published shall also be submitted to each member of the Board, and every member shall be entitled if publication be approved, to have published also a memorandum of any dissent or reservation he may express, together with a brief statement of his reasons therefore, should he so desire. The publication of a volume does not, however, imply that each member of the Board of Directors has read the manuscript and passed upon its validity in every detail.

7—The results of any inquiry shall not be published except with the approval of at least a majority of the entire Board and a two-thirds majority of all those members of the Board who shall have voted on the proposal within the time fixed for the receipt of votes on the publication proposed; such limit shall be 45 days from the date of the submission of the synopsis and manuscript of the proposed publication, except that the Board may extend the limit in its absolute discretion, and shall upon the request of any member extend the limit for a period not exceeding 30 days.

8—A copy of this memorandum shall, unless otherwise determined by the Board, be printed in each copy of every work published by the Bureau.

Adopted Oct. 25, 1926.

PREFACE

So far as the present writer is aware, no serious attempt was made by anyone to present an estimate of the aggregate income of our population until Dr. Charles B. Spahr published, in 1896, his book entitled *The Present Distribution of Wealth in the United States*. In 1912, Dr. Frank H. Streightoff set forth in the *Columbia University Studies* a careful analysis entitled *The Distribution of Incomes in the United States*, and, in 1915, the present writer followed with *The Wealth and Income of the People of the United States*.

These three publications represented careful attempts by individual students of the subject to get at the essential facts, but the preparation of any adequate analysis of the subject requires more labor than any one individual can devote to the task. So many questions pertaining to the economic welfare of the citizens and the political policy of the legislators hinge upon a knowledge of the facts concerning the distribution of income among different classes of citizens, that it is extremely important to have available figures which are as accurate as it is possible to obtain. It was with this situation in mind that the Directors of the National Bureau of Economic Research decided that the first study of the Bureau should be of the income of the people of the United States.

To guard against the possibility that one investigator might overlook vital points or go astray in his calculations, it was decided to make two independent calculations of the national totals. Dr. Oswald W. Knauth was instructed to make a computation using to the fullest extent possible the records of the Federal Income Tax authorities. The present writer was commissioned to base an estimate primarily upon the Census and data other than the Income Tax reports. The procedure used did not permit of a comparison of results until both estimates were complete. It was an exciting moment when the two sets of totals, each covering the years 1909 to 1918 inclusive, were brought together. All concerned were much gratified when it was discovered that the difference between the two estimates was in no year of much consequence.

The two estimates were scrutinized carefully by each of the members of the Board of Directors of the National Bureau—a Board representing many varied interests and points of view, and especially selected to guarantee impartiality in all the findings of the Bureau. These Directors offered many valuable suggestions which were utilized in improving many individual items. Dr. Wesley C. Mitchell, Director of Research, drew up a report embodying the two estimates. The Board then voted unanimously to accept the estimates of the two investigators as fair and unbiased and reasonably close to the truth. The estimates were published in the two volumes entitled *Income in the United States*—Vol. I in 1921 and Vol. II in 1922.

The interest aroused by our first estimate of the aggregate income of the inhabitants of the United States led the Board of Directors to continue the work and expand its scope. As Dr. Knauth had resigned from the Bureau's Staff, the continuation fell to the present writer. The work has gone on steadily since 1922, employing most of the time from two to six research assistants and computers. The original estimates have been revised section by section. The figures for the years 1919, 1920 and 1921 were, in part, published in 1925 in the report entitled *Income in the Various States*.

The income of the people of a vast country like the United States is derived from a great variety of industries. It accrues in the form of wages, salaries, pensions, rent, interest, dividends, and profits of individuals. To estimate these various quantities for each industry, it is necessary to obtain information from a multitude of sources. The basic data are, in most cases, derived from the reports of the Bureau of the Census and the Bureau of Internal Revenue, but since these figures fail to cover many important industries, and too often appear at rather widely spread intervals, the gaps must be filled in from other sources. It has been necessary to collect material from the reports of the various Departments and Bureaus of the Federal Government, of the States and the Cities, and also to secure from many private agencies series of figures necessary to supplement the Government's data. Hundreds of individuals and organizations have assisted materially in this work. Among those who deserve especial mention are:

Mr. W. M. Steuart, Director of the Census
Mr. W. F. Callander, Bureau of Agricultural Economics
Dr. L. C. Gray, Bureau of Agricultural Economics
Dr. Max O. Lorenz, Interstate Commerce Commission
Dr. Julius H. Parmelee, Bureau of Railway Economics
Mr. Seymour L. Andrew, American Telephone & Telegraph Co.
Mr. J. W. Rahde, Western Union Co.
Mr. Thomas H. Holden, F. W. Dodge Corporation

Dr. Paul H. Nystrom, Columbia University
Dr. O. C. Stine, Bureau of Agricultural Economics

In accordance with the National Bureau's regular procedure, the manuscript of this report was submitted to the scrutiny of the other members of the Research Staff. After all comments had been received and checked, the revised manuscript, with the recommendation of the Directors of Research, was submitted to the Board of Directors for formal review and approval for publication. Many helpful suggestions were received which led to improvements in the text of the study.

I am greatly indebted not only to the many outside agencies and persons who have furnished information and to those members of the National Bureau's Staff and Board who have helped with criticism, but also to the patience and faithfulness of my assistants.

While, in many fields, the present report goes into considerably greater detail than its predecessors, the really important new contribution which it presents is the study of that part of the income of investors derived from various classes of corporations. From the investor's standpoint, corporations are nothing more than intermediaries between industry and its owners. Investors have all too frequently discovered that reported corporate profits bear but a slight relationship to any profits which they can actually extract from their investments in corporate securities. This report is intended to give a financial picture, from the investor's viewpoint, of the results of corporate activity in the leading fields of industry—something which, so far as the writer is aware, has never before been undertaken seriously. To arrive at the underlying facts has required the entire time of several assistants for three years. It is felt, however, that the new understanding of the facts concerning corporate profits is well worth the time and money expended.

WILLFORD ISBELL KING.

TABLE OF CONTENTS

LIST OF TABLES

19

LIST OF CHARTS

THE NATIONAL INCOME

AND ITS

PURCHASING POWER

CHAPTER 1

INTRODUCTION

Income Studies First Work of National Bureau.

When the National Bureau of Economic Research was organized in 1920, the first task which it set for itself was to ascertain the approximate size and distribution of the total income of the people of the United States. In 1921 and 1922, the National Bureau published a two volume report presenting its estimates of income for the years 1909 to 1918 inclusive. Because there had been much controversy concerning the facts relating to income, it was deemed advisable to have the income totals estimated independently by two different investigators, each using a different method, and, to a considerable extent, different data.

When the two series of totals were compiled, it was found that they were closely in accord. This general agreement was believed to indicate that neither was widely in error,—and nothing which has developed since has upset the original conviction that the totals presented in 1921-22 are approximately correct, even though the constituent items have been modified in many respects.

Purposes of Present Study of Income.

The first findings, when published, aroused such widespread interest and general approval that it was felt worth while to pursue further investigations in this field, these investigations being directed toward two major goals:—

1. To make more trustworthy estimates of those items, which in the original study were but ill-supported by data.
2. To extend the inquiry into new fields.

Since 1920, the investigation of income in the United States has been carried on almost continuously. As a result, many concepts which were still somewhat hazy when the first report was published, have become clarified. New methods of attack have been developed. Most of these new concepts and new methods are discussed in the "Preliminary Statement" of the National Bureau's publication, entitled *Income in the Various States, 1919-1921.*

Reliability of Present Estimates.

Because of the large amount of additional work that has been done, it can confidently be asserted that the revised estimates now set forth are far more firmly buttressed than were those presented in Volumes 1 and 2.

However, even in these latest estimates, the various subdivisions vary greatly in dependability. Some items are so thoroughly supported by evidence that one feels little hesitancy in asserting that the errors probably do not exceed one or two per cent. For other items, satisfactory underlying data may be practically non-existent, and, in such cases, possible errors of 10, 20, or even 30 or 40 per cent may be present.

Gains of Individuals from Corporate Profits.

Much of the National Bureau's further study of income since 1922 has been devoted to the investigation of new fields. The most important unknown area is that of profits. Considerable information has been available concerning the reported profits of corporations, but it has been impossible to say to what extent these published figures represent anything real or tangible and to what extent they record merely nominal gains. Corporations are, of course, merely legal entities. In reality, they represent individual owners associated together for a particular end. Corporate profits are, then, significant as individual income only when they materialize in such a way as to affect the income of the individual owner. With a view to ascertaining how the combined individual owners who have invested in the securities of corporations operating in the respective industries have fared, a great volume of data has been analyzed, and the outstanding results of this inquiry are here presented.

The Mercantile Industry.

Another almost uncharted field is that of the mercantile industry. Although this has long been one of the major fields of activity in the United States, it has all but escaped the attention of both Federal and State statistical bureaus. True, an occasional effort has been made to estimate the total volume of goods sold by mercantile enterprises, but most of these estimates have been based upon nothing firmer than a few slight computations. The estimates here set forth represent the fruit of several years' work. Nevertheless, because of the difficulty of securing adequate data, the figures must, even yet, be presented as distinctly tentative in nature.

Necessity of Defining Income.

Before measuring the income of the people of the United States, it is obviously desirable to know what the term "income" signifies. As it happens, this word has been used to cover a variety of concepts, many vague, but some fairly clear-cut. In this series of income studies, the Bureau has naturally been compelled to confine its investigations to types of income translatable into terms of money units. Items upon which no money value can be placed have, necessarily, been omitted. Furthermore, some items having a definite money value have not been considered because it has proved impossible to estimate their total money value, even roughly. Among such omissions are the value of the services of persons to themselves and to their families. Several critics have urged the inclusion of an estimate of the value of the service of the housewife. If such services are evaluated, it is, of course, logical to include also the value of the services of the head of the household when he manages the family business and when he performs such physical labor as building fires, caring for the lawn, and shaving himself instead of going to the barber. The value of such home services is tremendous. Furthermore, in estimates like ours, in which the values of such services are not included, every transfer to the factory of work, formerly done at home, as for example, dressmaking and bread-making, gives an artificial and misleading upward slope to the curve representing estimates of the national income. Yet, because the difficulty of correctly evaluating such services is so very great, they have been excluded.

Another important item which has likewise been excluded from our totals consists of expense allowances to employees. Such income is received by many persons, in the form of board, room, laundry, travel, etc. Thus, for example, a salesman stays at a good hotel and perhaps takes his prospective customer to the theater—all at the expense of the company. There is no question but that income of this type is an important item, but it is extremely difficult even to approximate its total.

A third important type of income omitted from our estimates is that consisting of earnings from odd jobs. Presumably millions of persons earn a few dollars, and a considerable number many dollars each yearly, by performing such tasks as assisting with housework, caring for children, teaching, typing, cutting lawns, tending furnaces, selling newspapers and magazines, shining shoes, delivering packages, draying, cutting timber, and canvassing—all outside of their regular duties. Some of these persons are reported by the Census as "gainfully occupied" and others are not, but in neither case is the income from odd jobs likely to find its way into any of the statistical data upon which the estimates of national income are based; hence it does not appear in the national totals, even though it is an item of possibly great importance.

Total Book Income.

The concept of income which, from the statistician's standpoint, is the simplest, is that of total book income. It represents the income which would be shown by a correctly kept set of books if all of the entries in these books were made in terms of money of constant purchasing power.

Computation of Total Book Income.

To compute the total book income for any year, the first step is to add to the net value of the property used in the business at the beginning of the year the value of new investments in the business during the year. The resulting sum is next subtracted from the sum obtained by adding the value of money or property withdrawn from the business during the year to the net value of the property used in the business at the end of the year.

The fact must not be overlooked that, in times when the price level is changing rapidly, results obtained by this form of computation are meaningless unless all quantities are reduced to terms of money of constant purchasing power. That such is the case may readily be demonstrated by the use of a numerical example.

Suppose that the index of the general price level stands on January 1 at 0.90, and, at that date, a man buys a block of stock for $18,000. He receives during the year dividends amounting to $990. The average price level for the year is 1.10. By December 31, the price level has risen to 1.30. He sells the stock at the close of the year for $23,400.

To find his profit or loss we proceed as follows:—

$18,000 ÷ 0.90 = 20,000 constant dollars
$23,400 ÷ 1.30 = 18,000 constant dollars
Loss on principal = 2,000 constant dollars
$990 ÷ 1.10 = 900 constant dollars
Net loss on operation = 1,100 constant dollars.

The fact should be noted that it is as impossible to secure intelligible results by subtracting nominal dollars of January 1 from

nominal dollars of December 31 as it is to subtract cows from horses. Comparison is only possible when all quantities have been expressed in like units.

Book Income a Business Concept.

Book income is a business concept. The individual's book income is the measure of his gain from business operations. The typical employee receives most of his income from businesses directed by others, his wage or salary constituting his income from the business. The investor, on the other hand, draws interest on the money he has loaned or rent from the property he has leased. The entrepreneur gets his profits out of possible differentials between expenses and selling values.

Book Income Affected by Changes in Property Values.

In all entrepreneurial operations, changes in property values play important rôles. In many cases, it is impossible to segregate gains from changing property values from gains arising from other sources. For example, a merchant's income is, in the main, the result of selling goods for more than he pays for them. It is impracticable for the statistician to say what part of the merchant's gain is due to a rise in the prices of the goods sold, and what part has its origin in the amount of mark-up permitted by the usual conditions of competition. The merchant's profit cannot well be estimated without valuing his goods both at the beginning and at the end of the period under study. The statistician cannot tell whether any changes in inventory thus arrived at represent changes in the volume of physical stock on hand or changes in the values of the various goods on the shelves.

To a large extent all entrepreneurs are merchants, for all are engaged in buying and selling. For every enterprise, then, both an initial and a final valuation are necessary in computing the profit for a given period.

Many businesses, however, possess very valuable "fixed" assets such as land, mines, roadways, canals, buildings, machinery, and the like. These objects cannot be sold piecemeal and their values at any given moment must be matters of opinion rather than of fact. It is very difficult, therefore, to include such values in any inventory of the assets of a business. Nevertheless, these objects must be evaluated or a balance sheet cannot be completed and the income of the business calculated. The conservative business man usually values such objects at cost—less a somewhat arbitrary allowance for depreciation. Since increases in the value of fixed assets can rarely be used to pay dividends, it is quite generally agreed that sound business practice often requires the marking down of such values but rarely calls for marking them up.

When, however, all or part of a business enterprise is sold, it is often discovered that the fixed assets have tremendously increased in value. From the standpoint of the business man, the date of sale is usually the logical time to take cognizance of this increase in value. Experience shows also that this is the date at which the government can most conveniently step in and collect income tax on the increased value. However, one must differentiate carefully between the procedure which is logical from the standpoint of business and the fiscal authorities and the facts which the statistician, engaged in measuring income, must set forth if he is to give a true picture of the changes that have occurred.

It often happens, for example, that the value of a piece of land trebles in amount within a year or two and then remains stationary for a score of years. If the land is sold at the close of such a period of quiescence, it is obviously absurd to locate the change in value at a point two decades after it really occurred.

The correct goal of the measurer of income is easily discerned. He should give a true picture of the value of all assets, fixed or otherwise, at the beginning and at the end of each income period. These values should all be translated into terms of money of constant value, and the change in value of total net assets should be taken into account in computing the income for the period.

The procedure just outlined is sometimes attacked on the ground that a gain in the value of assets one year is offset by a loss the next, and that, therefore, there is no reason for taking the change into consideration. The answer to this objection is, that what may happen in the future is of no concern whatever to the accountant or statistician estimating the income of an enterprise for a given period. The books for the calendar year close on December 31. The year constitutes a unit in itself, and there is no legitimate reason for including in the measurements of income for the given year transactions or value changes taking place in some other year.

Estimating Property Values at Specified Dates.

While it is easy enough to outline the correct procedure for the statistician to follow, it is very difficult to secure the information

necessary to put this logical procedure into practice. To do so, it is necessary to have a correct statement of the net value of all assets at the beginning of and at the end of each period. Where are such statements to be obtained?

For reasons previously mentioned, one can place practically no faith in the published reports showing the net worth of a corporation at the end of its fiscal year, for the valuations placed upon fixed assets are at best rough approximations to the truth. In periods like 1915 to 1921, when the value of money was changing rapidly, the approximations became so rough as to take away all significance from the reported property values. The obvious result was to cast grave doubt on the reported net earnings, for the reported earnings were evidently dependent upon the property valuation. How to measure the income of corporations during such periods was, then, a puzzling question.

Corporate Property Value Assumed to Equal Value of Corporate Securities.

After much consideration, it was decided that the only feasible way to attack the problem of evaluating net assets was to fall back upon the recorded values of corporate securities. After all, the valuation put by interested parties upon the entire property of a corporation is represented by the aggregate market value of its stock and funded debt. Shares of stock and bonds are frequently sold, and, by assuming the sales as representative, a total value figure is easily arrived at by multiplying the market value per share by the number of shares outstanding.

Critics of this procedure have pointed out that, if an attempt were made to sell all of the stock outstanding at the market price, that price would be greatly depressed. True, but experience also shows that, when an attempt is made to buy the entire issue, the market price rises sharply. There is, then, apparently no sound reason for condemning the customary practice of evaluating all units at the prevailing market price of those units sold.

Calculating the Income of a Corporation-Controlled Industry.

The procedure used in calculating the income of an industry controlled by corporations is indicated by the following example.

Factories	Millions of Current Dollars	Index of Prices	Millions of Dollars of 1913	
Value of all common stock Dec. 31, 1919	30,336	1.7224	17,613	
" " " preferred stock " " "	7,561	1.7224	4,390	
" " " funded debt " " "	3,596	1.7224	2,088	
Value of all securities Dec. 31, 1919			24,091	
Value of all common stock Jan. 1, 1919	24,663	1.4958	16,488	
" " " preferred stock " " "	6,950	1.4958	4,646	
" " " funded debt " " "	3,637	1.4958	2,431	
Value of all securities Jan. 1, 1919			23,565	
Change in value of all securities				+526
New money invested in common stock	1,542	1.5814	975	
" " " " preferred stock	252	1.5814	159	
" " " " funded debt	75	1.5814	47	
New money invested in all securities			1,181	
Gain to owners from value changes				−655
Dividends on common stock	1,330	1.5814	841	
" " preferred stock	456	1.5814	288	
Interest on funded debt	206	1.5814	130	
Total dividends and interest			1,259	
Total income to owners of industry				604

It will be observed that three index numbers are required in this process of computation. Values of December 31 must be deflated by means of a price index for that date; values of January 1 require the use of the price index for that date; while, for deflating new money and also dividend and interest payments, an index representing average prices for the year is essential, since these payments are made at various times throughout the year.

Consumers' Price Indices Used as Deflators.

As in the study recorded in *Income in the Various States,* index numbers of the prices of consumers' goods have been used as

deflators. The quantities recorded as values in terms of 1913 dollars represent, then, the relative amounts of direct or consumers' goods which could have been purchased at the various dates with the money available.

Other index numbers might have been used and would have given different results, but, as we are dealing with income from the individual standpoint, and as all individuals consume direct goods, such an index seems the most generally applicable of any.

It will be noted that the data in the table just given are sufficient to enable us to compute separately the incomes of the common stockholders, the preferred stockholders, and the bondholders.

Property Values Very Unstable.

Values of securities are based primarily upon the anticipated future earnings of corporations. Anticipations are changed not only by changes in conditions affecting the industry but also by currency inflation or contraction, by rumors, and by waves of pessimism and optimism. As a result, the value of the total net assets of the security holders fluctuates greatly from year to year and the total book income of the owners of the industry is anything but stable, for the value of the assets, as compared to the annual net earnings, is so large that a small percentage change in the value of the former has a very large percentage effect upon the net income.

Effect Upon Owners of Changes in the Value of Their Property.

In the United States, vast quantities of securities change hands annually; hence the changes in market value affect the every day life of a large proportion of all stockholders. There are, however, a considerable proportion of all stockholders, and a larger proportion of bondholders, who retain their securities year after year and are not particularly interested in changes in the market price. To this latter class, dividends or interest are of much greater significance than changes in market value.

In industries not dominated by corporations, the turnover of fixed assets is presumably much slower than in the corporate field. While farmers are materially affected by changes in livestock values, farms change hands only occasionally, hence the typical farmer's mode of living is affected but slightly by shifts in land values. It follows, then, that large changes in total book income may occur without affecting to any great extent the consuming habits of the owners of an industry.

For Some Fields, Estimates of Property Values Are Very Unreliable.

In the industries controlled by corporations, it is possible to estimate, with some degree of confidence in the results, the total value of the industry at the beginning and at the end of the year. Thanks to the Bureau of the Census and the Bureau of Agricultural Economics, it is also possible to arrive at a moderately accurate statement of the value of farm property at yearly intervals. In other important fields, however, data are almost completely lacking, hence the values placed upon the business property utilized in such industries are nothing but guesses. This state of affairs prevails notably in the mercantile and unclassified industries.

Because many individuals are but slightly affected by temporary changes in the value of their property; because property values are so much affected by transitory psychological influences, and hence are so unstable; and, finally, because the net value of the assets in important industries cannot be estimated with any approach to precision, the figures for *total book income* appearing in this volume cannot legitimately be interpreted to represent current changes in the economic welfare of the people of the nation. It has, therefore, been deemed necessary to make the principal analyses of this book deal with another type of income, namely *realized income*.

Realized Income.

The term *realized income* covers exactly the same concept referred to in *Income in the Various States* as "current income," or that part of the aggregate income of individuals which remains if we eliminate income due to changes between January 1 and December 31 in values of inventories or property of any kind. *Realized income* like *total book income* is a concept based upon accounting practices as well as upon economic reasoning. It will be observed, however, that it applies solely to the income of individuals and not to that of business enterprises. Furthermore, it must be remembered that aggregate realized income includes only those types of money or commodity income the value of which can be estimated with some hope of success.

Realized income consists, in the main, of the amounts received by individuals in the form of wages, salaries, pensions, compensation for injuries, interest, dividends, rents, royalties, services of durable consumers' goods, and profits withdrawn from business.

All except the last two categories may be estimated with a reasonable degree of precision.

Chief Weaknesses in the Estimate of Total Realized Income.

The net value of the services rendered by durable consumers' goods such as owned homes, estates, automobiles, and the like can, at best, be only roughly approximated, and the amount of profits withdrawn from their own businesses by individual entrepreneurs is necessarily in a large degree a matter of conjecture. But, with the assistance of the Federal Income Tax reports, it is possible to estimate this last quantity within a margin of error believed to be not greater than 20 or 30 per cent.

Totals Refer to Individual Income.

Again the reader is reminded that, throughout this volume, although income has been classified by industries, the point of view is always that of the individual income recipient. The question is never how much does the industry earn, but how much income does the individual part-owner of the industry draw from it. Thus, for example, the manufacturing industry receives interest and dividends from other industries and itself pays out interest and dividends. It is, however, credited only with the excess of the latter over the former, in other words with the interest and dividends going to individuals which have been made possible by manufacturing activities.

CHAPTER II

THE INDUSTRIAL CLASSIFICATION OF THE POPULATION

Method of Estimating Population of United States.

Estimates of national income cannot be made without knowing the total and the working population of the country. Since the census of population is taken only once in a decade, it is necessary to estimate the population for each inter-censal year.

The method employed in interpolating population estimates has been to build up from the last census by calculating for each year the number of births and deaths and the net immigration. Evidently, if births and net immigration are added together and the number of deaths subtracted, the remainder represents the population increase during the given period. None of these three quantities can, however, be calculated with precision.

Reliability of Information Underlying Population Estimates.

During recent years, the Census registration area for deaths has come to cover the major portion of the population of the United States. The probabilities are that the great majority of deaths actually occurring within that area are reported to the proper registration official, and that, therefore, the statistics for the registration area are reasonably accurate. Since the registration area covers the majority of the inhabitants, it constitutes a sample which can now be safely used to represent the population as a whole.

One cannot feel a like degree of confidence in the estimates of the number of births. The Census birth registration has, until recently, included a much smaller proportion of the total population of the United States than has the death registration area, hence the birth-rates computed for the birth registration area are likely to be less representative of the country as a whole than are the death rates computed for the death registration area. There seems also, even within the registration area, to be a persistent tendency to neglect the registration of births. Studies which have been made both by the National Bureau of Economic Research and by other students in this field indicate that the actual birth rate is somewhat higher than the birth rate indicated by the registration figures. In the figures presented in Table I, an effort has been made to allow

for this error, but there is no way of knowing whether the allowance made for years since 1920 has been too great or too small. [1]

Our estimates of net immigration are probably even less trustworthy. True, the records made by the Federal Government of the number of persons entering the United States through customary channels are probably accurate in most cases, but, during the period of immigration restriction, many persons (sometimes asserted to run into the hundreds of thousands annually) have illegally entered the country.

Reliability of Population Estimate.

For the reasons just explained, the population estimates appearing in Table I presumably deviate from the truth to a greater or lesser extent. Since population counts are available for 1910 and 1920, the probabilities are that the interpolated estimates for dates preceding 1920 are but slightly in error. Since 1920, however, it has been necessary to extrapolate figures and, when extrapolation is resorted to, there is always a danger that the error grows greater with the passage of time. It will be observed that the figures for later years are marked with asterisks and that notes are appended explaining that these estimates are preliminary. This annotation signifies that the Bureau of the Census has not as yet published its complete reports on births and deaths in the registration area, and that it has been necessary in the present investigation to make estimates on the basis of such preliminary reports as are published. In the case of deaths, early information is available in sufficient quantity to make possible reasonably accurate estimates. Preliminary data on births are, however, scanty. Only because the number of births is fairly stable from year to year, is it possible to make population estimates for recent dates which have any claim to consideration. As it is, the tentative figures presented for the year 1928 may be as much as a million in error, though it is hoped that they are not this far from the truth. While a 1% error in the population count would not introduce a 1% error into the income estimate, it would, however, vitiate the income estimate by perhaps half a per cent.

[1] The correction necessary to cover the error of the original estimate built up to 1920 from 1910 was 1,064,000 for the decade. Since it is believed that the quality of available vital statistics is improving, the correction allowed since 1920 has been somewhat less, proportionally, than that required for the decade 1910-1920.

Estimation of the Gainfully Occupied Population.

As previously stated, the income of the country is dependent upon the volume of production, and production is dependent upon population. Not all of the inhabitants participate materially in the production of income. Children under 15 years of age are, for the most part, consumers and not producers. A considerable proportion of persons over 15 do not work directly for a money return, and hence do not fall within the category of the "gainfully occupied". To compute the income of the people of the United States, it is necessary to estimate the number of gainfully occupied persons in the country. We know, for each census date, what proportion of the entire population was composed of persons under 15 years of age. The reports of the Census Bureau also enable us to estimate for each year the number of persons born and the number of persons under 15 growing out of this age class or dying. It is possible also to estimate roughly the net number of immigrants under 15 years of age entering the United States. By combining these estimates, the population under 15 years of age can be calculated, and, the total population having been previously estimated, the population 15 years of age or over can evidently be obtained by subtraction.

We also know, for each Census date, what proportion of the population 15 years of age or over was represented by persons classed as gainfully occupied—that is, by those who were working for a money return. The fractions indicated for the census years have been plotted, and smooth curves have been drawn through the plotted points and extended to cover the other years.[1] Readings from these smooth curves have been taken and have been assumed to indicate the fractions for the years not covered by the Census. In this way, estimates of the number of persons gainfully occupied have been made for the beginning and middle of each year. These estimates appear in Table I.

Population Growth, 1909-1928.

This table indicates that the population has risen from 89 millions at the beginning of 1909 to 119 millions at the middle of 1928. In general, the growth of population has followed a straight line, but the annual increase was somewhat retarded during the period of the Great War, mainly because immigration to this coun-

---

[1] Our estimates all exclude workers on home farms other than farmers. On this basis, the percentage gainfully occupied has shown practically no tendency to fluctuate from decade to decade.

TABLE I

ESTIMATES OF THE POPULATION
OF THE CONTINENTAL UNITED STATES
(THOUSANDS OF PERSONS)

Date	Total[a]	15 Years of Age and Over[a]	Gainfully Occupied[b]	Date	Total[a]	15 Years of Age and Over[a]	Gainfully Occupied[b]
1909 Jan. 1	89,357	60,546	33,700	1919 Jan. 1	104,524	71,178	40,816
July 1	90,508	61,439	34,255	July 1	105,007	71,558	40,282
1910 Jan. 1	91,530	62,127	34,660	1920 Jan. 1	105,711	72,098	39,764
July 1	92,422	62,869	35,100	July 1	106,422	72,589	40,008
1911 Jan. 1	93,165	63,463	35,433	1921 Jan. 1	107,412	73,356	40,444
July 1	93,837	63,968	35,700	July 1	108,370	74,037	40,819
1912 Jan. 1	94,458	64,404	35,914	1922 Jan. 1	109,135	74,593	41,108
July 1	95,249	64,997	36,237	July 1	109,742	75,055	41,330
1913 Jan. 1	96,144	65,649	36,600	1923 Jan. 1	110,688	75,856	41,790
July 1	97,111	66,392	37,028	July 1	111,478	76,523	42,156
1914 Jan. 1	98,213	67,241	37,527	1924 Jan. 1	112,666	77,531	42,760
July 1	98,974	67,738	37,782	July 1	113,466	78,193	43,123
1915 Jan. 1	99,710	68,213	38,017	1925 Jan. 1	114,293	78,896	43,514
July 1	100,390	68,264	37,956	July 1	115,004	79,511	43,844
1916 Jan. 1	101,055	69,035	38,401	1926 Jan. 1	115,780[c]	80,219[c]	44,239[c]
July 1	101,787	69,515	38,638	July 1	116,380[c]	80,804[c]	44,912[c]
1917 Jan. 1	102,590	70,060	38,925	1927 Jan. 1	117,160[c]	81,546[c]	45,359[c]
July 1	103,234	70,484	39,373	July 1	117,843[c*]	82,204[c*]	45,747[c*]
1918 Jan. 1	103,852	70,859	39,916	1928 Jan. 1	118,673[c*]	82,976[c*]	46,215[c*]
July 1	104,377	71,132	40,383	July 1	119,306[c*]	83,600[c*]	46,580[c*]

[a] Figures for intercensal years estimated on basis of figures for births, deaths, and migration.

[b] Estimated on the basis of the Census of Occupations, the Censuses for various industries, and the various statistical reports of the Interstate Commerce Commission.

[c] This is a revised estimate made after the other tables in this volume had been completed, hence the figures therein differ very slightly from what they would be if they were based upon these figures.

[*] Preliminary estimate—basic data incomplete.

try was prevented by war conditions and by the interference of European Governments. Since 1919, however, the absolute rate of growth has been approximately as large as it was during the period preceding the Great War, even though the proportional rate of increase has somewhat declined. In the five years between January 1, 1909 and January 1, 1914, the growth in total population was approximately 8,856,000. In the five years ending January 1, 1928, the increase is estimated at 7,985,000.

Growth in Population 15 Years of Age and Over.

While inhabitants of all ages have increased in number during the past two decades, the total number of persons 15 years of age and over has grown somewhat more rapidly than has the total population; in other words, the percentage which those above the age of 15 years constitute of the total population appears to have increased. This increase is apparently accounted for by the fact that a reduced death rate among children has resulted in a larger proportion of the population surviving to the age of 15 years.

Growth in Gainfully Occupied Population.

The figures in Table I also indicate that there has recently been an increase in the proportion of the total population classed as gainfully occupied, the reason doubtless being the same as that causing the rise in the percentage of the population who are adults. However, the proportion of the adult population gainfully occupied is at present slightly smaller than was the case a score of years ago. This fall is probably due to the fact that, of persons over 15 years of age, a larger percentage attend school at the present time than was formerly the case. To some extent the diminution due to this source has, however, been offset by the tendency of women to cease work in the home in order to enter gainful occupations. The facts just discussed are illustrated in Chart 1.

Entrepreneurs, Salaried Employees, and Wage Workers.

This same chart also shows the apportionment of the "gainfully occupied" among the three classes of:

1. Entrepreneurs
2. Salaried workers
3. Wage workers.

The term entrepreneur is here applied to every person whose principal occupation is the conduct of an enterprise which he controls. Some entrepreneurs have other persons working for them. Others are merely independent workers, like many farmers, small merchants, physicians, lawyers, and real estate agents. The essential fact which distinguishes the entrepreneur from the employee is

CHART 1

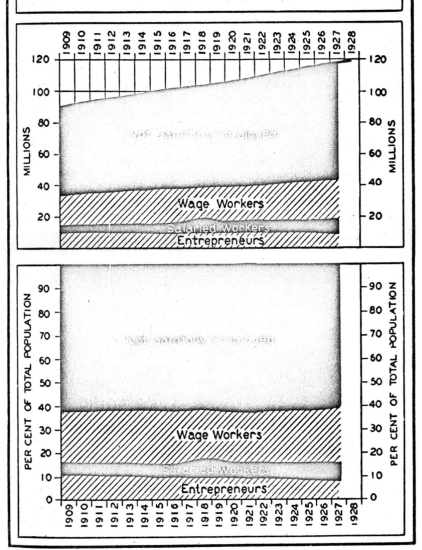

ESTIMATES OF THE POPULATION
OF THE CONTINENTAL UNITED STATES[a]

ᵃ For data, see Tables I, IV, V, and VI.

TABLE II

ESTIMATED APPORTIONMENT AMONG DIFFERENT INDUSTRIES OF THE TOTAL POPULATION NORMALLY ENGAGED IN GAINFUL OCCUPATIONS[a]

(AVERAGE NUMBER FOR YEAR EXPRESSED IN THOUSANDS)

Year	All Industries	Agriculture[b]	Manufacturing[c]	Mines, Quarries and Oil Wells[d]	Construction[e]	Banking[f]	Mercantile[g]	Government[h]	Unclassified[i]
1909	34,255	8,733	7,930	1,077	1,674	154	3,654	1,643	6,974
1910	35,100	8,814	8,176	1,099	1,650	158	3,783	1,709	7,115
1911	35,700	8,844	8,341	1,167	1,650	167	3,877	1,765	7,233
1912	36,237	8,800	8,604	1,173	1,676	172	3,970	1,821	7,308
1913	37,028	8,810	8,790	1,226	1,795	177	4,073	1,879	7,414
1914	37,782	8,792	8,943	1,204	1,795	183	4,176	1,947	7,858
1915	37,956	8,831	9,016	1,211	1,584	185	4,262	2,013	7,972
1916	38,638	8,801	10,009	1,180	1,375	188	4,345	2,013	7,780
1917	39,373	8,836	10,830	1,208	1,302	190	4,394	2,744	6,937
1918	40,383	8,862	11,276	1,191	1,037	197	4,278	5,210	5,256
1919	40,282	8,947	11,492	1,208	1,343	213	4,476	4,042	5,285
1920	40,008	8,871	11,389	1,239	1,092	232	4,618	2,719	6,355
1921	40,819	8,860	10,953	1,254	1,092	246	4,705	2,689	7,564
1922	41,330	8,643	10,928	1,269	1,363	252	5,126	2,618	7,693
1923	42,156	8,626	10,891	1,273	1,453	265	5,694	2,633	7,845
1924	43,123	8,672	10,654	1,214	1,532	271	5,485	2,674	9,176
1925	43,844	8,646	10,647	1,199	1,799	277	5,781	2,736	9,444
1926	44,560*	8,529*	10,829*	1,294	1,787*	288	5,906*	2,785*	9,794*
1927	45,373*	8,432*	10,746*	1,300*	1,753*	291*	6,122*	2,819*	10,599*
1928	47,100*								

* The figures here given include those temporarily idle as well as those actually at work.

[b] Based upon *Censuses of Occupations* and *Agriculture* and upon reports of the *Bureau of Agricultural Economics.*

[c] Based upon *Census of Manufactures* and State reports on manufactures. Includes only factories having total products valued at $5,000 and over.

[d] Based upon the *Census of Mines and Quarries* and reports of the *U. S. Bureau of Mines* and the *Pa. Dept. of Internal Affairs.*

[e] Estimated upon the basis of the volume of construction as reported by the F. W. Dodge Co. and upon the ratios of workers to construction volume shown by the Pennsylvania and Ohio State reports.

[f] Based upon the annual reports of the *Comptroller of the Currency.*

[g] Based upon the *Census of Occupations* and an original investigation of the volume of sales.

[h] Based upon reports of the *War Dept., Navy Dept.,* and *Civil Service Commission* and upon *Financial Statistics of Cities and States.*

[i] These figures are the difference between the total gainfully occupied and the summation for the separate industries.

that he takes the risk of the enterprise and does not receive for his services a fixed rate of compensation from an employer.

The distinction between salaried employees and wage workers

TABLE II—Continued

ESTIMATED APPORTIONMENT AMONG DIFFERENT INDUSTRIES OF THE TOTAL POPULATION NORMALLY ENGAGED IN GAINFUL OCCUPATIONS[a]

(AVERAGE NUMBER FOR YEAR EXPRESSED IN THOUSANDS)

Year	All Following Fields of Transportation	Railroads[j]	Pullman[k]	Express[l]	Transportation by Water[m]	Street Railways[n]	Private Electric Light and Power[o]	Telephones[p]	Telegraphs[q]
1909	2,417	1,620	18	59	226	250	55	150	39
1910	2,597	1,758	18	61	228	265	61	165	41
1911	2,657	1,763	18	61	235	279	67	185	49
1912	2,714	1,774	18	65	243	288	72	204	49
1913	2,865	1,895	21	64	249	293	77	218	48
1914	2,883	1,899	21	63	249	296	82	226	48
1915	2,882	1,883	20	64	250	298	87	230	50
1916	2,874	1,844	20	64	253	300	92	244	58
1917	2,929	1,852	20	74	250	301	96	268	67
1918	3,077	1,969	19	70	261	303	102	282	71
1919	3,275	2,075	20	77	322	306	108	297	71
1920	3,494	2,163	23	91	408	307	116	311	75
1921	3,456	2,122	23	82	403	308	126	318	75
1922	3,438	2,097	21	77	400	308	139	322	75
1923	3,476	2,080	22	74	395	319	161	350	76
1924	3,445	2,040	25	71	376	318	168	370	77
1925	3,314	1,891	26	68	362	318	187	377	86
1926	3,350	1,902	27	68	361	319	206	381	86
1927	3,311*	1,856*	27	66	349	322	221	385	86

j Includes switching and terminal companies. Based upon *Statistics of Railways.*
k Based upon *Preliminary Abstracts of Statistics of Common Carriers.*
l Based upon *Statistics of Express Companies* and other data from *Interstate Commerce Commission.*
m Based upon the *Census of Transportation by Water* and upon the reports of the *U. S. Commissioner of Navigation* and *Merchant Marine Statistics.*
n Based upon *Census of Electric Railways.*
o Based upon *Census of Electric Light and Power* and upon reports of the *Geological Survey.*
p Based upon *Census of Telephones* and reports of the *Bell Telephone Companies.*
q Based upon *Census of Telegraphs* and reports of the *Western Union Telegraph Co.*
* Preliminary estimate.

is often difficult to draw. In this, as in previous studies by the present author, the definition laid down by the Bureau of the Census has been followed, and the managerial staff, the office workers, and those having relatively high security of tenure have been counted as salaried employees, while all others have been classed as wage workers. All employees of Government and all employees of banks have been put in the salaried group because of lack of the data necessary for the segregation of the two classes. Chart 1 indicates that the salaried class was abnormally large during the years 1917 to 1919, an expansion accounted for almost entirely by the fact that a great number of men were serving in the Army, and hence are arbitrarily classified in this volume as salaried employees.

Chart 1 indicates that, while the absolute numbers of gainfully occupied, and also the absolute numbers working as employees, have grown steadily larger, the number of entrepreneurs has remained practically constant throughout the two decades. The comparison by percentages given in the lower part of the chart is perhaps more significant than are the absolute figures illustrated above. From it we see that the wage workers today include a slightly larger proportion of the total number of inhabitants than they did in 1909, their numbers having increased at the expense of those not gainfully occupied. Since the absolute number of entrepreneurs has remained approximately unchanged, while the population has grown, it obviously follows that the percentage of the population classed as entrepreneurs has diminished. The shrinkage in the entrepreneurial class is almost exactly balanced by an increase in the salaried class, the result being that the entrepreneurs and salaried employees, combined, form practically the same per cent of the population in 1927 as in 1909.

Changes in Industrial Connections of Gainfully Occupied.

Tables II and III record the estimated changes in the numbers of persons making their living in the various industries of the country. Chart 2 illustrates these tables both in absolute and in percentage form. A study of these tables and this chart indicates that agriculture is the only industry in which fewer people were engaged in 1927 than in 1909. The number of persons attached to this field showed little change until 1921, but a marked decline has since occurred. Manufacturing grew steadily until 1919, but, from that date on, a slow shrinkage is apparent. The construction industry, on the other hand, underwent a great depression between 1916 and 1922, but has recovered markedly in recent years. The railroad industry attained a high point in 1920 and has since tended to require a smaller proportion of the nation's working force than was formerly true. The express business has shown a similar ten-

TABLE III

ESTIMATED PERCENTAGE OF THE GAINFULLY OCCUPIED POPULATION ENGAGED IN EACH OF THE LEADING INDUSTRIES[*]

(AVERAGE FOR YEAR)

Year	All Industries	Agriculture	Manufacturing	Mines, Quarries and Oil Wells	Construction	Banking	Mercantile	Government	Specified Phases of Transportation	Unclassified
1909	100.00	25.49	23.15	3.14	4.89	0.45	10.67	4.80	7.05	20.36
1910	100.00	25.11	23.29	3.13	4.70	0.45	10.78	4.87	7.40	20.27
1911	100.00	24.77	23.36	3.27	4.62	0.47	10.86	4.94	7.44	20.26
1912	100.00	24.28	23.74	3.24	4.63	0.48	10.95	5.02	7.49	20.17
1913	100.00	23.79	23.74	3.31	4.85	0.48	11.00	5.08	7.74	20.02
1914	100.00	23.27	23.67	3.19	4.75	0.48	11.05	5.15	7.63	20.80
1915	100.00	23.27	23.75	3.19	4.17	0.49	11.23	5.30	7.59	21.00
1916	100.00	22.78	25.91	3.05	3.56	0.49	11.25	5.40	7.44	20.14
1917	100.00	22.44	27.51	3.07	3.31	0.48	11.16	6.97	7.44	17.62
1918	100.00	21.95	27.92	2.95	2.57	0.49	10.59	12.90	7.62	13.01
1919	100.00	22.21	28.53	3.00	3.33	0.53	11.11	10.03	8.13	13.12
1920	100.00	22.17	28.47	3.10	2.73	0.58	11.54	6.80	8.73	15.88
1921	100.00	21.71	26.83	3.07	2.67	0.60	11.53	6.59	8.47	13.53
1922	100.00	20.91	26.44	3.07	3.30	0.61	12.40	6.34	8.32	18.61
1923	100.00	20.46	25.84	3.02	3.45	0.63	13.51	6.25	8.25	18.61
1924	100.00	20.11	24.71	2.81	3.55	0.63	12.72	6.20	7.99	21.28
1925	100.00	19.72	24.28	2.73	4.10	0.63	13.19	6.24	7.56	21.54
1926	100.00	19.14	24.30	2.90	4.01	0.65	13.25	6.25	7.52	21.98
1927	100.00	18.58	23.68	2.86	3.86	0.64	13.49	6.21	7.30	23.36
1928	100.00									

[*] Calculated from the figures presented in Table II.

dency. Industries showing notable gains for the period 1909 to 1927, inclusive, are the following: banking, mercantile, government, Pullman, transportation by water, telephone, telegraph, private electric light and power, and unclassified industries. The increases between the years mentioned, expressed in percentages, are as follows:

Pullman	50%	Mercantile	67%	Telegraph	120%
Unclassified	52%	Government	71%	Telephone	156%
Transportation by water	54%	Banking	89%	Private electric light and power	300%

CHART 2

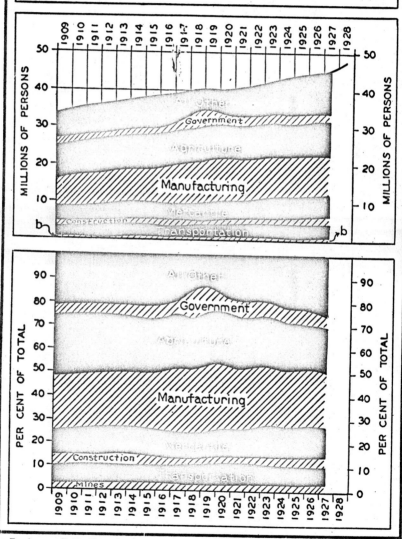

ESTIMATED APPORTIONMENT AMONG
DIFFERENT INDUSTRIES OF THE TOTAL
POPULATION NORMALLY ENGAGED IN
GAINFUL OCCUPATIONS[a]

ᵃ For data, see Tables II and III.
ᵇ Mines.

Since, during this eighteen year period, the total number of persons gainfully occupied expanded by less than 38%, it is evident that the industries just listed have been gaining at the expense of the other fields. It will be observed that the branches of industry which have been stationary or slow in growth are, in general, those commonly considered the more basic in their nature, such as agriculture, manufacturing, mining, construction, and railroad transportation. It appears, then, that, with increasing prosperity, the people of the country have demanded less of these old-fashioned products and more of the newer types of goods and services.

Rank of Industries in Man-Power.

Chart 2 shows that the man-power necessary to carry on our share in the World War was principally obtained by reducing the numbers engaged in construction, merchandising, and unclassified industries, agriculture showing practically no reduction on account of Government demands for men[1] and manufacturing showing an expansion during that period. Even though manufacturing has grown slowly as compared with some of the other fields of activity, it still includes a larger proportion of the gainfully occupied population than any other industry. If we except the heterogeneous group of the "unclassified," agriculture occupies the second place in the industrial field, and the mercantile industry the third. These three industries combined still employ considerably more than half of the total gainfully occupied population in the United States.

Industrial Attachments of Wage Workers.

Table IV shows the number of wage workers attached to each of the leading industrial fields. The fact should be noted at this point that the number of persons "attached" to a given industry is by no means the same thing as the number of persons actually at work in the industry. The phrase "attached to the industry" is here used to indicate the condition of all persons who normally obtain their living by working in the given industry, whether or not they were actually at work on the date specified. In a period of depression, such as 1921, there was of course a great shrinkage in the numbers of employees actually working in the factories of the United States. An investigation[2] made by the National Bureau of

[1] It is possible that our estimates for 1918 are too high for merchandising and agriculture and too low for unclassified industries. They are, however, based upon the best evidence available.

[2] See the publication of the National Bureau of Economic Research entitled, *Employment, Hours, and Earnings in Prosperity and Depression.*

TABLE IV

ESTIMATED NUMBERS OF WAGE WORKERS[a] ATTACHED TO THE VARIOUS INDUSTRIES[b]

(AVERAGE NUMBER FOR YEAR EXPRESSED IN THOUSANDS)

Year	All Industries	Agri-culture[c]	Manu-facturing[c]	Mines, Quarries and Oil Wells[c]	Con-struction[c]	Mer-cantile[d]	Unclas-sified[e]
1909	19,986	2,384	6,875	999	1,410	2,033	4,333
1910	20,543	2,447	7,012	1,023	1,379	2,120	4,454
1911	20,983	2,461	7,157	1,090	1,373	2,185	4,568
1912	21,330	2,403	7,379	1,096	1,392	2,252	4,625
1913	21,916	2,402	7,539	1,147	1,496	2,311	4,706
1914	22,466	2,376	7,698	1,124	1,492	2,375	5,074
1915	22,555	2,407	7,800	1,130	1,296	2,432	5,169
1916	23,074	2,370	8,735	1,098	1,101	2,477	4,988
1917	23,012	2,399	9,394	1,123	1,033	2,505	4,231
1918	21,707	2,419	9,696	1,099	793	2,516	2,745
1919	22,385	2,499	9,813	1,109	1,078	2,593	2,696
1920	23,208	2,419	9,735	1,142	850	2,693	3,626
1921	23,759	2,404	9,330	1,160	849	2,733	4,579
1922	24,256	2,309	9,334	1,175	1,091	3,065	4,601
1923	24,943	2,273	9,328	1,189	1,162	3,525	4,757
1924	25,616	2,282	9,112	1,128	1,230	3,338	5,844
1925	26,150	2,290	9,118	1,112	1,467	3,574	6,033
1926	26,781*	2,294	9,290*	1,208	1,449*	3,677*	6,286*
1927	27,298*	2,276	9,100*	1,215*	1,421*	3,852*	6,893*

[a] The term "wage workers" as here used excludes clerical workers and other salaried employees, all employees in banking, and all public employees.

[b] Workers are considered attached to an industry if they depend upon it for a living even though they are temporarily unemployed.

[c] Sources of information are same as those referred to in Table II.

[d] Based upon reports of *Michigan Dept. of Labor* and upon the *Census of Occupations.*

[e] Based upon *Census of Occupations.*

* Preliminary estimate.

Economic Research showed, however, that there was at that time little tendency on the part of employees to shift their industrial allegiance, mainly because, when employees were being laid off by millions in such fields as manufacturing and mining, no other industries were taking on workers, and hence there was no opportunity for the idle to obtain regular employment elsewhere.

In estimating the number of employees attached to a given industry, it has been assumed that every person continues to be attached to the last industry in which he has been employed until some other suitable industry, by adding to its working force, makes

TABLE IV—Continued

ESTIMATED NUMBERS OF WAGE WORKERS[a] ATTACHED TO THE VARIOUS INDUSTRIES[b]
(AVERAGE NUMBER FOR YEAR EXPRESSED IN THOUSANDS)

Year	All Following Fields of Transportation	Railroads[c]	Pullman[c]	Express[c]	Transportation by Water[c]	Street Railways[c]	Private Electric Light and Power[c]	Telephones[c]	Telegraphs[c]
1909	1,952	1,331	14	31	153	232	38	125	28
1910	2,109	1,453	14	32	154	245	42	140	29
1911	2,149	1,453	14	32	160	257	45	154	35
1912	2,183	1,455	14	34	167	264	48	166	35
1913	2,314	1,564	17	32	172	268	51	176	34
1914	2,327	1,564	17	32	172	270	54	183	34
1915	2,320	1,546	16	32	174	272	57	188	35
1916	2,305	1,506	16	31	177	273	60	202	40
1917	2,327	1,500	15	30	175	274	63	223	46
1918	2,439	1,591	15	25	182	275	67	235	49
1919	2,598	1,686	16	28	225	278	70	248	49
1920	2,743	1,746	18	33	285	278	75	258	51
1921	2,704	1,704	18	31	280	278	81	262	51
1922	2,681	1,679	16	29	278	277	88	264	51
1923	2,708	1,660	17	28	274	288	101	290	51
1924	2,682	1,625	20	26	260	286	105	308	52
1925	2,555	1,486	21	26	250	285	117	313	58
1926	2,577	1,495	21	25	249	286	128	315	58
1927	2,540*	1,455*	22	24	240	288	137	317	58

it possible for him to shift to a new industry.   This assumption avoids abrupt fluctuations in the number of persons attached to industry, and the changes recorded are, as a rule, gradual.

During the last 20 years, marked drifts have occurred in certain industries.   The changes in agriculture and manufacturing have already been noted.   Employment in mines and quarries rose from 1909 to 1913, showed little change between 1913 and 1925, but began to take on more wage workers since the last mentioned date. The construction industry was on a relatively high level between 1909 and 1914, dropped into a trough during the war period largely because of restrictions on private building, but emerged therefrom during the years 1922 to 1925.   Since that date, the number of wage workers employed in this field has been much the same as in the period 1909 to 1914. The mercantile industry has, throughout the period, been absorbing a constantly larger proportion of all wage earners. The same may be said of the unclassified industries, except for a marked depression during the years 1918 to 1920. Railroad wage workers grew in numbers from 1909 to 1920, but, since the last mentioned date, the railroads have operated with fewer employees of this class. The express and transportation by water industries have shown a trend similar to that for railways. The Pullman industry has, during the last twenty years, shown steady growth in the number of wage workers employed. Street railways took on more wage workers from 1909 to 1919, remained approximately on the same level for 4 years, but, since 1923, have again advanced to a higher level. In the telephone and telegraph, and especially in the private electric light and power industries, the number of wage workers has been increasing at a rapid rate.

Salaried Employees and Entrepreneurs.

Between 1909 and 1927 the number of wage workers attached to all industries gained 36%, while, during the same interval, the number of salaried employees was increased by 87%. At first thought, one would probably conclude from these figures that, as industry becomes more highly organized, a larger and larger proportion of the working force is required for managerial purposes. We have seen, however, that the percentage of the total population obtained by adding salaried employees and entrepreneurs has remained approximately constant for the last score of years. The true explanation of the relatively rapid increase in the number of salaried employees appears, then, to be that, as industry has been organized into larger and larger entrepreneurial units, those who formerly were independent entrepreneurs have accepted salaried positions, the total office and managerial force of the nation constituting a practically unchanging proportion of the gainfully occupied population.

Industrial Attachments of Salaried Employees.

Data concerning the number of employees working for salaries are more scanty, in general, than are those relating to wage workers. The estimates for the agricultural field, for example, appearing in Table V, represent little more than rough guesses. The same may be said of the figures for the construction industry, the mercantile industry, transportation by water, banking, and unclassified in-

CHART 3

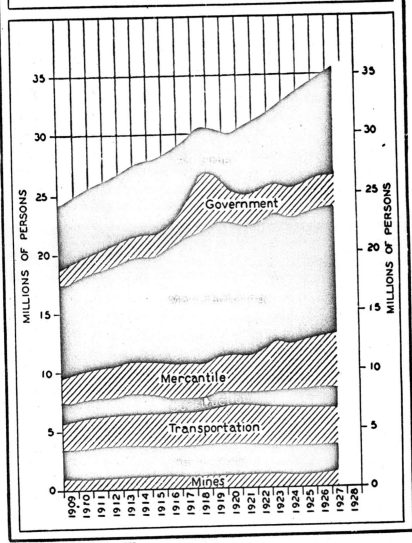

ESTIMATED NUMBERS OF EMPLOYEES
ATTACHED TO THE VARIOUS INDUSTRIES*

Government

Mercantile

Transportation

Mines

TABLE V

ESTIMATED NUMBERS OF SALARIED EMPLOYEES* ATTACHED TO THE VARIOUS INDUSTRIES[b]

(AVERAGE NUMBER FOR YEAR EXPRESSED IN THOUSANDS)

Year	All Industries	Agriculture°	Manufacturing°	Mines, Quarries and Oil Wells°	Construction°	Banking[d]	Mercantile°	Government[d]	Unclassified°
1909	4,424	60	790	43	90	151	398	1,643	794
1910	4,673	60	905	44	96	155	410	1,709	816
1911	4,811	60	930	45	102	163	421	1,765	826
1912	4,980	61	976	47	108	169	428	1,821	849
1913	5,162	62	1,007	50	121	174	452	1,879	875
1914	5,340	63	1,007	52	125	179	470	1,947	949
1915	5,407	65	983	54	112	181	481	2,013	965
1916	5,555	66	1,046	57	98	184	503	2,085	955
1917	6,367	68	1,214	61	95	187	526	2,744	878
1918	8,879	69	1,363	68	74	193	508	5,210	763
1919	7,968	70	1,468	77	103	209	509	4,042	820
1920	6,740	71	1,448	75	82	228	522	2,719	853
1921	6,991	69	1,424	74	83	243	565	2,689	1,102
1922	7,026	63	1,403	75	108	249	629	2,689	1,133
1923	7,185	55	1,385	65	115	262	712	2,618	1,197
1924	7,488	46	1,375	68	122	267	677	2,633	1,504
1925	7,697	39	1,370	70	146	274	723	2,674	1,587
1926	7,896*	35*	1,387*	70	145*	284	735*	2,736	1,689*
1927	8,274*	32*	1,498*	70*	142*	288*	771*	2,785*	1,892*

a Includes both managerial and clerical employees.

b Workers are considered attached to an industry if they depend upon it for a living, even though they are temporarily unemployed.

c Sources of information are same as those referred to in Table IV.

d Wage workers as well as salaried employees included here. For sources from which figures are derived, see notes to Table II.

* Preliminary estimate.

dustries. The last really dependable data for the whole group of electrical industries, with the exception of the telephone industry, are the Census figures for 1922, hence our estimates for more recent years may be considerably in error. For mines, quarries and oil-wells the only reliable figures available are those for 1909 and 1919. Fortunately, the estimates for manufacturing, government, and the railroad, Pullman, and express industries, rest on a firmer foundation.

We find that the number of salaried employees in manufacturing almost doubled between 1909 and 1919, but remained approximately

TABLE V—Continued

ESTIMATED NUMBERS OF SALARIED EMPLOYEES[a] ATTACHED TO THE VARIOUS INDUSTRIES[b]

(AVERAGE NUMBER FOR YEAR EXPRESSED IN THOUSANDS)

Year	All Following Fields of Transportation	Railroads[c]	Pullman[c]	Express[c]	Transportation by Water[c]	Street Railways[c]	Private Electric Light and Power[c]	Telephones[c]	Telegraphs[c]
1909	455	289	4	28	64	17	17	24	12
1910	479	305	4	29	65	20	20	25	12
1911	499	310	4	29	66	22	22	32	14
1912	522	318	4	31	68	24	24	39	14
1913	541	331	4	31	68	25	26	42	14
1914	547	335	4	31	67	25	28	42	14
1915	553	337	4	33	67	26	30	42	15
1916	561	338	4	33	67	27	31	42	18
1917	594	352	4	44	67	27	33	45	21
1918	629	377	4	45	70	28	35	47	23
1919	669	389	4	49	88	29	38	49	23
1920	742	417	5	58	114	29	41	53	24
1921	743	418	5	51	114	30	45	56	24
1922	749	418	5	48	114	31	51	58	24
1923	761	420	5	47	114	31	60	60	25
1924	755	416	5	44	109	32	63	62	25
1925	751	405	5	42	105	32	70	64	28
1926	766	408	6	43	105	33	78	66	28
1927	763*	401*	6	41	101	34	84	68	28

stationary since the latter date. While the number of persons employed by the Federal Government can be estimated with a fair degree of accuracy, the number serving the State and Local governments can be calculated but roughly. It appears, however, that, aside from the great war-time increase in the military and naval establishments, the number of employees of the various governmental units in the United States grew consistently from 1909 to 1917, and, since the War, has remained on a level materially higher than existed before the War. The number of salaried employees working for the railroads increased steadily between 1909 and 1920, but, since the last mentioned date, has been fairly constant. Much the same tendency is apparent in the express industry, although there has been more of a decline in that field in recent years.

TABLE VI

ESTIMATED NUMBERS OF ENTREPRENEURS[a] ATTACHED TO THE VARIOUS INDUSTRIES[b]
(AVERAGE NUMBER FOR YEAR EXPRESSED IN THOUSANDS)

Year	All Indus-tries	Agri-culture[c]	Manu-fac-turing[d]	Mines, Quarries and Oil Wells[e]	Con-struc-tion[f]	Bank-ing[g]	Mer-can-tile[h]	Trans-porta-tion by Water[i]	Un-clas-sified[f]
1909	9,845	6,289	264	35	174	4	1,223	9	1,847
1910	9,884	6,307	259	33	175	4	1,253	9	1,845
1911	9,906	6,322	254	31	176	4	1,271	9	1,839
1912	9,927	6,336	249	30	177	4	1,289	9	1,834
1913	9,950	6,346	244	29	178	4	1,309	9	1,832
1914	9,976	6,353	239	28	178	4	1,331	9	1,836
1915	9,994	6,359	233	27	176	4	1,348	9	1,838
1916	10,009	6,365	228	26	176	4	1,365	9	1,838
1917	9,994	6,369	222	25	174	4	1,364	8	1,828
1918	9,797	6,374	217	24	169	4	1,254	8	1,748
1919	9,929	6,378	211	23	162	4	1,374	8	1,769
1920	10,060	6,381	206	22	160	4	1,403	8	1,876
1921	10,069	6,387	200	21	160	4	1,408	8	1,882
1922	10,048	6,271	191	20	164	4	1,432	8	1,959
1923	10,028	6,297	178	19	176	4	1,456	8	1,890
1924	10,019	6,344	167	18	180	4	1,471	8	1,828
1925	9,997	6,317	159	17	185	4	1,484	8	1,824
1926	9,883*	6,200*	153*	16	192	4	1,493*	8	1,819
1927	9,801*	6,124*	148*	15	190	4	1,499*	7	1,814

[a] The term "entrepreneur," as here used, includes not only employers, but also individuals working on their own account, as, for example, farmers, merchants, lawyers, physicians, etc.

[b] Workers are considered attached to an industry if they depend upon it for a living, even though they are temporarily unemployed.

[c] Based upon *Census of Agriculture* and reports of the *U. S. Dept. of Agriculture.*

[d] Based upon *Censuses of Manufactures* and of *Occupations.*

[e] Based upon *Censuses of Mines and Quarries* and of *Occupations.*

[f] Based upon *Census of Occupations.*

[g] Based upon estimate of volume of banking business as indicated by figures in reports of *Comptroller of Currency.*

[h] Based upon *Census of Occupations* and original investigation of volume of sales.

[i] Based upon reports of the *Commissioner of Navigation* and upon *Merchant Marine Statistics.*

* Preliminary estimate.

Industrial Attachments of Entrepreneurs.

Table VI records the estimated numbers of entrepreneurs attached to the leading industries. These estimates are, however, subject to a large margin of error. The figures for banking are little more than guesses, while those for transportation by water are based upon data too fragmentary to command much respect. In

CHART 4

ESTIMATED NUMBERS OF ENTREPRENEURS ATTACHED TO THE VARIOUS INDUSTRIES[a]

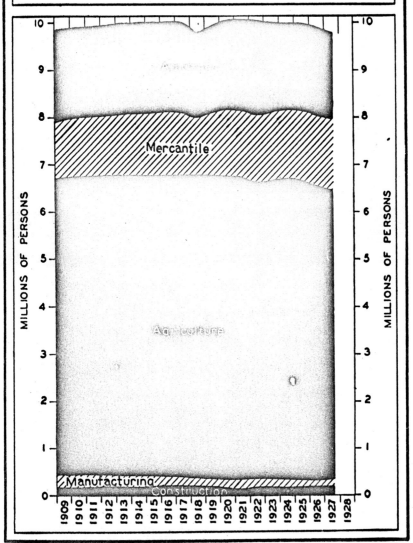

the construction industry and also in the unclassified field, information likewise is lamentably scanty. In general, the figures in Table VI represent estimates made upon the basis of the data contained in the *Census of Occupations* for 1910 and a similar census for 1920. Even for those two dates the totals are not entirely accurate, for the data for various occupations, as recorded in the reports of the Bureau of the Census, frequently fail to distinguish entrepreneurs from employees. Data compiled by the United States Bureau of Agricultural Economics enable us to calculate with some degree of confidence the number of entrepreneurs or farmers in agriculture for recent years. Furthermore, the *Census of Agriculture*, taken in 1925, gives us an additional basing point. Since farmers constitute approximately 3/5 of all entrepreneurs, it is fortunate that the single field for which fairly reliable information is available is the largest of all entrepreneurial groups. The *Census of Manufactures* gives us fairly dependable information for the years 1909, 1914, and 1919. For the period since 1919, our estimates of the number of individual entrepreneurs engaged in manufacturing have little to commend them. For mines, quarries, and oil-wells, reliable data are available only for the years 1909 and 1919. Dependable information for the mercantile industry can be obtained only for 1910 and 1920. The same is true of the estimates for the unclassified field. Despite the shortcomings of the data, there can be little doubt about the outstanding facts portrayed in Chart 4.

The Decline of the Individual Entrepreneur.

The decline in the number of entrepreneurs caused by the enrollment of men in the army during the war is also clearly indicated, as is the fact that the total number of entrepreneurs has tended to remain approximately stationary during the period when the numbers of employees in the various industries have been moving steadily upward. The decline since 1924 in the number of entrepreneurs in each of the three leading fields is also clearly shown. This chart, then, when taken in combination with those preceding, makes it perfectly plain that the independent entrepreneur is playing a relatively much less important rôle in industry than was the case a score of years ago.

CHAPTER III

INDEX NUMBERS FOR USE AS DEFLATORS

Dollar Has a Fluctuating Value.

The most convenient unit for measuring the income of the people of the United States is the dollar. But, as it happens, the dollar of 1909 was a very different unit from the dollar of 1919, and the latter in turn had little resemblance, in its purchasing power, to the dollar of 1921. Although, throughout the period, the United States Government has always been ready to redeem its money in gold dollars of constant weight, these gold dollars have varied greatly in their ability to purchase goods. If, therefore, we were to express the income of the people of the nation in terms of the dollars of the various years and make no further corrections, the changes in totals would have little real significance, and we might be accused of attempting to deceive the public as to the facts. What counts with the average citizen is not how many dollars he receives per annum, but how many goods a given number of dollars will buy. To ascertain this fact, it is necessary first to compute the number of dollars of income which he receives in each year and next to discover the relative quantities of goods purchasable in the various years with the income received. The most feasible way to accomplish this is first to construct a series of index numbers representing the relative changes in the average value of all goods bought, and then to divide the number of dollars received in each year by the appropriate index for that year.

Single Index Series Unsatisfactory as Deflator.

Evidently no two citizens buy in any given year exactly the same kinds and quantities of goods. Yet, to convert the income of a citizen to terms of constant purchasing power, the only accurate method is to divide by an index representing the average prices of goods which he has purchased. For this purpose it is necessary to have as many index numbers as there are purchasers. Under the circumstances the statistician must classify the inhabitants of the nation into a few broad classes, and then must arbitrarily calculate an index number presumably applicable to each class. This process manifestly does some violence to the facts. Were it true that the prices of goods bought by the various citizens in a class pursued radically different trends, it would, then, necessarily follow that the results obtained by putting citizens into classes would be wholly meaningless. Fortunately for the statistician, however, the prices of various classes of goods tend to have fluctuations resembling each other to a considerable extent; hence differences in the make-up of individual budgets do not affect greatly the course of the price averages. This fact explains why an average index number may give results which, after all, are not meaningless.

Upon What Commodities Should the Deflating Index Be Based?

Granted that we are to calculate separate index numbers for several classes of the population, we are still confronted by the fact that the members of each class of the population buy a great variety of goods. During the year they purchase consumers' goods, producers' goods, securities, life insurance, in fact a multitude of material goods and services. Which of these commodities shall be included in the list used in making up the index number used for purposes of deflation?

Why Indices of the Prices of Consumers' Goods Are Used as Deflators.

For several reasons it seems wisest to use, in the construction of an index number, the values of consumers' goods only. First, all other classes of goods are purchased not with a view to the service which they themselves will render, but in expectation that they will add to the possibilities of economic gain. The services anticipated from all classes of production goods, securities, etc. are then *indirect*, while the services rendered by consumers' goods are *direct*. This means that the market values of all indirect goods depend upon guesses as to the probable values in the future of the direct or consumers' goods into which the indirect goods are expected to mature. Thus, the present price of wheat is dependent upon the anticipated price of the bread into which it is ultimately to be converted; the present price of lumber depends largely upon the anticipated rent of the houses which are to be built from the lumber; the present worth of a share of stock depends upon the dividends which it is expected will be paid upon that stock in the future; and these dividends in turn depend upon income determined by future differentials existing between the prices of goods and services purchased by the corporation and prices of goods and services sold by the corporation. Evidently, then, prices of raw materials are at least one or two stages removed from the point at

which the consumer compares the gratification derivable from the consumption of the goods with the utility of the money which it takes to buy it. Security prices are several stages removed from this goal. Now, since the total income of the people of the nation varies but slowly, and since the total volume of wants and the total volume of goods produced to supply these wants fluctuate but little, the general tendency is for the average prices of direct or consumers' goods to vary but little from month to month and year to year, unless some marked change occurs in the currency supply of the country. The prices of indirect goods, however, show no such tendency to remain stable. It is, for example, generally true that the fluctuations occurring in the prices of wheat, steel, cotton, and the like are much greater than are the fluctuations in the prices of consumers' goods. Security prices, being still further removed from the ultimate goal of consumption, oscillate still more vigorously. Observation shows that the usual tendency is for index numbers representing the prices of indirect goods to fluctuate above and below a normal represented by the index series representing the prices of direct goods. The relationship doubtless arises from the fact that the prices of indirect goods are influenced by all kinds of guesses, rumors, and misconceptions, while the prices of direct goods are affected, in the main, by the immediate forces of supply and demand existing at the given time. Since the prices of direct goods represent reality, while the prices of indirect goods represent merely guesses as to future realities, there is always a tendency for the guesses to be corrected from time to time in the direction of reality. Hence we find the index numbers of commodities at wholesale fluctuating about a norm consisting of the index numbers of commodities at retail. For purposes of deflation, it is more convenient to use a series of index numbers which do not fluctuate widely, and it also seems more desirable to employ for this purpose index numbers representing actual conditions of supply and demand at the given time rather than those portraying changes in the psychology of the public. The facts just enumerated furnish, then, one strong argument for using as deflators indices of the prices of consumers' goods.

A second reason for using the prices of direct or consumers' goods in order to reduce the income of the people of the United States to dollars of constant purchasing power, is that the entire population are immediately interested in the prices of consumers' goods. Very many similarities exist in the consumption of goods by different families in a given income class in a specified locality. If you know

TABLE VII

ESTIMATED INDICES OF THE AVERAGE PRICES OF DIRECT OR CONSUMPTION GOODS USED BY DIFFERENT CLASSES OF THE POPULATION

(AVERAGE FOR 1913 = 1.000)

| DATE | SEMI-ANNUAL INDICES[a] | | | | | AVERAGE FOR YEAR INDICES | | | | |
| | Urban, Manual and Clerical Workers | Farm Laborers | Farmers | Families Spending for Direct Goods | | Urban, Manual and Clerical Workers | Farm Laborers | Farmers | Families Spending for Direct Goods | |
				$5,000	$25,000				$5,000	$25,000
1909 Jan. 1	.938	.976	.946	.929	.944					
July 1	.933	.980	.951	.927	.945	.945	.989	.968	.936	.951
1910 Jan. 1	.975	1.022	1.024	.961	.969					
July 1	.964	1.006	.971	.959	.969	.969	1.006	.995	.962	.969
1911 Jan. 1	.972	.991	1.012	.970	.971					
July 1	.957	.974	.939	.958	.960	.969	.977	.973	.966	.966
1912 Jan. 1	.991	.967	1.000	.980	.975					
July 1	.976	.967	.978	.971	.971	.982	.972	.987	.978	.978
1913 Jan. 1	.988	.988	.992	.992	.993					
July 1	.999	1.009	.983	.997	.999	1.000	1.000	1.000	1.000	1.000
1914 Jan. 1	1.015	.995	1.042	1.013	1.008					
July 1	1.009	.974	.992	1.006	1.000	1.017	.976	1.008	1.006	1.002
1915 Jan. 1	1.030	.960	1.006	1.001	1.002					
July 1	1.031	.949	.954	.983	.995	1.035	.962	.985	.996	1.005
1916 Jan. 1	1.057	.993	1.024	1.019	1.028					
July 1	1.100	1.036	1.083	1.050	1.056	1.116	1.040	1.108	1.064	1.064
1917 Jan. 1	1.183	1.094	1.242	1.139	1.118					
July 1	1.292	1.197	1.430	1.223	1.180	1.304	1.201	1.409	1.222	1.181
1918 Jan. 1	1.428	1.316	1.533	1.301	1.245					
July 1	1.589	1.474	1.565	1.419	1.348	1.572	1.472	1.613	1.422	1.346
1919 Jan. 1	1.750	1.622	1.789	1.550	1.442					
July 1	1.785	1.733	1.800	1.611	1.497	1.831	1.754	1.845	1.640	1.522
1920 Jan. 1	2.003	1.926	1.988	1.790	1.654					
July 1	2.172	2.032	2.115	1.940	1.779	2.088	1.963	2.001	1.872	1.739

(Continued on next page)

TABLE VII—Continued

ESTIMATED INDICES OF THE AVERAGE PRICES OF DIRECT OR CONSUMPTION GOODS USED BY DIFFERENT CLASSES OF THE POPULATION

(AVERAGE FOR 1913 = 1.000)

	SEMI-ANNUAL INDICES[a]					AVERAGE FOR YEAR INDICES				
DATE	Urban, Manual and Clerical Workers	Farm Laborers	Farmers	Families Spending for Direct Goods		Urban, Manual and Clerical Workers	Farm Laborers	Farmers	Families Spending for Direct Goods	
				$5,000	$25,000				$5,000	$25,000
1921 Jan. 1	1.980	1.861	1.787	1.816	1.745	1.800	1.584	1.557	1.681	1.667
July 1	1.766	1.522	1.457	1.657	1.655					
1922 Jan. 1	1.733	1.432	1.528	1.593	1.611	1.676	1.398	1.481	1.579	1.608
July 1	1.670	1.392	1.458	1.567	1.601					
1923 Jan. 1	1.693	1.376	1.481	1.587	1.620	1.707	1.436	1.452	1.598	1.615
July 1	1.700	1.447	1.420	1.596	1.611					
1924 Jan. 1	1.732	1.476	1.485	1.612	1.616	1.706	1.460	1.466	1.601	1.608
July 1	1.691	1.456	1.420	1.585	1.598					
1925 Jan. 1	1.730	1.452	1.540	1.621	1.620	1.744	1.451	1.588	1.637	1.641
July 1	1.745	1.438	1.573	1.635	1.642					
1926 Jan. 1	1.774	1.477	1.667	1.657	1.659	1.755	1.440	1.621	1.638	1.638
July 1	1.743	1.423	1.617	1.632	1.630					
1927 Jan. 1	1.751	1.437	1.583	1.632	1.632	1.722	1.416	1.529	1.611	1.618
July 1	1.718	1.403	1.501	1.605	1.608					
1928 Jan. 1	1.715	1.422	1.524	1.603	1.619	1.706	1.402	1.503	1.586*	1.598*
July 1	1.700	1.395	1.495	1.577	1.586					
1929 Jan. 1	1.708	1.398	1.498	1.589*	1.600*					

[a] For mode of estimation, see the report of this Bureau, entitled, *Income in the Various States*, pp. 25-27.

* Preliminary estimate.

the income of a family in a certain city at a particular date, you can predict with a reasonable degree of accuracy the grade of food they will eat, the size and furnishings of the house they will live in, the kind of clothes they will wear, the mode of transportation which they will enjoy, and the amusements in which they will indulge. It is, therefore, not impossible to construct an index number which will, in a broad way, represent the prices of goods used by a given income class.

To Deflate the Income of Different Sections of the Population Different Index Numbers Are Required.

To predict, however, in what classes of commodities or in what enterprises the various income classes will invest their surplus funds, is a matter of much greater difficulty. Statistics along this line are extremely scanty. It follows, then, that, even if it were desirable, it would be statistically impracticable to compile index numbers of indirect goods which could be depended upon to typify the expenditures of the various categories of the population.

Nature of Five Series of Index Numbers.

The index numbers appearing in Table VII represent the estimated average fluctuations in the prices of commodities supposed to have been consumed respectively by each of the five classes of families mentioned. For any given class, the index numbers are intended to show the relative changes in the prices of goods used by the average family in that group in the period 1919-1921. In order to make the figures fairly comparable from year to year, an effort has been made to compare prices of the same quantities of identical commodities in all years. Since most commodities are changing their form from time to time, it is, of course, in practice, impossible to compute index numbers which will completely satisfy this condition. We cannot be sure, for example, that certain of the commodities presented are of exactly the same quality at all the specified dates. In some instances, it has been necessary to substitute a new commodity for another which has gone out of use. The index numbers presented must, then, be understood to represent merely approximations to the truth, but care has been taken to make these approximations as close as is feasible, considering the resources at the command of the investigators. Those interested in a more detailed description of the method of computing these index series and of the weights applied to the various commodities, are referred to pages 25-27 of the publication of this Bureau entitled *Income in the Various States.*

Comparative Movements of Five Index Series.

Reference to the figures in Table VII and to Chart 5 shows that all five of these index series moved along a trend somewhat horizon-

CHART 5

INDICES OF THE PRICES OF CONSUMPTION GOODS[a]

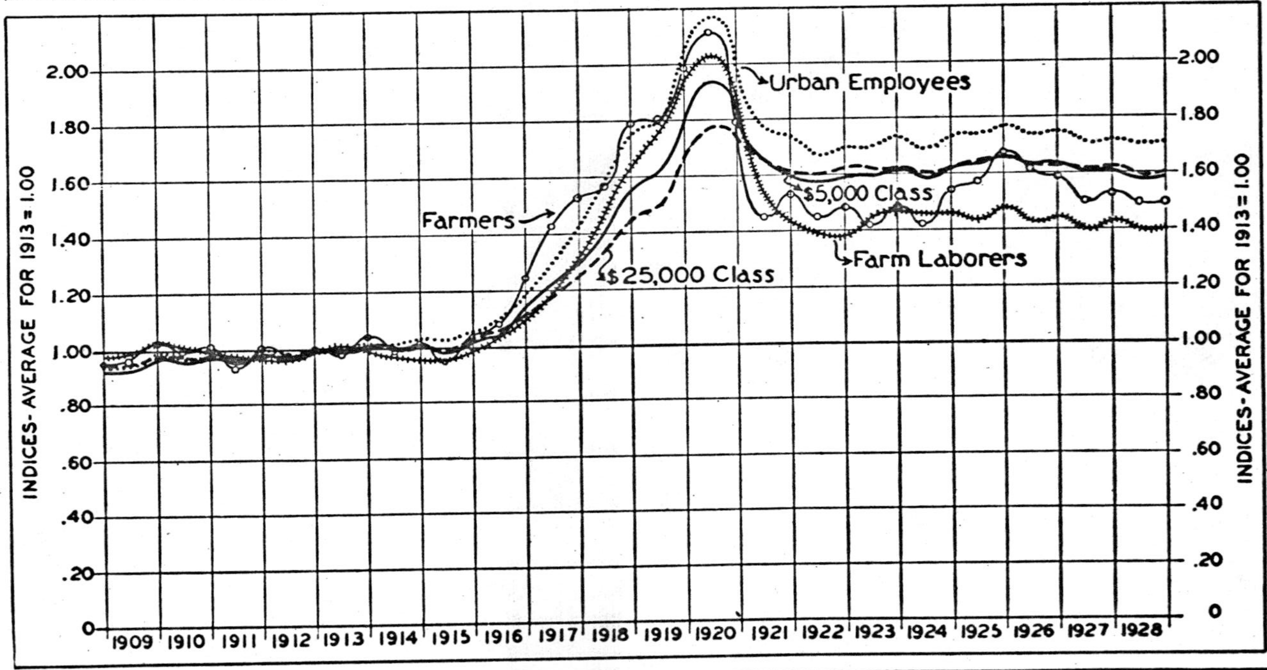
Urban Employees
$5,000 Class
Farmers
Farm Laborers
$25,000 Class
INDICES - AVERAGE FOR 1913 = 1.00
2.00
1.80
1.60
1.40
1.20
1.00
.80
.60
.40
.20
0
1909
1910
1911
1912
1913
1914
1915
1916
1917
1918
1919
1920
1921
1922
1923
1924
1925
1926
1927
1928

[a] For data, see Table VII.

tal, though perhaps sloping slightly upward, from January 1, 1909 to July 1, 1915. After the latter date, currency inflation had its effect, and all five index numbers rose rapidly along almost straight lines until the middle of 1920. The price rise in this period, although not nearly as great as that characterizing the increase in prices of commodities at wholesale, nevertheless amounted to from 78 to 122 per cent, and proved great enough to throw into confusion the whole economic life of the country. The prices of goods used by farmers and urban employees reached peaks higher than those of the other three index series, while the indices of the prices of goods used by the richer classes of consumers did not ascend so steeply. When the price crash came in the latter half of 1920 and the first half of 1921, it was the price indices representing the cost of goods purchased by farmers and farm laborers which fell fastest and farthest. These index numbers, being dependent to no small extent on the prices of home-produced commodities consumed on the farms of the producers, were pulled down by the collapse in the price of farm produce in 1920 and drifted downward until the middle of 1922. Since that date, four of the index numbers have pursued trends approximately horizontal, but having perhaps a slightly upward inclination. All five of the index series rose somewhat above the usual level at the close of 1925, but, around that date, the prices of consumers' goods used by farmers showed much more tendency to rise than did the prices of goods used by any of the other groups. In the middle of 1928, all five series stood at a point noticeably lower than the positions which they respectively occupied at the beginning of 1926. During the last half of 1928, however, a slightly rising tendency is apparent, but this may represent nothing more than a seasonal movement.

CHAPTER IV

INDUSTRIAL ORIGIN OF TOTAL REALIZED INCOME

Imputed Income.

Estimates of the aggregate realized income of the people of the Continental United States are presented in Table VIII. One of the important columns appearing in this table bears the title "Imputed Income." This column refers to the estimated value of the services rendered to their owners by durable direct or consumers' goods. Of the fact that durable consumable commodities render services having great economic value, there can be no doubt. For example, if each of two men working in the same office has accumulated $10,000, one man may purchase a house and the other invest in bonds and use the interest received on these bonds to pay the rent of his residence. Under these circumstances, both men have used similar amounts of accumulated funds to obtain similar services and, if the two houses are alike, there seems to be no logical reason for assuming that one man receives more income from his $10,000 than does the other. When we save money, we have the option of investing it and using the money return to buy such services of goods as we desire, or we can use the money to purchase the goods and thus control all of their future services. The services have equal value in either case. It seems only fair, then, to include in the income of the people of the nation an item representing the value of the services of the durable consumption goods which they own. Unfortunately, the total value of the services of such goods cannot be estimated with any degree of precision, since, for the most part, no statistical data on the value of these services are available. Under the circumstances, we have been forced to adopt for many of these goods the somewhat doubtful expedient of basing the estimated value of the services upon the market value of the goods rendering the services. The procedure for such goods has been to estimate the value in the hands of consumers, applying to that market value a fixed rate of interest, namely 6 per cent. This procedure has not, however, been applied to the services of residential property. We have estimated directly the rental value of urban homes occupied by their owners. The results of these computations

TABLE VIII

ESTIMATED REALIZED INCOME[*] OF THE PEOPLE OF THE CONTINENTAL UNITED STATES
(MILLIONS OF CURRENT DOLLARS)

YEAR	Total Including Imputed Income	SHARE OF ENTREPRENEURS AND OTHER PROPERTY OWNERS[b]			SHARE OF EMPLOYEES[c]				Total Excluding Imputed Income
		Imputed Income[a]	Money and Commodity Income[a]	Total	Wages	Salaries	Pensions, Compensations, etc.	Total	
1909	$29,605	$1,944	$12,571	$14,515	$10,529	$ 4,316	$ 246	$15,090	$27,661
1910	31,430	2,085	13,078	15,163	11,330	4,682	254	16,266	29,345
1911	31,858	2,198	13,162	15,360	11,325	4,918	256	16,498	29,660
1912	33,977	2,222	14,168	16,390	12,112	5,203	273	17,587	31,755
1913	35,723	2,330	14,571	16,901	13,017	5,503	302	18,822	33,393
1914	35,647	2,420	14,711	17,131	12,396	5,809	311	18,516	33,227
1915	37,205	2,515	15,330	17,845	13,117	5,926	317	19,361	34,690
1916	43,288	2,703	18,114	20,817	15,660	6,376	434	22,470	40,585
1917	51,331	3,017	22,512	25,529	17,741	7,665	396	25,802	48,314
1918	60,408	3,750	24,334	28,084	20,414	11,232	678	32,324	56,658
1919	65,949	4,321	26,229	30,550	23,029	11,576	794	35,399	61,628
1920	73,999	5,557	26,159	31,716	29,540	11,727	1,016	42,283	68,442
1921	63,371	5,100	22,057	27,157	23,353	11,855	1,006	36,213	58,271
1922	65,925	4,738	23,487	28,225	24,553	12,050	1,097	37,700	61,187
1923	74,337	5,042	26,402	31,444	28,691	13,156	1,046	42,893	69,295
1924	77,135	5,230	27,412	32,642	29,051	14,200	1,243	44,493	71,905
1925	81,931	5,370	29,705	35,076	30,762	15,008	1,085	46,855	76,561
1926	85,548*	5,264*	30,517*	35,781*	32,604*	15,991*	1,173*	49,767*	80,284*
1927	88,205*	5,284*	31,561*	36,845*	32,884*	17,243*	1,229*	51,360*	82,921*
1928	89,419*	5,300*	32,996*	38,296*	32,235*	17,823*	1,065*	51,123*	84,119*

[*] For definition of this term, see text.

[b] Includes also miscellaneous payments to non-investors, and entrepreneurial and investment income of employees.

[c] Excludes income derived from entrepreneurial activities or investments.

[*] Preliminary estimate.

appear in the third column of Table VIII.[1] It will be seen that this item of imputed income increased from not quite two billions of dollars in 1909 to 5 ¼ billions in 1927, at both dates representing approximately 6 per cent of the estimated total realized income of all the people.

[1] For further details concerning the mode of estimating miscellaneous and imputed income, see *Income in the United States*, Vol. II, Chapter 19. The figure here used for the rental value of homes is a *net* and not a *gross* estimate.

Since, as just stated, the estimates of imputed income are unavoidably based upon very scanty data and hence inspire no great degree of confidence, two totals of realized income are presented in Table VIII, the one at the left representing the total including imputed income, and the one at the right excluding imputed income.

Items Omitted from the Realized Income Here Recorded.

It will be remembered that neither of the totals of realized income here set forth includes any allowance for the income which might be imputed to housewives and householders for services rendered to their own families, nor do they include the value of services by individuals rendered to themselves, nor the value of goods and services received by employees in the guise of expense accounts, nor money earned through odd-job employment. The first two classes of items are so large in value that, were they included, the totals presented in Table VIII might be magnified much or little, depending upon the method of estimation used. All of these categories have been excluded because their computation is necessarily a matter of guess work. It will also be remembered that the total of *realized* income does not include any income arising from changes in the value of property.

Entire Realized Income in Current Dollars.

The totals including imputed income, appearing at the left hand side of Table VIII, indicate that the realized income of the people of the United States which, in 1909, was approximately 29½ billions of dollars, had risen by 1928 to 89½ billions, slightly more than trebling. This increase, however, must not be taken too seriously, for, to a considerable extent it represents nothing more than a change in the value of the dollar.

Shares in the Realized Income.

It will be observed that the total realized income is made up of two parts, first, the share of entrepreneurs and other property owners, and second, the share of the employees. As indicated by the sub-titles, the share of the employees consists of wages, salaries, pensions, and compensation for injuries. As here defined, this share represents income from employment and does not include income which employees may receive as a result of entrepreneurial activities or as a return on investments. Both of the latter types of income are included as a part of the share of entrepreneurs and other property owners. In short, the classification here adopted classifies the income and not the recipients. The share of the entrepreneurs and other property owners includes the item of imputed income previously discussed, and also a much larger item, entitled "Money and Commodity Income." Leading items comprised under the last-mentioned heading are dividends on stocks, interest on mortgages and funded debt, rents derived from real estate, royalties obtained from patents, copyrights, and the production of minerals, and miscellaneous net income accruing from ownership of property. The category "Money and Commodity Income" also includes the estimated total amount of profits withdrawn for personal use by entrepreneurs from the enterprises which they direct. Most of the income recorded in this column is received in the form of money or money equivalents, such as checks, but some is made up of commodities. For example, merchants may take from the stock in their stores goods for consumption at home. Farmers commonly derive a considerable fraction of their living from the wood, vegetables, fruits, honey, milk, butter, and meat produced on their own farms. These farm-grown products have been evaluated at the average prices prevailing on the farms of the United States at the given dates.

On account of the fact that records of entrepreneurial profits are difficult to obtain and even more difficult to apportion between savings and money withdrawn from the business, the figures showing the share of entrepreneurs and other property owners are subject to a much greater possibility of error than are those recording the total share of the employees, a share consisting of wages, salaries, pensions, and compensation for injuries.

Reference to Table VIII shows that the combined wage, salary, and pension bill of the nation is larger in every year than the share of the entrepreneurs and other property owners. The differential, which before 1917 was relatively small, has grown until, in 1927, the employees were receiving in realized income almost 40 per cent more than the entrepreneurs and other property owners. Roughly, two-thirds of the share of the employees consists of wages, while salaries account for something like one-third, pensions and compensations for injuries together forming but a relatively small item.

Entire Realized Income in Terms of 1913 Dollars.

The data contained in Table IX are of much greater significance than are those found in Table VIII, for all values in Table IX have

TABLE IX

PURCHASING POWER, IN 1913 DOLLARS,[a]
OF ESTIMATED REALIZED INCOME[c] OF THE PEOPLE
OF THE CONTINENTAL UNITED STATES
(MILLIONS OF 1913 DOLLARS)[b]

YEAR	Total Including Imputed Income	SHARE OF ENTREPRENEURS AND OTHER PROPERTY OWNERS[d]			SHARE OF EMPLOYEES[e]				Total Excluding Imputed Income
		Imputed Income[c]	Money and Commodity Income[c]	Total	Wages	Salaries	Pensions, Compensations, etc.	Total	
1909	$31,300	$2,079	$13,275	$15,354	$11,113	$ 4,573	$260	$15,946	$29,221
1910	32,380	2,173	13,441	15,614	11,668	4,836	262	16,766	30,207
1911	32,920	2,286	13,615	15,901	11,679	5,076	264	17,019	30,634
1912	34,656	2,283	14,460	16,743	12,336	5,299	278	17,913	32,373
1913	35,756	2,343	14,591	16,934	13,017	5,503	302	18,822	33,413
1914	35,250	2,409	14,602	17,011	12,216	5,717	306	18,238	32,841
1915	36,636	2,499	15,351	17,850	12,728	5,751	307	18,786	34,137
1916	39,559	2,563	16,783	19,346	14,081	5,742	390	20,214	36,996
1917	40,242	2,629	17,716	20,345	13,671	5,922	304	19,897	37,613
1918	40,150	2,889	16,573	19,462	13,036	7,220	433	20,688	37,261
1919	38,017	2,919	15,645	18,564	12,610	6,409	434	19,453	35,098
1920	37,573	3,225	13,963	17,188	14,194	5,703	488	20,385	34,348
1921	36,710	3,072	13,357	16,429	13,077	6,645	559	20,282	33,638
1922	40,565	2,942	14,941	17,883	14,785	7,242	655	22,682	37,623
1923	45,164	3,092	16,747	19,839	16,938	7,774	614	25,325	42,072 .
1924	46,758	3,181	17,309	20,490	17,148	8,389	730	26,267	43,577
1925	48,412	3,221	18,118	21,339	17,781	8,668	623	27,072	45,191
1926	50,421*	3,160*	18,684*	21,844*	18,729*	9,179*	669*	28,577*	47,261*
1927	52,892*	3,237*	19,596*	22,833*	19,251*	10,093*	713*	30,059*	49,655*
1928	54,022*	3,330*	20,725*	24,055*	18,895*	10,447*	624*	29,967*	50,692*

[a] "1913 Dollars" is an abbreviation for the phrase "dollars having purchasing power equivalent to that which they had in 1913."

[b] Computed from the corresponding items in Table VIII, by dividing by the appropriate price indices recorded in Table VII.

[c] For definition of this term, see text.

[d] Includes also miscellaneous payments to non-investors, and entrepreneurial and investment income of employees.

[e] Excludes income derived from entrepreneurial activities or investments.

* Preliminary estimate.

been reduced to terms of dollars having purchasing power equal to that which they possessed in 1913, and hence, fluctuations due to changes in the purchasing power of money have been eliminated. Including imputed income, the entire realized income of the people of the United States rose from 31 billions of constant dollars in 1909, to nearly 53 billions of the same dollars in 1927, representing an increase equal to more than two-thirds of the amount for the first date mentioned. The score of years covered by Table IX may well be divided into three parts. The first period, running from 1909 to 1916, was one of rapidly increasing income, broken only by a slight decline in 1914, doubtless caused by the business depression of that year. The second period, which includes the years 1918 to 1921, was characterized by a sharp decline in the total national income, presumably due partially to the disturbance of industry incident to its conversion from a war to a peace basis, and partially to the disrupting effect of the great price collapse of 1920 and 1921. The third period, which begins with 1922, and continues up to 1928, has witnessed a marked rise in the total income, the ascent being at a rate even more rapid than that characterizing the period 1909 to 1917; in fact, between 1921 and 1927, the purchasing power of the income of the people of the United States increased by approximately 44 per cent. It is probable that no other nation at any time in history has ever enjoyed such a marked advance in income in anything like the same space of time. In most of the older sections of the world, indeed, the attainment, even in a century, of such a proportionate increase of income would be regarded as remarkable.

Share of Enterprise and Property Measured in 1913 Dollars.

The figures in the fifth column of Table IX show that, during the two decades covered by the investigation, the dates and general nature of the oscillations occurring in the entire realized income of entrepreneurs and other property owners corresponded closely to those in the entire realized income of all classes, but that the income of the entrepreneurs and property owners was less stable than was the income of all gainfully occupied persons. From what has just been said, it follows that the total wage and salary income of employees has shown much less tendency to fluctuate than has the total income of the propertied classes. Two slight declines occurred in 1914, in 1918, and in 1921, but, in no case did any decline cover a period of years in succession, as was notably true of the income of entrepreneurs and property owners during the period 1918-1921. In the case of the employees, by contrast, the period 1917 to 1922 was merely one in which the income total remained nearly stationary, undergoing nothing more than minor fluctuations.

Share of Employees Measured in 1913 Dollars.

Salaries tend to be more stable than wages. The total purchasing power of all salaries shows no decline of any consequence, except in the years 1919 and 1920, the falling off in these years being primarily due to the disbanding of the Army, and the consequent reduction in the number of salaried workers, all soldiers having been included in the class of salaried employees. Total wages, on the other hand, when measured in dollars of constant purchasing power, register declines in 1914, 1917, 1918, 1919, and 1921, showing that wages are more susceptible than salaries to the fluctuations connected with the business cycles. The item, "Pensions, Compensations, etc." shows a definite tendency to advance to higher levels, being nearly three times as great in 1927 as in 1909. For many industries, however, data concerning this item are missing, hence the totals cannot be considered as complete.

Proportional Shares in Realized Income.

The figures in Table IX are, of course, affected materially by the fact that this is a growing country with a rapidly increasing population. The estimates presented in Table X, however, are particularly interesting because they record the approximate relative shares of the total realized income of the people obtained respectively from various sources.

This table and Chart 6 make it clear that, while the percentage of the total realized income represented by imputed income has remained approximately constant, the fraction representing money and commodity income going to entrepreneurs and other property owners has fallen off markedly since 1917. Before that date, it tended to remain steadily in the neighborhood of 41½ per cent. In 1917, however, it advanced sharply to nearly 44 per cent, but it then began an abrupt decline which continued until a figure of approximately 35 per cent was reached in 1920. Since that date, the percentage has remained roughly on this level.

The wage share in the entire realized income of the nation remained in the neighborhood of 35½ per cent between 1909 and 1916. During the next three years it fell off noticeably, the decline being accounted for in part by the entrance of a considerable proportion of the wage earning male population of the country into the Army when, according to our scheme of classification, they were ranked as salaried employees rather than wage earners and their earnings were, of course, transferred to the salary category. In 1920, the

TABLE X

ESTIMATED PERCENTAGES OF THE ENTIRE REALIZED INCOME OF THE PEOPLE OF THE CONTINENTAL UNITED STATES OBTAINED FROM VARIOUS SOURCES[a]

YEAR	All Sources	SHARE OF ENTREPRENEURS AND OTHER PROPERTY OWNERS[b]			SHARE OF EMPLOYEES[c]			
		Imputed Income	Money and Commodity Income	Total	Wages	Salaries	Pensions, Compensations, etc.	Total
1909	100.00	6.57	42.46	49.03	35.56	14.58	.83	50.97
1910	100.00	6.63	41.61	48.24	36.05	14.90	.81	51.75
1911	100.00	6.90	41.31	48.21	35.55	15.44	.80	51.79
1912	100.00	6.55	41.70	48.24	35.65	15.31	.80	51.76
1913	100.00	6.52	40.79	47.31	36.44	15.40	.85	52.69
1914	100.00	6.79	41.27	48.06	34.77	16.30	.87	51.94
1915	100.00	6.76	41.20	47.96	35.26	15.93	.85	52.04
1916	100.00	6.24	41.85	48.09	36.18	14.73	1.00	51.91
1917	100.00	5.88	43.86	49.73	34.56	14.93	.77	50.26
1918	100.00	6.21	40.28	46.49	33.79	18.59	1.12	53.51
1919	100.00	6.55	39.77	46.32	34.92	17.55	1.20	53.68
1920	100.00	7.51	35.35	42.86	39.92	15.85	1.37	57.14
1921	100.00	8.05	34.81	42.85	36.85	18.71	1.59	57.14
1922	100.00	7.19	35.63	42.81	37.24	18.28	1.66	57.19
1923	100.00	6.78	35.52	42.30	38.60	17.70	1.41	57.70
1924	100.00	6.78	35.54	42.32	37.66	18.41	1.61	57.68
1925	100.00	6.55	36.26	42.81	37.55	18.32	1.32	57.19
1926	100.00	6.15	35.68	41.83	38.11	18.69	1.37	58.17
1927	100.00	5.99	35.78	41.77	37.28	19.55	1.39	58.23
1928	100.00	5.93	36.90	42.83	36.05	19.93	1.19	57.17

[a] These percentages are derived from the data in Table VIII.
[b] Includes entrepreneurial and investment income of employees.
[c] Excludes entrepreneurial and investment income of employees.

proportion of the entire realized income going to wage workers jumped to its highest point, almost reaching the 40 per cent mark, but, in 1921 it broke sharply, and since that date has remained roughly on a level, hovering between 36 and 38½ per cent.

The salary share has, in general, been upward throughout the two decades. A fairly steady rise marked the period 1909 to 1914. The percentage then dropped off noticeably until 1917, but rose

CHART 6

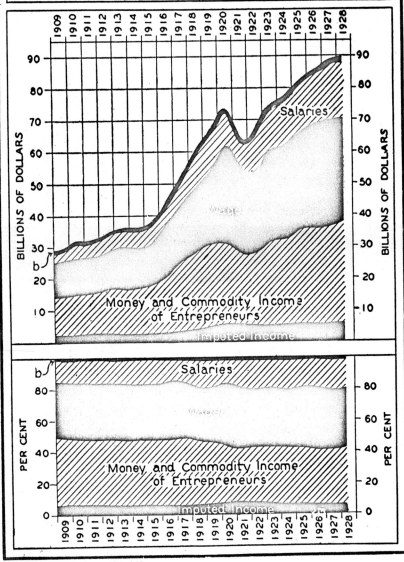

ESTIMATED REALIZED INCOME OF
THE PEOPLE OF THE CONTINENTAL
UNITED STATES[a]

* For data, see Tables VIII and X.
b Pensions, compensations, etc.

sharply in 1918 because of the inclusion of the soldiers among the salaried employees. With the return of the men from the Army to civil life, the percentage declined again. Advances in wage rates during 1919 and 1920 kept the proportion falling during those two years. The fact that salaried employees generally held their positions in 1921 and 1922, while wage workers were in many cases idle, again lifted the percentages for salaried employees to a higher level during that biennium, but the return of business activity in 1923 caused the share of the salaried employees to decline somewhat. Since that date, however, their share in the realized income of the nation has been steadily on the up-grade. The net result of these changes, is that, in 1928, the salaried employees of the country received in the form of salaries approximately 20 per cent of the total realized income, as compared with only 14½ per cent thus received in 1909.

To a considerable extent, this increase in the fraction of the entire national income which salaried employees are able to draw, is accounted for by the fact already noted, that salaried employees have, during recent years, constituted a steadily growing percentage of the entire gainfully occupied population. As entrepreneurs have ceased functioning as directors of business enterprises and have instead become salaried employees, there has of course been a tendency for the income previously going to the entrepreneurial class to be transferred to the salaried group.

The growth in the percentages of the entire realized income represented by pensions, compensations for injuries, etc. is to some extent the result of the growing tendency of corporations to make provision for the misfortunes of employees. A considerable proportion of the increase, however, is accounted for by the fact that, since the World War, the United States Government and some of the States have been paying out very considerable amounts to those who suffered injury because of their service in the army.

Table X shows us the extent to which salaried employees participate in the entire realized income of the nation. It must be remembered, however, that salaried employees are far from constituting a homogeneous group, for, under this title, are comprised grades of workers running in rank all the way from the President of the United States to the most poorly paid typists and filing clerks. The question naturally arises, therefore, as to whether the 10 billions of dollars disbursed in the form of salaries by various employers goes, in the main, to a small number of highly paid executives, or

whether it consists primarily of payments to clerical workers. Unfortunately, data are too scanty to enable us to answer this question for the nation as a whole with any degree of confidence. As it happens, however, scattered figures are obtainable from the reports of the Bureau of the Census and the Interstate Commerce Commission, which enable us to divide the total income of six industries in certain years into the following four divisions, namely:

1. The share of the entrepreneurs and other property owners.
2. Salaries of officials and managers.
3. Clerical salaries.
4. Wages.

These figures, when converted to percentages of the entire realized income of the given industries in the given years, appear in Table XI. This table shows us that the apportionment of the realized income differs widely in different industries. For example, in the field of manufacturing, entrepreneurs and property owners have received no more than 14 to 20 per cent of the realized income derived from the industry, whereas, in the private electric light and power industry, the same group have obtained between 53 and 58 per cent. Before 1914, the entrepreneurial and property owning interests were accustomed to obtaining about one-third of the entire realized income arising from railroading, but the percentage declined in 1919 to about 18½ per cent and continued on that level until 1923. Since the last mentioned date, their percentage has, however, been increasing. The percentage going to the owners in the telephone and street railway fields also fell off sharply between 1912 and 1922. There, as in the case of railroads, the decline was presumably due, in the main, to the increase in operating expenses, resulting from currency inflation, while at the same time selling rates for services were fixed by law or by public regulation and hence the owners of the industry could not adjust the rates upward in a degree sufficient to offset the effect of the diminished value of the dollar.

The various industrial fields show wide differences in the respective proportions of their totals of realized income which they find it necessary to disburse to executives in the form of salaries. Both railways and street railways are apparently able to operate successfully by paying to officials and managers less than 3 per cent of their entire realized income. Electric light and power companies in 1907 paid as much as 8½ per cent, but this percentage has been

TABLE XI

ESTIMATED APPORTIONMENT OF THE ENTIRE REALIZED INCOME RECEIVED BY INDIVIDUALS FROM CERTAIN INDUSTRIES DOMINATED BY CORPORATIONS[a]

CENSUS YEAR	PER CENT OF ENTIRE REALIZED INCOME											
	PROFITS, RENTS, DIVIDENDS AND INTEREST ON FUNDED DEBT						SALARIES OF OFFICIALS AND MANAGERS					
	Factories[b]	Mining[c]	Railroads[d]	Street Railways[e]	Private Electric Light and Power[e]	Telephones[e]	Factories[b]	Mining[c]	Railroads[d]	Street Railways[e]	Private Electric Light and Power[e]	Telephones[e]
1907				44.90	57.86	33.48				2.71	8.51	f
1909	20.07	28.55	35.38				7.97	3.83	2.12			
1912			32.24	45.24	55.85	31.15			2.14	3.02	7.33	6.34
1914	20.46		32.39				8.15		2.39			
1917			27.47	41.23	57.57	27.62			2.35	2.86	6.10	6.87
1919	15.23	24.47	18.47				9.09	5.65	1.99			
1921	16.64		18.63				f		2.81			
1922			19.80	29.22	52.96	22.31	f		2.88	3.07	5.62	5.61
1923	14.47		18.74				f		2.76			
1925	15.25		21.08				f		2.96			

[a] Total of four shares may equal slightly less than 100% owing to the fact that pensions, compensations for injuries, etc. are not included.

[b] Based upon *Census of Manufactures* and reports of a large number of corporations.

[c] Based upon *Census of Mines and Quarries* and reports of a large number of corporations.

[d] Based upon *Statistics of Railways* published by the *Interstate Commerce Commission*. Includes switching and terminal companies.

[e] Based upon *Census of Electrical Industries*.

[f] Data not available.

falling off until, in 1922, salaried executives and managers received but 5.6 per cent of the total realized income arising from that industry. In mining, on the other hand, between the census year of 1909 and the next census year of 1919, there was a marked increase in the proportion going to managerial employees. Presumably this represents the transfer of many mines from ownership by individual entrepreneurs to control by large corporations which were, of course, compelled to employ salaried managers to look after their property.

When it comes to clerk hire, the same wide discrepancies between different industries are noticeable. Railroads, which pay such a small proportion of their total income to officials and man-

TABLE XI—Continued

ESTIMATED APPORTIONMENT OF THE ENTIRE REALIZED INCOME RECEIVED BY INDIVIDUALS FROM CERTAIN INDUSTRIES DOMINATED BY CORPORATIONS*

Census Year	PER CENT OF ENTIRE REALIZED INCOME											
	CLERICAL SALARIES						WAGES					
	Factories^b	Mining^c	Railroads^d	Street Railways^e	Private Electric Light and Power^e	Telephones^e	Factories^b	Mining^c	Railroads^d	Street Railways^e	Private Electric Light and Power^e	Telephones^e
1907				2.00	5.67	*f*				50.39	27.97	48.45
1909	9.00	2.30	12.29				62.30	65.33	49.13			
1912			12.29	4.10	10.63	13.43			52.11	47.64	26.19	48.01
1914	10.57		14.21				59.75		49.72			
1917			12.52	4.60	10.80	12.45			56.43	51.31	25.53	51.18
1919	9.00	2.42	14.60				65.67	67.46	63.98			
1921	*f*		17.81				62.68		59.77			
1922			18.62	6.06	14.09	14.49			57.65	61.65	27.33	55.77
1923	*f*		17.18				66.26		60.20			
1925	*f*		17.50				64.57		57.07			

agers, make up for this saving by paying a larger proportion of their total income to clerks than do any of the other industries on the list. Furthermore, the percentage tends to increase rather than to diminish with the passage of time. This increase is accounted for, not so much by an increasing clerical salary bill as by the decline in the entrepreneurial income, a decline due to the shrinkage in profits brought about by the diminution in the value of the dollar. The reason just mentioned probably accounts, to a large extent also, for the fact that, between the years 1917 and 1922, the respective percentages of their total income paid out as clerical salaries showed an increase also in the case of street railways, private electric light and power plants, and telephone companies. Apparently, mining operations in general call for but little clerical work, for the clerks engaged in this field receive less than 2½ per cent of the total income, as contrasted with the 17 or 18 per cent of the railroad income which is paid to railroad clerks.

In manufacturing, the figures presented by the Bureau of the Census indicate that officials and managers secured about half of the total amount disbursed in salary payments. In mining, they secured the lion's share, leaving about one-third of the total salary roll for clerical work. Railway clerks, on the other hand, received in salaries about six times as much as did railway managers and officials. In 1907, street railway clerks received *in toto* even less than the officials and managers, but, by 1922, their salaries totalled almost twice as much as the salaries of the men higher in rank. A corresponding change, though even more marked in degree, has occurred in the case of private electric light and power companies. In 1912, the clerical workers in telephone companies received in total salaries about double the aggregate salaries paid to officials and managers. By 1922, the ratio was approaching three to one. The figures just quoted indicate that the division of the total salary bill between managerial employees and the clerical force is dependent upon the nature of the industry and changes with the passage of time. Hence, it is difficult to make any broad generalizations concerning the normal relationship existing between these two quantities.

Percentage of Realized Income Going to Wages.

The differences in the different industries as regards the percentages of the total realized income going to wages are not as marked as they are in the case of the percentages going to salaries. The general tendency in manufacturing appears to be to pay nearly two-thirds of the realized income to the wage earners, while the corresponding percentage in mining is a trifle higher. Before 1917, the railway wage workers secured something like half of the realized income of that industry, but, since that date, their share has tended to be nearly three-fifths. A similar increase has taken place in the case of street railways, the proportions there being roughly the same as in the case of the steam railways. Private electric light and power companies, on the other hand, are able to operate while paying only 25 to 28 per cent of their income to their wage workers. Telephone companies, like street railways, however, resemble the steam railroads in the proportions of total realized income paid out to wage workers.

Per Capita Realized Income in Current Dollars.

Table XII, shows the results obtained when the estimated realized income received by various classes has been divided by the number of recipients of the specified type of income, thus reducing

TABLE XII

ESTIMATED PER CAPITA RECEIPTS FOR VARIOUS CLASSES OF INDIVIDUALS

YEAR	CURRENT DOLLARS				DOLLARS OF 1913			
	REALIZED INCOME		AVERAGE ANNUAL EARNINGS		REALIZED INCOME		AVERAGE ANNUAL EARNINGS	
	Per Capita[b]	Per Person Gain-fully Oc-cupied	Per Salaried Em-ployee[a]	Per Wage Worker[a]	Per Capita[b]	Per Person Gain-fully Oc-cupied	Per Salaried Em-ployee[a]	Per Wage Worker[a]
1909	$327	$ 864	$ 976	$ 527	$346	$ 914	$1,034	$556
1910	340	895	1,002	552	350	923	1,035	568
1911	339	892	1,022	540	351	922	1,055	557
1912	357	938	1,045	568	364	956	1,064	578
1913	368	965	1,066	594	368	966	1,066	594
1914	360	943	1,088	552	356	933	1,071	544
1915	371	980	1,096	582	365	965	1,064	564
1916	425	1,120	1,148	679	389	1,024	1,034	610
1917	497	1,304	1,204	771	390	1,022	930	594
1918	579	1,496	1,265	940	385	994	813	601
1919	628	1,637	1,453	1,029	362	944	804	563
1920	695	1,850	1,740	1,273	353	939	846	612
1921	585	1,552	1,696	983	339	899	950	550
1922	601	1,595	1,715	1,012	370	981	1,031	610
1923	667	1,763	1,831	1,150	405	1,071	1,082	679
1924	680	1,789	1,896	1,134	412	1,084	1,120	669
1925	712	1,869	1,950	1,176	421	1,104	1,126	680
1926	735*	1,920*	2,025*	1,217*	433*	1,132*	1,162*	699*
1927	748*	1,928*	2,084*	1,205*	448*	1,156*	1,220*	705*
1928	749*	1,920*			452*	1,160*		

[a] These averages would be materially higher in bad years were they based upon the numbers actually employed rather than upon the numbers attached to industries.

[b] For entire population of the Continental United States.

* Preliminary estimate.

all figures to a per capita basis. In the second column of Table XII is recorded the average income going in each year to each inhabitant of the United States. While this figure, being an average, cannot of course show anything about the apportionment of income among different sections of the population, the changes from year to year do, nevertheless, have some significance. Per capita realized income, for example, when measured in the dollars current at the various dates, more than doubled between 1909 and 1923, and has since been steadily increasing until, in 1928, the average per capita income for all inhabitants of the United States amounted to $749. For the typical family of five this would make an income of $3,745. If, then, all of the income of the United States were equally divided among the inhabitants, and if this process of equal division did not reduce the productivity of the nation, (an assumption probably contrary to fact) it is clear that there would be income enough for all the families of the country to live comfortably, but that, according to American standards, none would be affluent. As a matter of fact, of course, the total realized income is far from being equally divided, some families receiving extremely large amounts and others being in poverty.

Per Capita Realized Income of Gainfully Occupied.

The division of the total income of the country among persons classed as gainfully occupied, is shown in the third column of Table XII. In 1928, the average person working for a money return still received materially less than $2,000 per annum. It is interesting to observe the close correspondence shown by Chart 7a between the average income per person gainfully occupied and the average salary per salaried worker. Apparently, the latter quantity normally lies about 10 per cent above the former, although the income per person gainfully occupied goes above the average salary level during the years 1917 to 1920, inclusive.

Average Wages and Average Salaries.

The figures in the 4th and 5th columns differ from those in the two preceding columns, in that they do not deal with an apportionment of the entire realized income of the people of the nation, but represent, respectively, merely the division of the total salary bill and the total wage bill of the nation by the number of persons normally occupied as salaried employees or wage workers as the case may be. These columns indicate that, when measured in terms of gold dollars, the average salary doubled between 1909 and 1925 and is still steadily on the up-grade, while the average wages doubled between 1909 and 1923 and have likewise been climbing higher in more recent years.

Per Capita Income in 1913 Dollars.

Owing to the fact that the value of money changed so radically during the period 1914 to 1921, the year to year comparisons shown in the first five columns of Table XII have comparatively little

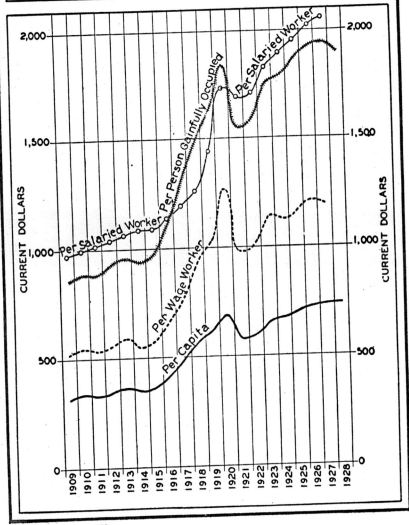

ESTIMATED PER CAPITA RECEIPTS
FOR VARIOUS CLASSES OF INDIVIDUALS[a]
(CURRENT DOLLARS)

[a] For data, see Table XII.

significance. One of the principal uses of the figures in those columns is to serve as a basis for deriving the results presented in the last four columns of the same table. In these latter columns, all amounts have been reduced to quantities indicating the relative amounts of consumers' goods which could have been purchased at the different dates by the average recipient of the given type of income. These figures indicate that per capita realized income, when measured in terms of constant purchasing power, had a marked upward trend between 1909 and 1916, declined between 1917 and 1921 until it was slightly lower than in 1909, and then began a sharp upward movement which continued steadily until 1928. It will be understood, of course, that, since the figures for 1926 and 1927 are merely preliminary estimates, the final computations may modify to some extent the course of the curve in the last two years recorded, though the probabilities are that the trend will not be materially altered. The course of this curve shows that the idea that the average inhabitant of the United States profited financially from the war is wholly fallacious, for not until 1922 did we begin to recover from the effects of those readjustments of industry made necessary by the war, and from the effects of currency inflation resulting from war finance here and abroad.

The growth in per capita income since 1921 must, however, be regarded as a remarkable phenomenon. The indications are that, in terms of immediate ability to buy goods for consumption purposes, the average American was approximately one-third better off in 1927 than he was in 1921. Under these circumstances, it is not surprising that a tremendous market has developed for furs, automobiles, radios, and other luxuries which were previously beyond the reach of the masses of the population.

The curve in Chart 7b, recording the changes in the average income per person gainfully occupied, shows approximately the same fluctuations as does the curve representing per capita income. This is true because, throughout the twenty years under consideration, the percentage of the total population classed as gainfully occupied has remained approximately constant.

Average Wages and Average Salaries in 1913 Dollars.

Chart 7b brings out forcefully the fact that the salaried employees of the United States suffered very materially from the effects of the inflation connected with the World War. The purchasing power of average salaries began to decline in 1915, and continued to fall

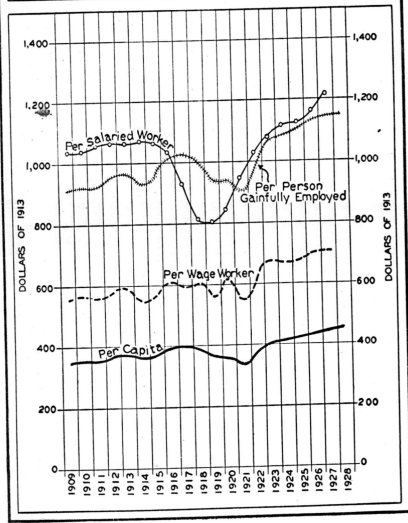

ESTIMATED PER CAPITA RECEIPTS
FOR VARIOUS CLASSES OF INDIVIDUALS[a]

(1913 DOLLARS)

a For data, see Table XII.

rapidly until 1918. The lowest point was reached in 1919. Since then, the ability of salaried employees to buy consumable commodities has risen rapidly, but it was not until 1923 that the average salaried employee in the United States was financially better off than he was in 1914. In 1927, however, his pay would buy approximately one-seventh more than it would in 1914 and more than half again as much as it would in 1919. The average annual earnings of the wage workers of the United States, when measured in terms of ability to buy consumers' goods, show fluctuations much less marked than do those of the salaried employees. The common assumption, therefore, that the position of the salaried man is relatively secure while that of the wage worker is fraught with risk, needs considerable emendation before it can be accepted. The truth apparently is that the salaried employee is much less affected by the ups and downs of the business cycle than is the wage worker. The average wage worker, for example, suffered a considerable cut in purchasing power in 1914 and in 1921, while for the average salaried employees of the nation there was no tendency in either of these years toward a decline in earnings. On the other hand, salaried employees are much more exposed to the evil effects of inflation. So far as can be seen by observing the graph in Chart 7b, the earnings of the average wage worker were not adversely affected by the currency inflation of 1915 to 1920—the trend of the purchasing power of average wages being approximately horizontal, with perhaps a slight upward tendency during the entire period extending from 1909 to 1921. Salaries, however, being fixed largely by custom in terms of the money legal tender at the time, are depressed by every wave of inflation, and are later adjusted upward slowly during a period covering several years. On the other hand, it is of course true that salaried workers gain during periods of deflation, for their salaries are not immediately reduced when commodity prices fall. Since 1923, the purchasing power of the average salary has risen materially more than has the purchasing power of the average wage, the increase between 1923 and 1927 being about 12½ per cent in the case of the average salaried employee as against 4 per cent in the case of the average wage worker.

Comparison of Salary and Wage Levels.

Table XIII presents some scattered data extracted from various reports of the Federal Government, comparing in various years average wages and average salaries as measured in terms of gold

TABLE XIII

COMPARATIVE FULL-TIME[a] ANNUAL PAY OF DIFFERENT CLASSES OF EMPLOYEES IN CERTAIN INDUSTRIES DOMINATED BY CORPORATIONS

CENSUS YEAR	FACTORIES[b]			MINES, QUARRIES AND OIL WELLS[c]			RAILROADS[d]		
	AVERAGE SALARY		AVERAGE WAGE[a]	AVERAGE SALARY		AVERAGE WAGE[a]	AVERAGE SALARY		AVERAGE WAGE[a]
	Managerial	Clerical		Managerial	Clerical		Managerial	Clerical	
1909	$2,060	$ 864	$ 518	$1,649	$ 829	$ 552	$2,637	$ 776	$ 674
1914	2,346	1,003	580				2,717	841	688
1919	3,513	1,392	1,158	2,685	1,260	1,321	3,483	1,494	1,453
1921			1,180				4,290	1,777	1,591
1923			1,254				4,321	1,776	1,536
1925			1,280				4,427	1,824	1,541
1927							4,524	1,882	1,570

CENSUS YEAR	STREET RAILWAYS[e]			PRIVATE ELECTRIC LIGHT AND POWER[e]			TELEPHONES[e]		
	AVERAGE SALARY		AVERAGE WAGE[a]	AVERAGE SALARY		AVERAGE WAGE[a]	AVERAGE SALARY		AVERAGE WAGE[a,g]
	Managerial	Clerical		Managerial	Clerical		Managerial	Clerical	
1907	$2,058	$ 677	$ 658	$1,282	$ 677	$ 691	[f]	[f]	$ 427
1912	2,305	815	674	1,590	742	695	$1,411	$ 709	438
1917	2,723	935	872	1,980	1,837	838	1,574	878	616
1922	3,600	1,534	1,436	2,898	1,363	1,320	2,565	1,426	1,064

a The averages here given represent the pay of those who remained on the payroll continuously and were subject to average conditions of overtime or short time.

b Based upon *Census of Manufactures*.

c Based upon *Census of Mines and Quarries*.

d Based upon *Statistics of Railways*, published by the *Interstate Commerce Commission*. Includes switching and terminal companies.

e Based upon *Census of Electrical Industries*.

f Data not available.

g Wages relatively low in telephone industry because women constitute unusually large proportion of workers.

dollars. The figures in this table do not, like those which we have just been studying, represent the total wage bill in industry divided among all persons attached to the industry. They represent, instead, the total wage bill or salary bill divided by the average number of wage earners or salaried employees, as the case may be, on the payroll in the field specified. They picture, then,

TABLE XIV

ENTIRE REALIZED INCOME* DRAWN BY INDIVIDUALS FROM THE VARIOUS INDUSTRIES

(MILLIONS OF CURRENT DOLLARS)

Year	All Industries	Agriculture	Manufacturing	Mines, Quarries and Oil Wells	Construction	Banking	Mercantile	Government	Unclassified	Miscellaneous
1909	$29,605	$4,988	$5,481	$ 833	$1,692	$ 337	$3,685	$1,554	$5,718	$2,747
1910	31,430	5,218	6,204	917	1,580	389	3,735	1,678	5,958	2,955
1911	31,858	4,815	6,251	910	1,607	409	4,034	1,767	6,142	3,020
1912	33,977	5,294	6,838	1,006	1,742	429	4,041	1,862	6,562	3,152
1913	35,723	5,133	7,332	1,153	1,527	453	4,488	1,981	7,126	3,316
1914	35,647	5,081	6,914	971	1,412	454	4,753	2,093	7,316	3,468
1915	37,205	5,488	7,362	983	1,394	463	4,839	2,192	7,627	3,605
1916	43,288	6,631	10,260	1,457	1,516	480	5,323	2,297	7,876	3,874
1917	51,331	9,188	12,477	1,810	1,206	509	6,342	3,044	8,357	4,330
1918	60,408	11,205	14,794	2,034	1,207	572	6,830	6,278	7,089	5,242
1919	65,949	12,182	16,090	1,875	1,846	646	8,019	6,136	7,476	5,882
1920	73,999	11,057	19,531	2,355	1,895	775	8,726	5,311	9,721	7,415
1921	63,371	6,967	13,274	1,843	1,740	848	8,440	5,629	11,435	7,104
1922	65,925	7,300	13,957	1,725	2,198	930	8,680	5,792	12,350	7,132
1923	74,337	8,026	16,835	2,396	2,465	997	10,772	5,783	13,056	7,505
1924	77,135	8,325	16,276	2,038	2,974	1,029	11,050	5,896	15,254	7,764
1925	81,931	9,089	16,866	2,169	3,458	1,094	11,996	6,130	16,452	7,940
1926	85,548*	8,214*				1,165	12,442*			8,020*
1927	88,205	8,371*					12,754*			
1928	89,419*	8,109*					13,137*			8,040*

* For definition of "entire realized income" see text. The totals in this table are the sums of the amounts received by entrepreneurs, other property owners, and employees as recorded in Tables XVII and XIX.

* Preliminary estimate.

the comparative earnings at different dates of those employees who were not laid off at any time but who were on the payroll throughout the year, and who performed the average amount of overtime work and suffered the average loss of pay due to short time work during the periods in which they remained on the payroll.

This table shows us that the pay of the average managerial employee in the manufacturing industry equals about 2½ times the wages of the average clerk, while the average clerk in turn is much better paid than the average wage worker. In the mining industry, the managerial force receive on the average, twice as much per annum as do the clerical workers, but the differential in favor of clerical workers over wage workers is not great. In the

TABLE XIV—Continued

ENTIRE REALIZED INCOME* DRAWN BY INDIVIDUALS FROM THE VARIOUS INDUSTRIES
(MILLIONS OF CURRENT DOLLARS)

Year	All Following Fields of Transportation	Railroads[b]	Pullman	Express	Transportation by Water	Street Railways	Private Electric Light and Power	Telephones	Telegraphs
1909	$2,569	$1,719	$21	$ 62	$211	$307	$ 93	$124	31
1910	2,795	1,872	22	69	232	331	99	137	33
1911	2,902	1,936	23	60	229	349	117	152	37
1912	3,051	2,029	23	60	241	367	126	165	40
1913	3,213	2,126	26	61	250	389	139	182	41
1914	3,186	2,061	26	57	252	411	152	188	40
1915	3,252	2,085	24	58	276	415	166	187	41
1916	3,574	2,249	26	72	339	439	182	216	51
1917	4,067	2,564	28	78	436	455	204	241	62
1918	5,156	3,457	32	97	504	489	232	266	79
1919	5,798	3,703	37	119	710	554	267	321	88
1920	7,214	4,610	44	167	896	654	323	408	113
1921	6,090	3,617	41	146	741	648	365	431	101
1922	5,862	3,530	37	125	555	630	413	468	104
1923	6,503	3,963	38	130	563	674	505	520	110
1924	6,531	3,836	42	124	602	674	571	569	114
1925	6,736	3,915	39	122	587	671	679	602	122
1926		4,043	42	122					
1927				122					
1928				118					

b Includes switching and terminal companies.

railroad industry, the managerial force formerly drew almost 4 times as much per capita as did the clerical force, but, by 1927, they were getting only about 2½ times as much. In this field, the clerical workers are, on the average, but slightly better paid than the wage workers. Managerial salaries in the street railway field average from 2½ to 3 times as much as clerical salaries, the latter being but slightly above the average wage rate. The managerial force in the private electric light and power industry receive, on the average, about double the pay of the clerical workers, while the clerical and wage workers are paid approximately the same rates per annum. In the telephone industry, the ratio between the pay of the average managerial employee and the pay of the clerk is about the same as in the electric light and power field, but the clerks are much better paid than are the wage workers. The low rate for the latter class in this field is largely due to the fact that a large proportion of the wage earners are of the female sex, telephone operators being included in the wage working class.

Total Realized Income in Current Dollars Derived from Each Industry.[1]

Table XIV compares the importance of the industrial sources from which the inhabitants of the United States have drawn their respective incomes in each of the years from 1909 to 1925, inclusive. The data for the various industries differ materially in dependability. In general, it may be said that the estimates for agriculture, manufacturing, mines, quarries and oil wells, government, and all of the fields of transportation except transportation by water, are fairly well authenticated throughout. It will be remembered that the quantities representing entire realized income are composed of two parts, the share of entrepreneurs and other property owners, and the share of the employees. Estimates of the share of the employees are reasonably accurate for unclassified industries, and are perhaps not widely in error in the construction industry, the mercantile industry, and transportation by water, although in the last-mentioned case the accuracy of the estimate must remain considerably in doubt. The share of the entrepreneurs and other property owners is well established for the banking industry, but figures on the share of employees in that field are very meager. The estimates of the share of the entrepreneurs and other property owners in construction, the mercantile industry, transportation by water, and the unclassified industries, are based upon data which are extremely fragmentary, and this fact makes the totals for these fields subject to wide margins of error. The preliminary estimates in agriculture, the mercantile industry, and unclassified industries for 1926, 1927, and 1928 are based upon sample data only and must, therefore, be viewed with considerable suspicion. The same lack of dependability characterizes all of the estimates of miscellaneous income.

Chart 8 shows that no less than seven industrial fields contribute important fractions to the realized income of the nation. In 1909, as far as production of income was concerned, the unclassified industries ranked first, manufacturing second, and agriculture third, all being roughly of the same magnitude. In 1925

[1] Includes imputed income which is not a product of industry.

CHART 8

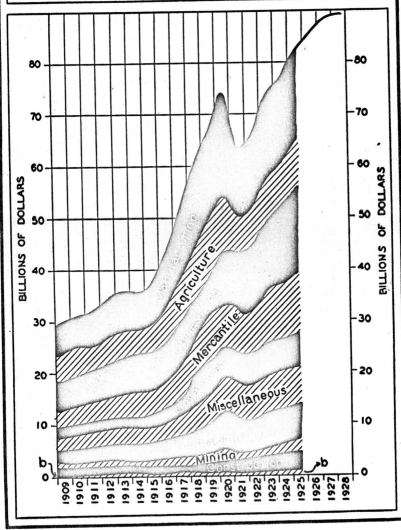

ENTIRE REALIZED INCOME DRAWN BY
INDIVIDUALS FROM THE VARIOUS
INDUSTRIES[a]

a For data, see Table XIV.
b Banking.

THE NATIONAL INCOME

TABLE XV

PER CENT OF ENTIRE REALIZED INCOME[*]
DRAWN BY INDIVIDUALS
FROM THE VARIOUS INDUSTRIES

Year	All Industries	Agriculture	Manufacturing	Mines, Quarries and Oil Wells	Construction	Banking	Mercantile	Government	Unclassified	Miscellaneous
1909	100.00	16.85	18.51	2.81	5.72	1.14	12.45	5.25	19.31	9.28
1910	100.00	16.60	19.74	2.92	5.03	1.24	11.88	5.34	18.96	9.40
1911	100.00	15.11	19.62	2.86	5.04	1.28	12.66	5.55	19.28	9.48
1912	100.00	15.58	20.13	2.96	5.13	1.26	11.89	5.48	19.31	9.28
1913	100.00	14.37	20.52	3.23	4.27	1.27	12.56	5.55	19.95	9.28
1914	100.00	14.25	19.40	2.72	3.96	1.27	13.33	5.87	20.52	9.73
1915	100.00	14.75	19.79	2.64	3.75	1.24	13.01	5.89	20.50	9.69
1916	100.00	15.32	23.70	3.37	3.50	1.11	12.30	5.31	18.19	8.95
1917	100.00	17.90	24.31	3.53	2.35	.99	12.36	5.93	16.28	8.44
1918	100.00	18.55	24.49	3.37	2.00	.95	11.31	10.39	11.74	8.68
1919	100.00	18.47	24.40	2.84	2.80	.98	12.16	9.30	11.34	8.92
1920	100.00	14.94	26.39	3.18	2.56	1.05	11.79	7.18	13.13	10.02
1921	100.00	10.99	20.95	2.91	2.75	1.34	13.32	8.88	18.04	11.21
1922	100.00	11.07	21.17	2.62	3.33	1.41	13.17	8.79	18.73	10.82
1923	100.00	10.80	22.65	3.22	3.31	1.34	14.49	7.78	17.56	10.10
1924	100.00	10.79	21.10	2.64	3.86	1.33	14.33	7.64	19.78	10.07
1925	100.00	11.09	20.59	2.65	4.22	1.34	14.64	7.48	20.08	9.69
1926	100.00	9.60				1.36	14.54			9.37
1927	100.00	9.49					14.46			9.11
1928	100.00	9.27					14.69			

[*] Calculated from figures presented in Table XIV.

unclassified industries and manufacturing competed for first place, but the mercantile industry had come up from fourth place to third, outranking agriculture to a marked degree. By this date, the value of the products of agriculture had declined until they equalled but little more than half the value of the manufacturing net output.

Relative Ranking of Industries as Producers of Realized Income.

The relative importance of the various industries is shown much more clearly by Table XV than by Table XIV, for, in Table XV, the income derived from the various fields has been reduced to percentages of the entire realized income of the nation. The relative importance of agriculture declined slightly between 1909 and 1914, increased vigorously during the war period, declined abruptly between 1919 and 1921, and has since merely been able to

TABLE XV—Continued

PER CENT OF ENTIRE REALIZED INCOME•
DRAWN BY INDIVIDUALS
FROM THE VARIOUS INDUSTRIES

Year	All Following Fields of Transportation	Railroads	Pullman	Express	Transportation by Water	Street Railways	Private Electric Light and Power	Telephones	Telegraphs
1909	8.68	5.81	.07	.21	.71	1.04	.31	.42	.10
1910	8.89	5.96	.07	.22	.74	1.05	.31	.44	.10
1911	9.12	6.08	.07	.19	.72	1.10	.37	.48	.12
1912	8.98	5.97	.07	.18	.71	1.08	.37	.49	.12
1913	8.99	5.95	.07	.17	.70	1.09	.39	.51	.11
1914	8.94	5.78	.07	.16	.71	1.15	.43	.53	.11
1915	8.74	5.60	.06	.16	.74	1.12	.45	.50	.11
1916	8.26	5.20	.06	.17	.78	1.01	.42	.50	.12
1917	7.92	5.00	.05	.15	.85	.89	.40	.47	.12
1918	8.54	5.72	.05	.16	.83	.81	.38	.44	.13
1919	8.79	5.61	.06	.18	1.08	.84	.40	.49	.13
1920	9.75	6.23	.06	.23	1.21	.88	.44	.55	.15
1921	9.61	5.71	.06	.23	1.17	1.02	.58	.68	.16
1922	8.89	5.35	.06	.19	.84	.96	.63	.71	.16
1923	8.75	5.33	.05	.17	.76	.91	.68	.70	.15
1924	8.47	4.97	.05	.16	.78	.87	.74	.74	.15
1925	8.22	4.78	.05	.15	.72	.82	.83	.73	.15
1926		4.73	.05	.14					
1927				.14					
1928				.13					

maintain itself approximately on the level reached in 1921, now producing somewhat less than 10 per cent of the income of the nation in contrast to 18½ per cent produced in 1918. This decline in the proportion of the national income going to agriculture has, of course, been responsible for the shift of workers from agriculture to other industries, a fact previously noted in this volume. The percentage of the national income derived from manufacturing remained about constant between 1909 and 1915, the share of this industry constituting throughout these years about one-fifth of the total for all industries. The relative share of manufacturing rose after 1915 until, in 1920, it constituted over one-fourth of the national income, but fell back rapidly in 1921 and since that date has remained approximately constant at a level representing slightly more than

TABLE XVI

PURCHASING POWER, IN 1913 DOLLARS,[*] OF THE ENTIRE REALIZED INCOME[c] DRAWN BY INDIVIDUALS FROM THE VARIOUS INDUSTRIES

(MILLIONS OF 1913 DOLLARS)[b]

Year	All Industries	Agriculture	Manufacturing	Mines, Quarries and Oil Wells	Construction	Banking	Mercantile	Government	Unclassified	Miscellaneous
1909	$31,300	$5,139	$5,808	$ 882	$1,798	$357	$3,922	$1,645	$6,064	$2,963
1910	32,380	5,239	6,411	947	1,635	402	3,869	1,732	6,157	3,098
1911	32,920	4,948	6,455	940	1,660	423	4,169	1,824	6,341	3,163
1912	34,656	5,376	6,970	1,026	1,776	437	4,123	1,896	6,685	3,258
1913	35,756	5,133	7,332	1,153	1,527	453	4,488	1,981	7,126	3,349
1914	35,250	5,063	6,821	958	1,393	447	4,700	2,060	7,206	3,456
1915	36,636	5,591	7,185	959	1,366	451	4,775	2,124	7,423	3,581
1916	39,559	6,032	9,326	1,330	1,382	434	4,897	2,067	7,120	3,720
1917	40,242	6,643	9,789	1,434	939	396	5,055	2,353	6,504	3,720
1918	40,150	7,015	9,705	1,351	782	372	4,604	4,030	4,625	4,284
1919	38,017	6,644	9,084	1,063	1,033	359	4,667	3,423	4,190	4,281
1920	37,573	5,540	9,618	1,165	932	379	4,432	2,607	4,770	4,583
1921	36,710	4,459	7,519	1,042	984	477	4,859	3,161	6,440	4,333
1922	40,565	4,974	8,434	1,042	1,330	560	5,337	3,480	7,458	4,411
1923	45,164	5,538	10,013	1,425	1,468	591	6,530	3,416	7,749	4,574
1924	46,758	5,681	9,688	1,214	1,777	609	6,701	3,483	9,043	4,676
1925	48,412	5,795	9,826	1,266	2,017	634	7,117	3,542	9,540	4,751
1926	50,421*	5,163*				671	7,347*			4,816*
1927	52,892*	5,539*					7,666*			
1928	54,022*	5,456*					7,993*			4,924*

[*] "1913 Dollars" is an abbreviation for the phrase "dollars having purchasing power equivalent to that which they had in 1913."

[b] Computed from the corresponding items in Table XIV by dividing the various sub-items for each industry by the appropriate price indices recorded in Table VII.

[c] For definition of this term, see text.

[*] Preliminary estimate.

one-fifth of the total. Mines, quarries and oil wells have accounted throughout the period for between 2½ and 3½ per cent of the national income, the importance of this industry being greatest during the war years. Although the construction industry has recently been regarded as unusually active, our estimates indicate that a smaller proportion of the national income has been derived therefrom than was the case in the period 1909 to 1912. For this industry, the period 1917 to 1921 was one of both absolute and relative depression. The product of banking, which constituted about 1¼ per cent of the national income in the pre-war period,

TABLE XVI—Continued

PURCHASING POWER, IN 1913 DOLLARS,[a]
OF THE ENTIRE REALIZED INCOME[c]
DRAWN BY INDIVIDUALS
FROM THE VARIOUS INDUSTRIES

(MILLIONS OF 1913 DOLLARS)[b]

Year	All Follow-ing Fields of Trans-portation	Rail-roads[d]	Pull-man	Ex-press	Trans-por-tation by Water	Street Rail-ways	Private Electric Light and Power	Tele-phones	Tele-graphs
1909	$2,721	$1,821	$22	$66	$224	$325	$ 99	$132	$33
1910	2,889	1,935	23	71	240	342	102	142	34
1911	2,997	1,999	24	61	236	360	121	156	38
1912	3,111	2,068	23	61	246	374	129	168	40
1913	3,213	2,126	26	61	250	389	139	182	41
1914	3,145	2,035	25	56	248	406	150	185	39
1915	3,179	2,037	24	56	268	408	163	182	40
1916	3,251	2,045	23	65	307	402	167	195	46
1917	3,199	2,013	22	60	341	362	164	188	49
1918	3,383	2,259	21	62	328	328	160	173	52
1919	3,273	2,082	21	65	398	319	159	179	50
1920	3,548	2,260	22	80	436	328	167	199	56
1921	3,436	2,039	23	81	415	368	211	242	57
1922	3,537	2,128	23	75	332	382	253	281	63
1923	3,861	2,350	22	76	330	404	306	307	65
1924	3,884	2,278	25	73	353	404	347	337	68
1925	3,923	2,276	23	70	338	393	404	349	71
1926		2,339	24	70					
1927				71					
1928									

d Includes switching and terminal companies.

declined to less than 1 per cent during war time, but has since risen until it now amounts to over one and one-third per cent of the total. The mercantile industry yielded approximately one-eighth of the national income between 1909 and 1922. Since then, its share has tended to approximate one-seventh of the total. The share of government accounted for between 5 and 6 per cent of all realized income during the period 1909 to 1917, jumped abruptly to 10 per cent in 1918, declined abruptly in 1920 to 7 per cent, and has since remained somewhat above that figure, showing, during the period since 1922, a slight tendency to decline. The reader should remember that the term "government," as here used, includes not only the activities of the national government, but also those of the state, local, and municipal governments, including school districts. The income from government, as here computed, consists of wages and salaries paid to employees of the various branches of government, pensions and compensation for injuries, paid to present and past employees, and interest on the public debt paid to individuals.

Individuals tended to derive something less than one-fifth of their total income from unclassified fields during the period 1909 to 1916. With the coming on of the war, this percentage declined rapidly until, in 1919, unclassified industries produced but one-ninth of the total income of the nation. After 1920, however, the percentage again rose rapidly, and, by 1925, it had reached its old level, and unclassified industries again accounted for one-fifth of the national income. Miscellaneous income, which is composed, in the main, of the estimated rent paid for leased homes not on farms and of the imputed value of the services of durable consumers' goods including the rental value of urban homes occupied by the owners has, in general, constituted from one-eleventh to one-tenth of the income of the nation. Those fields of transportation for which adequate records are available, namely those dominated by corporations, account for a slightly smaller percentage of the total income, their combined share running around one-eleventh of the aggregate. In this field, railways are dominant, about 60 per cent of the transportation income originating in this one industry. Although the most rapid growth within the transportation field has been shown by the private electric light and power industry, it still does not rank as a major industry, for, even in 1925, (the last year for which estimates are made) it did not account for 1 per cent of the nation's total income.

The Entire Realized Income Measured in 1913 Dollars.

While Tables XIV and XV both help in making clear the relative standings of the various industries at each date, neither of these tables reveals the facts concerning the absolute growth of each industry as measured by its ability to produce income for the individuals depending upon it as a chief source of livelihood. These facts are shown in Table XVI and Charts 9, 10a, and 10b. The last two charts reveal striking differences in the stability of income derived from the various industries. Railroads, public utilities, and merchandising show a marked tendency to stability as income

CHART 9

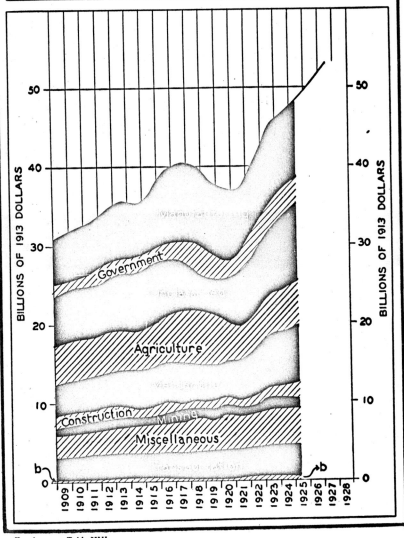

PURCHASING POWER, IN 1913 DOLLARS,
OF THE ENTIRE REALIZED INCOME
DRAWN BY INDIVIDUALS FROM THE
VARIOUS INDUSTRIES[a]

[a] For data, see Table XVI.
[b] Banking.

producers. Manufacturing, agriculture, government, mining, and transportation by water, all participated during the general period 1916-1920 in a great expansion of income as measured in 1913 dollars, but this expansion was offset by a great shrinkage in both the construction and unclassified fields, and a considerable depression in banking and street railways.

Every industrial field except the express business yielded to individuals more "deflated" income in 1925 than in 1909, though the gains were small in the Pullman industry. The manufacturing, unclassified, mercantile, telephone, private electric light and power, mining, and governmental industries all experienced marked growth in income producing ability.

The fact should be made clear in this connection that a large yield of income does not necessarily involve an increase, and is not a necessary outcome of large physical productivity. For example, the great rise and decline in income from agriculture, occurring between 1915 and 1921, was not accompanied by any great variation in the physical productivity of agricultural operations. It was caused, instead, by the fact that, during that time, farm produce was greatly in demand, commanded an unusual price, and hence produced a large income for the person engaged in that line of work. Similarly, the depression in the street railway income which occurred between 1916 and 1920 did not signify that the street railways were carrying fewer passengers, but merely that rate regulation kept fares down while expenses rose.

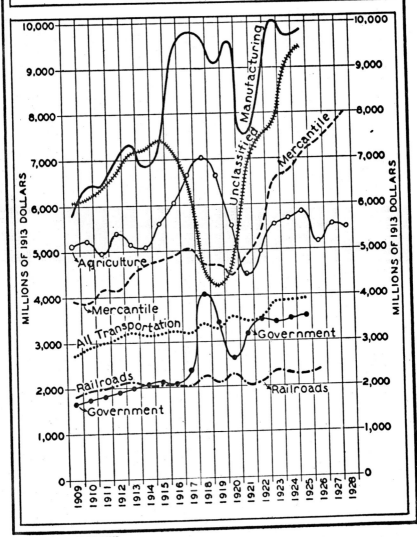

PURCHASING POWER, IN 1913 DOLLARS,
OF THE ENTIRE REALIZED INCOME
DRAWN BY INDIVIDUALS FROM THE VARIOUS
INDUSTRIES[a]

[a] For data, see Table XVI.

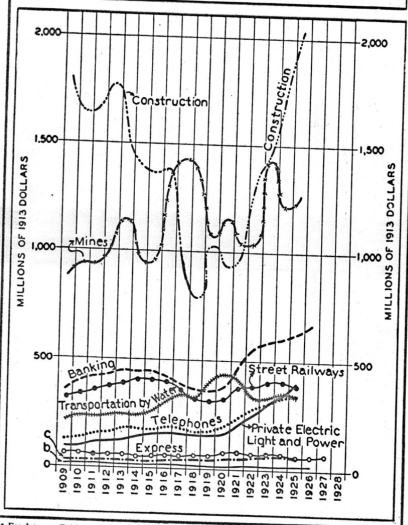

PURCHASING POWER, IN 1913 DOLLARS,
OF THE ENTIRE REALIZED INCOME
DRAWN BY INDIVIDUALS FROM THE VARIOUS
INDUSTRIES[a]

CHAPTER V

THE SHARE OF PROPERTY AND ENTERPRISE

Realized Entrepreneurial and Property Income By Industries.

Table XVII presents a comparison of the industrial sources from which entrepreneurs and other property owners have drawn their realized income during the last 20 years. It will be remembered that the term "realized income," as here used, excludes all gains due to changes in property values and that, therefore, "the realized income of entrepreneurs and other property owners" is made up, in the main, of interest on funded debt, dividends on stocks, rents and royalties derived from leased property, and profits withdrawn from their own enterprises by individual entrepreneurs. It will be observed that the figures presented for the years 1926-1928 are indicated as being preliminary. These figures, in fact, are highly tentative and may be widely in error. In general, the estimates of entrepreneurial income are less trustworthy than are the corresponding figures for wages and salaries, the reason being that it is extremely difficult to tell how much income individual entrepreneurs have withdrawn from their enterprises.

The industry yielding the largest aggregate of returns to all owners combined is agriculture. The returns in agriculture have been estimated by deducting from the total value of farm products estimated to have been sold or consumed at home the business expenses incurred in production. While the errors in the estimates so obtained may, in some years, be considerable, it is not believed that they are large enough seriously to vitiate the results. The data in the third column of Table XVII include not only the income of farmers and their families but also the receipts obtained by landlords from farm rentals and by mortgage holders from interest on farm mortgages.

The mercantile industry ranks second. The estimates of mercantile income must be considered as nothing more than crude approximations based mainly upon three estimated quantities: first, the total value of goods sold by merchants; second, the average rates of profits to total sales; third, the fraction of total profits saved. Much effort has been devoted to obtaining year by year estimates of the total value of goods sold by merchants, but one

TABLE XVII

REALIZED INCOME[a] DRAWN BY ENTREPRENEURS AND OTHER PROPERTY OWNERS FROM THE VARIOUS INDUSTRIES

(MILLIONS OF CURRENT DOLLARS)

Year	All Industries	Agriculture[b]	Manufacturing[c]	Mines, Quarries and Oil Wells[d]	Construction[e]	Banking[f]	Mercantile[g]	Government[h]	Unclassified[i]	Miscellaneous[j]
1909	$14,515	$4,271	$1,103	$238	$663	$222	$2,048	$ 142	$2,156	$2,747
1910	15,163	4,504	1,246	261	566	266	2,024	178	2,165	2,955
1911	15,360	4,065	1,323	240	620	272	2,305	197	2,307	3,020
1912	16,390	4,539	1,378	281	648	280	2,351	201	2,534	3,152
1913	16,901	4,357	1,479	351	354	293	2,580	216	2,879	3,316
1914	17,131	4,326	1,425	275	536	290	2,666	232	2,830	3,468
1915	17,845	4,715	1,485	282	520	280	2,684	257	2,902	3,605
1916	20,817	5,803	2,380	575	548	266	2,952	272	2,998	3,874
1917	25,529	8,159	2,681	705	268	279	3,696	361	3,830	4,330
1918	28,084	9,991	2,550	658	204	291	3,867	537	3,547	5,242
1919	30,550	10,692	2,465	459	395	284	4,536	1,064	3,525	5,882
1920	31,716	9,394	2,422	507	448	346	4,566	1,078	4,293	7,415
1921	27,157	5,562	2,223	429	424	367	4,306	1,065	4,427	7,104
1922	28,225	6,097	1,946	410	516	436	4,293	1,130	4,973	7,132
1923	31,444	6,796	2,449	564	584	469	5,474	1,083	5,110	7,505
1924	32,642	7,092	2,329	528	877	470	5,790	973	5,304	7,764
1925	35,076	7,836	2,583	611	919	498	6,347	979	5,721	7,940
1926	35,781*	6,941*				529	6,347*			8,020*
1927	36,845*	7,119*					6,472*			8,040*
1928	38,296*	6,830*					6,602*			

[a] For definition of this term, see text.
[b] Based upon *Census of Agriculture* and reports of the U. S. Dept. of Agriculture.
[c] Based upon *Census of Manufactures, Statistics of Income,* published by the U. S. Bureau of Internal Revenue, and a study of a large number of sample corporations made by the National Bureau of Economic Research.
[d] Based upon *Census of Mines & Quarries, Statistics of Income,* published by the U. S. Bureau of Internal Revenue, and upon a study of the reports of numerous corporations made by the National Bureau of Economic Research.
[e] Based upon volume of construction as reported by the F. W. Dodge Co. and upon *Statistics of Income,* published by the U. S. Bureau of Internal Revenue.
[f] Based upon reports of the Comptroller of the Currency.
[g] Based upon reports of various research bureaus and upon *Statistics of Income,* published by the U. S. Bureau of Internal Revenue.
[h] Based upon reports of the Secretary of the Treasury.
[i] Based upon *Statistics of Income,* published by the U. S. Bureau of Internal Revenue.
[j] Includes income from urban gardens, poultry and cows, imputed rent of owned homes, imputed interest on the value of durable consumption goods in the hands of consumers, income from foreign investments, and rent of leased homes. Based upon Census data, bulletins of the Dept. of Commerce and F. W. Dodge figures on the value and volume of residential construction.
* Preliminary estimate.

cannot be certain that even these sales figures do not contain a considerable margin of error. To these estimates of total sales, profit ratios have been applied, the products presumably representing

TABLE XVII—Continued

REALIZED INCOME[a] DRAWN BY ENTREPRENEURS AND OTHER PROPERTY OWNERS FROM THE VARIOUS INDUSTRIES

(MILLIONS OF CURRENT DOLLARS)

Year	All Following Fields of Transportation	Railroads[k]	Pullman[l]	Express[l]	Transportation by Water[m]	Street Railways[n]	Private Electric Light and Power[o]	Telephones[p]	Telegraphs[q]
1909	$ 926	$614	$8	$19	$39	$139	$ 53	$43	$12
1910	997	653	9	22	51	151	54	45	12
1911	1,009	659	9	9	46	158	66	48	12
1912	1,025	662	9	6	46	166	70	53	13
1913	1,077	691	9	6	46	179	77	56	13
1914	1,085	676	9	4	49	189	86	58	13
1915	1,116	688	9	6	53	190	95	60	15
1916	1,150	683	9	15	65	196	104	63	15
1917	1,220	714	9	4	103	188	117	68	17
1918	1,196	691	9	3	87	177	137	72	19
1919	1,248	694	9	3	120	178	149	76	19
1920	1,248	703	9	4	87	176	164	84	20
1921	1,251	684	9	6	74	176	186	97	19
1922	1,293	709	10	5	34	184	219	108	24
1923	1,410	755	9	5	18	206	276	120	21
1924	1,516	804	9	5	15	199	328	134	23
1925	1,643	839	5[r]	5	22	196	404	150	23
1926		871	7	5					
1927				5					
1928				5					

k Based upon *Statistics of Railways* published by the Interstate Commerce Commission. Includes switching and terminal companies.

l Based upon *Preliminary Abstract of Statistics of Common Carriers*, issued by the Interstate Commerce Commission.

m Based upon *Statistics of Income*, published by the U. S Bureau of Internal Revenue.

n Based upon *Census of Electric Railways* and upon records of a large number of sample corporations.

o Based upon *Census of Electric Light and Power* and upon the records of a large number of sample corporations.

p Based upon *Census of Telephones*, reports of *Bell Telephone Companies* and reports of other telephone corporations.

q Based upon the reports of the telegraph companies given in Moody's *Manual of Public Utilities*.

r Decrease in income due to split in the Pullman Co., all the manufacturing being given over to the Pullman Car & Manufacturing Co. which is owned by the Pullman Co.

the aggregate gains which merchants have made on their sales. These profit ratios are based on the investigations of a number of public and private agencies and are much more dependable in the later than in the earlier years of the period covered by this study, since, for the earlier years, data along this line are almost non-existent. It is, therefore, possible that considerable errors have been made in calculating the profits of merchants, especially in the pre-war period. We know, further, very little about the proportion of mercantile profits withdrawn by owners for private use, hence a third source of error is introduced into the figures.

The estimates for unclassified industries and for miscellaneous returns are both little more than careful guesses. Since 1916, the figures covering the unclassified industries are based, to a considerable extent, upon data in the reports published by the United States Bureau of Internal Revenue, entitled *Statistics of Income*, and are therefore less likely to be widely in error than are the figures for the years 1909 to 1915. The estimates for the construction industry and for transportation by water, especially in the earlier years, are also subject to considerable margins of error. It is believed that the data for the other fields covered, namely, manufacturing, mining, government, banking, railways, Pullman, express, street railways, telephones, telegraphs, and private electric light and power—are reasonably dependable. Even in those industries in which the estimates are extremely crude, the changes from year to year presumably have considerable significance, the indications of change being much more reliable than those of absolute size. The figures in the column headed "government" represent an estimate of the amount of interest paid by the Federal, state, and local governments in the various years.

Table XVII indicates that the owners of the agricultural industry derive from farming approximately three times as much revenue as the owners of the manufacturing industry obtain from their factories. The fact that entrepreneurs and property owners in the manufacturing industry received total income so much less than the aggregate for the agricultural or mercantile fields is obviously due to the fact that in the latter fields the number of entrepreneurs devoting full time to the industry is relatively great. The magnitude of the total profits in the unclassified industries is accounted for in the same way, for it must be remembered that the unclassified industries are largely made up of the various so-called hand trades, and they also include a great variety of small enterprises conducted by the proprietor himself or with the help of his family. The manufacturing industry, on the other hand, is owned largely by corporations, and a great majority of the holders of corporate securities devote almost no time to the management of the industry.

CHART 11

REALIZED INCOME DRAWN BY ENTREPRENEURS AND OTHER PROPERTY OWNERS FROM THE VARIOUS INDUSTRIES[a]

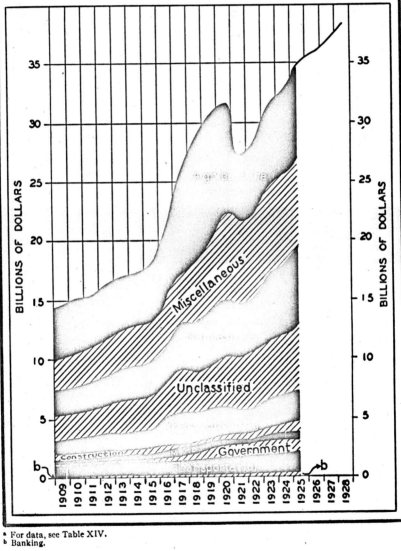

[a] For data, see Table XIV.
[b] Banking.

TABLE XVIII

PURCHASING POWER, IN 1913 DOLLARS,[a] OF THE REALIZED INCOME DRAWN BY ENTREPRENEURS AND OTHER PROPERTY OWNERS FROM THE VARIOUS INDUSTRIES

(MILLIONS OF 1913 DOLLARS)[b]

Year	All Industries	Agriculture	Manufacturing	Mines, Quarries and Oil Wells	Construction	Banking	Mercantile	Government	Unclassified	Miscellaneous
1909	$15,354	$4,414	$1,169	$252	$708	$235	$2,188	$150	$2,293	$2,963
1910	15,614	4,528	1,290	270	589	275	2,104	184	2,243	3,098
1911	15,901	4,179	1,369	248	642	281	2,386	204	2,384	3,163
1912	16,743	4,600	1,409	288	663	286	2,403	206	2,584	3,258
1913	16,934	4,357	1,479	351	354	293	2,580	216	2,879	3,349
1914	17,011	4,290	1,418	274	532	286	2,649	230	2,796	3,456
1915	17,850	4,789	1,484	282	522	274	2,693	254	2,857	3,581
1916	19,346	5,237	2,235	540	515	242	2,774	252	2,749	3,720
1917	20,345	5,792	2,230	587	219	219	3,025	296	3,033	3,930
1918	19,462	6,194	1,841	475	144	193	2,719	378	2,371	4,284
1919	18,564	5,796	1,557	290	241	161	2,765	653	2,033	4,281
1920	17,188	4,694	1,340	281	239	174	2,439	580	2,170	4,583
1921	16,429	3,572	1,328	256	253	210	2,562	625	2,545	4,333
1922	17,883	4,116	1,222	257	327	266	2,719	698	3,056	4,411
1923	19,839	4,681	1,526	351	365	281	3,426	663	3,094	4,574
1924	20,490	4,837	1,452	329	548	282	3,617	597	3,210	4,676
1925	21,339	4,935	1,576	373	561	292	3,877	588	3,386	4,751
1926	21,844*	4,282*				309	3,874*			4,816*
1927	22,833*	4,656*					4,018*			4,924*
1928	24,055*	4,546*					4,162*			

[a] "1913 Dollars" is an abbreviation for the phrase "dollars having purchasing power equivalent to that which they had in 1913."

[b] Computed from corresponding items in Table XVII by dividing by the appropriate price indices recorded in Table VII.

* Preliminary estimate.

It is interesting to note that, in recent years, the share of the owners of the construction industry has been larger than the corresponding share derived from the operation of the railroads of the country.

Realized Entrepreneurial and Property Income in 1913 Dollars.

In Table XVIII, entrepreneurial and property income are expressed in terms of dollars having purchasing power equal to that prevailing in 1913. In the latter table, therefore, the quantities shown indicate the relative amounts of consumable commodities

TABLE XVIII—Continued

PURCHASING POWER, IN 1913 DOLLARS,[a] OF THE REALIZED INCOME DRAWN BY ENTREPRENEURS AND OTHER PROPERTY OWNERS FROM THE VARIOUS INDUSTRIES

(MILLIONS OF 1913 DOLLARS)[b]

Year	All Following Fields of Transportation	Rail- roads[c]	Pull- man	Ex- press	Trans- por- tation by Water	Street Rail- ways	Private Electric Light and Power	Tele- phones	Tele- graphs
1909	$ 982	$651	$8	$20	$42	$147	$ 56	$46	$12
1910	1,033	676	9	23	53	157	56	47	13
1911	1,044	682	10	9	47	164	69	50	13
1912	1,048	677	9	6	47	170	72	54	13
1913	1,077	691	9	6	46	179	77	56	13
1914	1,079	673	9	4	49	188	86	58	13
1915	1,114	687	9	6	53	190	95	59	15
1916	1,080	642	9	14	61	184	98	58	14
1917	1,014	594	8	3	86	156	98	55	14
1918	863	499	7	2	63	128	99	50	14
1919	787	439	6	2	76	113	94	46	13
1920	689	389	5	2	48	97	91	46	11
1921	746	409	6	4	44	105	111	58	12
1922	810	445	6	3	21	115	137	68	15
1923	876	470	6	3	11	128	172	75	13
1924	943	501	6	3	9	124	204	84	14
1925	1,000	512	3[d]	3	13	119	246	92	14
1926		532	4	3					
1927				3					

[c] Includes switching and terminal companies.
[d] Decrease in income due to split in the Pullman Co., all the manufacturing being given over to the Pullman Car & Manufacturing Co. which is owned by the Pullman Co.

which would have been purchasable in the various years had there been no changes in the general price level. The figures in the second column of Table XVIII indicate that the ability of entrepreneurs and other property owners combined to purchase direct or consumers' goods has increased during the 19 years between 1909 and 1927 by almost one-half. The share of the owners in the aggregate moved up rapidly from 1909 to 1917, declined sharply between 1917 and 1921, then climbed upward again passing the 1917 high in 1924, and continuing on until, in 1927, it was nearly 50 per cent above the 1909 figure.

From Charts 11, 12a, and 12b, it is seen that the entrepreneurial and property income from agriculture remained approximately constant from 1909 to 1914, rose rapidly until 1918, then fell with even greater speed until 1921, since which date a gradual recovery is evident. Though the level attained in 1927 was well above that of 1909, the recovery had not yet succeeded in bringing the share of the farmers, landlords, and mortgage holders, as measured in purchasing power, to anything like as high as the level of 1918.

The gains of the owners in the manufacturing industry have, in many respects, fluctuated in the same way as have those of the agriculturists, although, in manufacturing, the high point was reached in 1916 and the decline continued until 1922. Data are not available for years since 1925, but, in that year, the share of the entrepreneurs and other property owners, though materially higher than in 1909, was still only about two-thirds as great as in 1916.

The figures for mines, quarries, and oil wells likewise show that the years 1916 and 1917 were the most profitable for the owners, and that their gains declined thereafter rapidly until 1921. The recovery up to 1925 had not as yet brought profits up to the 1916 level.

In the construction industry, the years preceding our entry into the World War, though characterized by declining profits, were much more profitable to the entrepreneurs than were those during and after the war, although conditions improved after 1918. From the profit standpoint, the construction industry has, in fact, been steadily on the up-grade since the close of the war, real profits in 1924 and 1925 having again approached, though not attained, the average pre-war level.

The share of the entrepreneurs and other property owners in banking was apparently a little larger in 1925 than in the period 1911 to 1914. Due primarily to the reduced purchasing power of the dollar, profits were greatly depressed during the whole period of inflation, reaching their lowest point in 1919.

In the mercantile field, total profits rose rapidly from 1909 to 1917, declined between 1917 and 1920, rose sharply to 1925, and have since been tending slowly upward. There is no evidence that the period of inflation brought to merchants unusual profits. Only in the year 1917 does it seem that the rise in prices really brought to merchants any considerable net gain. Of course, in the other years likewise, they made nominal gains, but, when the figures are de-

CHART 12a

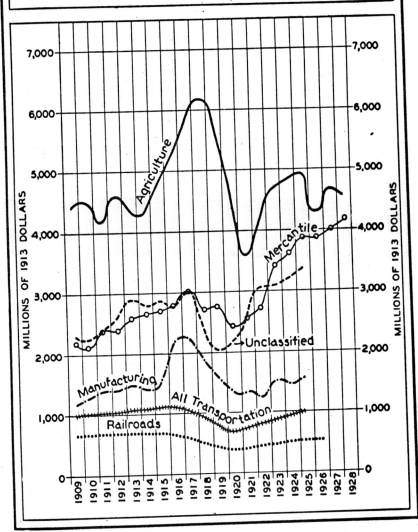

PURCHASING POWER, IN 1913 DOLLARS,
OF THE REALIZED INCOME DRAWN BY
ENTREPRENEURS AND OTHER PROPERTY
OWNERS FROM THE VARIOUS INDUSTRIES•

• For data, see Table XVIII.

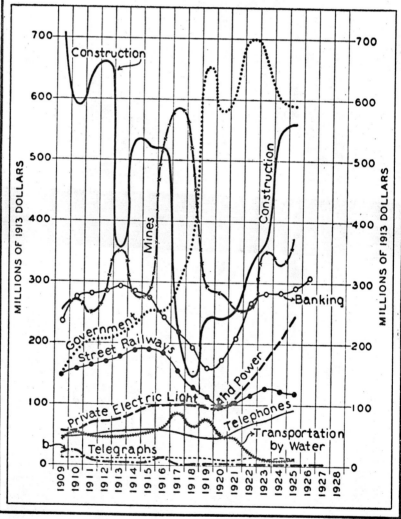

PURCHASING POWER, IN 1913 DOLLARS,
OF THE REALIZED INCOME DRAWN BY
ENTREPRENEURS AND OTHER PROPERTY
OWNERS FROM THE VARIOUS INDUSTRIES[a]

[a] For data, see Table XVIII.
[b] Express.

flated, their apparently excessive profits shrink to figures indicating that gains were only average in size.

As previously stated, the items appearing under the caption "Government" represent payments to holders of the funded debt. Interest payments were, of course, greatly expanded by the war, hence it is not surprising to see that the rise which had been going on steadily but slowly between 1909 and 1917 was, at the last-mentioned date, sharply accentuated, the rise to 1919 being almost vertical. Since 1922, there has been a decline in the total, due primarily to the paying off of some of its debt by the Federal government. The irregular changes from year to year observable in this column are due primarily, not to variations in the amount of interest paid, but rather to fluctuations in the index numbers used as deflators.

Figures purporting to show, in deflated dollars, the share of entrepreneurs and other property owners in the unclassified industries are not sufficiently trustworthy to deserve much comment. They indicate a marked decline in this class of income during the war period, due to the fact that the number of persons attached to this industry at that time fell off so sharply. Aside from this temporary depression, there is a steady general upward tendency in the items in this column. The figures for miscellaneous income, made up as they are largely of rents of homes and imputed income on the value of various durable consumers' goods, tend to parallel the general increase in the wealth of the inhabitants.

The graph in Chart 12a, recording the returns received by the owners of the railroads of the country, shows that such returns remained approximately constant between 1909 and 1915. With the advent of deflation, however, their income declined sharply until, in 1920, it was only three-fifths as large as it was in 1913. Since 1920, however, the lot of the railway stock and bondholders has slowly but steadily improved, though in 1925, the last year for which figures have been computed, their annual income would still buy but about three-fourths as much as in the years before the World War. What has been said of the railroad industry applies with practically equal force to the Pullman industry.

The erratic behavior of the figures for the express industry is caused by the various transformations which that industry has undergone, and by the liquidation of some of the concerns in that field, resulting in payment of enormous dividends in some years.

Figures for transportation by water are far from being highly dependable as to details, but they indicate conclusively that the owners profited greatly by the high returns from carrying freight during war time, despite the loss of numerous vessels. After the close of the World War, the profits in this field declined rapidly and, since 1923, have been at an extremely low ebb.

Until the year 1915, the security holders in street railways gained steadily in their income from this industry as measured in terms of constant dollars. Inflation, however, forced their income sharply downward during the years 1916 to 1920 until, in the last mentioned year, it was but about half what it was in 1915. Since 1920, there has been a slow recovery, but, presumably mainly because of the strenuous competition of the automobile, earnings are still at a low level and the share of the stock and bondholders remains small as compared to what it was in pre-war times.

Private electric light and power plants and telephone and telegraph companies were affected less severely by the effects of inflation accompanying the war than were the other corporation-controlled industries studied. Since 1921, the owners of all three of these industries have been prospering, although the most marked growth in dividends and interest is in the field of electric light and power, the owners of that industry receiving 2½ times as large an income in 1925 as in 1920. However, for the entire field of transportation, the income was lower in 1925 than in any year before the war, except 1909.

Perhaps the most important fact brought out by the figures in Table XVIII and the graphs in Chart 13 is that, to the owners of American industries, the Great War, and especially its aftermath of inflation, brought, in the main, severe losses instead of gains. It is true that, before the United States entered the World War, the industries of agriculture, manufacturing, mining, and transportation by water did profit materially on account of the new business given them by the European countries participating in the war. When, in 1918, however, the United States Government really became engaged in earnest, profits shrank in practically all of the industries except agriculture. Farmers' gains continued on a high level throughout 1918 and 1919, but then began a swift descent. In practically all of the other fields of private industry, the decline in profits continued until 1920, and in some cases until 1921, despite the supposedly tremendous post-war boom of 1919 and early 1920. Of course, during this boom, many entrepreneurs secured large nominal profits, which, when translated into dollars of constant purchasing power, often shrank until they were materially smaller than normal.

CHART 13

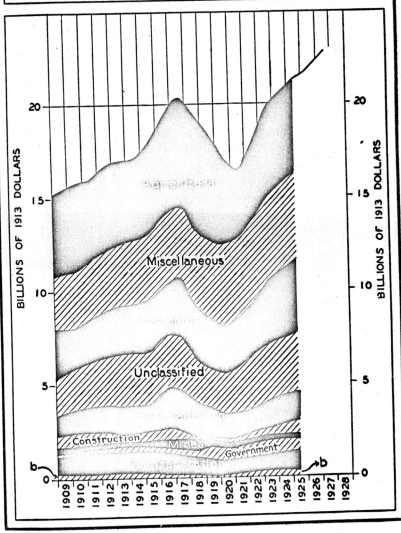

PURCHASING POWER, IN 1913 DOLLARS,
OF THE REALIZED INCOME DRAWN BY
ENTREPRENEURS AND OTHER PROPERTY
OWNERS FROM THE VARIOUS INDUSTRIES[a]

[a] For data, see Table XVIII
[b] Banking.

CHAPTER VI

THE SHARE OF THE EMPLOYEES

Absolute Share of Employees in Each Industry.

In Table XIX are recorded figures of the absolute share of the employees in the realized income derived from each of the leading branches of industry. All amounts in this table are recorded in the dollars current in the given year. The reader will note that, although agriculture is one of the most important industries when ranked on the basis of the total value of its products, it is relatively insignificant when considered from the standpoint of the amount disbursed to employees. The reason for this is that the largest part of the work in the agricultural field is performed by farmers and members of their families, hired employees playing but a minor rôle. We see that manufacturing and the unclassified industries are the leading dispensers of wages and salaries, each paying out approximately double the amount disbursed in this form by any other single industry. In the next group are the mercantile, government, and transportation industries, each distributing in wages and salaries some 5 or 6 billions of dollars annually. Railroads pay, in the aggregate, somewhat more to their employees than all of the remaining transportation industries for which records are available.

Percentage of Entire Realized Income Received by Employees.

The figures in the second column of Table XX and the heavy line in Chart 15a show that there has been a marked change in the percentage of the total realized income going to employees. From 1909 to 1917, the trend of this proportionate share was nearly horizontal, the average fraction received by the employees being in the neighborhood of 52 or 53 per cent. Between 1917 and 1920, this percentage moved sharply upward, rising, in the last mentioned year, above the 57 per cent level. Since that date, it has constantly remained in the neighborhood of 57 per cent. The increase taking place between 1917 and 1920 in the proportionate share going to the employees appears to be adequately explained by the inflation of the currency during that period. As we have previously seen, wages were promptly adjusted to allow for the change in value of the dollar, and wages are by far the most important item in the total

share of the employees. When, because of disturbances in industry connected with the World War, the total realized income, as measured in terms of purchasing power, declined, it is obvious that the shares of the salaried employees and entrepreneurs would bear the brunt of the loss. Evidently the shrinkage in the share of the relatively small salaried class was not sufficiently large to offset the gain in the share of the wage workers, hence the total share of the employees increased. The question arises, however, as to why this increase was retained after the disturbances connected with the war had quieted down, and the realized income of the country had therefore risen again. This phenomenon is probably due to complex causes. It is, however, doubtless accounted for in part, at least, by the diminution in the percentage of the population conducting enterprises on their own account.

In general it appears that the proportion of the realized income going to employees varies inversely with the percentage of the work of the industry performed by entrepreneurs and also inversely with the amount of capital invested in the industry. The tendency toward an increase since 1916 in the proportion of the total realized income of the industry going to employees is found in the case of every industry in the list except government. In the case of government, the share of the property owners consists entirely of interest on funded debt. The enormous issues of bonds for war financing tended, of course, to increase the share of the property owners and diminish the share of the employees in the income derived by individuals directly from government.

Since 1922, a tendency toward decline in the proportionate share of the employees in the realized income of the industry, is noticeable in the case of mining, banking, agriculture, construction, electric light and power, railroading, and the telephone industry. Whether this declining tendency will later extend to other industries or whether the share of the employees in general will again move upward, it is, of course, now impossible to say.

Purchasing Power of Absolute Share of Employees by Industries.

In Table XXI the shares of the employees in leading industries are shown in terms of dollars having the same value which they had in 1913. The total column in Table XXI shows that the employees of the United States were able to purchase with their combined wages and salaries nearly twice as many goods in 1927 as they could have bought in 1909. We have here an adequate ex-

TABLE XIX

TOTAL WAGES, SALARIES, PENSIONS, COMPENSATION FOR INJURIES, ETC., RECEIVED BY EMPLOYEES FROM THE VARIOUS INDUSTRIES[a]

(MILLIONS OF CURRENT DOLLARS)

Year	All Indus-tries	Agri-cul-ture	Manu-fac-turing	Mines, Quarries and Oil Wells	Con-struc-tion	Bank-ing	Mer-can-tile	Gov-ern-ment	Un-clas-sified
1909	$15,090	$ 717	$4,378	$ 595	$1,030	$115	$1,637	$1,412	$3,563
1910	16,266	715	4,958	656	1,014	123	1,711	1,500	3,792
1911	16,498	751	4,927	670	987	137	1,729	1,570	3,834
1912	17,587	754	5,460	725	1,094	149	1,689	1,661	4,029
1913	18,822	776	5,854	803	1,172	161	1,908	1,766	4,247
1914	18,516	756	5,489	695	876	164	2,087	1,861	4,486
1915	19,361	773	5,877	701	874	183	2,155	1,936	4,725
1916	22,470	828	7,881	881	968	214	2,370	2,025	4,879
1917	25,802	1,029	9,796	1,105	938	230	2,647	2,683	4,526
1918	32,324	1,213	12,244	1,376	1,003	281	2,963	5,741	3,542
1919	35,399	1,491	13,624	1,416	1,451	362	3,482	5,072	3,951
1920	42,283	1,663	17,109	1,848	1,447	429	4,161	4,232	5,428
1921	36,213	1,405	11,052	1,414	1,316	481	4,134	4,564	7,009
1922	37,700	1,203	12,010	1,315	1,682	493	4,387	4,662	7,377
1923	42,893	1,231	14,385	1,832	1,881	528	5,298	4,699	7,946
1924	44,493	1,232	13,947	1,510	2,097	559	5,260	4,923	9,951
1925	46,855	1,253	14,283	1,558	2,539	596	5,649	5,151	10,731
1926	49,767*	1,272*	15,010*	1,768*	2,624*	636	6,095*	5,640*	11,441*
1927	51,360*	1,252*	14,985*	1,646*	2,639*	649*	6,281*	5,927*	12,713*
1928	51,123*	1,279*	14,422*		2,805*		6,535*		

   [a] The totals in this table are the sums of the amounts received by employees as recorded in Tables XXII and XXIV plus amounts paid out as pensions, compensation for injuries, etc.
   * Preliminary estimate.

planation of the remarkable development of those industries depending for their success upon mass production of goods. A study of the totals indicates that the period may well be divided into three parts. From 1909 to 1916, there was a rather rapid rise in the purchasing power of the combined wages and salaries of all employees. From 1918 to 1921, there was a very slight decline, wholly inconsequential in comparison with the great loss suffered by entrepreneurs and other property owners during the same period. Even the industrial depression of 1921 did not force down the total share of the employees to any noticeable extent; all that happened was that it was kept from rising. After 1921, the purchasing power

TABLE XIX—Continued

TOTAL WAGES, SALARIES, PENSIONS, COMPENSATION FOR INJURIES, ETC., RECEIVED BY EMPLOYEES FROM THE VARIOUS INDUSTRIES[a]
(MILLIONS OF CURRENT DOLLARS)

Year	All Following Fields of Transportation	Railroads	Pullman	Express	Transportation by Water	Street Railways	Private Electric Light and Power	Telephones	Telegraphs
1909	$1,643	$1,105	$13	$ 43	$172	$168	$ 41	$ 81	$19
1910	1,798	1,219	14	47	181	179	45	92	21
1911	1,893	1,277	14	51	183	190	51	103	25
1912	2,027	1,367	14	54	196	201	56	113	27
1913	2,136	1,434	17	55	204	210	61	126	28
1914	2,101	1,385	16	52	203	222	66	129	27
1915	2,136	1,397	15	52	223	225	70	128	26
1916	2,423	1,566	16	58	274	243	78	154	36
1917	2,848	1,851	18	74	333	267	86	173	45
1918	3,960	2,766	23	93	417	312	96	194	60
1919	4,550	3,009	28	116	590	376	118	246	69
1920	5,966	3,907	34	162	809	478	159	323	94
1921	4,838	2,933	32	140	666	472	180	334	82
1922	4,569	2,821	27	120	521	446	194	360	80
1923	5,093	3,208	28	125	545	468	229	400	89
1924	5,015	3,031	33	119	587	476	244	434	91
1925	5,094	3,076	34	116	566	475	275	452	99
1926	5,281	3,172	35	117	570	480	313	479	114
1927	5,268*	3,133*	36	117	547	480	342	501	111

of the share of the employees again moved upward at a rate even more rapid than in the first period. Since that date, in fact, the total share of the employees has increased by about 50 per cent. Industries in which the increase since 1920 has been noticeably large are construction, banking, the mercantile field, unclassified industries, private electric light and power plants, and government. The absolute share of the employees has remained approximately constant in the railroad industry, and the same is true in agriculture. In the express industry and transportation by water, there has been some tendency for the absolute share of the employees to decline. In every industrial field mentioned, however, the share of the employees, when measured in purchasing power, was materially greater

TABLE XX

PER CENTS[a] WHICH TOTAL AMOUNTS RECEIVED BY EMPLOYEES AS WAGES, SALARIES, PENSIONS, ETC., CONSTITUTE OF THE ENTIRE REALIZED INCOME DRAWN BY INDIVIDUALS FROM THE VARIOUS INDUSTRIES

Year	All Industries	Agriculture	Manufacturing	Mines, Quarries and Oil Wells	Construction	Banking	Mercantile	Government	Unclassified
1909	51.0	14.4	79.9	71.4	60.8	34.2	44.5	90.9	62.3
1910	51.8	13.7	79.9	71.5	64.2	31.5	45.8	89.4	63.7
1911	51.8	15.6	78.8	73.6	61.4	33.5	42.9	88.8	62.4
1912	51.8	14.3	79.8	72.1	62.8	34.7	41.8	89.2	61.4
1913	52.7	15.1	79.8	69.6	76.8	35.5	42.5	89.1	59.6
1914	51.9	14.9	79.4	71.6	62.0	36.2	43.9	88.9	61.3
1915	52.0	14.1	79.8	71.3	62.7	39.6	44.5	88.3	61.9
1916	51.9	12.5	76.8	60.5	63.8	44.6	44.6	88.2	61.9
1917	50.3	11.2	78.5	61.0	77.8	45.2	41.8	88.1	54.2
1918	53.5	10.8	82.8	67.7	83.1	49.1	43.4	91.4	50.0
1919	53.7	12.2	84.7	75.5	78.6	56.0	43.5	82.7	52.9
1920	57.1	15.0	87.6	78.5	76.4	55.3	47.7	79.7	55.8
1921	57.1	20.2	83.3	76.7	75.6	56.7	49.0	81.1	61.3
1922	57.2	16.5	86.1	76.2	76.5	53.1	50.6	80.5	59.7
1923	57.7	15.3	85.5	76.4	76.3	53.0	49.1	81.3	60.9
1924	57.7	14.8	85.7	74.1	70.5	54.3	47.6	83.5	65.2
1925	57.2	13.8	87.8	71.8	73.4	54.5	47.1	84.0	65.2
1926	58.2	15.5				54.6	49.0		
1927	58.2	15.0					49.2		
1928	57.2	15.8					49.7		

[a] Calculated from figures presented in Tables XIV and XIX.

in 1927 than it was in 1909. The most striking increases for the entire 18 year interval were in the banking, telephone, and telegraph industries, in all three of which the share of the employees trebled, and in the electric light and power industry where employees received, in 1927, more than 4 times the total purchasing power they had in 1909.

Wage Totals in Current Dollars by Industries.

We have now considered the share of the employees taken as a whole. The next step will be to treat separately the two main divisions of wages and salaries. Table XXII records the total amount paid in wages by each industrial field, all amounts being expressed in terms of the dollars current in various years. The total

TABLE XX—Continued

PER CENTS* WHICH TOTAL AMOUNTS RECEIVED BY EMPLOYEES AS WAGES, SALARIES, PENSIONS, ETC., CONSTITUTE OF THE ENTIRE REALIZED INCOME DRAWN BY INDIVIDUALS FROM THE VARIOUS INDUSTRIES

Year	All Following Fields of Transportation	Railroads	Pullman	Express	Transportation by Water	Street Railways	Private Electric Light and Power	Telephones	Telegraphs
1909	63.9	64.3	62.5	69.8	81.4	54.8	43.7	65.4	62.1
1910	64.3	65.1	61.2	68.3	78.1	54.2	45.8	66.8	62.3
1911	65.2	65.9	60.2	85.1	80.0	54.6	43.3	68.1	66.7
1912	66.4	67.4	59.8	90.1	81.1	54.8	44.2	68.1	68.3
1913	66.5	67.5	64.1	90.8	81.7	54.0	44.2	69.2	69.2
1914	66.0	67.2	63.7	92.2	80.4	54.0	43.5	68.9	68.3
1915	65.7	67.0	62.0	90.3	80.8	54.3	42.4	68.1	63.2
1916	67.8	69.6	63.6	79.7	80.7	55.3	42.7	71.0	70.0
1917	70.0	72.2	66.4	95.2	76.4	58.8	42.4	71.7	72.7
1918	76.8	80.0	71.1	96.4	82.7	63.8	41.1	73.0	76.0
1919	78.5	81.3	75.0	97.5	83.1	67.9	44.2	76.5	78.3
1920	82.7	84.7	78.9	97.3	90.2	73.1	49.3	79.3	82.7
1921	79.5	81.1	77.6	95.9	90.0	72.8	49.2	77.6	80.9
1922	77.9	79.9	72.8	95.9	94.0	70.8	47.0	76.9	76.7
1923	78.3	80.9	75.5	96.3	96.8	69.5	45.3	77.0	81.1
1924	76.8	79.0	78.5	92.8	97.5	70.6	42.7	76.4	80.1
1925	75.6	78.6	88.0	95.7	96.3	70.8	40.6	75.0	81.2
1926		78.5	83.3	95.7					
1927				95.7					
1928				95.5					

of nominal wage payments more than trebled between 1909 and 1928, but we cannot attach any particular significance to this difference because of the changing value of the dollar. From the point of view of total wages paid, manufacturing is the industry dominant in the United States. The unclassified industries, the mercantile industry, construction, and transportation rank next in the order named.

Chart 17 shows that, in practically all industries, the nominal amount paid in wages rose sharply to a peak in 1920 and declined thereafter. The unclassified industries, the telephone industry, and private electric light and power plants furnished exceptions to this general rule, in each of these fields the total wage bill being higher in 1921 than in 1920.

CHART 14

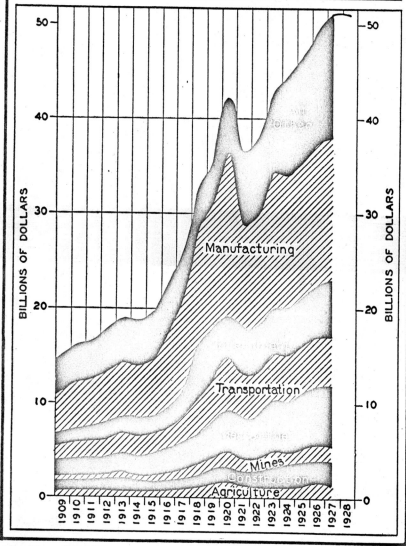

TOTAL WAGES, SALARIES, PENSIONS,
COMPENSATION FOR INJURIES, ETC., RECEIVED
BY EMPLOYEES FROM THE VARIOUS INDUSTRIES[a]

[a] For data, see Table XIX

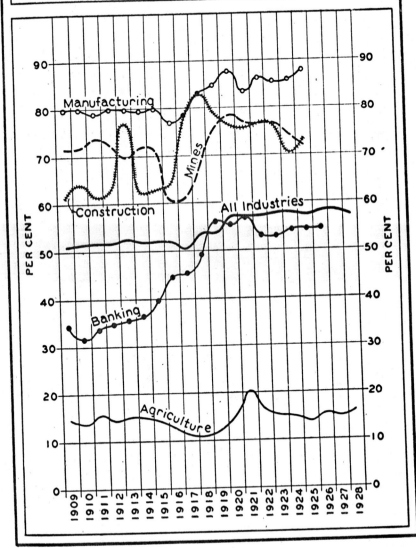

PER CENTS WHICH TOTAL AMOUNTS RECEIVED
BY EMPLOYEES AS WAGES, SALARIES, PENSIONS,
ETC., CONSTITUTE OF THE ENTIRE REALIZED
INCOME DRAWN BY INDIVIDUALS FROM THE
RESPECTIVE INDUSTRIES[a]

* For data, see Table XX.

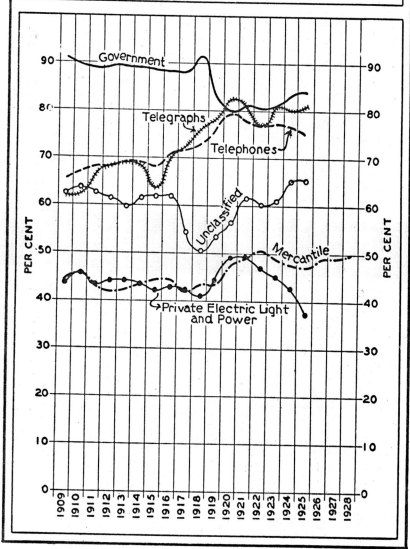

PER CENTS WHICH TOTAL AMOUNTS RECEIVED
BY EMPLOYEES AS WAGES, SALARIES, PENSIONS,
ETC., CONSTITUTE OF THE ENTIRE REALIZED
INCOME DRAWN BY INDIVIDUALS FROM THE
RESPECTIVE INDUSTRIES[a]

[a] For data, see Table XX.

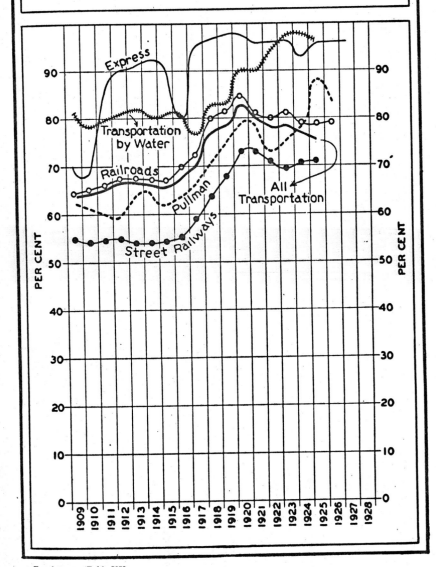

PER CENTS WHICH TOTAL AMOUNTS RECEIVED
BY EMPLOYEES AS WAGES, SALARIES, PENSIONS,
ETC., CONSTITUTE OF THE ENTIRE REALIZED
INCOME DRAWN BY INDIVIDUALS FROM THE
RESPECTIVE INDUSTRIES[a]

[a] For data, see Table XX.

TABLE XXI

PURCHASING POWER, IN 1913 DOLLARS,[a] OF TOTAL WAGES, SALARIES, PENSIONS, COMPENSATION FOR INJURIES, ETC., RECEIVED BY EMPLOYEES FROM THE VARIOUS INDUSTRIES

(MILLIONS OF 1913 DOLLARS)[b]

Year	All Indus- tries	Agri- cul- ture	Manu- fac- turing	Mines, Quarries and Oil Wells	Con- struc- tion	Bank- ing	Mer- can- tile	Gov- ern- ment	Un- clas- sified
1909	$15,946	$726	$4,640	$ 630	$1,090	$122	$1,733	$1,495	$3,771
1910	16,766	711	5,121	677	1,046	127	1,766	1,548	3,914
1911	17,019	769	5,086	692	1,018	141	1,784	1,620	3,956
1912	17,913	775	5,560	738	1,113	152	1,720	1,691	4,101
1913	18,822	776	5,854	803	1,172	161	1,908	1,766	4,247
1914	18,238	773	5,403	683	861	161	2,051	1,830	4,410
1915	18,786	802	5,702	678	845	177	2,083	1,871	4,565
1916	20,214	794	7,090	790	867	192	2,124	1,814	4,371
1917	19,897	851	7,559	847	719	177	2,030	2,058	3,471
1918	20,688	821	7,865	875	638	179	1,885	3,652	2,253
1919	19,453	848	7,527	773	792	197	1,901	2,770	2,157
1920	20,385	847	8,278	885	693	205	1,992	2,027	2,599
1921	20,282	888	6,191	786	731	267	2,297	2,536	3,895
1922	22,682	858	7,213	785	1,004	294	2,618	2,782	4,402
1923	25,325	856	8,487	1,073	1,102	309	3,104	2,753	4,655
1924	26,267	844	8,236	886	1,229	328	3,084	2,886	5,834
1925	27,072	861	8,250	893	1,456	342	3,240	2,954	6,154
1926	28,577*	880*	8,618*	1,007*	1,495*	362	3,473*	3,213*	6,519*
1927	30,059*	882*	8,776*	956*	1,533*	377*	3,648*	3,443*	7,384*
1928	29,967*	910*							

[a] "1913 Dollars" is an abbreviation for the phrase "dollars having purchasing power equivalent to that which they had in 1913."

[b] Computed from corresponding items in Table XIX by dividing the sub-items pertaining to the various columns by the appropriate price indices recorded in Table VII.

* Preliminary estimate.

Wage Totals in 1913 Dollars by Industries.

The record of total wages in terms of 1913 dollars appears in Table XXIII. This table makes it clear that the wage earners of the nation, *in toto*, were able to buy, in 1927, somewhat less than twice the quantity of goods which they could have purchased in 1909. In general, the purchasing power of the aggregate wage bill of the nation rose along a line somewhat irregular but having a steady upward trend between 1909 and 1921. Since 1921, the total has risen very sharply, the increase since that date being approximately 50 per cent.

TABLE XXI—Continued

PURCHASING POWER, IN 1913 DOLLARS,* OF TOTAL WAGES, SALARIES, PENSIONS, COMPENSATION FOR INJURIES, ETC., RECEIVED BY EMPLOYEES FROM THE VARIOUS INDUSTRIES

(MILLIONS OF 1913 DOLLARS)[b]

Year	All Following Fields of Transportation	Railroads[c]	Pullman	Express	Transportation by Water	Street Railways	Private Electric Light and Power	Telephones	Telegraphs
1909	$1,739	$1,169	$14	$46	$182	$178	$ 43	$ 86	$20
1910	1,856	1,258	14	49	187	185	47	95	21
1911	1,953	1,317	14	52	189	196	52	106	26
1912	2,063	1,391	14	55	199	205	57	115	28
1913	2,136	1,434	17	55	204	210	61	126	28
1914	2,065	1,362	16	51	199	218	65	127	' 27
1915	2,064	1,350	15	51	215	218	68	123	25
1916	2,172	1,403	15	52	245	218	70	138	32
1917	2,185	1,419	14	57	255	206	66	132	35
1918	2,520	1,759	14	59	265	200	61	124	38
1919	2,486	1,643	15	63	322	207	64	134	38
1920	2,858	1,871	16	78	387	230	76	155	45
1921	2,690	1,630	18	78	370	263	100	186	45
1922	2,727	1,683	16	72	311	267	116	215	48
1923	2,985	1,879	17	73	319	275	134	234	52
1924	2,941	1,777	19	70	344	280	143	255	54
1925	2,922	1,764	20	67	324	273	158	259	57
1926	3,010	1,807	20	67	325	275	179	273	65
1927	3,059*	1,820*	21	68	318	280*	197	291	65

* Includes switching and terminal companies.

In agriculture, the total amount of purchasing power paid to wage earners increased steadily from 1909 to 1917, then remained roughly on a level until 1924, when an upward movement again began. There was a slow upward trend in manufacturing between 1909 and 1915, with a sharp rise from 1915 to 1920, a heavy break in 1921, recovery during the next two years, and, since then, a trend which is nearly horizontal. In mining, the purchasing power of the total wage bill has fluctuated greatly, but the general trend was apparently upward between 1909 and 1923. Since that date, there has been a slight downward drift. The trend of aggregate real wages in the construction industry was approximately horizontal between 1909 and 1913; there was a marked decline from 1914 to

TABLE XXII

TOTAL WAGES DRAWN BY EMPLOYEES FROM THE VARIOUS INDUSTRIES[a]

(MILLIONS OF CURRENT DOLLARS)

Year	All Industries	Agri- culture[b]	Manu- facturing[c]	Mines, Quarries and Oil Wells[d]	Con- struction[e]	Mer- cantile[f]	Unclas- sified[g]
1909	$10,529	$ 680	$ 3,417	$ 544	$ 943	$1,204	$2,539
1910	11,330	678	3,822	605	919	1,263	2,717
1911	11,325	713	3,714	616	884	1,277	2,732
1912	12,112	715	4,173	667	983	1,240	2,845
1913	13,017	736	4,502	740	1,045	1,442	2,983
1914	12,396	715	4,130	631	742	1,562	3,121
1915	13,117	731	4,574	636	751	1,602	3,278
1916	15,660	783	6,315	807	858	1,749	3,385
1917	17,741	977	7,815	1,002	816	1,957	3,093
1918	20,414	1,146	9,710	1,240	887	2,247	2,202
1919	23,029	1,416	10,559	1,265	1,271	2,708	2,476
1920	29,540	1,581	13,628	1,672	1,282	3,273	3,722
1921	23,353	1,324	8,318	1,249	1,150	3,167	4,768
1922	24,553	1,129	9,301	1,147	1,486	3,367	4,962
1923	28,691	1,165	11,151	1,675	1,669	4,086	5,335
1924	29,051	1,177	10,502	1,346	1,857	4,053	6,623
1925	30,762	1,204	10,898	1,389	2,251	4,358	7,117
1926	32,604*	1,228	11,466*	1,599*	2,323*	4,777*	7,529*
1927	32,884*	1,213	11,063*	1,475*	2,337*	4,860*	8,288*
1928	32,235*	1,243*	10,366*		2,484*	5,057*	

[a] The few wage workers employed in *Banking* and *Government* are included with salaried employees.
[b] Based upon *Census of Agriculture* and reports of the U. S. Dept. of Agriculture.
[c] Based upon *Census of Manufactures* and various State reports.
[d] Based upon *Census of Mines and Quarries*, and reports of U. S. Bureau of Mines and of the Pennsylvania Dept. of Internal Affairs.
[e] Based upon volume of construction reported by F. W. Dodge Co. and upon ratios derived from Pennsylvania and Ohio reports.
[f] Based upon various State reports.
[g] Based upon large sample of average wages taken from reports throughout the country.
* Preliminary estimate.

1918; but a year or two later an upward trend began which has continued until 1927. In the mercantile industry, the trend has been upward throughout the entire period, although there was a temporary drop in the total real value of wage payments in the years 1917-1918. The course of aggregate real wages among the unclassified industries has been much the same as in the mercantile industry, but the depression in the years 1917 to 1919 inclusive was very marked. The total purchasing power of wages paid by rail-

TABLE XXII—Continued

TOTAL WAGES DRAWN BY EMPLOYEES FROM THE VARIOUS INDUSTRIES[a]

(MILLIONS OF CURRENT DOLLARS)

Year	All Following Fields of Transportation	Rail-roads[h]	Pull-man[i]	Ex-press[i]	Transportation by Water[j]	Street Railways[k]	Private Electric Light and Power[l]	Tele-phones[m]	Tele-graphs[n]
1909	$1,202	$ 844	$ 7	$16	$ 87	$149	$ 26	$ 61	$12
1910	1,326	942	7	17	92	158	28	70	13
1911	1,388	982	7	19	93	166	30	76	16
1912	1,488	1,057	6	20	100	175	33	79	18
1913	1,569	1,108	9	20	104	183	36	89	19
1914	1,496	1,025	9	19	103	193	38	92	18
1915	1,544	1,066	7	18	113	196	39	91	·15
1916	1,761	1,210	8	20	138	211	45	107	22
1917	2,082	1,447	9	24	166	233	52	123	28
1918	2,981	2,226	12	28	207	272	59	139	37
1919	3,334	2,369	15	37	292	325	74	180	42
1920	4,381	3,091	20	53	401	417	100	238	61
1921	3,376	2,162	19	48	332	411	108	244	52
1922	3,161	2,035	15	41	260	388	113	261	48
1923	3,610	2,386	15	43	272	409	133	296	55
1924	3,495	2,204	19	42	294	416	140	325	56
1925	3,545	2,234	20	41	283	414	157	337	59
1926	3,680	2,310	21	41	285	417	177	356	74
1927	3,649*	2,265*	21	40	273	416	191	370	72
1928		2,159*							

h Based upon *Statistics of Railways*, published by the Interstate Commerce Commission. Includes switching and terminal companies.

i Based upon *Preliminary Abstracts of Statistics of Common Carriers*, published by the Interstate Commerce Commission.

j Based upon *Census of Transportation by Water, Merchant Marine Statistics*, and U. S. Bureau of Labor Statistics.

k Based upon *Census of Electric Railways* and upon index of wage rates given in Moody's *Rating Book of Public Utilities*.

l Based upon *Census of Electric Light and Power* and various State reports.

m Based upon *Census of Telephones* and upon reports of Bell Telephone Companies.

n Based upon *Census of Telegraphs* and upon reports of Western Union Telegraph Company.

ways rose from 1909 to 1911, remained on a plateau until 1916, went higher during the war years, fell off in 1921, recovered somewhat in the next year or two, and has since remained on a practically horizontal plane. The course of total real wages in the express industry has closely paralleled the movements in the railway industry. In the Pullman industry, the trend of the total has been rather

CHART 16

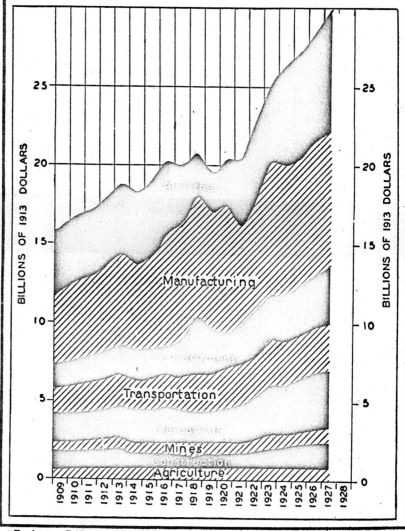

PURCHASING POWER, IN 1913 DOLLARS,
OF TOTAL WAGES, SALARIES, PENSIONS,
COMPENSATION FOR INJURIES, ETC., RECEIVED
BY EMPLOYEES FROM THE VARIOUS INDUSTRIES*

* For data, see Table XXI.

CHART 17

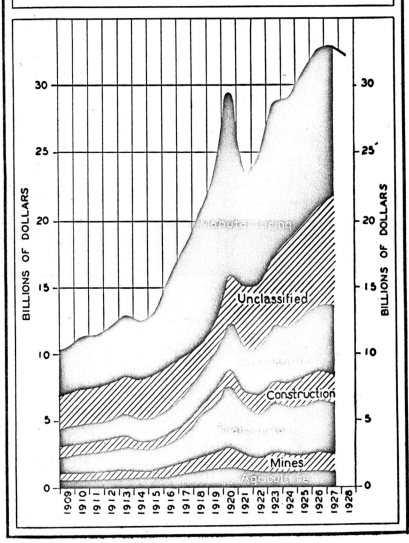

TOTAL WAGES DRAWN BY EMPLOYEES
FROM THE VARIOUS INDUSTRIES[a]

[a] For data, see Table XXII.

TABLE XXIII

PURCHASING POWER, IN 1913 DOLLARS,[a] OF TOTAL WAGES DRAWN BY EMPLOYEES FROM THE VARIOUS INDUSTRIES

(MILLIONS OF 1913 DOLLARS)[b]

Year	All Industries	Agri- culture	Manu- facturing	Mines, Quarries and Oil Wells	Con- struction	Mer- cantile	Unclas- sified
1909	$11,113	$687	$3,617	$576	$ 998	$1,274	$2,688
1910	11,668	673	3,945	624	949	1,303	2,804
1911	11,679	730	3,832	636	913	1,318	2,819
1912	12,336	736	4,248	679	1,000	1,263	2,819
1913	13,017	736	4,502	740	1,045	1,442	2,983
1914	12,216	732	4,060	620	729	1,536	3,068
1915	12,728	759	4,420	615	726	1,548	3,168
1916	14,081	754	5,658	723	769	1,567	3,033
1917	13,671	813	5,993	768	626	1,501	2,372
1918	13,036	779	6,177	789	564	1,429	1,401
1919	12,610	807	5,766	691	694	1,479	1,352
1920	14,194	805	6,526	801	614	1,568	1,782
1921	13,077	836	4,622	694	639	1,760	2,650
1922	14,785	808	5,550	684	887	2,009	2,961
1923	16,938	811	6,533	981	978	2,394	3,126
1924	17,148	806	6,157	789	1,089	2,376	3,883
1925	17,781	830	6,250	797	1,291	2,499	4,082
1926	18,729*	853	6,533*	911*	1,324*	2,722*	4,289*
1927	19,251*	857*	6,426*	857*	1,357*	2,823*	4,814*
1928	18,895*	886*					

[a] "1913 Dollars" is an abbreviation for the phrase "dollars having purchasing power equivalent to that which they had in 1913."

[b] Computed from corresponding items in Table XXII by dividing by the appropriate price indices recorded in Table VII.

* Preliminary estimate.

steadily upward. In transportation by water, the purchasing power of the total wage bill rose rather steadily from 1909 to 1920, more than doubling during this period. There followed a sharp decline until 1922, and since then slow recovery. The tendency in the street railway field was upward between 1909 and 1914, slightly downward between 1914 and 1918, and upward between 1918 and 1924, since which time the trend has been approximately horizontal. Wage payments of private electric light and power plants have grown steadily larger each year. In 1927, the combined wage earners in this field could buy with their wages about 4 times as

TABLE XXIII—Continued

PURCHASING POWER, IN 1913 DOLLARS,[a]
OF TOTAL WAGES DRAWN BY EMPLOYEES
FROM THE VARIOUS INDUSTRIES

(MILLIONS OF 1913 DOLLARS)[b]

Year	All Following Fields of Transportation	Railroads[c]	Pullman	Express	Transportation by Water	Street Railways	Private Electric Light and Power	Telephones	Telegraphs
1909	$1,273	$ 894	$ 7	$17	$ 92	$158	$ 27	$ 65	$13
1910	1,369	972	7	18	95	163	28	73	13
1911	1,432	1,013	7	19	96	171	31	79	16
1912	1,515	1,076	6	21	102	178	34	81	18
1913	1,569	1,108	9	20	104	183	36	89	19
1914	1,470	1,007	8	18	101	190	37	91	17
1915	1,492	1,030	7	17	109	189	38	88	15
1916	1,578	1,084	7	18	123	189	40	96	20
1917	1,597	1,110	7	18	127	179	40	95	22
1918	1,896	1,416	8	18	132	173	38	88	23
1919	1,821	1,294	8	20	159	178	40	98	23
1920	2,098	1,480	10	26	192	200	48	114	29
1921	1,876	1,202	10	26	185	229	60	136	29
1922	1,886	1,214	9	24	155	232	67	156	29
1923	2,115	1,398	9	25	160	240	78	174	32
1924	2,049	1,292	11	25	172	244	82	191	33
1925	2,033	1,281	11	24	162	237	90	193	34
1926	2,097	1,316	12	23	162	237	101	203	42
1927	2,117*	1,316*	12	23	158	242	109	215	42

• Includes switching and terminal companies.

much as they could have done in 1909. The courses of total real wages in the telephone and telegraph industries have also been marked by this same steady upward trend, the wage bill in both fields slightly more than trebling during the same period.

Salary Totals Compared with Wage Totals.

A comparison of the figures in Table XXIV with those in Table XXII shows that, in 1928, the salary bill of the nation was slightly more than half as large as the wage bill. Between 1909 and 1928, the wage bill trebled, while the salary bill quadrupled.

TABLE XXIV

TOTAL SALARIES DRAWN BY EMPLOYEES FROM THE VARIOUS INDUSTRIES

(MILLIONS OF CURRENT DOLLARS)

Year	All Industries	Agriculture[a]	Manufacturing[a]	Mines, Quarries and Oil Wells[a]	Construction[a]	Banking[a,b]	Mercantile[a]	Government[a,b]	Unclassified[a]
1909	$4,316	$37	$ 926	$ 51	$ 87	$115	$ 434	$1,226	$1,023
1910	4,682	37	1,093	51	95	123	448	1,314	1,075
1911	4,918	38	1,171	54	103	137	452	1,384	1,102
1912	5,203	39	1,239	58	111	149	449	1,465	1,102
1913	5,503	40	1,289	62	127	161	466	1,558	1,184
									1,265
1914	5,809	41	1,287	64	134	164	525	1,656	1,365
1915	5,926	42	1,220	65	123	183	553	1,734	1,447
1916	6,376	45	1,377	74	109	214	621	1,821	1,493
1917	7,665	53	1,846	103	122	230	690	2,464	1,433
1918	11,232	67	2,368	136	116	281	716	5,272	1,340
1919	11,576	75	2,904	151	180	362	774	4,489	1,475
1920	11,727	82	3,243	176	165	429	887	3,519	1,706
1921	11,855	81	2,591	165	166	481	967	3,751	2,240
1922	12,050	74	2,550	169	196	493	1,020	3,775	2,416
1923	13,156	66	3,046	157	212	528	1,212	3,898	2,611
1924	14,200	56	3,130	165	240	559	1,207	4,053	3,328
1925	15,008	49	3,180	169	289	596	1,292	4,338	3,614
1926	15,991*	44*	3,332*	169	300*	636	1,318*	4,750*	3,913*
1927	17,248*	39*	3,700*	172*	302*	649*	1,421*	4,992*	4,425*
1928	17,823*	36*			321*		1,478*		

[a] Sources of information are same as those referred to in Table XXII.
[b] Includes all wage workers in this field.
* Preliminary estimate.

Salary Totals in Current Dollars by Industries.

While in 1927 the manufacturing industry had by far the largest wage bill, government led in the salary bill. Attention should, however, be called to the fact that the figures for salaries entered under the heading "government" include an unknown amount which ought to be counted as wages. Lack of information as to the facts has prevented the division of the amount paid to employees into the two usual categories. It is believed, however, that, even if the wage item were isolated, the total of salaries proper paid by government would still exceed the total for any other field of industry. Unclassified industries come next in importance, with manufacturing slightly lower. In the same year, the government salary bill made

TABLE XXIV—Continued

TOTAL SALARIES DRAWN BY EMPLOYEES FROM THE VARIOUS INDUSTRIES
(MILLIONS OF CURRENT DOLLARS)

Year	All Following Fields of Transportation	Railroads[ac]	Pullman[a]	Express[a]	Transportation by Water[a]	Street Railways[a]	Private Electric Light and Power[a]	Telephones[a]	Telegraphs[a]
1909	$ 417	$248	$3	$20	$ 85	$19	$ 15	$ 20	$ 7
1910	446	263	3	22	89	22	18	21	7
1911	477	279	4	24	90	24	20	26	9
1912	508	293	4	26	96	26	23	33	9
1913	535	308	4	26	100	27	26	36	9
1914	574	342	4	26	99	29	28	36	9
1915	560	313	4	27	110	30	31	35	10
1916	621	337	4	28	136	31	33	39	13
1917	724	381	5	41	167	34	34	47	16
1918	936	517	5	54	210	40	36	51	22
1919	1,167	614	6	66	298	51	44	62	25
1920	1,521	780	8	93	408	61	59	81	32
1921	1,413	746	8	79	334	60	72	86	28
1922	1,357	759	7	67	261	57	81	94	30
1923	1,426	790	7	69	273	59	96	99	32
1924	1,462	794	8	65	293	60	104	105	33
1925	1,482	801	9	63	282	61	118	110	38
1926	1,529	816	9	65	285	63	137	118	38
1927	1,548*	822*	9	65	274	64	151	125	37
1928		820*							

* Includes switching and terminal companies.

up slightly less than one-third of the total for all industries, while the unclassified industries and manufacturing industries each accounted for about one-fourth of the total. Salaries in the mercantile field ranked next in importance, but their total was well below that for either unclassified industries or manufacturing.

Salary Totals in 1913 Dollars by Industries.

The total column of Table XXV shows that the salaried employees of the nation could buy with their aggregate income more than twice as many goods in 1927 as in 1909. The total purchasing power of salaries in the mercantile, transportation, and manufacturing fields respectively, all climbed steadily upward through-

TABLE XXV

PURCHASING POWER, IN 1913 DOLLARS,[a] OF TOTAL SALARIES DRAWN BY EMPLOYEES FROM THE VARIOUS INDUSTRIES

(MILLIONS OF 1913 DOLLARS)[b]

Year	All Industries	Agriculture	Manufacturing	Mines, Quarries and Oil Wells	Construction	Banking	Mercantile	Government	Unclassified
1909	$ 4,573	$38	$ 985	$54	$ 92	$122	$459	$1,298	$1,083
1910	4,836	37	1,132	53	98	127	462	1,356	1,110
1911	5,076	39	1,210	56	106	141	466	1,428	1,110
1912	5,299	40	1,264	59	113	152	457	1,428	1,137
1913	5,503	40	1,289	62	127	161	466	1,491	1,205
								1,558	1,265
1914	5,717	41	1,272	63	132	161	516	1,627	1,342
1915	5,751	43	1,200	63	119	177	534	1,675	1,398
1916	5,742	41	1,262	67	98	192	557	1,632	1,338
1917	5,922	37	1,461	79	93	177	529	1,890	1,099
1918	7,220	42	1,581	86	74	179	455	3,354	853
1919	6,409	41	1,672	83	98	197	423	2,451	805
1920	5,703	41	1,637	84	79	205	425	1,685	817
1921	6,645	52	1,488	92	92	267	537	2,084	1,245
1922	7,242	50	1,567	101	117	294	609	2,252	1,441
1923	7,774	45	1,843	92	124	309	710	2,284	1,530
1924	8,389	38	1,893	97	141	328	708	2,376	1,951
1925	8,668	31	1,880	97	166	342	741	2,488	2,073
1926	9,179*	27*	1,963*	96	171*	362	751*	2,706*	2,229*
1927	10,093*	26*	2,220*	100*	175*	377*	825*	2,899*	2,570*
1928	10,447*	24*							

[a] "1913 Dollars" is an abbreviation for the phrase "dollars having purchasing power equivalent to that which they had in 1913."

[b] Computed from corresponding items in Table XXIV by dividing by the appropriate price indices recorded in Table VII.

* Preliminary estimate.

out the period 1909 to 1927, though the rise has been much more marked since 1920 than before. Because of the inclusion of the pay of the Army in the total salary bill of the government, there was, of course, an enormous increase in this figure during the period 1918 and 1919. By 1920, however, the aggregate purchasing power of government salaries dropped back to its usual trend, and, if the war period be omitted, we could say that, from 1909 to 1927, the tendency of the purchasing power of aggregate government salaries has been steadily upward along a reasonably smooth line. The purchasing power of the amounts estimated to have been paid out

TABLE XXV—Continued

PURCHASING POWER, IN 1913 DOLLARS,[a]
OF TOTAL SALARIES DRAWN BY EMPLOYEES
FROM THE VARIOUS INDUSTRIES
(MILLIONS OF 1913 DOLLARS)[b]

Year	All Following Fields of Transportation	Railroads[c]	Pullman	Express	Transportation by Water	Street Railways	Private Electric Light and Power	Telephones	Telegraphs
1909	$441	$262	$4	$21	$ 90	$20	$16	$21	$ 7
1910	460	271	4	23	92	23	18	21	8
1911	492	288	4	24	93	25	21	27	9
1912	517	298	4	26	98	27	23	33	9
1913	535	308	4	26	100	27	26	36	9
1914	564	336	4	25	98	29	28	35	9
1915	542	303	4	26	106	29	30	34	10
1916	557	302	4	25	122	29	30	35	11
1917	556	292	3	31	128	27	26	36	12
1918	597	329	3	34	133	27	23	33	14
1919	639	336	3	36	163	29	24	34	14
1920	730	374	4	44	196	31	28	39	15
1921	787	415	4	44	186	35	40	48	16
1922	811	453	4	40	156	35	49	56	18
1923	837	463	4	41	160	36	56	58	19
1924	858	465	5	38	172	36	61	61	19
1925	851	459	5	36	162	36	68	63	22
1926	873	465	5	37	162	37	78	67	22
1927	901*	478*	5	38	159	39*	88	73	21

[c] Includes switching and terminal companies.

by unclassified industries in the form of salaries increased regularly from 1909 to 1916, but then declined abruptly until 1919, the shrinkage being due to the fact that so many of the salaried employees in this field were pressed into government service. From 1919 to date, on the other hand, there has been a very rapid increase, the total trebling during this eight year period. In the various branches of transportation, there has, in general, been a steady increase in the purchasing power of total salaries, the trend being very steeply upward in the case of private electric light and power plants and telephone and telegraph companies. The banking industry has likewise had a remarkable increase in the total salary bill, its purchasing power trebling between 1909 and 1927.

CHART 18

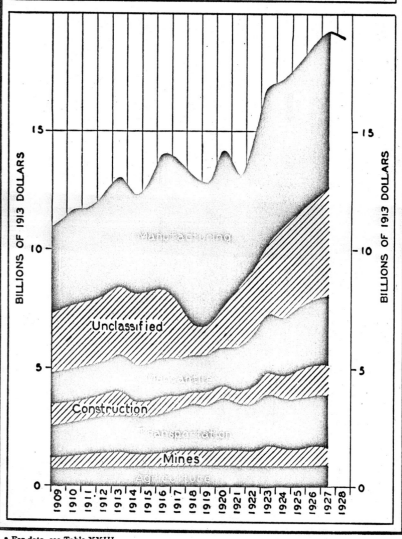

PURCHASING POWER, IN 1913 DOLLARS,
OF TOTAL WAGES DRAWN BY EMPLOYEES
FROM THE VARIOUS INDUSTRIES[a]

BILLINGS OF 1913 DOLLARS

BILLIONS OF 1913 DOLLARS

15

10

5

0

15

10

5

0

Manufacturing

Unclassified

Construction

Mines

Agriculture

1909 1910 1911 1912 1913 1914 1915 1916 1917 1918 1919 1920 1921 1922 1923 1924 1925 1926 1927 1928

[a] For data, see Table XXIII.

CHART 19

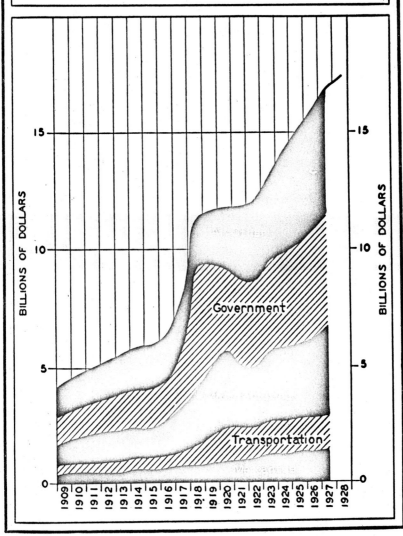

TOTAL SALARIES DRAWN BY EMPLOYEES
FROM THE VARIOUS INDUSTRIES[a]

[a] For data, see Table XXIV.

Average Earnings of Employees Attached to Industry.

The estimated amount received in wages during the year by
the average wage worker is shown in Table XXVI. In considering
these figures, one should always bear in mind the fact that these
averages apply to workers *attached to the industry*, and not to those
actually at work. For this reason, the averages appearing in Table
XXVI are much lower in years of depression, like 1921, than are
the averages for persons actually at work, the reason being, of
course, that the number of persons idle, being included in the
divisor, pulls down the size of the quotient. The figures in Table
XXVI, however, throw much more light on the question of the
welfare of the average working family than do figures showing average full time pay, for, in general, it is true that the workers attached
to an industry and also their families are dependent, in the main,
upon the pay received from that industry. Hence, if part of the
workers are unemployed, the average welfare of the workers in that
field and also the welfare of their dependents obviously tends to
decline.

**Average Earnings in Current Dollars of Wage Workers Attached to
Industry.**

For some industries the estimates of average wages rest on
insecure statistical foundations. We have, for example, no information, in most years, concerning the amount of unemployment in
agriculture, and hence it is probable that the actual fluctuations in
the averages are somewhat greater than are those shown in Table
XXVI. It is believed, however, that both the general level of agricultural wages and the trend are reasonably accurate. Data concerning wages in the field of mines, quarries, and oil wells are reasonably adequate in the case of coal mining which, fortunately for our
purposes, constitutes the most important phase of mining. Data
for metal mining are much more scanty and for oil wells are practically non-existent, except in the census years. The averages for
all mineral extraction are therefore subject to a moderate error.
The averages for the construction industry have been built up
largely from data on wage rates used in connection with estimates
of the value of the total volume of construction in the United States
and are probably much less reliable than are those for the mining
industry. The figures for the mercantile industry are based upon
data extracted from a limited number of state reports, and these
state reports may or may not be representative of the nation as a

CHART 20

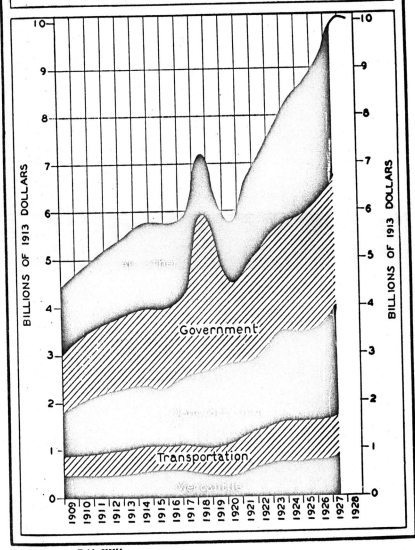

PURCHASING POWER, IN 1913 DOLLARS,
OF TOTAL SALARIES DRAWN BY EMPLOYEES
FROM THE VARIOUS INDUSTRIES[a]

Government

Transportation

Mercantile

TABLE XXVI

AVERAGE ANNUAL EARNINGS[a] OF WAGE WORKERS ATTACHED TO THE VARIOUS INDUSTRIES[b]
(ESTIMATES TAKE ACCOUNT OF UNEMPLOYMENT)

Year	All Industries	Agri-culture	Manu-facturing	Mines, Quarries and Oil Wells	Con-struction	Mer-cantile	Unclas-sified
1909	$ 527	$285	$ 497	$ 544	$ 669	$ 592	$ 586
1910	552	277	545	591	667	596	610
1911	540	290	519	565	644	585	598
1912	568	298	566	608	706	551	615
1913	594	306	597	645	699	624	634
1914	552	301	536	561	497	658	615
1915	582	304	586	563	580	659	634
1916	679	331	723	735	779	706	679
1917	771	407	832	892	790	781	731
1918	940	474	1,001	1,129	1,118	893	802
1919	1,029	567	1,076	1,141	1,180	1,044	918
1920	1,273	653	1,400	1,464	1,510	1,216	1,026
1921	983	551	892	1,077	1,355	1,159	1,041
1922	1,012	489	996	976	1,362	1,099	1,078
1923	1,150	513	1,195	1,408	1,437	1,159	1,121
1924	1,134	516	1,152	1,193	1,510	1,214	1,133
1925	1,176	526	1,195	1,250	1,534	1,219	1,180
1926	1,217*	535	1,234*	1,324*	1,603*	1,299*	1,198*
1927	1,205*	533	1,216*	1,224*	1,644*	1,262*	1,202*
1928		530*	1,140*		1,645*	1,276*	

[a] Derived from Tables IV and XXII.

[b] Figures derived by dividing total pay of all wage workers in industry by total number of persons depending upon this industry for wages.

* Preliminary estimate.

whole. In this industry, therefore, the averages are not such as to be thoroughly dependable. The averages for transportation by water are likewise constructed from very scanty data and may be materially in error. Except in census years, the same is true of the averages for private electric light and power plants. The fact, however, that we have census figures for 1907, 1912, 1917, and 1922 probably eliminates the chance of any serious errors in this field for years previous to 1923. In general, it is felt that the figures for the manufacturing, steam railway, street railway, Pullman, express, telephone, and telegraph industries are reasonably satisfactory, the errors not being large enough to be of much consequence. It is believed also that the figures for unclassified industries are ap-

TABLE XXVI—Continued

AVERAGE ANNUAL EARNINGS[a] OF WAGE WORKERS ATTACHED TO THE VARIOUS INDUSTRIES[b]
(ESTIMATES TAKE ACCOUNT OF UNEMPLOYMENT)

Year	All Following Fields of Transportation	Railroads	Pullman	Express	Transportation by Water	Street Railways	Private Electric Light and Power	Telephones	Telegraphs
1909	$ 616	$ 642	$ 720	$ 518	$ 572	$ 642	$ 666	$ 490	$440
1910	629	656	722	536	595	643	663	506	449
1911	646	684	734	584	580	646	676	499	456
1912	682	735	711	590	598	661	688	482	524
1913	678	718	759	636	608	683	696	511	567
1914	643	664	750	576	598	715	692	508	534
1915	666	698	699	562	647	719	687	488	443
1916	764	814	764	662	778	774	738	558	568
1917	895	977	894	792	947	851	825	561	627
1918	1,222	1,410	1,144	1,142	1,137	989	888	603	767
1919	1,284	1,417	1,396	1,338	1,296	1,171	1,052	737	886
1920	1,597	1,787	1,490	1,692	1,406	1,501	1,337	935	1,219
1921	1,248	1,280	1,350	1,567	1,185	1,480	1,338	943	1,046
1922	1,179	1,224	1,246	1,433	937	1,401	1,287	1,001	972
1923	1,333	1,452	1,254	1,575	994	1,421	1,310	1,035	1,106
1924	1,303	1,372	1,219	1,768	1,130	1,451	1,325	1,068	1,111
1925	1,387	1,524	1,243	1,640	1,134	1,449	1,341	1,088	1,045
1926	1,428	1,568	1,248	1,646	1,146	1,457	1,380	1,142	1,311
1927	1,436*	1,580*	1,258	1,649	1,138	1,445	1,398	1,180	1,274
1928		1,597*							

proximately correct as to trend and general level, though the fluctuations due to cyclical movements in this field are perhaps not portrayed with any near approach to accuracy.

In 1927, the construction and express industries paid higher wages than any other industry. The fact should, however, be kept in mind that in these industries employees are largely male; and men everywhere receive higher pay than women.

According to our estimates for 1909, industries in which the average wage was materially lower than the average for all industries were agriculture, manufacturing, the telegraph, and telephone industries, and the express business. In 1927, wages in the manufacturing industry had risen until they equalled the average for all industries, but telephone and agricultural wage workers still ranked

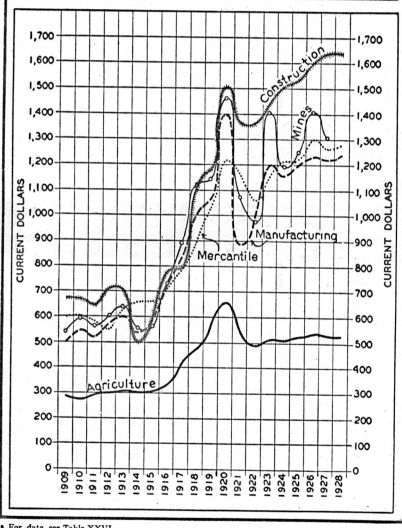

AVERAGE ANNUAL EARNINGS OF WAGE WORKERS
ATTACHED TO THE VARIOUS INDUSTRIES[a]

[a] For data, see Table XXVI.

CHART 21b

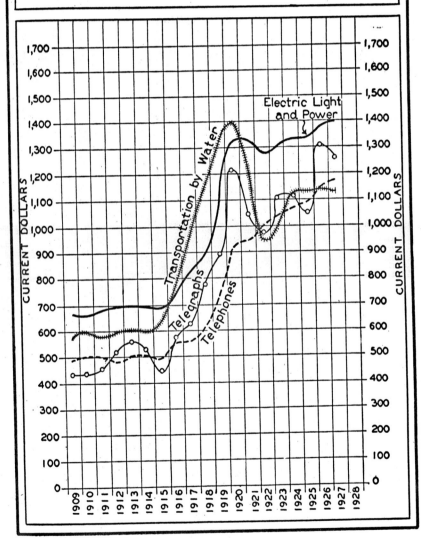

AVERAGE ANNUAL EARNINGS OF WAGE WORKERS
ATTACHED TO THE VARIOUS INDUSTRIES*

* For data, see Table XXVI.

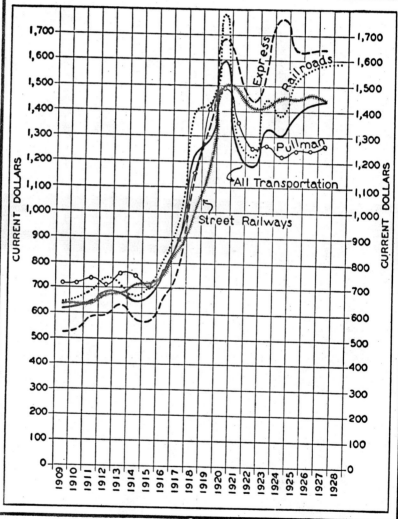

AVERAGE ANNUAL EARNINGS OF WAGE WORKERS
ATTACHED TO THE VARIOUS INDUSTRIES[a]

[a] For data see Table XXVI.

below the average in pay, and those in transportation by water
now were added to this low paid group. The low average of pay in
the telephone industry is explained primarily by the fact that such
a large proportion of its wage workers are female, all telephone
operators being classified as wage workers. The most striking fact
as regards comparative wage levels brought out by Table XXVI is,
however, the fact that agricultural wage workers received in 1927
less than half the pay of wage workers in any other field of industry.
Even in 1909, their pay was not much more than half of that in the
other lower-paid industries. In a country in which movement from
place to place is so easy, this striking discrepancy in wages is
somewhat difficult to explain. At the present time, when other
industries flourish in nearly all sections of the country, when travel
is extremely common so that the average farm hand is presumably
familiar either directly or through hearsay with the conditions of
city life, and in fact when a large proportion of agricultural laborers
own automobiles and visit towns and cities frequently, it can scarcely
be said that the farm hand remains on the farm merely because he
is not familiar with conditions in other industries, or even that he
stays there purely through inertia. Among the true reasons why
agricultural laborers receive pay so markedly lower than that obtained by employees in other fields, the following are probably the
major ones:—

1. Although the averages for agricultural labor include an
   allowance for board and room, agricultural laborers frequently receive other perquisites, as for example, pasturage
   for their horses, garage room for their automobiles, and
   garden plots in which to raise vegetables.
2. Because the very high costs involved in transportation and
   selling are eliminated, foodstuffs are far cheaper on the
   farm than in the city, and hence every dollar of the employee's earnings goes further when spent for sustenance.
   House rent is also cheaper in the country, and, in many
   instances, the same may be said of fuel.
3. Rural customs are such that the farm hand is not required
   to spend as many dollars per annum for clothing and other
   costs connected with the maintenance of personal appearance as is the case with the city worker.
4. To a considerable fraction of the population, the spacious-
   ness and sense of freedom associated with rural life possess
   high value.

TABLE XXVII

PURCHASING POWER, IN 1913 DOLLARS, OF AVERAGE ANNUAL EARNINGS[a] OF WAGE WORKERS ATTACHED TO THE VARIOUS INDUSTRIES[b]
(COMMAND OVER CONSUMERS' GOODS AT PRICES OF 1913)

Year	All Industries	Agriculture	Manufacturing	Mines, Quarries and Oil Wells	Construction	Mercantile	Unclassified
1909	$556	$288	$526	$576	$708	$627	$620
1910	568	275	563	610	688	615	630
1911	557	297	535	583	665	603	617
1912	578	306	576	619	719	561	626
1913	594	306	597	645	699	624	634
1914	544	308	527	552	489	647	605
1915	564	315	567	544	560	637	613
1916	610	318	648	659	698	633	608
1917	594	339	638	684	662	599	561
1918	601	322	637	718	711	568	510
1919	563	323	588	623	644	570	501
1920	612	333	670	701	723	582	492
1921	550	348	495	599	753	644	579
1922	610	350	595	582	813	655	644
1923	679	357	700	825	842	679	657
1924	669	353	676	699	885	712	664
1925	680	362	686	627	880	699	677
1926	699*	372	703*	754*	913*	740*	682*
1927	705*	376*	706*	711*	955*	733*	698*
1928		378*	668*		964*	748*	

[a] Derived from Tables IV and XXIII by division.
[b] Figures derived by dividing total pay of all wage workers in industry by total number of persons depending upon this industry for wages.
* Preliminary estimate.

The fact that wages have advanced in all fields is so well known as to require no comment. Much of this advance represents merely changes in the purchasing power of the dollar. Charts 21a, 21b and 21c show that, in practically all fields of industry, average nominal wages were approximately stationary from 1909 to 1915, inclusive, rose sharply during the inflation period covering 1916 to 1920, fell with other prices from 1920 to 1921, or, in some cases, to 1922, and, since then, again moved upward until, in some instances, the averages in 1925 were above the 1920 level. In the construction, mercantile, electric light and power, telephone, express, and street railway industries, the depression of 1921 and 1922 was either small

TABLE XXVII—Continued

PURCHASING POWER, IN 1913 DOLLARS, OF AVERAGE ANNUAL EARNINGS[a] OF WAGE WORKERS ATTACHED TO THE VARIOUS INDUSTRIES[b]

(COMMAND OVER CONSUMERS' GOODS AT PRICES OF 1913)

Year	All Following Fields of Transportation	Railroads	Pullman	Express	Transportation by Water	Street Railways	Private Electric Light and Power	Telephones	Telegraphs
1909	$652	$679	$762	$548	$606	$680	$705	$519	$465
1910	649	677	746	554	614	663	684	523	463
1911	666	706	758	603	598	666	698	514	470
1912	694	749	724	601	609	673	700	491	533
1913	678	718	759	636	608	683	696	511	567
1914	632	653	737	567	587	703	680	499	525
1915	643	675	675	543	625	695	664	471	428
1916	684	729	685	593	697	694	661	500	509
1917	686	749	686	608	726	653	633	431	481
1918	777	897	728	726	723	629	565	384	488
1919	701	774	762	731	708	640	575	402	484
1920	765	856	714	810	673	719	640	448	584
1921	694	711	750	871	658	822	743	524	581
1922	704	730	744	855	559	836	768	597	580
1923	781	851	735	923	582	832	767	607	648
1924	764	804	715	1,036	663	851	777	626	651
1925	796	874	713	940	650	831	769	624	599
1926	814	894	711	938	653	830	786	651	747
1927	834*	918*	731	958	661	839	812	685	740
1928		936*							

in amplitude or brief in its influence, though in the last-mentioned field wages have advanced very slowly since 1922. On the other hand, in mining, manufacturing, agriculture, transportation by water, telegraphs, railroads, and the Pullman industry, the decline in wages between 1920 and 1922 was severe. The Pullman wage workers have not had any material increase in earnings since 1922, and the earnings of agricultural laborers and street railway employees have also remained nearly on a level. In all other fields, the trend of wages since 1922 has been sharply upward.

Average Earnings in 1913 Dollars of Wage Workers Attached to Industry.

The figures for wages of agricultural employees in Table XXVII have been deflated by use of a special index of the prices of goods

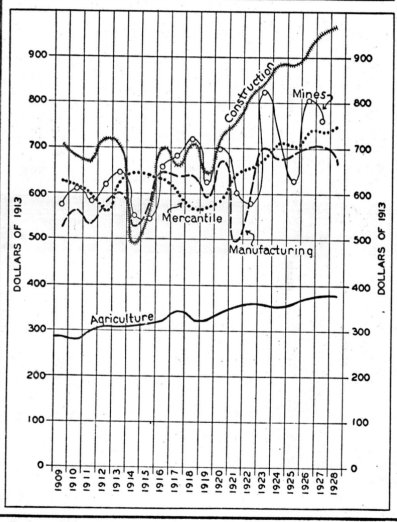

PURCHASING POWER, IN 1913 DOLLARS,
OF AVERAGE ANNUAL EARNINGS OF WAGE
WORKERS ATTACHED TO THE VARIOUS
INDUSTRIES[a]

CHART 22b

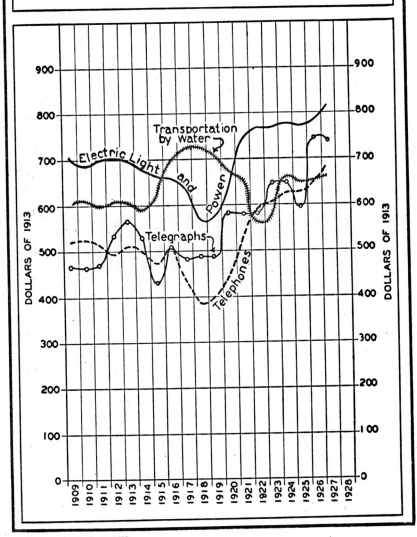

PURCHASING POWER, IN 1913 DOLLARS, OF AVERAGE ANNUAL EARNINGS OF WAGE WORKERS ATTACHED TO THE VARIOUS INDUSTRIES[a]

* For data, see Table XXVII.

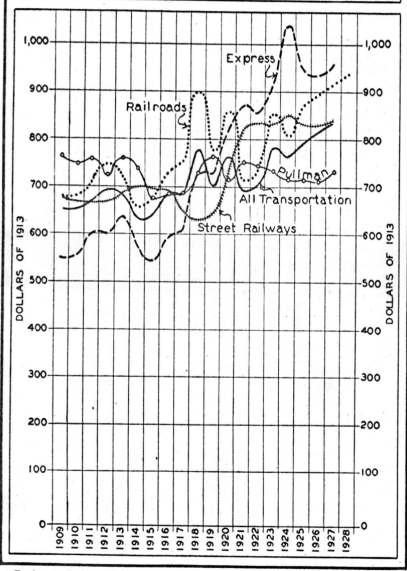

PURCHASING POWER, IN 1913 DOLLARS, OF
AVERAGE ANNUAL EARNINGS OF WAGE WORKERS
ATTACHED TO THE VARIOUS INDUSTRIES[a]

[a] For data, see Table XXVII.

used by agricultural employees. In the deflation of all other average wage figures, a common index has been used, namely, the United States Bureau of Labor index of the "cost of living," extended back from 1913 to 1909 by the National Bureau of Economic Research. The reader will note that the figures given in Table XXVII take into account all workers attached to the industry, whether or not they were actually working in the industry at the date specified. In interpreting these figures, one should remember also that wage workers receive some income from investments, the keeping of boarders and lodgers, gardening, cow-keeping, and the performance of odd jobs, and that none of this income enters into the average wage.

From Charts 22a, 22b and 22c it is seen that wages in terms of constant purchasing power show, in most industries, a marked upward trend throughout the period under consideration. In the construction industry, there was a notable depression in the purchasing power of the average wage during the years 1913 to 1915, inclusive, but, since 1919, the gains of the average wage worker in that field have been 50 per cent larger than those of the average wage worker in any other line. Our figures indicate that the purchasing power of the wages of the average worker tended downward between 1909 and 1918 in the case of the mercantile, telephone, and electric light and power industries. Since 1919, however, the condition of the wage workers in all three of these fields has shown rapid improvement. For wage earners in the field of transportation by water, the period 1915 to 1921 constituted an era of prosperity. The years 1922 and 1923 were, however, bad and, though there has since been considerable recovery, the purchasing power of their average pay was still approximately the same in 1927 as in 1921. Street railway employees could buy less for their wages in 1918 than they could in 1909, but, between 1918 and 1922, their condition improved markedly. Since the latter date, their wage level has been approximately stationary. Only the employees of the Pullman industry are, at present, no better off than they were in 1909. The trend of the wages of agricultural employees has come nearer to approximating a straight line during the score of years covered by our study than has the trend in any other industry.

Average Earnings in Current Dollars of Salaried Employees Attached to Industry.

The salaried employees covered in Table XXVIII include executives, officials, managers, and clerks. Persons in these callings

TABLE XXVIII

AVERAGE ANNUAL EARNINGS OF SALARIED EMPLOYEES ATTACHED TO THE VARIOUS INDUSTRIES[a]

(ESTIMATES TAKE ACCOUNT OF UNEMPLOYMENT)

Year	All Industries	Agriculture	Manufacturing	Mines, Quarries and Oil Wells	Construction	Banking	Mercantile	Government	Unclassified
1909	$ 976	$ 616	$1,172	$1,177	$ 965	$ 766	$1,088	$ 746	$1,289
1910	1,002	621	1,208	1,173	987	793	1,092	769	1,318
1911	1,022	626	1,260	1,198	1,008	839	1,072	784	1,334
1912	1,045	640	1,270	1,239	1,030	883	1,049	805	1,394
1913	1,066	645	1,281	1,235	1,053	925	1,029	829	1,445
1914	1,088	650	1,278	1,232	1,074	917	1,115	850	1,438
1915	1,096	655	1,241	1,215	1,096	1,012	1,149	861	1,499
1916	1,148	679	1,315	1,314	1,116	1,164	1,234	874	1,564
1917	1,204	776	1,520	1,688	1,285	1,232	1,312	898	1,632
1918	1,265	970	1,737	1,985	1,559	1,454	1,410	1,012	1,757
1919	1,453	1,067	1,977	1,964	1,751	1,726	1,521	1,111	1,798
1920	1,740	1,164	2,240	2,343	2,006	1,879	1,698	1,294	2,001
1921	1,696	1,164	1,820	2,244	1,992	1,980	1,713	1,395	2,033
1922	1,715	1,174	1,818	2,257	1,821	1,985	1,622	1,442	2,132
1923	1,831	1,188	2,199	2,414	1,839	2,018	1,701	1,480	2,181
1924	1,896	1,213	2,277	2,437	1,962	2,092	1,784	1,516	2,213
1925	1,950	1,237	2,321	2,400	1,973	2,179	1,787	1,585	2,277
1926	2,025*	1,251*	2,402*	2,404	2,068*	2,239	1,792*	1,706*	2,317*
1927	2,084*	1,242*	2,470*	2,454*	2,129*	2,259*	1,844*	1,771*	2,339*
1928		1,232*			2,123*		1,862*		

[a] Derived from Tables V and XXIV by division.
* Preliminary estimate.

are, as a rule, hired by the year or at least by the month, and hence they are affected less than wage workers by cyclical fluctuations in industry and materially less by the minor irregular and seasonal swings. The figures in Table XXVIII, then, are much closer to full-time earnings than are those in Table XXVI, but allowance has been made in every case for a certain amount of unemployment. A comparison of the total columns of Tables XXVI and XXVIII shows that the average salaried employee normally receives from 70 to 85 per cent more pay per annum than does the average wage worker.

On the whole, the data upon which our estimates of average salaries are based are less reliable than are those underlying the estimates of average wages. The figures for agriculture are nothing

TABLE XXVIII—Continued

AVERAGE ANNUAL EARNINGS OF SALARIED EMPLOYEES ATTACHED TO THE VARIOUS INDUSTRIES*

(ESTIMATES TAKE ACCOUNT OF UNEMPLOYMENT)

Year	All Following Fields of Transportation	Railroads	Pullman	Express	Transportation by Water	Street Railways	Private Electric Light and Power	Telephones	Telegraphs
1909	$ 916	$ 892	$ 826	$ 733	$1,317	$1,099	$ 899	$ 815	$ 604
1910	930	897	822	777	1,382	1,105	911	830	606
1911	956	938	839	825	1,363	1,109	928	838	639
1912	974	956	860	841	1,423	1,112	939	844	635
1913	989	967	875	848	1,467	1,109	985	850	652
1914	1,048	1,058	854	843	1,478	1,136	1,020	855	653
1915	1,012	964	915	834	1,639	1,134	1,034	858	709
1916	1,107	1,034	975	875	2,014	1,162	1,057	966	723
1917	1,219	1,122	1,070	932	2,494	1,237	1,046	1,054	771
1918	1,487	1,408	1,298	1,209	2,987	1,419	1,034	1,114	1,008
1919	1,744	1,623	1,349	1,357	3,382	1,770	1,168	1,279	1,145
1920	2,050	1,920	1,623	1,602	3,570	2,071	1,427	1,544	1,339
1921	1,901	1,830	1,587	1,561	2,920	2,012	1,575	1,558	1,195
1922	1,812	1,863	1,425	1,402	2,280	1,882	1,589	1,641	1,284
1923	1,875	1,929	1,523	1,492	2,399	1,892	1,618	1,673	1,334
1924	1,935	1,957	1,581	1,485	2,698	1,893	1,652	1,710	1,355
1925	1,973	2,033	1,590	1,511	2,700	1,892	1,688	1,740	1,365
1926	1,998	2,057	1,599	1,532	2,722	1,917	1,745	1,815	1,365
1927	2,028*	2,104*	1,614	1,606	2,705	1,914	1,795	1,880	1,335
1928		2,177*							

more than guesses. For the construction industry and transportation by water, the data are so scanty as to preclude the possibility of securing results that inspire confidence. The data for street railways, private electric light and power plants, and telephone and telegraph concerns, are presumably fairly accurate in the census years 1907, 1912, 1917, and 1922. The chances are, also, that the figures for the other years in these fields are not widely in error. Supplementary data make the intercensal estimates for the telephone and telegraph industries more trustworthy than are those for street railways and electric light and power plants. The figures for the banking industry are subject to a wide margin of error. In manufacturing, mining, merchandising, government, railroading, and the Pullman, express, and unclassified industries, the figures

CHART 23a

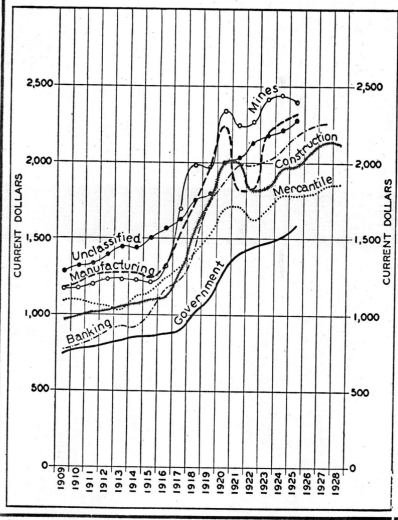

AVERAGE ANNUAL EARNINGS OF SALARIED
EMPLOYEES ATTACHED TO THE VARIOUS
INDUSTRIES[a]

[a] For data, see Table XXVIII.

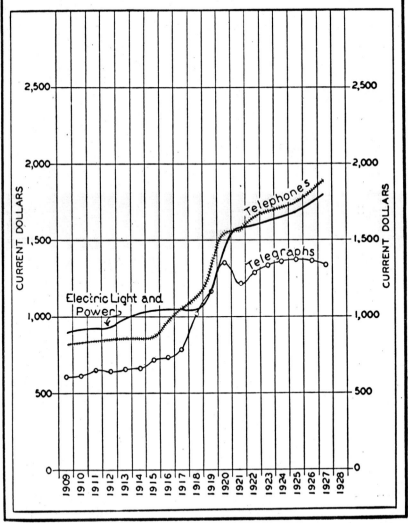

AVERAGE ANNUAL EARNINGS OF SALARIED
EMPLOYEES ATTACHED TO THE VARIOUS
INDUSTRIES[a]

[a] For data, see Table XXVIII.

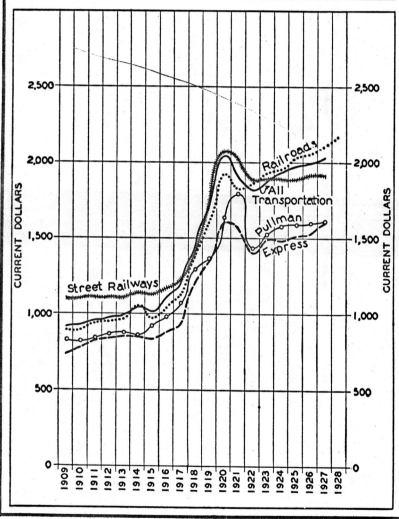

AVERAGE ANNUAL EARNINGS OF SALARIED
EMPLOYEES ATTACHED TO THE VARIOUS
INDUSTRIES[a]

* For data see Table XXVIII

given in Table XXVIII are believed to be essentially correct, though in the case of mining there may be errors of consequence in some years because the Census of Mines and Quarries is taken but once in ten years.

Whether the average salary in a given field is high or low depends primarily upon the proportion which managers and executives constitute of the total number of salaried employees. Our figures for 1927 indicate that salaries were well above the average in manufacturing, mining, banking, transportation by water, and unclassified industries, while salaries were relatively low in agriculture, merchandising, government, and the Pullman, express, electric light and power, and telegraph fields.

Charts 23a, 23b, and 23c show clearly that the fluctuations in average salaries have been much less marked during the last two decades than have the fluctuations in average wages. Just as in the case of wages, the rise in average salaries was accentuated by inflation, but not to the same extent. In most cases, salaries declined somewhat between 1920 and 1922, but, in some, the decline was too small to be of consequence. The fall at that time was most marked in the case of manufacturing, telegraphs, street railways, the express industry, and the Pullman business. Banking, government, telephones, electric light and power, and unclassified industries registered no decline in salaries during the deflation period. Since 1922, salaries have had a marked upward trend in all industries except street railways. The charts just mentioned make it evident that, when salaries and wages are both measured in current dollars, salary trends have much greater stability than wage trends, for they were rising in the period 1909 to 1915 when wages were approximately stationary; the hump in 1920 was less marked in the case of salaries; and the increases since 1922 tend to be similar to those during the period 1909 to 1916.

Average Earnings in 1913 Dollars of Salaried Employees Attached to Industry.

The figures in Table XXIX do not include income from investments. In the case of clerical workers, and even with executive and managerial employees, it is, however, probably true that the figures in Table XXIX represent the major portions of their incomes, and hence it is reasonable to assume that the trends in their income are not widely different from the trends in their average salaries. In so far as salaried employees have recently been receiving a larger

TABLE XXIX

PURCHASING POWER, IN 1913 DOLLARS, OF
AVERAGE ANNUAL EARNINGS OF SALARIED EMPLOYEES
ATTACHED TO THE VARIOUS INDUSTRIES[a]

(COMMAND OVER CONSUMERS' GOODS AT PRICES OF 1913)

Year	All Indus- tries	Agri- cul- ture	Manu- fac- turing	Mines, Quarries and Oil Wells	Con- struc- tion	Bank- ing	Mer- can- tile	Gov- ern- ment	Un- clas- sified
1909	$1,034	$ 637	$1,247	$1,246	$1,022	$ 811	$1,152	$ 790	$1,365
1910	1,035	624	1,252	1,210	1,019	819	1,127	794	1,361
1911	1,055	643	1,301	1,236	1,040	866	1,106	809	1,377
1912	1,064	649	1,296	1,262	1,048	899	1,068	819	1,419
1913	1,066	645	1,281	1,235	1,053	925	1,029	829	1,445
1914	1,071	644	1,263	1,211	1,056	901	1,096	836	1,414
1915	1,064	665	1,221	1,174	1,059	978	1,110	832	1,448
1916	1,034	613	1,206	1,177	1,000	1,043	1,106	783	1,401
1917	930	551	1,203	1,295	986	945	1,006	689	1,252
1918	813	601	1,160	1,262	992	925	897	644	1,118
1919	804	578	1,139	1,072	956	943	831	606	982
1920	846	582	1,131	1,122	961	900	813	620	958
1921	950	747	1,046	1,247	1,107	1,100	952	775	1,130
1922	1,031	792	1,117	1,347	1,087	1,184	968	860	1,272
1923	1,082	819	1,330	1,414	1,077	1,182	997	867	1,278
1924	1,120	827	1,377	1,429	1,150	1,227	1,046	889	1,297
1925	1,126	779	1,373	1,376	1,131	1,250	1,025	909	1,306
1926	1,162*	772*	1,415*	1,370	1,168*	1,275	1,021*	972*	1,320*
1927	1,220*	812*	1,482*	1,425*	1,232*	1,312*	1,071*	1,029*	1,358*
1928		820*			1,244*		1,091*		

[a] Derived from Tables V and XXV by division.

* Preliminary estimate.

proportion of their income from investments than was formerly the
case, the actual trends of their incomes would be somewhat steeper
than the trends of the salaries here indicated.

Charts 24a, 24b, and 24c show how salaried employees in general
suffered severely from the inflation of the period 1917 to 1920. In
nearly every case the curve representing the purchasing power of
the average salaried employee's stipend shows a sharp dip between
1915 and 1920. This decline is especially marked in the case of the
salaries of employees in mercantile, manufacturing, electric light
and power, and the street railway and unclassified industries. This
means that, in these fields, salaried employees were unable to get
their normal salaries raised rapidly enough to offset the increases in

TABLE XXIX—Continued

PURCHASING POWER, IN 1913 DOLLARS, OF
AVERAGE ANNUAL EARNINGS OF SALARIED EMPLOYEES
ATTACHED TO THE VARIOUS INDUSTRIES[a]
(COMMAND OVER CONSUMERS' GOODS AT PRICES OF 1913)

Year	All Following Fields of Transportation	Railroads	Pullman	Express	Transportation by Water	Street Railways	Private Electric Light and Power	Telephones	Telegraphs
1909	$ 970	$ 946	$874	$776	$1,395	$1,169	$ 951	$ 863	$639
1910	960	926	848	802	1,426	1,144	940	857	626
1911	986	968	865	851	1,406	1,146	958	865	659
1912	992	973	876	856	1,448	1,134	955	859	646
1913	989	967	875	848	1,467	1,109	985	850	652
1914	1,031	1,042	840	829	1,452	1,122	1,003	840	641
1915	979	937	884	805	1,583	1,116	999	829	685
1916	993	934	874	784	1,805	1,066	947	865	648
1917	936	869	821	714	1,913	979	802	808	591
1918	948	907	826	769	1,900	948	658	709	641
1919	955	898	737	741	1,847	1,019	638	698	625
1920	984	1,026	777	767	1,710	1,046	683	739	641
1921	1,058	1,089	882	868	1,623	1,156	875	866	664
1922	1,083	1,120	850	837	1,360	1,157	948	979	766
1923	1,100	1,140	892	874	1,405	1,145	948	980	782
1924	1,136	1,158	927	870	1,582	1,145	969	1,002	794
1925	1,133	1,178	912	867	1,549	1,119	968	998	783
1926	1,140	1,184	911	873	1,551	1,130	994	1,034	778
1927	1,180*	1,235*	937	933	1,571	1,149*	1,043	1,092	776
1928		1,226*							

the prices of the commodities they purchased. Even before 1916, the salaried employees in some industries were finding it difficult to secure salary increases sufficient to offset the shrinkage in the purchasing power of the dollar. This was notably true in the case of those employed in factories, mines, merchandising, telephone and telegraph concerns, street railways, and the Pullman and express fields. In all of these, a tendency toward decline appeared as early as 1911. In some industries, the fall in the purchasing power was stopped as early as 1918 and 1919, but, in most instances, it continued until 1920. In manufacturing, the buying power of the average salary did not improve until after 1921.

Although salaries, measured in current dollars, increased materially between 1909 and 1925, measured in terms of dollars of constant purchasing power, the average salaried employee in some industries was receiving less in 1925 than he was before the World War. This is the case in the mercantile and unclassified industries. Only very recently, in the electric light and power, street railway, Pullman, and express industries, have salaried employees been able to buy as much with their salaries as they could in pre-war days. In all of these four industries, the increases over the pre-war level have been too small to be of much significance. But in the banking, telegraph, railway, mining, and construction industries the salaried employees are much better off than they were before 1916. Government employees have also shown some gain.

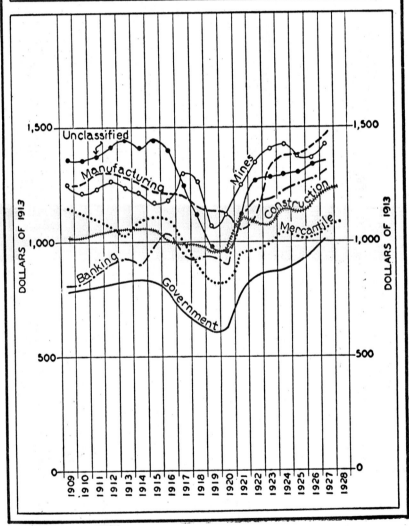

PURCHASING POWER, IN 1913 DOLLARS, OF
AVERAGE ANNUAL EARNINGS OF SALARIED
EMPLOYEES ATTACHED TO THE VARIOUS
INDUSTRIES[a]

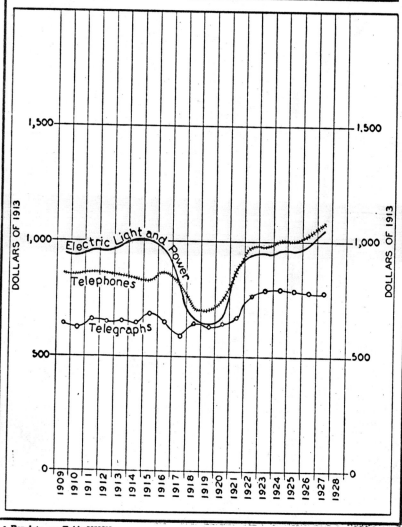

CHART 24b

PURCHASING POWER, IN 1913 DOLLARS,
OF AVERAGE ANNUAL EARNINGS OF SALARIED
EMPLOYEES ATTACHED TO THE VARIOUS
INDUSTRIES[a]

[a] For data, see Table XXIX.

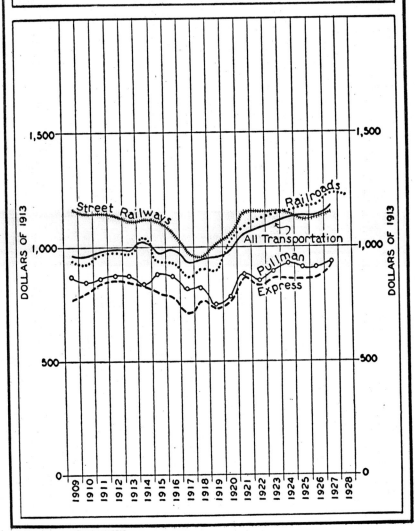

PURCHASING POWER, IN 1913 DOLLARS,
OF AVERAGE ANNUAL EARNINGS OF SALARIED
EMPLOYEES ATTACHED TO THE VARIOUS
INDUSTRIES[a]

* For data, see Table XXIX.

CHAPTER VII

CHANGES IN CONCENTRATION OF INCOME

Procedure in Estimating Distribution of Income.

The preceding analysis of the division of the total realized income of the people of the United States has been confined to a functional or industrial apportionment. Figures now available throw some light upon the relative proportions of the total income going to different strata of income recipients when the stratification is based upon the size of the total income received by the recipient.[1] Tables XXX to XXXIII, inclusive, analyze the facts in this respect for each of the years from 1914 to 1926, inclusive. The study is limited to these years because they are the only ones covered by the statistics of the Federal Income Tax, and it is upon these statistics that we must place our chief reliance in analyzing the gradations of income among persons having the larger incomes. Little light is thrown on the annual changes in distribution by the *Statistics of Income*, of the United States Bureau of Internal Revenue, because they are expressed in dollars having purchasing power differing from year to year. It is, therefore, necessary to convert all quantities to dollars of constant purchasing power. To simplify matters, the data presented in the Federal reports have all been divided by a common price index which is believed to represent approximately the *average for the year* relative prices of goods consumed by all consumers in the United States. This price index is as follows:

1914	1.0077	1921	1.6926
1915	1.0070	1922	1.5829
1916	1.0913	1923	1.5977
1917	1.2858	1924	1.6024
1918	1.5175	1925	1.6517
1919	1.7571	1926	1.6617
1920	1.9801		

An effort has been made to apportion among different income classes the total number of income recipients. The number of income recipients recorded in Table XXXII includes all gainfully

[1] Col. M. C. Rorty points out that another excellent method of comparison is to show the percentages of those gainfully employed receiving various multiples of the average income.

TABLE XXX

APPROXIMATE NUMBERS OF PERSONS REPORTING TO THE FEDERAL GOVERNMENT INCOMES ABOVE THE AMOUNTS SPECIFIED AS MEASURED IN 1913 DOLLARS AND THE TOTAL INCOME OF EACH CLASS[a]

YEAR	INDIVIDUAL INCOME IN 1913 DOLLARS ABOVE								
	$5,000[b]			$25,000[b]			$150,000[b]		
	Class Income in Current Dollars (Millions)	Number of Income Recipients	Class Income in 1913 Dollars (Millions)	Class Income in Current Dollars (Millions)	Number of Income Recipients	Class Income in 1913 Dollars (Millions)	Class Income in Current Dollars (Millions)	Number of Income Recipients	Class Income in 1913 Dollars (Millions)
1914	$3,630	252,000	$3,602	$1,562	25,700	$1,550	$ 453	1,600	$ 450
1915	4,270	245,000	4,240	2,270	32,200	2,254	864	2,620	858
1916	5,690	282,000	5,214	3,420	46,400	3,134	1,561	5,610	1,430
1917	6,465	332,000	5,028	3,330	42,300	2,590	1,145	2,860	890
1918	5,290	268,000	3,486	2,240	28,700	1,476	547	1,260	360
1919	6,420	292,000	3,654	2,485	28,200	1,414	531	1,220	302
1920	5,620	248,000	2,838	1,710	20,100	864	272	440	137
1921	4,625	246,000	2,732	1,395	20,200	824	192	390	113
1922	6,145	315,000	3,882	2,290	31,200	1,447	478	950	302
1923	6,690	352,000	4,187	2,375	32,300	1,487	476	940	298
1924	7,880	392,000	4,918	3,070	39,600	1,916	622	1,350	388
1925	10,520	465,000	6,369	4,585	51,200	2,776	1,348	2,550	816
1926	10,660	479,000	6,415	4,565	49,700	2,747	1,388	2,450	835

[a] Based upon *Statistics of Income*, published by the U. S. Bureau of Internal Revenue, and upon an average price-index series derived from Table VII.

[b] The equivalents of $5,000, $25,000 and $150,000 in 1926 dollars are $8,309, $41,543 and $249,255 respectively.

occupied persons, plus the number of wives filing separate returns with the Federal income tax authorities. Since nearly everyone receives some slight money income, this limitation on the number of income recipients is of course an arbitrary one, but it has the advantage of yielding results satisfactorily comparable from year to year, even though the absolute amounts for any given year may be materially in error.

The figures for individual income reported to the United States Bureau of Internal Revenue have been taken as reported, no adjustments having been made except for changes in the purchasing power

TABLE XXXI

APPROXIMATE NUMBERS OF PERSONS
AND AMOUNTS OF INCOME
INDICATED BY THE FEDERAL TAX RETURNS
AS FALLING BETWEEN THE AMOUNTS SPECIFIED
MEASURED IN 1913 DOLLARS[a]

| | INDIVIDUAL INCOME IN 1913 DOLLARS | | | | | | | |
| | UNDER $5,000[b] | | $5,000–$25,000[b] | | $25,000–$150,000[b] | | $150,000 AND OVER[b] | |
YEAR	Number of Income Recipients	Class Income in 1913 Dollars (Millions)	Number of Income Recipients	Class Income in 1913 Dollars (Millions)	Number of Income Recipients	Class Income in 1913 Dollars (Millions)	Number of Income Recipients	Class Income in 1913 Dollars (Millions)
1914	37,530,000	$31,648	226,300	$2,052	24,100	$1,100	1,600	$450
1915	37,711,000	32,396	212,800	1,986	29,580	1,396	2,620	858
1916	38,363,635	34,345	235,600	2,080	40,790	1,704	5,610	1,430
1917	39,061,530	35,214	289,700	2,438	39,440	1,700	2,860	890
1918	40,150,942	36,664	239,300	2,010	27,440	1,116	1,260	360
1919	40,048,534	34,363	263,800	2,240	26,980	1,112	1,220	302
1920	39,837,558	34,735	227,900	1,974	19,660	727	440	137
1921	40,662,634	33,978	225,800	1,908	19,810	711	390	113
1922	41,116,319	36,683	283,800	2,435	30,250	1,145	950	302
1923	41,974,573	40,977	319,700	2,700	31,360	1,189	940	298
1924	42,904,225	41,840	352,400	3,002	38,250	1,528	1,350	388
1925	43,499,358	42,043	413,800	3,593	48,650	1,960	2,550	816
1926	44,194,550	44,006*	429,300	3,668	47,250	1,912	2,450	835

[a] Derived from Table XXX.
[b] The equivalents of $5,000, $25,000 and $150,000 in 1926 dollars are $8,309, $41,543 and $249,255 respectively.
* Preliminary estimate.

of the dollar. To obtain the number of income recipients and the amount of income above the specified limits of $5,000, $25,000, and $150,000, all measured in terms of 1913 purchasing power, it was necessary to plot the figures for each year in terms of 1913 dollars, to connect the plotted points by smooth curves, and then to read off from these smooth curves the numbers for the points specified. It is in this manner that the figures in Table XXX have been arrived at. Such errors as exist in the final results are believed to depend mainly upon errors in the index series used for reducing the original quantities to a constant purchasing power and upon errors

TABLE XXXII

PERCENTAGES OF ALL INDIVIDUAL INCOME RECIPIENTS IN THE UNITED STATES
REPORTING TO THE FEDERAL AUTHORITIES INCOMES BETWEEN THE LIMITS SPECIFIED*

YEAR	INCOME RECIPIENTS IN THE UNITED STATES[b]	PER CENTS HAVING INDIVIDUAL INCOMES IN 1913 DOLLARS			
		Under $5,000[c]	$5,000-$25,000[c]	$25,000-$150,000[c]	$150,000 and Over[c]
1914	37,782,000	99.333	0.599	0.064	0.004
1915	37,956,000	99.355	0.561	0.078	0.007
1916	38,645,635	99.270	0.610	0.106	0.015
1917	39,393,530	99.157	0.735	0.100	0.007
1918	40,418,942	99.337	0.592	0.068	0.003
1919	40,340,534	99.276	0.654	0.067	0.003
1920	40,085,558	99.381	0.569	0.049	0.001
1921	40,908,634	99.399	0.552	0.048	0.001
1922	41,431,319	99.240	0.685	0.073	0.002
1923	42,326,573	99.168	0.755	0.074	0.002
1924	43,296,225	99.095	0.814	0.088	0.003
1925	43,964,358	98.942	0.941	0.111	0.006
1926	44,673,550	98.928	0.961	0.106	0.005

* Derived from Table XXXI.

b Includes gainfully occupied persons, plus the number of wives filing separate returns with the Federal Income Tax authorities.

c The equivalents of $5,000, $25,000 and $150,000 in 1926 dollars are $8,309, $41,543 and $249,255 respectively.

in reporting by the various income tax payers, and not upon the method of interpolation used. The figures in Table XXXI are obtained from those in Table XXX merely by a process of subtraction. The significant analysis begins with Table XXXII. In this table, we find recorded for each year the proportion of the total number of income recipients having incomes between the specified limits when these incomes are measured in terms of dollars of constant purchasing power.

Distribution of Individual Incomes Measured in 1913 Dollars.

The figures in Table XXXII indicate that, even in the present era of prosperity, only one out of 100 income recipients is fortunate enough to attain the limit of $5,000 in terms of 1913 dollars. This amount was equal to $8,309, measured in dollars of 1926. While an income of this size doubtless represents a high standard of comfort, it can scarcely be thought of as indicating affluence. Chart 25 makes it further clear that the great bulk of the American population still consists of people who are not in a position to live lives of luxurious leisure.

At the close of the period under consideration, approximately one income recipient in a thousand could boast of an income equal to $25,000 in 1913 purchasing power, while but one in 20,000 had an income as large as $150,000. In numbers, then, the very opulent represent a negligible fraction of the total population, and this has been true throughout the period 1914 to 1926.

Shifts in the Distribution of Income Recipients.

Perhaps the most interesting comparisons disclosed by Table XXXII are those showing the changes, as the years passed, in the percentages of the inhabitants falling in each class. Is it true that the rich are getting richer and the poor poorer? If so, we should find a constantly increasing percentage of income recipients falling in the lowest income class, and a constantly increasing percentage falling in the highest income class. Chart 26 shows the actual facts to have been as follows: The percentages of income recipients having incomes under $5,000, while fluctuating somewhat, had an approximately horizontal trend between 1914 and 1921. Since that date, the trend has been steadily downward, that is the proportion of the population included in the lowest income class is growing smaller.

Examination of the two right-hand columns of Table XXXII, and of the lower two graphs in Chart 26 shows that the classes having incomes above $25,000 increased rapidly in numbers between 1914 and 1916. This change in numbers is doubtless explained in part by the fact that business in the United States was moving from depression into prosperity, and in part by the fact that war orders from European combatants tended to give very large incomes to a limited number of Americans. With the entrance of the United States into the war in 1917, came a shrinkage in the percentages of income recipients included in the two highest income classes. This shrinkage continued rapidly until 1920, being unchecked by the boom of 1919 and 1920. Its effect was most marked in the case of the class having the highest incomes, the percentage in this class being reduced from 0.015 to 0.001 during this period; in other words, in 1921 there was only one person in the highest income class as compared to 15 in the year 1916. Since 1921, the numbers in

CHART 25

RELATIVE PROPORTIONS OF
ALL RECIPIENTS OF INCOME
IN THE UNITED STATES IN 1926
HAVING INCOMES OF THE CLASSES SPECIFIED*

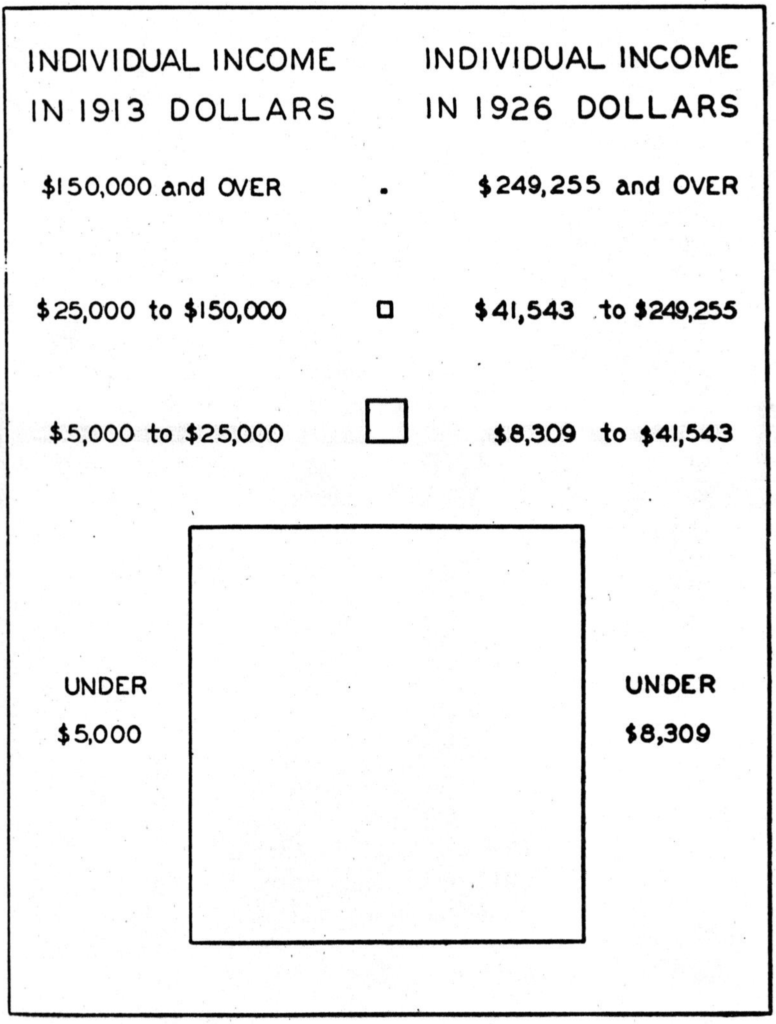

INDIVIDUAL INCOME
IN 1913 DOLLARS

INDIVIDUAL INCOME
IN 1926 DOLLARS

$150,000 and OVER   • $249,255 and OVER

$25,000 to $150,000   □ $41,543 to $249,255

$5,000 to $25,000   □ $8,309 to $41,543

UNDER
$5,000

UNDER
$8,309

* For data, see Table XXXI.

the three higher income classes have again grown. The number receiving incomes from $25,000 to $150,000 doubled before 1926, while the number receiving incomes of $150,000 and over, was multiplied by 5. The net result of the changes between 1914 and 1926 was to leave the proportion receiving incomes of more than $150,000 approximately the same as at the beginning of the period, while the proportion of income recipients obtaining incomes of $25,000 to $150,000 was about half as large again in 1926 as in 1914. The number of income recipients in the group having incomes between $5,000 and $25,000 has fluctuated somewhat less violently than have the numbers located in the higher income classes. There was, however, an increase in number between 1914 and 1917, and a diminution between 1917 and 1921, just as was the case with the still more prosperous sections of the population. Since 1921, there has been a steady and marked increase in the proportion of all income recipients falling within this class.

The general evidence of Table XXXII indicates, then, that the lower incomes are the more stable, and that the very highest class of incomes fluctuates most of all. When the entire period is taken into consideration, the most marked increase in any of the four classes is in that comprising incomes between $5,000 and $25,000. There has been a tendency for those in the lowest income class to climb up into this class. There has also been some tendency for those in the $5,000 to $25,000 class to ascend into the higher classes, but this tendency has been much less marked. Since 1921, apparently all classes of the population have been participating in the prevailing widespread prosperity.

The Apportionment Among Income Classes of Total Realized Income Measured in 1913 Dollars.

The figures in Table XXXII give us a good picture of the proportions of income recipients found in each of the four classes under consideration, but they tell us but little concerning the proportions of the total realized income of the nation going to the persons in each class. Is it true that, although income recipients receiving more than $150,000 in 1913 purchasing power are few in number, they nevertheless control the lion's share of the national income, while the masses with incomes below $5,000, on the 1913 basis, have the smaller part of the total income? Table XXXIII is designed to throw light upon this question. This table and Chart 27 show that the persons in the lowest of the four classes of income recipients

CHART 26

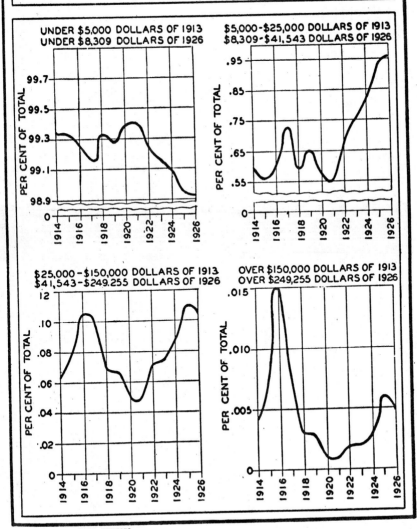

PERCENTAGES OF INDIVIDUAL INCOME
RECIPIENTS INCLUDED BETWEEN
FIXED INCOME LIMITS[a]

[a] For data see Table XXXII.

TABLE XXXIII

PERCENTAGES OF THE ENTIRE REALIZED INCOME OF ALL THE INHABITANTS OF THE UNITED STATES CONSTITUTED BY THE AMOUNTS REPORTED TO THE FEDERAL GOVERNMENT[a]

YEAR	REALIZED INCOME OF ALL INHABITANTS OF THE UNITED STATES[b] (Millions of 1913 Dollars)	PER CENTS INCLUDED IN INDIVIDUAL INCOMES IN 1913 DOLLARS			
		Under $5,000[c]	$5,000- $25,000[c]	$25,000- $150,000[c]	$150,000 and Over[c]
1914	$35,250	89.782			
1915	36,636	88.427	5.821	3.121	1.277
1916	39,559	86.820	5.421	3.810	2.342
1917	40,242	87.506	5.258	4.307	3.615
1918	40,150	91.318	6.058	4.224	2.212
			5.006	2.780	.897
1919	38,017	90.389			
1920	37,573	92.447	5.892	2.925	.794
1921	36,710	92.558	5.254	1.935	.365
1922	40,565	90.430	5.197	1.937	.308
1923	45,164	90.729	6.003	2.823	.744
			5.978	2.633	.660
1924	46,758	89.482			
1925	48,412	86.844	6.420	3.268	.830
1926	50,421*	87.277	7.422	4.049	1.686
			7.275	3.792	1.656

[a] Derived from Table XXXI.
[b] See Table IX.
[c] The equivalents of $5,000, $25,000 and $150,000 in 1926 dollars are $8,309, $41,543 and $249,255 respectively.
* Preliminary estimate.

received, in 1926, approximately 7/8 of the entire realized income of the nation, while those having incomes of $150,000 obtained, in the aggregate, only 1/60 of the entire realized income of the nation's inhabitants. If all of the income of persons having more than $5,000 of 1913 purchasing power, or, in other words, $8,309 having the value current in 1926, were distributed proportionately among the persons having less than the $8,309 specified, the incomes of this poorer group would be increased by only 1/7; in fact this change would be less than that which was caused between 1922 and 1926 by the general increase in the productiveness of American industry.[1]

[1] If the wealthier persons were allowed to retain $8,309 each and *excess* incomes only were distributed the average income in the poorest class would be increased but 1/11.

CHART 27

RELATIVE PROPORTIONS OF THE
REALIZED INCOME OF ALL THE PEOPLE
RECEIVED BY PERSONS
HAVING INCOMES OF THE CLASSES SPECIFIED[a]

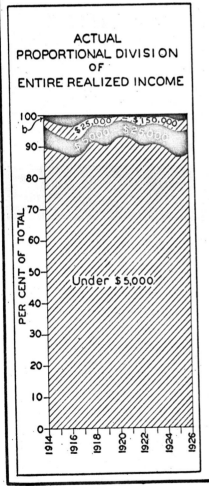

ACTUAL
PROPORTIONAL DIVISION
OF
ENTIRE REALIZED INCOME

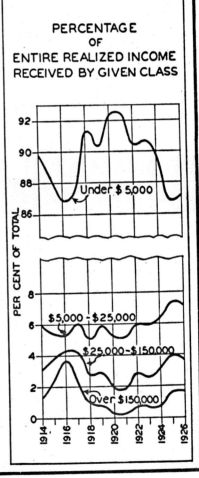

PERCENTAGE
OF
ENTIRE REALIZED INCOME
RECEIVED BY GIVEN CLASS

[a] For data, see Table XXXIII.
[b] Over $150,000.

Changes in Apportionment of Aggregate Income.

A year-to-year comparison of the percentages entered in Table XXXIII and Chart 27 shows that the fraction of the total income going to the poorest of the four income classes diminished between 1914 and 1916, increased between 1916 and 1921, and has since been declining.

There is a manifest tendency for the less prosperous classes of the population to receive in periods of depression a larger percentage of the total national income than that which they receive in times of marked prosperity. High incomes, also, are more responsive to the ups and downs of business than are low incomes. This phenomenon may, to a considerable extent, be explained by the fact that the lower incomes consist, in very large part, of wages and salaries, and, as we have seen, wages, in terms of dollars of constant purchasing power, form a much more stable fraction of the total realized income than do profits. The percentages of the national income going respectively to the classes having incomes of $25,000 to $150,000 and to those having incomes over $150,000 fluctuated in much the same way during the period under consideration. Both percentages rose sharply from 1914 to 1916, declined from 1916 to 1921, and have since been steadily rising. The fluctuations were, however, much more severe in the case of the most opulent class than they were in those receiving the incomes next lower in size. The percentages of the entire realized income received by these two classes were both slightly larger in 1926 than they were in 1914, but were both smaller in 1926 than they were in 1915. One might conclude, therefore, that the long-time trend of these percentages tends to be approximately horizontal. On the other hand, the percentage of the entire realized income going to the class receiving between $5,000 and $25,000, although it fluctuated considerably during the 13 years, closed the period at a level materially higher than that which it occupied in 1914. It appears that there is some slight tendency toward a concentration both of numbers of persons and of income in the prosperous class having incomes in 1926 between $8,309 and $41,543, but that there is practically no tendency towards the putting of more income into the hands of the extremely opulent sections of the community.

CHAPTER VIII

DIVIDENDS AND INTEREST ON CORPORATE FUNDED DEBT

Having considered the division of the national income between different grades of income recipients, we may now observe the part played by corporations in collecting and disbursing the national income.

Gross Dividends Actually Paid.

Tables XXXIV and XXXV, respectively, represent careful estimates of the gross amount of dividends paid out by corporations in the various fields of industry in each of the years 1909 to 1925, inclusive. For the years before 1922, the figures on gross dividends are not entirely accurate, as the Federal authorities did not collect and publish information for all the different fields. Since 1922, however, the totals have appeared regularly in *Statistics of Income,* ssued by the United States Bureau of Internal Revenue

In calculating the figures for both gross and net[1] dividends, the figures just mentioned have been taken as they stand in the case of both the manufacturing and the mining industries in 1922 and the years following. For earlier years, estimates for these two industries are based upon the dividend payments of sample groups of corporations. These samples include practically all of the larger corporations, reports for which are found in Moody's and Poor's *Manuals.* Assistance has also been given by the *Annual Reports* of the Bureau of Internal Revenue for earlier years. Data for the railways are taken from or estimated upon the basis of figures in *Statistics of Railways,* published by the Interstate Commerce Commission. The data for the Pullman and express companies are likewise based upon reports of the Interstate Commerce Commission. In the case of the electrical industries, namely, street railways, telephones, telegraphs, and private electric light and power plants, the Census figures for 1907, 1912, 1917, and 1922 have been used as basing points, the estimates for the inter-censal years being inserted on the basis of the trends of totals taken from a considerable number of sample corporations in each industry. This method can be relied

[1]Dividends paid from one corporation to another are excluded from *net* dividends but included in gross dividends.

181

TABLE XXXIV

ESTIMATED GROSS DIVIDENDS[a] ON PREFERRED STOCK PAID OUT BY VARIOUS CLASSES OF CORPORATIONS

YEAR	MILLIONS OF DOLLARS PAID BY								
	All Industries[b]	Factories[c]	Mines, Quarries and Oil Wells[c]	Railroads[d]	Street Railways[e]	Electric Light and Power[e]	Telephones[e]	Telegraphs[f]	All Other
1909	$ 459	$284	$ 4	$50	$11	$ 3	$1	$2	$104
1910	494	308	5	51	11	3	2	2	112
1911	506	318	8	45	11	5	2	2	115
1912	528	333	9	46	12	6	2	2	118
1913	562	354	15	42	14	7	2	2	126
1914	539	349	11	30	16	8	2	2	121
1915	587	369	9	47	16	10	2	2	132
1916	645	416	14	42	14	11	2	2	144
1917	780	501	19	58	12	12	2	2	174
1918	766	502	17	44	10	17	2	2	172
1919	715	456	17	46	11	21	2	2	160
1920	796	512	16	50	12	25	2	2	177
1921	759	478	15	51	11	31	2	2	169
1922	645	462	14	54	16	34	3	2	136
1923	697	500	15	63	21	55	4	2	128
1924	671	510	18	62	19	77	4	3	163
1925	849	508	22	63	18	105	5	3	223
1926				63					

[a] For definition of this term see text; inter-company dividend payments are included.
[b] Based upon *Statistics of Income*, published by the U. S. Bureau of Internal Revenue.
[c] Based upon *Statistics of Income* and upon a study of the reports of a large number of sample corporations.
[d] Based upon *Statistics of Railways*, published by the Interstate Commerce Commission. Include switching and terminal companies.
[e] Based upon *Census of Electrical Industries* and upon special study of reports of a large number of sample corporations.
[f] Based upon reports of various telegraph companies.

upon to give reasonably accurate results for figures which are interpolated, but is less dependable for extrapolations; hence the estimates for the years since 1922 are, in these industries, less reliable than are the figures for the earlier years.

The figures in Table XXXIV show that gross dividend payments on preferred stock approximately doubled between 1909 and 1926, while gross dividends on common stock were roughly trebled during the same period. Evidently the junior securities of corporations have been coming to play a more prominent rôle in so far

as disbursement of cash to stockholders is concerned. Throughout the entire period covered, the manufacturing corporations of the country have constantly tended to pay out in the neighborhood of half of all preferred dividends disbursed. Their rôle in regard to common dividends has, however, been slightly less prominent. In the earlier years of the period, they were responsible for considerably less than 1/3 of the total in this field, whereas, in recent years, their share has grown relatively but is still considerably less than half. As regards disbursements of preferred dividends, railroad corporations and electric light and power corporations are the only single groups, outside of the manufacturing field, paying out a considerable sum in this manner. The gross dividends on the preferred stocks of railroads fell off between 1909 and 1914, but have since increased again. In 1926, however, they totalled only about 1/4 more than in 1909. The record of railways in this respect is in striking contrast to the record of the electric light and power corporations, which have increased their preferred dividends from 3 millions in 1909 to 105 millions in 1925, the latter group of corporations having risen from a position of minor importance as regards preferred dividends to one in which they outclass the railroad companies and take a place next to manufacturing. Corporations engaged in the operation of mines, quarries, and oil wells have also shown a marked tendency to increase their payments of preferred dividends, the total rising from 4 millions, in 1909, to 22 millions in 1925. Under the caption "All Other" appears a record of the preferred dividends paid by numerous classes of corporations conducting activities in widely scattered fields. As the records for this miscellaneous group are based upon relatively scanty information, one is not justified in placing much dependence upon the figures.

Table XXXV shows that, as far as gross common dividends are concerned, banking comes next to manufacturing in size of payments. Corporations engaged in the extraction of minerals occupied third place, with railroads and electric light and power companies taking respectively the 4th and 5th positions. Between 1909 and 1925, the gross total of dividends paid by banking corporations doubled. The same was true in mining and in the operation of telegraphs. Factory dividends on common stock were multiplied by more than 4, while electric light and power companies paid out some 7 times as many dollars in 1925 as in 1909. On the other hand, corporations engaged in the operation of both steam railways and street railways paid as common dividends but a

TABLE XXXV

ESTIMATED GROSS DIVIDENDS[a] ON COMMON STOCK PAID OUT BY VARIOUS CLASSES OF CORPORATIONS

YEAR	All Indus-tries[b]	Bank-ing[c]	Fac-tories[b]	Mines, Quarries and Oil Wells[b]	Rail-roads[b]	Pull-man[d]	Ex-press[d]	Street Rail-ways[b]	Electric Light and Power[b]	Tele-phones[b]	Tele-graphs[b]	All Other
	MILLIONS OF DOLLARS PAID BY											
1909	$1,461	$223	$ 402	$160	$213	$ 8	$20	$49	$25	$24	$ 7	$330
1910	1,724	253	509	180	243	9	24	56	27	26	7	390
1911	1,790	272	573	154	242	9	11	58	32	27	7	405
1912	1,878	280	612	184	235	9	8	59	29	30	7	425
1913	2,112	286	685	251	260	9	7	61	38	30	7	478
1914	2,025	279	646	184	298	9	5	62	46	30	8	458
1915	2,065	270	688	183	289	10	6	60	51	32	9	467
1916	3,621	279	1,528	503	300	10	15	66	56	35	10	819
1917	4,058	293	1,739	602	329	10	4	61	52	38	12	918
1918	3,776	294	1,623	526	298	10	2	51	66	39	13	854
1919	3,428	287	1,589	306	293	10	•	47	70	39	12	775
1920	3,213	347	1,452	221	285	10	1	44	74	39	13	727
1921	3,048	389	1,279	286	213	10	2	41	84	43	12	689
1922	2,792	425	1,059	209	216	11	3	38	96	55	16	588
1923	3,472	439	1,527	285	229	11	2	54	122	61	13	638
1924	3,668	429	1,393	237	245	11	2	47	142	71	12	893
1925	4,340	451	1,740	313	259	11	2	52	185	78	13	1,138

[a] For definition of this term see text; inter-company dividend payments are included.

[b] Sources of information are same as those referred to in Table XXXIV.

[c] Includes small amount of preferred dividends. Based upon reports of *Comptroller of the Currency*.

[d] Based upon *Preliminary Abstract of Statistics of Common Carriers*, published by the Interstate Commerce Commission.

[e] Less than $500,000.

slightly greater number of dollars in 1925 than they did in 1909. When we consider the change in the purchasing power of the dollar, it is obvious that the buying power of the aggregate dividend payments by these two classes of corporations was actually less at the close of the period than at the beginning. Telephone companies, by contrast, approximately trebled their aggregate of dividends, while express companies reduced their payments to a mere fraction of the amounts disbursed in the years 1909 and 1910.

Total Interest on Funded Debt Actually Received by Individuals.

In Table XXXVI are recorded estimates of the total amount of net interest paid to individuals holding the evidences of funded

debt issued by various classes of corporations. These net amounts received by individuals are, of course, somewhat smaller than the gross amounts paid out by corporations, for, in some instances, one corporation holds the bonds or mortgages of another, and then the interest payments evidently do not directly reach any individual.

The available information is not sufficient to enable one to say for some of the industries what proportion of the interest paid out is paid to other corporations. The necessary facts are, for example, lacking in the case of manufacturing, mining, transportation by water, and miscellaneous corporations. Under the circumstances only a rough guess of the percentage could be made. The estimates of interest payments by corporations in manufacturing, mining, and transportation by water are based upon data from sample corporations, and may, therefore, be considerably in error. The probabilities are that, for these fields, the year-to-year comparisons are much more significant than are the absolute amounts indicated.

The data for street railways, electric light and power companies, and telephone and telegraph corporations are presumably reasonably accurate in the census years 1907, 1912, 1917, and 1922. It is believed that there are no considerable errors in the data for any of those industries, except perhaps in the case of electric light and power companies, in which instance, the changes since 1922 have been very rapid, and hence the data for the last two or three years may be subject to larger error. The figures for railway and express companies are reasonably complete.

The estimates in Table XXXVI indicate that, in the year 1925, the total interest paid on the funded debt amounted to about one-third as much as the total dividends paid on common and preferred stock. The ratio of interest payments to dividend payments has declined during the period covered, for, in 1909, the total of interest payments was approximately half as great as the gross total of dividends on common and preferred stocks combined. Between 1909 and 1928, the total amount of interest paid on the funded debt, as measured in current dollars, slightly more than doubled. The change in the purchasing power of the dollar has, however, been so great that it nearly offsets this normal increase in interest payments. The fact is, then, that the holders of bonds and mortgages could buy only about the same amount of goods with their 1928 interest money as could have been purchased in 1909 with the total of the same type of receipts.

Chart 28 makes it plain that, of all the individual industries

TABLE XXXVI

ESTIMATED NET INTEREST[a] ON FUNDED DEBT PAID TO INDIVIDUALS BY VARIOUS CLASSES OF CORPORATIONS

YEAR	MILLIONS OF DOLLARS PAID BY										
	All Industries[b]	Factories[b]	Mines, Quarries and Oil Wells[b]	Railroads[b]	Express[b]	Transportation by Water[c]	Street Railways[b]	Electric Light and Power[b]	Telephones[b]	Telegraphs[b]	All Other
1909	$ 993	$162	$16	$371	$1	$28	$ 83	$ 30	$14	$2	$286
1910	1,012	165	17	378	1	27	88	29	13	2	292
1911	1,047	168	18	390	1	22	94	36	14	2	302
1912	1,085	170	20	401	1	25	99	38	16	2	313
1913	1,127	174	21	410	d	26	109	41	19	2	325
1914	1,131	178	23	399	d	24	115	42	22	2	326
1915	1,208	182	25	437	d	27	119	46	22	2	348
1916	1,234	186	27	436	1	32	121	50	23	2	356
1917	1,255	191	29	440	d	31	119	57	25	1	362
1918	1,270	197	32	433	0	24	119	70	27	2	366
1919	1,321	206	36	436	0	30	124	75	31	2	381
1920	1,390	218	41	462	0	24	122	83	37	2	401
1921	1,461	227	47	477	0	27	125	93	42	2	421
1922	1,502	223	52	490	0	13	132	114	42	2	433
1923	1,568	231	56	503	0	14	133	132	44	3	452
1924	1,639	252	60	527	0	11	134	149	47	3	456
1925	1,678	248	66	539	0	11	128	166	50	3	467
1926	1,792*			529							
1927	1,933*										
1928	2,051*										

[a] For definition of this term, see text; intercorporate payments are excluded.
[b] Sources of information are same as those referred to in Table XXXV.
[c] Based upon *Statistics of Income*, published by the U. S. Bureau of Internal Revenue and reports of various sample corporations.
[d] Less than $500,000.
* Preliminary estimate.

for which data are available, railroads pay the largest amount of interest on funded debt. Manufacturing corporations occupy second, and electric light and power corporations third place, with street railway corporations a close fourth. Clearly, in the case of both the steam and street railways, interest charges on funded securities make up a far larger proportion of the total income yielded by the industry than is the case elsewhere.

In the earlier years of the period, street railways paid nearly three times as much money in the form of net interest on the funded

CHART 28

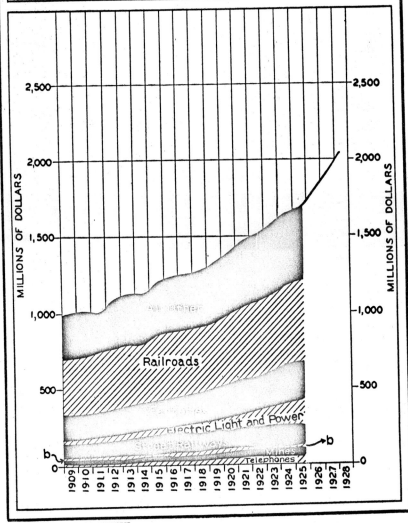

ESTIMATED NET INTEREST
ON FUNDED DEBT PAID TO INDIVIDUALS
BY VARIOUS CLASSES OF CORPORATIONS[a]

ᵃ For data, see Table XXXVI.
ᵇ Transportation by Water.

debt as did electric light and power corporations, but, in the year 1924, the rapid growth of the corporations in the last mentioned group brought their interest payments above those of the street railways. Payments to the holders of the funded debt in the mining industries approximately quadrupled between 1909 and 1925, and the same was true in the telephone field. The most rapid growth is shown by the records from electric light and power corporations, the interest on funded debt in that field being multiplied by 5. Manufacturing, railroading, and street railway corporations did not even double the payments on their funded debt, while transportation by water reduced its payments by one half and the funded debt of express companies entirely disappeared.

A striking characteristic of the graphs in Chart 28 is the regularity of the different zones representing the volume of net interest payments by the various industries. Only in the case of transportation by water is there any evidence of violent change, a marked shrinkage in interest payments taking place about 1922. In every other field, there has been a constant tendency for interest on funded debt to grow steadily larger throughout the period 1909 to 1925. The most marked expansion occurred in the case of electric light and power corporations.

The 16 years between 1909 and 1925 saw a total increase of approximately 70 per cent in the aggregate payments of interest on funded debt to individuals by all industries. When, however, an allowance is made for changes in the purchasing power of the dollar this apparent increase is about cancelled.

Total Dividends on Preferred Stock Received by Individuals.

In Table XXXVII, the attempt is made to show only the amounts actually received by individuals, excluding all dividends paid to other corporations. In certain of the industries, this process of elimination has necessarily been only an approximation. This is especially true in the case of manufacturing and mining corporations.

In general, it appears that individuals receive only about 50 per cent as much income from dividends on preferred stock as they do from interest on the funded debt of corporations. In a rough way, this ratio has remained approximately constant throughout the period 1909-1925. Nearly half of the total of net dividend payments on preferred stocks in all industries goes to the holders of this class of securities of manufacturing corporations. Preferred stock dividends of electric light and power corporations which, in 1909, ac-

TABLE XXXVII

ESTIMATED NET DIVIDENDS[b] ON PREFERRED STOCK RECEIVED BY INDIVIDUALS FROM VARIOUS CLASSES OF CORPORATIONS

YEAR	MILLIONS OF DOLLARS PAID BY								
	All Indus- tries[a]	Fac- tories[a]	Mines, Quarries and Oil Wells[a]	Rail- roads[a]	Street Rail- ways[a]	Electric Light and Power[a]	Tele- phones[a]	Tele- graphs[a]	All Other
1909	$451	$284	$ 4	$45	$10	$ 3	$1	$2	$102
1910	488	308	5	47	11	3	1	2	111
1911	498	318	8	41	11	5	1	2	112
1912	523	333	9	41	12	6	2	2	118
1913	557	354	15	38	14	6	2	2	126
1914	533	349	11	25	16	7	2	2	121
1915	569	369	9	34	15	9	2	2	129
1916	629	416	14	30	13	10	2	2	142
1917	758	501	19	40	12	11	2	2	171
1918	748	502	17	32	9	15	2	2	169
1919	696	456	17	33	10	18	2	2	158
1920	774	512	16	34	11	22	2	2	175
1921	741	478	15	38	11	27	2	2	168
1922	623	386	14	42	15	29	4	2	131
1923	674	409	15	52	20	48	4	2	124
1924	646	325	18	53	18	67	5	3	157
1925	821	410	22	56	17	92	5	3	216
1926	941*	469*	26*	52			6*		
1927	1,042*						6*		
1928	1,171*						7*		

[a] Sources of information are same as those referred to in Table XXXIV.

[b] For definition of this term, see text; intercorporate payments are excluded.

* Preliminary estimate.

counted for but 3 millions of dollars out of the 451 millions paid by all industries, rose to such an extent that, in 1925, they made up 1/9 of the total dividends on preferred stock paid by all corporations. This type of income has also risen rapidly in the case of holders of preferred stock in mining corporations, dividends in this field having risen from about 4 millions in 1909 to 25 millions in 1925. A large part of this increase is due to the growth of the petroleum industry. Telephone corporations have also expanded rapidly their preferred stock dividends, but the total still remains very small. The growth in this particular type of income has been slow in the case of steam and street railway and telegraph corporations.

Total Dividends on Common Stock Received by Individuals.

Very frequently, for purposes of control, the common stock of one corporation is largely held by some superior corporation. For this reason, there is a marked difference between the gross total of dividends and the net total of dividends received by individuals. In Table XXXVIII are recorded estimates of the *net* dividends paid by each industry on common stock, an attempt having been made to eliminate all inter-corporate payments. According to this table, net dividends on common stock trebled between 1909 and 1925. The annual payments fluctuate widely; a high point was reached in 1917 with a decline thereafter until 1922, since which date a marked upward movement has again occurred.

Of the individual industries for which records are available, manufacturing is far in the lead in net payment of dividends on common stock. This class of dividends accounted in recent years for almost half of the total for all industries. Manufacturing dividends rose rapidly from 1909 to 1917, the increase between 1915 and 1917 being especially steep. From 1917 to 1922, there was a continuous decline, most marked between 1919 and 1922. The year 1923 was characterized by an extremely sharp recovery, and, since that date, a large volume of dividends has been maintained. The course of total net common dividends in the mining industry has paralleled closely the record for manufacturing. Railroads increased the total volume of their payments on common stock at a slow rate between 1909 and 1914. With the beginning of inflation, and the subsequent rise in operating costs, the railroads, because of rate control, were unable to continue paying dividends as freely, hence the total gradually declined until the year 1921. After that date, conditions affecting the railway stockholders were gradually ameliorated and common dividends rose until, in 1925, they were at a level but slightly below that existing just before the World War. What has been said of common dividends of steam railway corporations applies with almost equal force to the street railway companies. Telephone and telegraph companies have been able to expand their dividend payments on common stock throughout most of the period, although the tendency to expansion in the telegraph field apparently ceased after 1922. Electric light and power corporations have been extremely liberal in their disbursements to their common stockholders, the total paid out being some 7 times as great in 1925 as in 1909. Practically every year has seen expansion in the amount of dividends paid by this branch of trans-

TABLE XXXVIII

ESTIMATED NET DIVIDENDS* ON COMMON STOCK RECEIVED BY INDIVIDUALS FROM VARIOUS CLASSES OF CORPORATIONS

MILLIONS OF DOLLARS PAID BY

YEAR	All Industries[b]	Banking[b]	Factories[b]	Mines, Quarries and Oil Wells[b]	Railroads[b]	Pullman[b]	Express[b]	Street Railways[b]	Electric Light and Power[b]	Telephones[b]	Telegraphs[b]	All Other
1909	$1,119	$ 88	$ 337	$131	$192	$ 8	$16	$44	$20	$ 24	$ 6	$253
1910	1,351	120	426	146	221	9	19	51	21	25	7	306
1911	1,383	120	479	124	221	9	6	53	25	26	7	313
1912	1,448	119	513	148	212	9	3	54	27	28	7	328
1913	1,630	122	574	197	235	9	3	55	30	29	7	369
1914	1,522	111	541	140	245	9	2	56	37	29	8	344
1915	1,505	99	576	134	209	9	3	55	40	31	9	340
1916	2,707	81	1,279	357	209	9	12	61	44	34	9	612
1917	3,016	81	1,456	410	224	9	1	56	49	37	11	682
1918	2,796	87	1,359	342	217	9	1	47	52	38	12	632
1919	2,530	67	1,330	190	214	9	*	43	55	38	12	572
1920	2,337	108	1,216	133	192	9	1	40	58	39	12	529
1921	2,217	148	1,071	168	159	9	2	38	66	44	11	501
1922	2,026	176	936	126	167	10	2	34	75	58	15	427
1923	2,672	182	1,371	208	188	9	1	50	96	64	12	491
1924	2,863	164	1,344	195	211	9	2	43	112	74	12	697
1925	3,337	170	1,518	247	231	5	2	48	146	83	12	875
1926	3,823*	181*	1,670*	300*	276	7	2			89*		
1927	4,233*	169*					2			100*		
1928	4,760*									106*		

* For definition of this term, see text; intercorporate payments are excluded.
b Sources of information are same as those referred to in Table XXXV.
* Negative figure of less than $500,000; more dividends received than paid out.
* Preliminary estimate.

portation. The banks of the United States increased their total dividends on common stock between 1909 and 1913 at a rapid rate. Between 1913 and 1919, however, their dividends declined sharply until they were well below the 1909 level. In the year 1920 a rapid expansion began, which continued until 1923. After 1923, a slight tendency to decline is noticeable.

Totals of Net Interest on Funded Debt and Net Dividends, as Measured in 1913 Dollars.

A large part of this increase in dividend payments represents nothing more than shrinkage in the value of the dollar. Chart 30

CHART 29

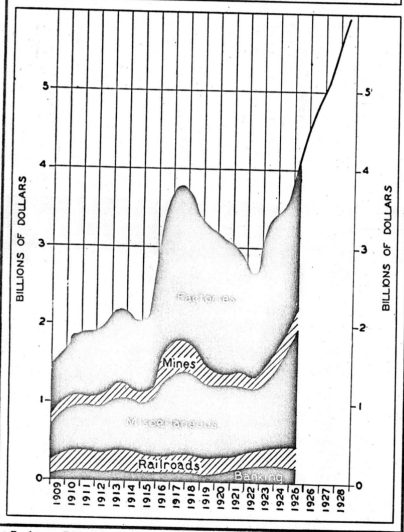

ESTIMATED NET DIVIDENDS
ON CAPITAL STOCK RECEIVED BY INDIVIDUALS
FROM VARIOUS CLASSES OF CORPORATIONS*

* For data, see Tables XXXVII and XXXVIII.

shows that, when all quantities are expressed in terms of dollars of constant purchasing power, the total of preferred dividends was actually lower in 1924 than in 1909, and in 1922 the total of common dividends was lower than in 1910. Total interest payments on funded debt were less in 1925 than in 1909. Even after the great rise since 1922, the purchasing power of the total of interest payments on the funded debt was but 22 per cent greater, and of dividends on preferred stock but 54 per cent greater in 1928 than in 1909. The class of securities in which the striking increase in disbursements has occurred is common stocks, the purchasing power of the net dividends on this class of securities being 1 1/2 times as great in 1928 as in 1909.

The total payments in 1913 dollars, for the various years are as follows:

Millions of 1913 Dollars

Year	Interest	Preferred Dividends	Common Dividends
1909	1,052	478	1,185
1910	1,048	505	1,399
1911	1,084	516	1,432
1912	1,109	535	1,481
1913	1,127	557	1,630
1914	1,126	531	1,516
1915	1,208	569	1,505
1916	1,160	591	2,544
1917	1,044	631	2,509
1918	918	540	2,020
1919	836	440	1,600
1920	770	429	1,294
1921	873	443	1,324
1922	942	391	1,271
1923	976	420	1,664
1924	1,022	403	1,785
1925	1,024	501	2,036
1926	1,094*	574*	2,334*
1927	1,198*	646*	2,623*
1928	1,288*	736*	2,984*

*Preliminary estimate.

CHART 30

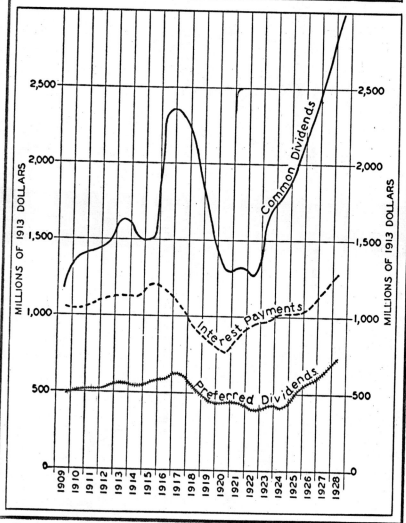

PURCHASING POWER, IN 1913 DOLLARS,
OF NET INTEREST AND NET DIVIDENDS
RECEIVED BY INDIVIDUALS
FROM VARIOUS CLASSES OF CORPORATIONS[a]

[a] For data, see text.

Changes in Fractions Which Interest and Dividends Constitute of Total Realized Income.

We now hear so much about investments in corporate securities and their influence on American welfare, that we are inclined to feel that they have come more and more to dominate the income of the nation. Table XXXIX and Chart 31 furnish surprisingly little evidence for any such conclusion. In 1909, for example, the total volume of interest paid on the funded debt constituted a much larger proportion of the entire realized income of all individuals in the nation than it did in 1928. Total dividend payments, while slightly larger relatively in the most recent years than at the beginning of the period, form a distinctly smaller proportion of the total realized income of the nation than they did in 1916 and 1917. Furthermore, interest and dividends combined account for but one-eleventh of the entire realized income of all individuals in the United States.

When we consider not the entire income but merely the income of entrepreneurs and other property owners, we find that interest on funded debt constitutes a much smaller proportion of the total than was the case in the period before the war, but that the relative share made up of dividends was approximately one-fourth greater than in that earlier period. In 1916, however, it was even larger than in 1928. Entrepreneurs and other property owners have, in recent years, tended to derive between one-sixth and one-fifth of their income from corporate sources, the great bulk still coming from investments in individual enterprises and from private entrepreneurial activities such as farming and merchandising.

Total Par Values of Funded Debt and Preferred Stock.

It is by no means easy to estimate the par value of the various types of securities outstanding for the corporations in each industry. During recent years, the United States Bureau of Internal Revenue has requested all corporations to report the amount of securities of each class outstanding, but an examination of the figures indicates that, in many fields, the corporations have been extremely remiss in complying with this request. It appears, however, that the figures secured by the United States Bureau of Internal Revenue are reasonably complete for manufacturing corporations, and Federal figures have been used as basing points in this industry. In the case of mines, quarries, and oil wells, such a large proportion of the corporations have failed to report that it has seemed best to

TABLE XXXIX

RELATIVE IMPORTANCE OF THE CONTRIBUTIONS MADE BY DIVIDENDS AND INTEREST ON THE FUNDED DEBT OF CORPORATIONS TO THE REALIZED INCOME OF INDIVIDUALS

	PER CENT[a] WHICH CORPORATE INTEREST AND DIVIDENDS CONSTITUTE OF					
YEAR	ENTIRE REALIZED INCOME OF INDIVIDUALS		REALIZED ENTREPRENEURIAL AND PROPERTY INCOME			
			INCLUDING IMPUTED INCOME		EXCLUDING IMPUTED INCOME	
	Interest on Funded Debt	Dividends	Interest on Funded Debt	Dividends	Interest on Funded Debt	Dividends
1909	3.35	5.30	6.84	10.82	7.90	12.49
1910	3.22	5.85	6.67	12.13	7.74	14.06
1911	3.29	5.90	6.82	12.25	7.95	14.29
1912	3.19	5.80	6.62	12.03	7.66	13.91
1913	3.15	6.12	6.67	12.94	7.73	15.01
1914	3.17	5.76	6.60	12.00	7.69	13.97
1915	3.25	5.57	6.77	11.62	7.88	13.53
1916	2.85	7.71	5.93	16.03	6.81	18.42
1917	2.44	7.35	4.92	14.78	5.57	16.76
1918	2.10	5.87	4.52	12.62	5.22	14.56
1919	2.00	4.89	4.32	10.56	5.04	12.30
1920	1.88	4.20	4.38	9.81	5.31	11.89
1921	2.31	4.67	5.38	10.89	6.62	13.41
1922	2.28	4.02	5.32	9.39	6.40	11.28
1923	2.11	4.50	4.99	10.64	5.94	12.67
1924	2.12	4.55	5.02	10.75	5.98	12.80
1925	2.05	5.08	4.78	11.85	5.65	14.00
1926	2.09	5.57	5.01	13.31	5.87	15.61
1927	2.19	5.98	5.25	14.32	6.12	16.71
1928	2.29	6.63	5.36	15.49	6.22	17.97

[a] Derived from Tables VIII, XXXVI, XXXVII and XXXVIII.

present in the accompanying tables estimates based entirely upon data secured from a large number of sample corporations. Figures in this industry represent, then, merely data from the larger active corporations in the mining field, and do not take into account the thousands of inactive and practically defunct concerns which still have securities outstanding. The United States Interstate Commerce Commission secures practically complete data from the rail-

CHART 31

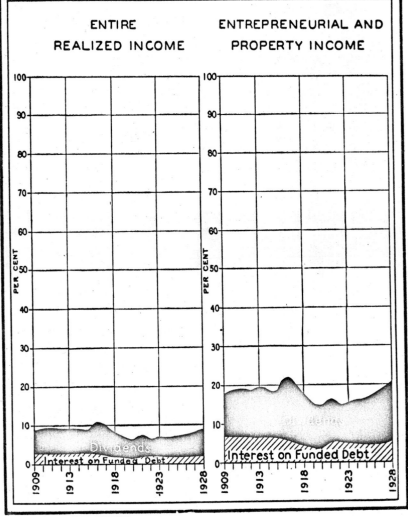

RELATIVE IMPORTANCE OF THE
CONTRIBUTIONS MADE BY DIVIDENDS AND
INTEREST ON THE FUNDED DEBT OF
CORPORATIONS[a]

ENTIRE
REALIZED INCOME

ENTREPRENEURIAL AND
PROPERTY INCOME

[a] For data, see Table XXXIX.

ways, the Pullman Company, and the express companies, and hence it is believed that figures relating to these fields are free from any considerable error. Once in five years, the Bureau of the Census collects data from street railways, telephone and telegraph companies, and private electric light and power plants. These figures have been used for the years 1907, 1912, 1917 and 1922. The estimates for the other years are based upon sample data consisting of the annual reports of a large number of representative corporations operating in these fields.

Table XL serves to set forth estimates of the par value of the gross funded debt outstanding, on the average, during the years 1909 to 1925, inclusive. An examination of the figures in this table shows that, throughout the period, the funded debt of the railways of the United States has had a face value larger than the funded debt of all the other corporations covered in this study. Manufacturing corporations come next, with street railways and electric light and power companies having practically equal amounts outstanding in 1925. Corporations engaged in the operation of mines, quarries, and oil wells have funded securities outstanding in an amount slightly larger than the volume of those issued by telephone corporations.

During the period under consideration, manufacturing and telegraph companies have increased their funded debt by something more than one-third, railways by two-fifths, street railway companies by three-quarters, while telephone and mining companies have trebled the amount of their funded debt, and electric light and power corporations have multiplied theirs by 5. The general tendency is for the funded debt to grow steadily larger, with few fluctuations. The decline in the case of the express companies was caused largely by the consolidation of a number of the companies. In 1918, the entire business was taken over by a single corporation, the American Railway Express Company.

Table XLI presents for the various industries estimates of the gross par value of preferred stock outstanding in each of the years covered by this study. A comparison of the figures in this table with those in Table XL shows that the respective industries rank very differently as regards the volume of preferred stock issues and the volume of bond issues. In 1925, manufacturing corporations, for example, had outstanding twice as much preferred stocks as bonds, while the funded debt of railroads and street railways totalled 7 times as much as the aggregate of their preferred stock issues.

TABLE XL

ESTIMATED TOTAL FOR ALL CORPORATIONS IN THE GIVEN INDUSTRY OF THE PAR VALUE OF THE GROSS FUNDED DEBT OUTSTANDING ON THE AVERAGE DURING THE YEAR
(MILLIONS OF CURRENT DOLLARS)

Year	Factories[a]	Mines, Quarries and Oil Wells[a,f]	Railroads[b]	Express[c]	Street Railways[d]	Electric Light and Power[d]	Telephones[d]	Telegraphs[e]
1909	$3,203	$319	$ 9,969	$36	$1,909	$ 647	$316	$61
1910	3,270	344	10,644	36	2,031	715	300	61
1911	3,379	372	11,284	36	2,157	789	332	61
1912	3,446	401	11,751	36	2,279	864	373	57
1913	3,453	430	11,832	28	2,378	859	432	53
1914	3,501	460	12,268	20	2,493	824	482	53
1915	3,572	493	11,919	19	2,654	893	478	52
1916	3,644	529	11,796	19	2,825	1,022	488	52
1917	3,724	568	11,706	18	2,983	1,191	509	52
1918	3,786	608	11,624	0	3,077	1,368	502	52
1919	3,846	651	11,610	0	3,114	1,474	577	52
1920	3,897	705	12,034	0	3,139	1,676	664	52
1921	3,913	768	12,467	0	3,143	2,027	720	59
1922	3,892	836	12,639	0	3,129	2,237	733	67
1923	4,005	918	13,112	0	3,151	2,474	768	67
1924	4,397	1,011	13,728	0	3,214	2,832	826	67
1925	4,368	1,098	14,035	0	3,258	3,203	901	67
1926	4,366		14,009	0	3,299		993	80

a Based upon a special study of the reports of a large number of sample corporations.

b Based upon *Statistics of Railways* published by the Interstate Commerce Commission. Includes switching and terminal companies.

c Based upon *Preliminary Abstract of Statistics of Common Carriers*, published by the Interstate Commerce Commission.

d Based upon *Census of Electrical Industries* and upon a study of the reports of a large number of sample corporations.

e Based upon reports of various telegraph companies.

f The figures in this column represent estimates for the larger *active* corporations only. A great number of mining corporations having an unknown amount of funded debt are inactive. For example, in the year 1926, out of 19,252 mining corporations reporting to the U. S. Bureau of Internal Revenue only 4,820 reported net income and only 11,641 reported the amount of their capital stock. These 11,641 had outstanding $1,008,031,898 in bonded debts and mortgages. See *Statistics of Income*, 1926, pp. 356 and 365.

Mining corporations depend more upon funded debt in obtaining their operating funds than they do upon preferred stock. This is even more emphatically true of electric light and power corporations and telephone and telegraph companies.

While railroad corporations are dominant in the use of bond issues, manufacturing concerns are foremost in the use of preferred

TABLE XLI

ESTIMATED TOTAL FOR ALL CORPORATIONS IN THE GIVEN INDUSTRY OF THE PAR VALUE OF THE GROSS PREFERRED STOCK OUTSTANDING ON THE AVERAGE DURING THE YEAR

(MILLIONS OF CURRENT DOLLARS)

Year	Factories[a]	Mines, Quarries and Oil Wells[a][c]	Rail- roads[a]	Street Rail- ways[a]	Electric Light and Power[a]	Tele- phones[a]	Tele- graphs[a]
1909	$4,855	$ 78	$1,476	$344	$ 89	$34	$50
1910	5,075	97	1,411	360	118	37	50
1911	5,310	119	1,404	375	150	38	50
1912	5,505	139	1,381	396	171	41	50
1913	5,720	159	1,396	419	190	41	50
1914	5,955	178	1,394	432	215	40	50
1915	6,175	199	1,356	440	233	40	50
1916	6,470	221	1,432	449	248	41	50
1917	6,825	241	1,632	458	264	42	50
1918	7,110	262	1,817	464	283	43	50
1919	7,350	282	1,850	469	322	46	50
1920	7,580	300	1,895	474	398	48	57
1921	7,815	318	1,845	479	467	58	67
1922	8,030	334	1,813	484	520	76	70
1923	8,160	351	1,838	486	b	88	70
1924	8,255	368	1,878	486	b	100	70
1925	8,355	384	1,922	485	b	112	70
1926			1,928	485		123	70

[a] Sources of information are same as those referred to in Table XL.

[b] Because of the extremely rapid changes occurring in this industry reasonably dependable estimates cannot well be made until the data for the 1927 Census become available. Data in *Statistics of Income,* published by U. S. Bureau of Internal Revenue are incomplete.

[c] The figures in this column represent estimates for the larger *active* corporations only. A great number of mining corporations, having a very large but unknown amount of preferred stock, are inactive. For example, in the year 1926, out of 19,252 mining corporations reporting to the U. S. Bureau of Internal Revenue only 4,820 reported net income and only 11,641 reported the amount of their capital stock. These 11,641 had outstanding $538,017,502 in preferred stock. See *Statistics of Income,* 1926, pp. 356 and 365.

stock, the preferred stock issues of manufacturing corporations aggregating in 1925 approximately 3 times as much as the issues of the 6 other classes of corporations represented in Table XLI. The evidence of the figures presented in this table is that the issue of preferred stock as a means of raising funds did not increase in favor with either steam and street railways, or telegraph corporations during the last two decades, for, in each case, their issues increased by only about one-third between 1909 and 1925. Companies engaged in manufacturing operations have, in the same period, nearly

TABLE XLII

RATIO OF THE TOTAL INTEREST PAID ON THE
FUNDED DEBT OF ALL CORPORATIONS IN THE INDUSTRY
TO THE TOTAL PAR VALUE OF THAT DEBT[a]

Year	Factories[c]	Mines, Quarries and Oil Wells[c]	Railroads	Express	Street Railways	Electric Light and Power	Telephones	Telegraphs[c]
1909	.0506	.0502	.0378	.0400	.0465[c]	.0474[c]	.0419[c]	.0441
1910	.0505	.0494	.0362	.0400	.0465[c]	.0423[c]	.0410[c]	.0442
1911	.0497	.0484	.0353	.0400	.0464[c]	.0472[c]	.0420[c]	.0440
1912	.0493	.0499	.0349	.0400	.0465	.0471	.0408	.0446
1913	.0504	.0488	.0354	.0283	.0488[c]	.0490[c]	.0432[c]	.0438
1914	.0508	.0500	.0366	.0390	.0494[c]	.0526[c]	.0442[c]	.0438
1915	.0510	.0507	.0404	.0401	.0479[c]	.0534[c]	.0453[c]	.0443
1916	.0510	.0510	.0419	.0383	.0457[c]	.0507[c]	.0464[c]	.0441
1917	.0513	.0511	.0417	.0404	.0425	.0517	.0483	.0403
1918	.0520	.0526	.0416	b	.0414[c]	.0526[c]	.0528[c]	.0441
1919	.0536	.0553	.0424	b	.0423[c]	.0526[c]	.0532[c]	.0441
1920	.0559	.0582	.0430	b	.0415[c]	.0512[c]	.0545[c]	.0441
1921	.0580	.0612	.0400	b	.0425[c]	.0473[c]	.0560[c]	.0440
1922	.0573	.0622	.0407	b	.0449	.0525	.0549	.0488
1923	.0577	.0610	.0401	b	.0451[c]	.0549[c]	.0559[c]	.0464
1924	.0573	.0594	.0411	b	.0446[c]	.0541[c]	.0554[c]	.0465
1925	.0568	.0601	.0401	b	.0419[c]	.0533[c]	.0540[c]	.0468

[a] Derived from figures for gross interest paid and gross funded debt outstanding.
[b] No funded debt outstanding.
[c] As estimated from a large sample of corporations.

doubled the amount of preferred stock outstanding. Telephone corporations have more than trebled their issues, while those engaged in the operations of mines, quarries, and oil wells have multiplied their issues by 5, and the increase in the case of private electric light and power corporations has been even more rapid.

Ratio of Interest Paid to Par Value of Funded Debt.

In Table XLII there is given a record of the ratio of the total amount of interest paid to the total par value of funded debt outstanding as estimated for the various industries. For corporations engaged in the operation of factories, mines, quarries, and oil wells, the data are based solely upon the reports of a large number of sample corporations, the samples consisting of those corporations annually reported in Moody's and Poor's *Manuals*. For street railways, telephone and telegraph companies, and electric light and power corporations, the data for the years 1912, 1917, and 1922 are taken from the reports of the United States Census, while the figures for the other years are interpolated or extrapolated on the basis of the records of sample corporations. The figures for railroads and express companies are taken from the reports of the Interstate Commerce Commission and are believed to be substantially accurate. The fact should be carefully noted that the rates here given represent neither the average normal rate of payment on securities outstanding nor the rate paid upon securities upon which payments are actually made, but instead represent the ratio of total interest payments made to total par value outstanding, whether the securities were or were not in default.

We see that, for the sample corporations covered, the rate paid in 1925 was highest for those engaged in the operation of mines, quarries, and oil wells, with manufacturing corporations coming next, and telephone companies and electric light and power corporations occupying third and fourth places respectively. The lowest rate was paid by steam railways, with street railways and telegraph companies paying slightly more. For corporations engaged in manufacturing, mining, and the operation of telephones and electric light and power plants, there was a tendency for the rate to decline for a year or two at the beginning of the period, but, after that, in all four cases, rates moved upward, the high point being reached in the period 1921 to 1923. Since that date, the rates have declined somewhat in all four industries. The trend of rates in railways was much the same, except that the maximum was reached in 1920. Street railway corporations paid a slightly lower rate in 1925 than in 1909, but, in every other group of corporations included in Table XLII, the rate was higher in 1925 than in 1909.

Ratio of Dividend Payments to Par Value of Preferred Stock.

The figures in Table XLIII indicate that, in the case of manufacturing, mining, and telephone corporations, there was a distinct tendency in pre-war years for preferred stocks actually to pay, on the average, a higher return on par value than that yielded by bonds. In the case of the railroads, street railways, telegraph companies, and electric light and power corporations, however, the preferred stockholders fared worse than the bondholders during the pre-war period. This condition continued in the post-war period in the case of telegraph and telephone companies, both

TABLE XLIII

RATIO OF THE TOTAL DIVIDENDS PAID THEREON TO THE TOTAL PAR VALUE OF THE PREFERRED STOCK OF ALL CORPORATIONS IN THE INDUSTRY[a]

Year	Factories[d]	Mines, Quarries and Oil Wells[d]	Railroads	Street Railways	Electric Light and Power	Telephones	Telegraphs[d]
1909	.0585	.0513	.0338	.0320[d]	.0337[d]	.0294[d]	.0400
1910	.0607	.0515	.0361	.0306[d]	.0254[d]	.0541[d]	.0400
1911	.0601	.0672	.0321	.0293[d]	.0333[d]	.0526[d]	.0400
1912	.0603	.0647	.0333	.0303	.0351	.0488	.0400
1913	.0617	.0943[b]	.0301	.0334[d]	.0368[d]	.0488[d]	.0400
1914	.0584	.0618	.0215	.0370[d]	.0372[d]	.0500[d]	.0400
1915	.0596	.0452	.0347	.0364[d]	.0429[d]	.0500[d]	.0400
1916	.0640	.0633	.0293	.0312[d]	.0444[d]	.0488[d]	.0400
1917	.0731[b]	.0788[b]	.0355	.0262	.0455	.0476	.0400
1918	.0705	.0649	.0242	.0216[d]	.0601[d]	.0465[d]	.0400
1919	.0618	.0603	.0249	.0235[d]	.0651[d]	.0435[d]	.0400
1920	.0672	.0533	.0264	.0253[d]	.0638[d]	.0417[d]	.0351
1921	.0608	.0472	.0276	.0230[d]	.0657[d]	.0345[d]	.0299
1922	.0575	.0419	.0298	.0331	.0646	.0395	.0286
1923	.0613	.0427	.0343	.0432[d]	[c]	.0455[d]	.0286
1924	.0618	.0489	.0330	.0391[d]	[c]	.0400[d]	.0429
1925	.0608	.0573	.0328	.0371[d]	[c]	.0446[d]	.0429

a Derived from Tables XXXIV and XLI.
b Seemingly high dividend rates due to payment of back dividends.
c Because of the extremely rapid changes occurring in this industry reasonably dependable estimates cannot well be made until the data for the 1927 Census become available.
d As estimated from a large sample of corporations.

steam and electric railways, and corporations engaged in manufacturing and the operation of mines, quarries, and oil wells. Preferred stockholders in electric light and power corporations have received, on the average, in recent years a rate of return higher than that paid to the bondholders of the same class of corporations. From the facts just stated it is clearly evident that, in general, one cannot count on the junior class of securities yielding on the average a higher rate of return than that obtained on the supposedly safer class of investments. Apparently, in most instances, the higher nominal yield on preferred stocks during the post-war period was insufficient to cover the greater degree of risk involved.

CHAPTER IX

THE VALUES OF CORPORATIONS TO THEIR OWNERS

What are the great corporation-dominated industries of the United States worth to their owners? This is a question upon which heretofore, very little light has been thrown. There are, of course, numerous index numbers of the prices of bonds and of stocks, but a single bond represents a varying fraction in the total value of the industry, and a share of stock is an even more fluctuating unit, for the number of shares of stock issued by a given corporation varies from time to time and the fraction of the business of the industry done by that corporation changes from day to day. Manifestly, therefore, movements in index numbers of stock prices or bond prices throw little light on fluctuations in the value of the industry as a whole.

The Process of Valuing Corporate-Controlled Industries.

Some attempts have been made to estimate the value of the property used in industry by estimating the value of each unit, piece-meal, and afterward adding together all such estimates. Such a process is, however, necessarily futile, for most of the property used by the industries dominated by corporations has little value except when taken in conjunction with other dissimilar units. No one, for example, wishes to buy a railroad roundhouse except for use in conjunction with the railway. The roadbed, aside from its function of carrying railway traffic, is, in many cases, merely a nuisance, having negative rather than positive value.

The genuine market value of industries of the type specified lies in the market prices of their securities. These securities are actually bought and sold from day to day, and each share, for the moment, represents a definite fraction of the value of the whole enterprise. If, then, we add together the values at a given instant of time of all of the shares of all the enterprises in the given industry, we have a figure which possesses precise significance. Whether or not the *absolute* quantities thus arrived at have much meaning, there can be little doubt but that the *changes* in these totals from time to time have very great significance.

The process used in calculating the values presented in Table

XLIV is as follows: In each industry, an estimate has been made of the total par value of the funded debt, the total par value of the preferred stock, and the total number of shares of common stock in the hands of individuals. For a large number of sample corporations in the industry, both the price of each type of security and the number of shares outstanding at the end of the year have been ascertained. In this way, it has been possible to make an estimate of the average price per unit of each class of security in the given industry. These average prices per unit have, then, been multiplied by the estimated number of units outstanding in order to approximate the total value of the securities of a given class at the close of a year. In a number of industries, these results have been tested by ascertaining the ratio of the market price of the given class of securities to the total amount of dividends or interest, as the case may be, paid on the given class of securities. The entire value of the corporate property in each industry has been estimated by adding together the respective values of the funded debt, the preferred stock, and the common stock. In the case of the manufacturing and mining industries, in which a small fraction of the property of the industry still remains in the hands of private entrepreneurs, the total value of the corporate holdings has been increased by a specified ratio in order to estimate the total value of the entire property rights of the owners of the industry. The ratio used in making this adjustment has been determined on the basis of the number of employees working for corporations and for individual entrepreneurs, as shown by the reports of the Bureau of the Census.

Causes for Fluctuations in Values of Industries.

Since the estimates in Table XLIV are based upon sample data, they are of course subject to a considerable margin of error, but it is believed that they are sufficiently accurate to reveal fairly completely the important changes which have taken place in the values of the various industries to their owners. The figures indicate that these values fluctuate widely from year to year. A considerable part of this fluctuation is ascribable to the fact that the purchasing power of the dollar shifted so materially during the 18 years under consideration; but this factor must not be thought of as explaining all of the oscillations. The value of an enterprise always looks to the future rather than to the past; hence the question of whether it is worth much or little to its owners depends primarily upon general anticipations concerning the future income

TABLE XLIV

TOTAL MARKET VALUE AT CLOSE OF YEAR OF THE PROPERTY RIGHTS OF INDIVIDUAL SECURITY OWNERS IN INDUSTRIES DOMINATED BY CORPORATIONS[a]

(MILLIONS OF CURRENT DOLLARS)

December 31	Mines, Quarries and Oil Wells	Factories	Railroads[b]	Pullman	Express	Street Railways	Electric Light and Power	Telephones	Telegraphs
1908	$2,343	$15,403	$16,447	$166	$165	$3,133	$1,641	$ 709	$ 228
1909	2,520	19,585	17,237	185	239	3,361	1,725	759	242
1910	2,544	19,559	17,216	186	193	3,377	1,969	774	231
1911	3,712	21,457	17,096	187	172	3,563	2,345	834	225
1912	4,307	22,876	17,991	193	143	3,682	2,503	931	218
1913	4,387	21,700	16,617	179	101	3,610	2,246	908	192
1914	5,416	22,761	15,364	178	79	3,649	2,376	1,006	188
1915	7,054	31,050	17,712	195	104	3,772	2,692	1,042	229
1916	8,357	32,953	17,165	191	106	3,831	3,359	1,136	219
1917	6,070	29,019	14,256	133	c	3,091	2,665	1,022	195
1918	6,507	35,250	15,550	137	c	3,137	2,782	1,063	221
1919	7,148	41,494	13,762	132	c	2,620	2,629	1,141	217
1920	4,510	36,124	13,519	122	c	2,332	2,679	1,177	223
1921	5,848	36,171	13,717	141	c	2,516	3,457	1,604	243
1922	7,027	38,579	15,596	163	c	3,136	3,958	1,809	309
1923	6,492	38,080	16,446	142	c	3,035	d	2,025	314
1924	8,468	45,416	17,715	166	29	3,442	d	2,332	357
1925	9,500	51,900	20,053	99	28	3,484	d	2,691	392

[a] The totals in this table are the sums of the aggregate market values of funded debt, preferred stock and common stock as recorded in Tables LIII, LIV, LV, and LXXXI.

[b] Includes switching and terminal companies. Based on *Statistics of Railways*, published by the Interstate Commerce Commission.

[c] Information not available.

[d] Because of the extremely rapid changes occurring in this industry reasonably dependable estimates cannot well be made until the data for the 1927 Census become available.

derivable from the ownership of the property in the industry. Market value is, then, necessarily largely dependent upon subjective factors. A change in public sentiment from pessimism to optimism may, for example, increase the value of the manufacturing industry hundreds of millions of dollars in a single day.

As just stated, market values are arrived at on the basis of subjective values, and subjective values, in turn, are in part the result of discounting anticipated future income at a given subjective interest rate. When in general, subjective interest rates are low, the value of the industry is large, and *vice versa*.

The market value of an industry is also affected materially by the action of government. No matter how perfect the physical plant, or how effectively it is operated, the industry may be practically valueless to its owners because of the fact that government is taking most of the net earnings by taxation or is, by rate regulation, preventing the owners from securing any considerable amount of net income. To sum up, then, we may say that the values in Table XLIV are affected by:

1. Prevailing interest rates.
2. Actual volume of physical activity.
3. Optimism or pessimism concerning the future outlook.
4. Public policies as to taxation and rate regulation.

Table XLIV shows that, in 1925, the factories of the United States were worth far more than the steam and electric railways, mines, quarries, and oil wells, and the telephone, telegraph, and electric light and power plants combined. The steam railways had, in turn, a value about double as great as that of all the mines, quarries, and oil wells. The telephone and telegraph equipment of the country was worth nearly as much as the street railways.

Only the Pullman and express, of all the industries covered by the entries in this table, failed to show an increase in current-dollar value between 1908 and 1925. The increases in the nominal value of the other industries have little significance because they fail to take account of the changing value of the dollar. In Table XLV the nominal figures have been deflated in order to eliminate as far as possible the effect of the changing value of gold.

Industries Valued in Terms of Direct Goods.

It is not easy to devise a wholly satisfactory means of deflating the value of an industry. The property used in the operation of the various industries dealt with in Table XLV is of such a complex nature that it is not feasible to find units which are comparable from year to year, and hence there is little chance of constructing index numbers on the basis of articles actually representing the physical wealth of each industry or of all industries combined. Since this method is not practicable, recourse has been had to a procedure which has its advantages and disadvantages. This procedure is to ascertain the comparative physical quantities of direct or consumers' goods which could have been obtained by the owners of the industries in question, at the various dates, had they sold their securities at the market prices prevailing and used the money thus obtained to buy direct goods. This concept is definite and specific.

Changes in the Real Value of Industries.

Table XLV and Charts 32a and 32b show that, during the period 1909 to 1915 inclusive, of the 9 industries included in the table, the aggregate values were increasing in the case of manufacturing, mining, electric light and power, and telephone corporations. The value of the Pullman and street railway industries was almost stationary, while the telegraph and the express industries began declining in value in 1910 and the railroad industry started downward in 1913. In the case of manufacturing, the up-grade movement was terminated before 1916, but the value of the mining industry continued to rise until the following year. From the beginning of 1917 until the end of 1920, the purchasing power of the combined value of all the securities fell off sharply in every one of the industries for which records are available; in other words, the total value of the securities failed to keep pace with the rise in the value of consumers' goods. This decline is doubtless ascribable in part to the high interest rates prevailing during this period, for, other things being equal, the higher the interest rates, the lower the value of securities. This relationship obtains because securities represent anticipated income discounted at some given interest rate, and the interest rate used in the discounting process is likely to be similar to the one prevailing at the time when the discount is calculated. Another reason, probably accounting in part for the decline in real value of corporations between 1917 and 1920 was that security holders were doubtless skeptical that the income of the corporations in the future would increase sufficiently to offset the increase in the price level. A third factor which doubtless played an important rôle was custom. People were accustomed to thinking of corporate income in terms of past experience and did not immediately revise their views. More important still, custom frequently congealed into law and thus, in many cases, prevented price increases—a most notable example being found in the rates charged by railways and public utility corporations. For these three, and perhaps for other reasons, the aggregate value of each of the 9 industries covered continued to fall until the general price level turned downward in 1920. By that time, the factories of the United States had a real value to their owners of only about two-thirds as much and both

TABLE XLV

COMMAND OVER DIRECT OR CONSUMERS' GOODS,
AT 1913 PRICES, GIVEN TO INDIVIDUAL SECURITY OWNERS
BY THE TOTAL MARKET VALUE OF THEIR
PROPERTY RIGHTS
IN INDUSTRIES DOMINATED BY CORPORATIONS[a]

(MILLIONS OF DOLLARS HAVING THE PURCHASING POWER OF 1913)

December 31	Mines, Quarries and Oil Wells	Factories	Railroads[b]	Pullman	Express	Street Railways	Electric Light and Power	Telephones	Telegraphs
1908	$2,502	$16,445	$17,560	$176	$176	$3,345	$1,752	$ 756	$241
1909	2,612	20,300	17,866	191	248	3,484	1,788	784	250
1910	2,622	20,160	17,744	192	199	3,480	2,029	798	238
1911	3,798	21,956	17,493	192	176	3,646	2,400	849	231
1912	4,340	23,049	18,127	194	144	3,709	2,522	939	220
1913	4,341	21,469	16,440	177	99	3,571	2,221	897	190
1914	5,408	22,730	15,343	177	79	3,644	2,373	995	188
1915	6,892	30,334	17,303	190	102	3,685	2,630	1,006	223
1916	7,405	29,199	15,209	171	94	3,394	2,977	990	195
1917	4,768	22,796	11,198	107	c	2,428	2,093	772	156
1918	4,351	23,566	10,396	95	c	2,097	1,860	672	153
1919	4,150	24,091	7,990	80	c	1,521	1,526	628	131
1920	2,533	20,286	7,591	70	c	1,309	1,504	637	128
1921	3,650	22,579	8,562	87	c	1,571	2,158	974	151
1922	4,382	24,058	9,726	101	c	1,955	2,468	1,108	191
1923	4,022	23,673	10,190	88	c	1,881	d	1,224	194
1924	5,226	28,030	10,933	103	13	2,124	d	1,407	220
1925	5,729	31,301	12,094	60	14	2,101	d	1,586	236

a The totals in this table are the sums of the purchasing power in 1913 dollars of the market values of unded debt, preferrred stock and common stock, as recorded in Tables LIX, LX, LXI, and LXXX.

b Includes switching and terminal companies.

c Information not available.

d Because of the extremely rapid changes occurring in this industry reasonably dependable estimates cannot well be made until the data for the 1927 Census become available.

steam and electric railways were worth less than half as much as at the beginning of 1916, and the owners of the Pullman Company had suffered nearly as large a percentage of loss as that last mentioned. The decline in the value of all mining corporations was considerably more than half of their 1917 value. The owners of the telephone industry suffered a smaller loss than most of the others, but, even in their case, the command over consumers' goods was one-third less at the beginning of 1920 than it was at the beginning of 1916.

Between the beginning of 1921 and the end of 1925, the purchasing power represented by the total value of the securities increased markedly in the case of all but two of the industries covered by Table XLV. At the close of 1925, however, the manufacturing and telephone industries, and presumably the private electric light and power industry, were the only ones worth as much to their owners as they had been at some time during the pre-war period. The increase in value in 1925 over that of 1916 was very slight in the case of manufacturing but amounted to approximately 60 per cent in the case of the telephone industry. The telegraph industry was worth somewhat more at the close of 1925 than at the beginning of 1916, but not quite as much as at the beginning of 1910. We have, then, the strange situation in which, although the income of the country as measured in dollars of constant purchasing power had risen materially above the pre-war level, the value of the great corporate industries still remained, at the end of 1925, below the pre-war level in the case of steam and electric railways and the telegraph, Pullman, and express businesses.

Forces Causing the Value of an Industry to Change.

If the price level never changed, if interest rates always remained constant, and if government never stepped in to regulate the prices charged for the output of the industry, it would presumably be true that the total value of the industry to its owners would vary with the demand for its products and the prospective ability of the industry to meet such demand. In general, under such circumstances, we would expect that, when the physical plant of an industry increased, the value of the industry would also increase.

Under existing conditions, an increase in the size of the physical plant normally requires an increase in investment. The industry may draw the excess funds for this additional investment from:

1. Savings within the industry.
2. New money invested by outsiders.

Estimation of Positive and Negative "New Money."

New money may be temporarily secured by borrowing from banks, but such loans are not as a rule continued indefinitely. In order to secure funds for permanent investment, it is ordinarily necessary for the industry, if under corporate control, to sell to the investing public issues of short-term notes, bonds, or preferred or common stocks. Receipts thus obtained account for most of the

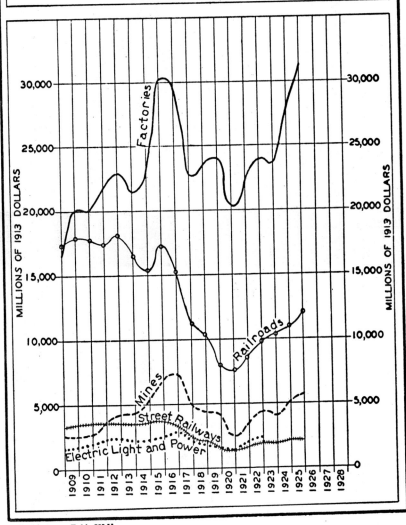

COMMAND OVER DIRECT OR CONSUMERS' GOODS,
AT 1913 PRICES, GIVEN TO INDIVIDUAL
SECURITY OWNERS BY THE TOTAL MARKET
VALUE OF THEIR PROPERTY RIGHTS IN
INDUSTRIES DOMINATED BY CORPORATIONS[a]

ᵃ For data, see Table XLV.

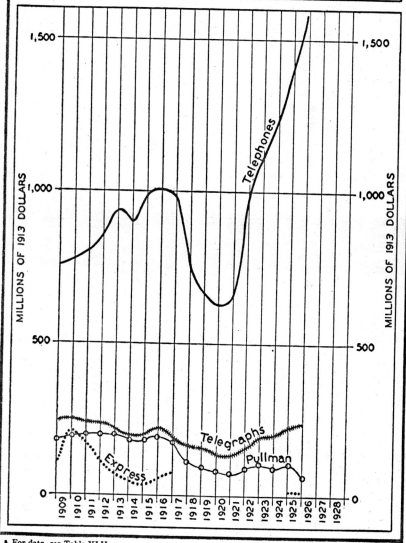

COMMAND OVER DIRECT OR CONSUMERS' GOODS, AT 1913 PRICES, GIVEN TO INDIVIDUAL SECURITY OWNERS BY THE TOTAL MARKET VALUE OF THEIR PROPERTY RIGHTS IN INDUSTRIES DOMINATED BY CORPORATIONS[a]

[a] For data, see Table XLV.

positive entries of new money used in the calculation of the figures in Table XLVI.

If the profits within an industry are large, it is frequently possible for the corporations in the field to use part of their corporate savings to pay off some of their funded debt or even to retire part of their preferred stock. This process is evidently the reverse of that employed when new money is secured. For the purposes of our study, we shall designate amounts thus removed from the industry as "negative new money."

Table XLVI represents the results of an effort to estimate, on the basis of a large number of sample corporations, the "net amount of new money" invested in these corporations during each of the years 1909 to 1925, inclusive. When the amounts invested were larger than the amounts withdrawn from the industry, the sums recorded in the table are positive. When withdrawals exceeded investments, the entries are negative.

Making these estimates proved to be an extremely laborious task. Most corporations are constantly engaged either in retiring certain securities or issuing new ones. Especially for the earlier years, it is extremely difficult to ascertain the terms upon which new securities were issued or old ones retired. The difficulties are still further accentuated by the fact that, in many instances, corporations are consolidated, securities of one being issued to replace the securities of another. Furthermore, securities are often exchanged for property the value of which cannot be estimated with any degree of accuracy. For the reasons just mentioned, it was necessary to study each security of the sample corporations with meticulous care. Poor's *Manuals*, Moody's *Manuals* and *Rating Books*, the records prepared by the Standard Statistics Company, and the files of *The Commercial and Financial Chronicle*, were all ransacked for information. All estimates have been verified by some worker other than the one making the original computations.

While, in the case of many individual securities, the estimates must of necessity be rough, it is believed that the number of corporations studied is large enough in the case of mines, factories, and electric light and power corporations to make the samples reasonably representative of the industry as a whole. An attempt has been made to secure complete data for the telegraph, Pullman, and express industries. The telephone industry is, of course, dominated by the American Telephone and Telegraph Company. The figures for steam railroads are computed from approximately complete

TABLE XLVI

ESTIMATED NET NEW MONEY*
INVESTED BY INDIVIDUAL SECURITY OWNERS
IN INDUSTRIES DOMINATED BY CORPORATIONS[b]
(MILLIONS OF CURRENT DOLLARS)

Year	Mines, Quarries and Oil Wells	Factories	Railroads[c]	Pullman	Express	Street Railways	Electric Light and Power	Telephones	Telegraphs
1909	$112	$1,584	$330	0	0	$148	$114	$ 4	$ −2
1910	384	1,111	432	0	16	162	285	32	0
1911	580	1,930	472	0	d	161	181	62	0
1912	301	268	377	0	d	155	119	77	−8
1913	119	1,002	335	0	−12	120	32	50	0
1914	137	951	−456	0	e	205	150	39	0
1915	198	1,610	−522	0	−6	184	149	8	−1
1916	168	503	65	0	−5	177	184	96	0
1917	133	1,428	364	0	0	163	279	11	0
1918	379	2,084	−193	0	f	44	180	21	0
1919	180	1,869	42	0	f	30	178	129	0
1920	143	627	698	0	f	14	453	36	17
1921	91	1,914	−116	0	f	1	553	192	22
1922	70	352	62	15	0	4	387	81	3
1923	146	248	583	0	0	57	g	182	d
1924	153	−145	473	0	0	62	g	207	d
1925	126	508	−40	0	0	38	g	198	d

* For definition of this term, see text.

[b] The totals in this table are the sums of the new money invested in funded debt, preferred stock, and common stock, as recorded in Tables LVI, LVII, LVIII, and LXXXI.

[c] Includes switching and terminal companies. Based upon *Statistics of Railways* published by the Interstate Commerce Commission.

[d] Positive figure of less than $500,000.

[e] Negative figure of less than $500,000.

[f] Information not available.

[g] Because of the extremely rapid changes occurring in this industry, reasonably dependable estimates cannot well be made until the data for the 1927 Census become available.

data appearing in the various issues of *Statistics of Railways*, published by the United States Interstate Commerce Commission. It is believed, therefore, that the figures for various fields of transportation are reasonably accurate except in the instances given in the footnotes to Table XLVI, and, in so far as the sample corporations are representative, the chances are that the errors in the manufacturing and mining industries are not serious. The sample corporations have necessarily been chosen from among those large enough to have their reports in such Manuals as Moody's and Poor's, and

hence it is possible that they may not be representative of smaller concerns. It is believed, however, that they constitute an adequate sample of the larger corporations.

New Money Measured in Current Dollars.

The supply of new money which corporations have drawn from outside has been extremely variable. As might be expected in the case of a rapidly developing nation like the United States, the general tendency has been to invest far more money than has been withdrawn. Net withdrawals of cash apparently occurred primarily in the railroad, express, and telegraph industries. Throughout the period, the general tendency has been for the manufacturing industry to absorb more investment funds than have mines, quarries, oil wells, and all fields of transportation combined.

Money flowed into the manufacturing industry in large volume during the period 1909 to 1921 inclusive, but, thereafter, the investments in manufacturing became smaller. Investments in the mining industry have, in general, been on a lower level since 1920 than they were before, the lowest point being reached in 1922. *Positive* net investments were made in the railroad industry for each year between 1909 and 1913, inclusive. Since that date, net increases have frequently been followed by net decreases. In street railways, new money flowed in freely during the years 1909 to 1917, inclusive, but remained at a very low level from 1918 to 1922. Since then, the street railways have succeeded in securing a moderate amount of new funds, but not more than one-third as much annually as was customary before the war. The net new money secured by telephone and electric light and power corporations, while variable, has, in general, shown an upward tendency.

New Money Measured in 1913 Dollars.

In Table XLVII the results are given of dividing new money in current dollars by price indices representing the average-for-the-year relative prices of consumers' goods to well-to-do purchasers. From the standpoint of the corporation receiving the new money, this method of deflation is obviously illogical, for it does not picture with any reasonable degree of precision the change taking place in the physical quantity of equipment purchasable by the corporation with the new money received. From the standpoint of the investor, however, the method of deflation followed is thoroughly defensible. The investor is always being compelled to choose between buying

TABLE XLVII

VALUE, IN 1913 DOLLARS, OF THE ESTIMATED NET NEW MONEY[f] INVESTED BY INDIVIDUAL SECURITY OWNERS IN INDUSTRIES DOMINATED BY CORPORATIONS[a]

(MILLIONS OF 1913 DOLLARS)

Year	Mines, Quarries and Oil Wells	Factories	Railroads[b]	Pullman	Express	Street Railways	Electric Light and Power	Telephones	Telegraphs
1909	$119	$1,680	$349	$0	$ 0	$156	$120	$ 4	$—2
1910	397	1,151	447	0	17	167	295	33	0
1911	600	1,997	489	0	c	167	187	64	0
1912	307	274	385	0	c	158	122	79	—9
1913	119	1,002	335	0	—12	120	32	50	0
1914	137	947	—454	0	d	204	150	39	0
1915	198	1,609	—521	0	—6	184	149	8	d
1916	158	473	61	0	—5	167	173	89	0
1917	111	1,188	303	0	0	136	232	9	0
1918	274	1,506	—140	0	c	32	130	15	0
1919	114	1,182	27	0	c	19	113	78	0
1920	79	347	387	0	c	8	251	19	10
1921	54	1,144	—69	0	c	c	330	112	13
1922	50	221	39	9	0	2	243	50	2
1923	91	154	363	0	0	36	g	111	c
1924	95	—90	295	0	0	38	g	127	c
1925	77	310	—24	0	0	23	g	118	

   [a] The totals in this table are the sums of the purchasing power in 1913 dollars of new money invested in funded debt, preferred stock, and common stock as recorded in Tables LXII, LXIII, LXIV, and LXXX.
   [b] Includes switching and terminal companies.
   [c] Positive figure of less than $500,000.
   [d] Negative figure of less than $500,000.
   [e] Information not available.
   [f] For definition of this term, see text
   [g] Because of the extremely rapid changes occurring in this industry reasonably dependable estimates cannot well be made until the data for the 1927 Census become available.

securities and purchasing consumers' goods. The quantities entered in Table XLVII represent, then, the relative amounts of direct or consumers' goods which investors have sacrificed or foregone in the various years in order to finance the needs of the corporations in the fields covered. Even in terms of 1913 dollars, the tendency to invest new money was downward in mining and manufacturing industries between 1918 and 1925. In street railways, the declining tendency began in 1915. Since 1913, investors have shown an increasing tendency to put money into private electric light and power plants, and, since approximately the same date, the trend has also

been upward in the case of the telephone corporations. New investments in the railroad industry were steadily large only during the period 1909 to 1913, and thereafter were highly irregular.

Gains Above New Money in the Values of Industries.

The fact that a business enterprise has changed in value during a given interval of time tells us nothing whatever about whether this change in value has resulted in a gain or loss to the owner. If, for example, an enterprise is worth $10,000 at the beginning of the year and $12,000 at the end of the year, although its value has increased $2000, the owner may still have lost money, for he may have invested in the meantime $3,000 in new money. Similarly, the value of the enterprise might decline from $10,000 to $9,000, but if, in the meantime, the owner had withdrawn $2,000 in cash, the enterprise would still be netting him a gain. What is true of a single enterprise is equally true of an industry as a whole. Table XLVIII represents the facts for the 9 industries data for which are available in a reasonably accurate form.

In arriving at the quantities presented in Table XLVIII, it has been necessary to proceed as follows: The value of the industry has been calculated for the beginning and end of each year and both amounts have been reduced to dollars of constant purchasing power by dividing by the price indices for January 1 and December 31 respectively. Similarly, the new money invested during the year has been converted to terms of the same kind of dollars by dividing by the average-for-the-year price index. The net value of new money invested has then been added to the value of the industry at the beginning of the year, and the sum thus obtained has been subtracted from the value of the industry at the end of the year. The remainder represents the net gain or loss to the owners of the industry arising from changes in the value of the industry, all quantities being expressed in terms of 1913 dollars. The results of calculations of this type are recorded in Table XLVIII.

Gains and losses incurred through fluctuations in the value of the securities have varied tremendously from year to year. In 1915, for example, the owners of the mining industry profited by more than 1⅛ billions of constant dollars, while in 1917 they lost nearly 3 billions of the same dollars. On the other hand, in the manufacturing industry, the owners gained more than 7 billions of the same dollars. Similar wild fluctuations may be observed in the other fields. Certain years are characterized by losses in nearly all

TABLE XLVIII

GAINS,[a] ABOVE NEW MONEY INVESTED, IN VALUE TO INDIVIDUALS, IN TERMS OF 1913 DOLLARS, OF THEIR PROPERTY RIGHTS IN INDUSTRIES DOMINATED BY CORPORATIONS[a]

(MILLIONS OF 1913 DOLLARS)

Year	Mines, Quarries and Oil Wells	Factories	Railroads[b]	Pullman	Express	Street Railways	Electric Light and Power	Telephones	Telegraphs
1909	$ —10	$ 2,818	$ —43	$ 16	$ 107	$ —18	$ —85	$ 29	$ 11
1910	—421	—1,640	—568	c	—59	—171	—54	—13	—12
1911	625	—255	—740	c	—59	—1	184	—8	—7
1912	254	1,023	249	2	—39	—95	c	14	—3
1913	—128	—3,190	—2,022	—17	—10	—258	—333	—93	—30
1914	1,004	383	—643	b	—13	—132	2	58	—3
1915	1,383	7,233	2,482	13	27	—143	108	2	36
1916	381	—1,917	—2,155	—19	24	—458	173	—107	—27
1917	—2,946	—8,936	—4,314	—64	—1	—1,102	—1,116	—232	—39
1918	—741	—855	—663	—12	—7	—362	—363	—118	—3
1919	—336	—754	—2,432	—15	d	—595	—447	—121	—22
1920	—1,811	—4,716	—785	—10	e	—219	—271	—20	—13
1921	1,133	1,291	1,040	17	e	261	326	209	10
1922	726	1,397	1,124	4	e	382	248	23	38
1923	—479	—592	102	—13	e	—110	f	6	3
1924	1,177	4,832	448	15	e	205	f	151	26
1925	452	3,183	1,185	—43	e	—46	f	185	16

[a] Derived from figures presented in Tables LXV, LXVII, and LXIX.

[b] Includes switching and terminal companies. Based upon *Statistics of Railways*, published by the Interstate Commerce Commission.

[c] Positive figure of less than $500,000.

[d] Negative figure of less than $500,000.

[e] For definition of this term, see text.

[f] Because of the extremely rapid changes occurring in this industry, reasonably dependable estimates cannot well be made until the data for the 1927 Census become available.

industries. Among such years are 1910, 1911, 1913, 1917, 1918, 1919, and 1920. In other years, the owners of nearly all industries gained. This was noticeably true in 1921, 1922, and 1924, and to a very considerable extent in 1925. Strangely enough, we see that the years in which owners have profited most from changes in values of their securities have been years characterized by depression rather than by boom. This means that, in such years, security values have either risen while prices of consumers' goods have been falling, or that, if both have fallen, the prices of consumers' goods have fallen the more.

TABLE XLIX

GAINS,[a] ABOVE NEW MONEY INVESTED,
IN VALUE TO INDIVIDUALS, IN TERMS OF
CURRENT DOLLARS, OF THEIR PROPERTY RIGHTS
IN INDUSTRIES DOMINATED BY CORPORATIONS[a]

(MILLIONS OF CURRENT DOLLARS)

Year	Mines, Quarries and Oil Wells	Factories	Railroads[b]	Pullman	Express	Street Railways	Electric Light and Power	Telephones	Telegraphs
1909	$ —9	$ 2,658	$ —41	$ 15	$ 101	$ —17	$ —80	$ 28	$ 10
1910	—407	—1,583	—549	c	—57	—165	—52	—13	—11
1911	604	—246	—715	c	—57	—1	178	—7	—7
1912	248	1,001	243	2	—38	—93	c	14	—3
1913	—128	—3,190	—2,022	—17	—10	—258	—333	—93	—30
1914	1,008	385	—646	b	—13	—132	2	58	—3
1915	1,384	7,239	2,484	13	27	—143	108	2	36
1916	405	—2,040	—2,294	—20	25	—487	184	—116	—29
1917	—3,538	—10,734	—5,182	—76	—1	—1,324	—1,341	—287	—46
1918	—1,025	—1,184	—918	—17	—10	—501	—502	—171	—4
1919	—531	—1,192	—3,846	—23	d	—941	—707	—202	—34
1920	—3,271	—8,515	—1,418	—17	1	—396	—489	—38	—23
1921	1,897	2,161	1,741	29	e	436	545	358	16
1922	1,157	2,227	1,791	7	e	609	395	38	61
1923	—770	—952	163	—21	e	—177	f	10	5
1924	1,889	7,751	719	24	e	329	f	248	42
1925	741	5,216	1,943	—70	e	—75	f	310	26

[a] Derived from figures presented in Tables LXVI, LXVIII, and LXX.
[b] Includes switching and terminal companies.
[c] Positive figure of less than $500,000.
[d] Negative figure of less than $500,000.
[e] For definition of this term, see text.
[f] Because of the extremely rapid changes occurring in this industry, reasonably dependable estimates cannot well be made until the data for the 1927 Census become available.

For convenience in some of the computations that follow, and
in order to facilitate comparison with other figures, the quantities
presented in Table XLVIII have been multiplied by index numbers
representing the prices of direct goods used by the wealthier classes
of families and the results have been entered in Table XLIX.
These entries show the gains above new money invested which have
accrued to all the owners of the 9 industries covered, when such gains
are expressed in terms of gold dollars.

In Table L, there are heterogeneous figures representing the
estimated amount of net gains, in terms of 1913 dollars, which in-

TABLE L

ROUGH ESTIMATE OF NET GAINS[e] TO INDIVIDUALS, IN TERMS OF 1913 DOLLARS,[h] ARISING FROM INCREASES IN THE VALUE OF THEIR PROPERTY RIGHTS IN VARIOUS INDUSTRIES

(MILLIONS OF 1913 DOLLARS)[b]

Year	Agriculture[a]	Construction[b]	Transportation by Water[c]	Power Laundries[b]	Banking[d]	Mercantile[e]	Unclassified[b]	Miscellaneous[f]
1909	$ —1,827	$278	$10	$2	$101	$292	$583	$ —565
1910	1,206	253	37	4	120	475	714	1,199
1911	1,012	180	14	3	111	211	520	441
1912	3,027	239	36	4	94	238	522	—272
1913	—708	69	32	3	55	174	348	529
1914	2,795	86	—1	3	61	138	335	2,036
1915	3,743	114	37	3	69	181	396	32
1916	—4,922	167	99	4	116	247	622	—5,929
1917	—2,998	66	22	4	127	259	712	—6,546
1918	—1,710	24	33	4	140	141	599	—8,177
1919	—930	37	8	5	213	176	764	—2,993
1920	1,097	3	1	3	122	27	470	5,214
1921	—2,396	3	—33	2	73	34	330	12,381
1922	170	72	—12	4	91	206	544	941
1923	—645	152	1	4	100	403	583	—477
1924	—2,013	67	1	4	128	152	550	1,758
1925	—3,243	67	4	5	177	229	768	—1,612

[a] Based upon *Census of Agriculture* and various reports of the U. S. Department of Agriculture.
[b] Based upon ratios of savings to income in mercantile and banking industries.
[c] Based upon *Statistics of Income* published by the U. S. Bureau of Internal Revenue and upon reports of a number of sample corporations.
[d] Based upon reports of the Comptroller of the Currency.
[e] Based upon *Statistics of Income*, published by the U. S. Bureau of Internal Revenue.
[f] Based upon a crude estimate of changing realty values.
[g] For definition of this term, see text.
[h] "1913 Dollars" is an abbreviation for the phrase "dollars having purchasing power equivalent to that which they had in 1913."

dividuals have secured because of their property holdings in various industries not covered in Table XLVIII. The figures for agriculture, while not precisely accurate, are believed to represent general tendencies. The relative dependability of these figures is due to the fact that the United States Department of Agriculture collects annually a large amount of data concerning the value of farm land, crops, and live stock, and, on the basis of these figures, it is possible to approximate the total value of the property represented

TABLE LI

ROUGH ESTIMATE OF NET GAINS
TO INDIVIDUALS, IN TERMS OF CURRENT DOLLARS,
ARISING FROM INCREASES IN THE VALUE OF
THEIR PROPERTY RIGHTS IN VARIOUS INDUSTRIES

(MILLIONS OF CURRENT DOLLARS)[a]

Year	Agri-culture	Con-struc-tion	Trans-portation by Water	Power Laun-dries	Bank-ing	Mer-cantile	Unclas-sified	Mis-cella-neous
1909	$ −1,768	$261	$10	$2	$ 96	$273	$548	$ − 533
1910	1,199	244	36	3	116	457	690	1,158
1911	985	174	13	3	107	203	503	426
1912	2,987	234	35	4	92	233	512	−266
1913	−708	69	32	3	55	174	348	529
1914	2,818	86	−1	3	61	139	338	2,045
1915	3,685	114	37	3	69	180	402	32
1916	−5,453	178	105	5	124	263	678	−6,311
1917	−4,223	80	27	5	153	317	899	−7,863
1918	−2,758	34	46	5	194	201	897	−11,316
1919	−1,716	61	13	8	336	289	1,326	−4,733
1920	2,195	6	2	6	221	51	931	9,414
1921	−3,731	4	−56	4	123	57	575	20,723
1922	252	114	−19	6	145	324	884	1,499
1923	−937	243	2	7	160	643	963	−766
1924	−2,952	108	2	6	206	244	910	2,821
1925	−5,150	110	7	8	289	374	1,297	−2,642

[a] Computed from corresponding items in Table L by multiplying by the appropriate price indices recorded in Table VII.

by the farms of the United States and the equipment thereon. The values originally expressed in terms of dollars current in the given year have been converted to dollars of 1913 purchasing power by dividing by indices representing the relative values of those consumers' goods purchased by the farmers of the United States.

Since the Comptroller of the Currency gives annually figures covering most of the banks of the United States, it is believed that the data for the banking industry are not widely in error, although attention should be called to the fact that many private banks do not report to the Comptroller of the Currency, and hence their assets are excluded from these totals. Unfortunately, the data for the industries other than agriculture and banking are calculated from data so fragmentary and on the basis of so many hypotheses, that they are here presented merely for what they are worth.

TABLE LII

ESTIMATED TOTAL INCOME[e] OF THE PEOPLE
OF THE CONTINENTAL UNITED STATES INCLUDING
INCREASES IN THE TOTAL VALUE OF PRIVATE PROPERTY

YEAR	INCOME IN 1913 DOLLARS				INCOME IN CURRENT DOLLARS			
	GAINS IN PURCHASING POWER OF PROPERTY VALUES[a] (MILLIONS)	ENTIRE REALIZED INCOME[b] (MILLIONS)	TOTAL INCOME		GAINS IN PURCHASING POWER OF PROPERTY VALUES[c] (MILLIONS)	ENTIRE REALIZED INCOME[d] (MILLIONS)	TOTAL INCOME	
			Of All People (Millions)	Per Capita			Of All People (Millions)	Per Capita
1909	$ 1,700	$31,300	$33,000	$365	$ 1,553	$29,605	$31,158	$344
1910	1,071	32,380	33,450	362	1,066	31,430	32,496	352
1911	2,230	32,920	35,150	375	2,162	31,858	34,020	363
1912	5,294	34,656	39,950	419	5,205	33,977	39,182	411
1913	−5,578	35,756	30,178	311	−5,578	35,723	30,145	310
1914	6,109	35,250	41,358	418	6,150	35,647	41,798	422
1915	15,714	36,636	52,351	521	15,672	37,205	52,877	527
1916	−13,699	39,559	25,860	254	−14,781	43,288	28,506	280
1917	−27,104	40,242	13,138	127	−33,135	51,331	18,196	176
1918	−12,071	40,150	28,079	269	−17,028	60,408	43,380	416
1919	−7,442	38,017	30,575	291	−11,891	65,949	54,058	515
1920	−908	37,573	36,666	345	−1,340	73,999	72,659	683
1921	14,681	36,710	51,392	474	24,884	63,371	88,254	814
1922	5,958	40,565	46,523	424	9,490	65,925	75,416	687
1923	−1,021	45,164	44,141	396	−1,518	74,337	72,819	653
1924	7,945	46,758	54,703	482	13,056	77,135	90,191	795
1925	1,969	48,412	50,381	437	3,438	81,931	85,369	741

[a] Derived from Tables XLVIII and L.
[b] See Table IX.
[c] Derived from Tables XLIX and LI.
[d] See Table VIII.
[e] For definition of this term, see text.

The same inaccuracies appearing in Table L are found, to an extent perhaps even greater, in Table LI. In this table, the amounts expressed in dollars of constant purchasing power have been converted into dollars current in the various years, and hence an additional error may have arisen from defects in the index numbers used in the multiplying process.

The Total Income of the Inhabitants.

The purpose of Tables L and LI is to arrive at some estimate of the total income of the people of the Continental United States,

CHART 33

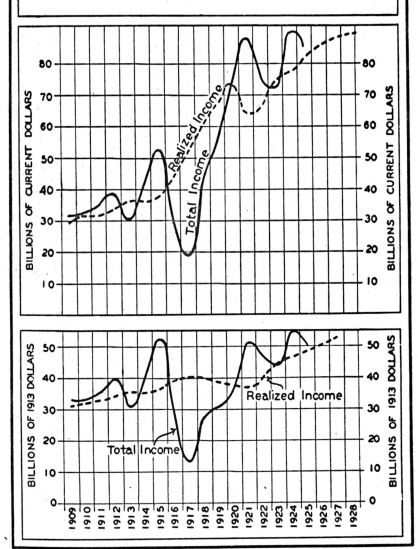

COMPARISON OF TOTAL INCOME, INCLUDING
INCREASES IN THE TOTAL VALUE OF PRIVATE
PROPERTY, AND ENTIRE REALIZED INCOME
OF THE PEOPLE OF THE CONTINENTAL UNITED
STATES[a]

[a] For data, see Table LII.

since no estimate of the income of individuals is complete which fails to take into consideration year-to-year changes in the value of the property which they own. In Table LII, we find estimates of the total income of the people of the United States expressed both in terms of dollars of constant purchasing power and in terms of the dollars current in the various years. The results are more easily comprehended from the graphs in Chart 33.

They show that, while the entire realized income pursues a relatively stable course, the total income, because of the extreme changes occurring in the value of property used in the business enterprises of the United States, fluctuates violently, showing very large cyclical oscillations. Presumably, over any considerable period of time, if the estimates are correct, the figures for total income should tend, on the average, to lie above the figures for entire realized income, the difference between the trends of the two graphs representing total business savings. Actually, however, the depression in total income covering the years 1916, 1917, 1918, and 1919 as shown in Chart 33 is so great that it practically offsets all of the gains in other years. This leads one to question the validity of the calculations. The appearance of the graphs makes it seem not impossible that the losses in the years 1916 to 1919 have been estimated at too high a figure. It will be seen that, in general, peaks in total income tend to be reached during or immediately after periods of depression rather than in boom years. Were the figures in Table LII based upon dependable data, the results appearing in that table and in Chart 33 would necessarily be considered of the very highest significance. Because, however, of the possibility of large errors in the figures, we are not justified in attaching much importance to these findings.

CHAPTER X

GAINS AND LOSSES OF INVESTORS IN EACH OF THE THREE CLASSES OF SECURITIES

In marked contrast to the figures in Tables L to LII inclusive, stand the entries in Table LIII to LV, for the latter are based upon evidence which is believed in most instances to be reasonably accurate.

The Net Funded Debt Valued in Current Dollars.

The data in Table LIII represent the approximate market value at the close of each year of that part of the corporate funded debt which is in the hands of individuals. In some industries we do not know just what proportion of the funded debt was in the hands of individuals, and hence there may be considerable error in comparing industry with industry, especially in the earlier years. The year-to-year comparisons for any given industry are, however, not affected by this error, and are believed to be reasonably dependable. The figures have been arrived at by ascertaining the average price per thousand dollar unit outstanding in the case of all securities quoted for the leading corporations. This average has been applied to all corporations in the field by relating it to our estimates of the total par value of the funded debt in the hands of individuals and also to the estimated total amount of interest paid to individuals.

The figures indicate that, as far as funded debt is concerned, railroad securities are decidedly in the forefront, their total market value at the end of 1925 being almost as great as the combined market value of this class of securities in the 7 other industries covered. At the end of 1928, their position was even more preeminent. Manufacturing concerns, electric light and power companies, and street railways had funded debts next in magnitude, when measured in terms of total market value at the end of 1925. At the same date, the funded debts of mining companies and of telephone companies were about equal in importance. In practically all cases, the general trend of the total market value of the funded debts, as expressed in current dollars, has been upward throughout the period. The most marked increases have occurred in the case of manufacturing and mining corporations, telegraph

225

TABLE LIII

ESTIMATED MARKET VALUE AT CLOSE OF YEAR OF THAT PART OF THE CORPORATE FUNDED DEBT WHICH WAS IN THE HANDS OF INDIVIDUALS[a]
(MILLIONS OF CURRENT DOLLARS)

December 31	Factories	Mines, Quarries and Oil Wells	Railroads[c]	Express	Street Railways	Electric Light and Power	Telephones	Telegraphs
1908	$3,295	$ 287	$8,518	$33	$1,554	$ 579	$ 330	$48
1909	3,362	321	8,755	33	1,667	658	261	49
1910	3,405	329	8,772	33	1,706	700	299	47
1911	3,541	351	8,985	30	1,830	800	298	45
1912	3,540	384	8,965	29	1,919	858	370	40
1913	3,446	386	8,769	14	1,993	756	412	38
1914	3,388	416	8,309	14	2,072	745	471	41
1915	3,565	458	9,592	16	2,192	908	440	42
1916	3,762	507	9,483	15	2,266	994	525	34
1917	3,514	499	8,228	12	1,925	1,084	461	27
1918	3,637	553	8,535	b	1,994	1,266	508	34
1919	3,596	597	7,877	b	1,655	1,251	613	33
1920	3,400	589	7,989	b	1,484	1,412	630	34
1921	3,749	754	8,946	b	1,711	1,935	810	39
1922	3,799	867	9,480	b	2,087	2,127	792	59
1923	3,924	911	10,289	b	1,982	2,426	912	53
1924	4,277	1,035	10,586	b	2,222	2,806	938	54
1925	4,398	1,108	11,557	b	2,166	3,257	1,114	55

[a] Based upon the average price of corporate securities in each industry, as determined from large samples, and upon the data presented in Table XL showing the total par value in each field.
[b] No funded debt outstanding.
[c] Includes switching and terminal companies.

companies, and electric light and power plants, the funded securities of the mining and telephone corporations having trebled in value and those of the electric light and power plants having grown more than five fold.

The Net Preferred Stock Valued in Current Dollars.

Table LIV contains similar figures for the preferred stock of 6 different classes of corporations. It was not feasible to estimate separately the total market value of the preferred stocks and common stocks of railway corporations, hence the figures for this industry are missing. The 6 industries covered are completely dominated by the preferred stocks of manufacturing corporations,

TABLE LIV

ESTIMATED MARKET VALUE AT CLOSE OF YEAR OF THAT PART OF THE PREFERRED STOCK OF CORPORATIONS WHICH WAS IN THE HANDS OF INDIVIDUALS[a]

(MILLIONS OF CURRENT DOLLARS)

December 31	Factories	Mines, Quarries and Oil Wells	Street Railways	Electric Light and Power	Telephones	Telegraphs
1908	$4,599	$ 55	$251	$ 57	$20	$35
1909	5,232	81	282	80	26	39
1910	5,122	64	273	108	24	38
1911	5,333	102	296	127	27	35
1912	5,544	128	322	146	28	34
1913	5,344	114	264	140	25	33
1914	5,444	110	255	172	24	34
1915	6,438	174	233	188	28	33
1916	6,902	159	235	202	29	33
1917	6,344	149	189	165	29	29
1918	6,950	244	206	220	26	32
1919	7,561	260	189	285	24	32
1920	6,749	244	165	287	29	33
1921	7,092	299	180	336	41	38
1922	8,233	299	246	431	59	46
1923	8,189	294	315	b	65	49
1924	8,936	307	308	b	80	53
1925	9,577	302	311	b	88	54

[a] Based upon the average price of preferred stock in each industry, as determined from large samples and upon the data presented in Table XLI showing the total par value in each field.

[b] Because of the extremely rapid changes occurring in this industry, reasonably dependable estimates cannot well be made until the data for the 1927 Census become available.

but the rate of growth in the total market value of preferred stock in the hands of individuals has been greater in the case of mines, quarries, and oil wells, electric light and power plants, and telegraph and telephone companies than it has been in the case of concerns operating factories. The total market value of the preferred stock of street railways has increased but slowly. It is the only one of the fields in which the total value was very greatly depressed during 1920 and 1921.

It is interesting to note that the preferred stock of manufacturing corporations was, at the close of 1925, worth twice as much as the funded debt of corporations in that industry. On the other hand, the funded debt was many times more valuable than the preferred stock in the case of each other industry for which records are available, except in the case of telegraph companies, in which both funded debt and preferred stock had approximately equal values.

The Net Common Stock Valued in Current Dollars.

In Table LV are estimates of the total market value in each of the specified industries of the common stock then in the hands of individuals. As might be expected, the aggregate value of the common stock is, in most cases, far larger than the aggregate value of the preferred stock. In manufacturing, at the end of 1925, common stocks were worth, *in toto*, 4 times as much as the preferred stocks and nearly 9 times as much as the bonds. In mining, the common stocks had a market value 26 times as great as the preferred stock, but only about 7 times as great as the funded debt. The common stocks of street railways, however, at the same date, would sell for only about 3 times as much as the preferred stocks and half as much as the funded debt. In the case of electric light and power corporations, common stocks and funded debt were nearly equal in value. The preferred stock issued by telephone corporations is insignificant in amount, while the common stock has an aggregate value somewhat greater than the total value of the funded debt. In the case of telegraph companies, preferred stock and funded debt were about equal in total value at the end of 1925, but the common stock was worth about 5 times as much as either one of the other types of securities. The figures just cited make it obvious that different fields of industry behave very differently in their methods of financing.

The total value of the common stock in the hands of individuals has shown a remarkable growth in manufacturing and mining corporations. The stock of the Pullman Company was worth no more at the end of 1924 than at the end of 1908. The sharp decline in the aggregate value as recorded for the end of 1925 is due to the split up of the Pullman Company into manufacturing and operating sections—the latter only being included in this account. The common stock of all the street railways in the United States was worth much less in 1925 than at the end of 1908, though its value rose greatly between 1921 and 1925. The aggregate value of the common stock of electric light and power companies has fluctuated greatly, rising markedly between 1909 and 1916, then declining sharply until 1920, after which it rose rapidly until the end of 1925.

TABLE LV

ESTIMATED MARKET VALUE AT CLOSE OF YEAR OF THAT PART OF THE COMMON STOCK OF CORPORATIONS WHICH WAS IN THE HANDS OF INDIVIDUALS

(MILLIONS OF CURRENT DOLLARS)

December 31	Factories[a]	Mines, Quarries and Oil Wells[a]	Pullman[b]	Express[b]	Street Railways[c]	Electric Light and Power[c]	Telephones[c]	Telegraphs[d]
1908	$ 7,509	$2,001	$166	$132	$1,329	$1,005	$ 358	$145
1909	10,992	2,118	185	205	1,412	988	472	155
1910	11,033	2,150	186	160	1,397	1,161	451	147
1911	12,584	3,259	187	141	1,437	1,418	508	146
1912	13,792	3,795	193	114	1,440	1,498	532	144
1913	12,910	3,887	179	87	1,353	1,350	471	121
1914	13,929	4,889	178	65	1,322	1,459	510	114
1915	21,046	6,422	195	89	1,347	1,596	574	154
1916	22,289	7,692	191	91	1,329	2,163	582	152
1917	19,161	5,422	133	*	977	1,416	532	138
1918	24,663	5,711	137	*	937	1,296	529	155
1919	30,336	6,291	132	*	775	1,093	505	152
1920	25,975	3,678	122	*	683	980	518	156
1921	25,330	4,795	141	*	625	1,186	753	166
1922	26,547	5,862	163	*	803	1,401	958	204
1923	25,967	5,287	142	*	738	1,553	1,048	211
1924	32,203	7,126	166	29[f]	912	2,296	1,313	250
1925	37,925	8,090	99	28[f]	1,007	3,806	1,489	284

[a] Based upon the average price of common stock in each industry, as determined from large samples and upon the par values of all common stock or the total dividends paid in the specified industries.

[b] Based upon *Preliminary Abstracts of Statistics of Common Carriers*, publ'shed by the Interstate Commerce Commission and upon the average prices per share quoted in the financial journals.

[c] Based upon the *Censuses of Electrical Industries* and upon the prices of securities as quoted in the financial journals.

[d] Based upon the reports of various telegraph companies and upon the prices of stocks quoted in the financial journals.

[*] Information not available.

[f] Based upon the market value of American Railway Express stock.

The value of the entire common stock of telephone and telegraph corporations has, on the other hand, been characterized by a relatively high degree of stability, increasing steadily throughout the period.

The aggregate market value of all the common stock of manufacturing corporations was approximately 5 times and that of mining corporations approximately 4 times as great at the end of 1925 as at the end of 1908. The increase in the total market value of the common stock of electric light and power companies was in approximately the same proportion applying to mines, quarries, and oil wells, and the same may be said of the change in the value of the common stock of telephone corporations. The common stock of telegraph companies doubled in value during the period, while the aggregate for street railways diminished by about one-third. The fact should be kept in mind that all of the aggregate values described in Tables LIII, LIV, and LV are expressed in terms of current dollars.

The Effect of Security Conversion Upon Estimates of New Money

In Table XLVI, we found estimates of the total amount of new money invested by individuals in those leading industrial fields dominated by corporations. This "net new money" was, however, invested in various types of securities. Tables LVI, LVII, and LVIII furnish the basic information used in the construction of Table XLVI. In considering the data entered in the three tables just mentioned, it is necessary to take into account the fact that frequently one security is converted into another. It is, for example, especially common to convert bonds into stock. In such instances, for purposes of our computations, it has been assumed that money is paid out on the bonds and received on the stock. In other words, the amount transferred is entered as a negative quantity under the heading of new money for funded debt, and as a positive quantity under the heading of new money for stock. In Tables LVII and LVIII no data are found for railways. The reason for this omission is that the reports of the Interstate Commerce Commission are in such a form that it is not easy to distinguish between investments of new money in preferred stock, and similar investments in common stock. Owing to lack of available time, it has been found necessary to omit the analysis of individual railway corporations in this connection, and hence the segregated data do not appear in these tables. An estimate of the net amount of new money invested in all railway stocks appears, however, in Table LXXXI.

Investments of New Money in Funded Debt (Current Dollars).

Table LVI shows that, of the industries therein listed, electric light and power companies and railways have, during recent years, been the leading consumers of new money for funded debt, although, in both 1923 and 1924, the manufacturing industry absorbed a large amount of this type of capital, and the telephone industry also

TABLE LVI

ESTIMATED NET NEW MONEY[f] INVESTED BY INDIVIDUALS IN THE FUNDED DEBT OF CORPORATIONS
(MILLIONS OF CURRENT DOLLARS)

Year	Factories[a]	Mines, Quarries and Oil Wells[a]	Railroads[a,d]	Street Railways[a]	Electric Light and Power[a]	Telephones[a]	Telegraphs[a]
1909	$46	$22	$483	$100	$ 73	$ -81	$-2
1910	77	27	641	100	63	50	0
1911	86	28	538	116	84	17	0
1912	—4	24	265	107	67	66	—8
1913	42	30	250	72	—79	55	0
1914	74	29	39	126	9	48	0
1915	75	28	--210	162	131	—56	—1
1916	76	34	—99	156	125	75	0
1917	72	40	—32	145	213	—32	0
1918	50	39	—119	29	141	20	0
1919	75	48	95	25	72	136	0
1920	31	60	667	10	333	42	0
1921	0	65	102	—3	368	71	15
1922	— 93	52	213	—2	210	—53	0
1923	223	85	689	45	383	119	0
1924	210	122	463	49	268	—1	0
1925	9	77	102	23	398	147	•

[a] Sources of information are the same as those referred to in Table XL.
[b] Negative figure of less than $500,000.
[c] No information available.
[d] Includes switching and terminal companies.
[e] Positive figure of less than $500,000.
[f] For definition of this term, see text.

attracted extensive additional money for investment in funded debt in 1923 and 1925. In general, the investment of money in the bonds of electric light and power companies increased rapidly between 1914 and 1921, since which date the flow has remained upon a high level. Investment in the funded debt of street railways, on the other hand, declined rapidly between 1915 and 1921, and up to the end of 1925 had risen but slowly.

Investments of New Money in Preferred Stock (Current Dollars).

Figures in Table LVII show the net amount of new money invested by individuals in the preferred stock of various groups of corporations. Most of the money put into this type of security has

TABLE LVII

ESTIMATED NET NEW MONEY[c] INVESTED BY INDIVIDUALS IN THE PREFERRED STOCK OF CORPORATIONS

(MILLIONS OF CURRENT DOLLARS)

Year	Factories[a]	Mines, Quarries and Oil Wells[a]	Street Railways[a]	Electric Light and Power[a]	Tele-phones[a]	Tele-graphs[a]
1909	$154	$18	$18	$25	$ 5	$0
1910	244	20	13	33	—1	0
1911	220	22	15	29	4	0
1912	168	19	25	13	1	0
1913	264	19	18	25	—1	0
1914	197	19	7	26	—2	0
1915	230	22	6	9	2	0
1916	321	21	9	20	b	0
1917	344	21	6	13	2	0
1918	211	22	4	24	2	0
1919	252	19	4	65	2	0
1920	177	35	4	76	3	6
1921	180	16	4	59	17	3
1922	257	16	4	23	18	0
1923	165	16	b	d	16	0
1924	222	14	b	d	19	0
1925	192	19	—1	d	5	0

[a] Sources of information are same as those referred to in Table XLI.
[b] Negative figure of less than $500,000.
[c] For definition of this term, see text.
[d] Because of the extremely rapid changes occurring in the industry, reasonably dependable estimates cannot be made until the data for the 1927 Census become available.

gone into manufacturing. There has, however, been a growing tendency toward this form of investment in the case of electric light and power companies and telephone companies. Although new investments in the preferred stock of street railways were never very large, they fell off approximately two-thirds during the period 1913 to 1918, and remained at a very low level until the last date recorded.

Investments of New Money in Common Stock (Current Dollars).

Table LVIII makes it plain that the volume of new money invested in common stocks during the years preceding 1926 has been far larger than the amount invested either in funded debt or in preferred stock. Furthermore, the heavy investments of new

TABLE LVIII

ESTIMATED NET NEW MONEY[a] INVESTED BY INDIVIDUALS
IN THE COMMON STOCK OF CORPORATIONS

(MILLIONS OF CURRENT DOLLARS)

Year	Fac-tories[b]	Mines, Quarries and Oil Wells[b]	Pull-man[b]	Ex-press[b]	Street Rail-ways[b]	Electric Light and Power[b]	Tele-phones[b]	Tele-graphs[b]
1909	$1,385	$ 72	$ 0	$ 0	$30	$16	$80	$ 0
1910	790	336	0	16	49	188	−18	0
1911	1,624	530	0	c	31	68	42	0
1912	105	257	0	c	23	39	10	0
1913	696	69	0	c	30	85	−3	0
1914	681	89	0	c	72	116	−7	0
1915	1,306	148	0	−5	16	9	61	0
1916	106	114	0	−4	12	39	22	0
1917	1,012	73	0	c	12	52	42	0
1918	1,823	318	0	c	10	16	d	0
1919	1,542	114	0	c	1	41	−9	0
1920	419	49	0	c	1	45	−8	11
1921	1,735	10	0	0	c	126	104	4
1922	188	11	15	0	2	153	116	3
1923	−140	45	0	0	12	161	56	c
1924	−577	16	0	0	13	211	190	c
1925	307	29	0	0	15	399	46	c

a For definition of this term, see text.
b Sources of information are same as those referred to in Table LV.
c Positive figure of less than $500,000.
d Negative figure of less than $500,000.
e No information available.

money in common stock have all tended to be concentrated in the
field of mining, most of it doubtless going into the petroleum business. While the amount of new money furnished to individuals for
common stock fluctuated radically from year to year, the general
tendency was to put approximately a billion dollars a year into
manufacturing corporations during the period 1909 to 1921. After
the last mentioned date, there was a very marked decline in this regard, 1923 and 1924 showing actually more money withdrawn than
invested. In general, the same tendencies as regards investments
have been shown in mining corporations as in the case of manufacturing corporations, but, in mining, the decline in investment
began as early as 1919. In the street railway and electric light and
power fields, there was a tendency for the amount invested in com-

mon stocks to fall off between 1910 and 1918. Since 1918, electric light and power stocks have found favor with the public, and their output has multiplied remarkably. Investment in street railway stocks, on the other hand, diminished almost to the zero point in 1921, but has since risen slightly. The year 1921, the end of the period of large investment in manufacturing, marked the beginning of the period of large investment in the common stock of telephone corporations. The tendency for individuals to put more money into the last mentioned class of stocks was maintained between 1921 and 1925.

We have already seen how the owners of various industries have fared at different times during the period 1908 to 1925, but, in the case of industries dominated by corporations, the investors are not necessarily to be considered as a single group. The interests of the holders of the funded debt may not be identical with those of the preferred or common stockholders. In some industries, one group furnishes most of the money, and in other industries another. It is, therefore, a matter of interest to see how the market values of each of these 3 great classes of securities have varied in the different industrial fields.

The Net Funded Debt Valued in 1913 Dollars.

Table LIX gives the approximate total value of the funded debt of the corporations in several important industries at the close of each year. The figures have been compiled on the assumption that each unit of the funded debt outstanding has the same value as an identical unit which happens to be bought or sold at or near the date mentioned. All quantities are expressed in terms of command over direct goods; in other words, the figures represent the comparative physical quantities of consumers' goods that could have been purchased with the total nominal value of the funded debt at each date mentioned. A study of Table LIX indicates that, at the close of 1908, the funded debt of railroads was worth far more and, in 1925 nearly as much as the funded debt of all the other 7 classes of corporations covered by this table. As regards funded debt, therefore, the railways have occupied a position of first importance throughout the entire 18 years. During the same period, also, manufacturing corporations have occupied second place. Until 1920, the third place was filled by street railways, but, since that date, the total funded debt of electric light and power companies has been more valuable than that of street railways.

TABLE LIX

MARKET VALUE, IN 1913 DOLLARS,[a] OF THAT PART OF THE CORPORATE FUNDED DEBT WHICH WAS IN THE HANDS OF INDIVIDUALS

(MILLIONS OF DOLLARS' WORTH OF DIRECT OR CONSUMERS' GOODS PURCHASABLE THEREWITH AT 1913 PRICES)[b]

December 31	Factories	Mines, Quarries and Oil Wells	Railroads[c]	Express	Street Railways	Electric Light and Power	Telephones	Telegraphs
1908	$3,518	$307	$ 9,094	$35	$1,659	$ 618	$352	$51
1909	3,484	333	9,074	35	1,728	682	270	50
1910	3,509	340	9,041	34	1,758	721	308	49
1911	3,623	359	9,194	31	1,873	819	303	46
1912	3,566	387	9,033	30	1,933	865	374	41
1913	3,410	382	8,675	14	1,972	748	407	38
1914	3,383	416	8,297	14	2,069	744	466	41
1915	3,483	448	9,370	15	2,141	887	425	41
1916	3,333	449	8,402	13	2,008	880	458	30
1917	2,761	392	6,464	9	1,512	852	348	22
1918	2,431	370	5,706	d	1,333	846	321	23
1919	2,088	347	4,573	d	961	726	338	20
1920	1,909	331	4,486	d	834	793	341	19
1921	2,340	471	5,584	d	1,068	1,208	492	24
1922	2,369	540	5,912	d	1,302	1,326	485	36
1923	2,431	564	6,375	d	1,228	1,503	552	33
1924	2,639	639	6,534	d	1,371	1,732	566	33
1925	2,653	668	6,970	d	1,306	1,964	657	33

a "1913 Dollars" is an abbreviation for the phrase "dollars having purchasing power equivalent to that which they had in 1913."

b Computed from corresponding items in Table LIII by dividing by the appropriate price indices recorded in Table VII.

c Includes switching and terminal companies.

d No funded debt outstanding.

The trends of the aggregate market values of the funded debts of the companies in the different industries have been anything but uniform. In manufacturing, the total command over consumers' goods represented by the aggregate funded debt remained about constant between 1908 and 1915, then declined abruptly until the close of 1920, and, after that date, rose moderately until the close of 1925. However, at the end of 1925, all the bond and mortgage holders in the manufacturing industry held securities worth but about three-quarters as much as the total value outstanding in the same industry at the end of 1909. The market value of the funded

TABLE LX

MARKET VALUE, IN 1913 DOLLARS,[a] OF THAT PART OF THE PREFERRED STOCK OF CORPORATIONS WHICH WAS IN THE HANDS OF INDIVIDUALS

(MILLIONS OF DOLLARS' WORTH OF DIRECT OR CONSUMERS' GOODS PURCHASABLE THEREWITH AT 1913 PRICES)[b]

December 31	Factories	Mines, Quarries and Oil Wells	Street Railways	Electric Light and Power	Telephones	Telegraphs
1908	$4,910	$ 59	$268	$ 61	$22	$37
1909	5,423	83	292	83	27	40
1910	5,279	66	282	111	25	39
1911	5,457	105	303	130	28	35
1912	5,586	129	325	147	28	34
1913	5,286	113	261	138	24	32
1914	5,436	110	255	172	24	33
1915	6,290	170	228	184	27	32
1916	6,116	141	209	179	25	29
1917	4,983	117	148	130	22	23
1918	4,646	163	138	147	16	22
1919	4,390	151	110	165	13	19
1920	3,790	137	93	161	16	19
1921	4,427	187	112	210	25	23
1922	5,134	186	153	269	36	28
1923	5,074	182	195	c	39	31
1924	5,515	189	190	c	48	33
1925	5,776	182	188	c	52	32

[a] "1913 Dollars" is an abbreviation for the phrase "dollars having purchasing power equivalent to that which they had in 1913."

[b] Computed from corresponding items in Table LIV by dividing by the appropriate price indices recorded in Table VII.

[c] Because of the extremely rapid changes occurring in the industry, reasonably dependable estimates cannot be made until the data for the 1927 Census become available.

debt of both steam and electric railways has shown about the same trend as manufacturing, the decline in the aggregate market value amounting to about 23 per cent in the case of the steam railways and 21 per cent in the case of the electric railways. The purchasing power of the securities of the telegraph companies has shown a shrinkage even greater in proportion, the decline amounting to over one-third. On the other hand, the aggregate market value of the funded debt, when reduced to dollars of constant purchasing power, increased more than 80 per cent in the case of telephone companies, more than doubled in the case of mining corporations and trebled in the case of electric light and power corporations.

The Net Preferred Stock Valued in 1913 Dollars.

The market value of preferred stock in 1913 dollars has undergone no such shrinkage as has characterized the funded debt. Investors in the preferred stock of manufacturing corporations, when considered *en masse*, found their holdings somewhat more valuable at the end of 1925 than at the end of 1909. The total holdings of preferred stockholders in telegraph companies were worth slightly less at the close of 1925 than at the close of 1908, but the only marked decline is found in the case of street railways, in which a 30 per cent shrinkage is apparent. The aggregate market value of the preferred stock of mining corporations more than trebled during the 17 years. The upward trend in the case of telephone companies was slightly less regular, but preferred stocks of electric light and power corporations showed gains even greater than those of mining corporations.

The value of the preferred stocks of manufacturing corporations has, throughout the period of the investigation, been equal to several times the total value of all the preferred stocks in all of the other 5 industries studied. Unfortunately, it is not possible to make a comparison with the railway industry, because of the fact that computations have not been made for this field. In 1925, the preferred stock of the manufacturing corporations was valued at approximately twice as much as the funded debt of the corporations in the same industry. In the other industries, the value of the preferred stock issue is in no case as large as the value of the funded debt.

The Net Common Stock Valued in 1913 Dollars.

Table LXI furnishes an opportunity to compare the value of the common stock with that of the other securities. The value of the common stock of manufacturing corporations far exceeded that of the common stock of the other seven industries listed. Railway corporations, for reasons before stated, have been excluded from the list. At the close of 1925, in every industry studied, the common stock was, as a whole, worth more than either the funded debt or the preferred stock. The common stock of the corporations in the manufacturing industry had, in fact, a market value nearly 9 times as great as the funded debt in the same industry. The ratio in the case of corporations engaged in the operation of mines, quarries, and oil wells was almost as great. The aggregate value of the funded

TABLE LXI

MARKET VALUE, IN 1913 DOLLARS,ᵃ OF THAT PART OF THE COMMON STOCK OF CORPORATIONS WHICH WAS IN THE HANDS OF INDIVIDUALS

(MILLIONS OF DOLLARS' WORTH OF DIRECT OR CONSUMERS' GOODS PURCHASABLE THEREWITH AT 1913 PRICES)ᵇ

December 31	Factories	Mines, Quarries and Oil Wells	Pullman	Express	Street Railways	Electric Light and Power	Telephones	Telegraphs
1908	$ 8,017	$2,136	$176	$141	$1,419	$1,073	$383	$153
1909	11,393	2,195	191	213	1,464	1,024	487	160
1910	11,372	2,216	192	165	1,440	1,196	465	151
1911	12,876	3,335	192	144	1,470	1,451	518	150
1912	13,896	3,824	194	115	1,451	1,510	537	145
1913	12,772	3,845	177	86	1,339	1,335	465	120
1914	13,910	4,882	177	65	1,321	1,457	504	114
1915	20,561	6,274	190	87	1,316	1,559	555	150
1916	19,749	6,815	171	80	1,178	1,917	507	136
1917	15,052	4,259	107	°	767	1,111	402	111
1918	16,488	3,818	95	°	626	867	334	107
1919	17,613	3,652	80	°	450	635	278	92
1920	14,586	2,065	70	°	383	550	281	89
1921	15,812	2,993	87	°	390	740	457	103
1922	16,555	3,655	101	°	501	873	587	126
1923	16,168	3,276	88	°	457	962	634	131
1924	19,875	4,398	103	18	563	1,417	793	154
1925	22,873	4,879	60	17	608	2,295	878	171

ᵃ "1913 Dollars" is an abbreviation for the phrase "dollars having purchasing power equivalent to that which they had in 1913."

ᵇ Computed from corresponding items in Table LV by dividing by the appropriate price indices recorded in Table VII.

° No information available.

debt of street railways, however, was more than twice as great as the value of the common stock.

The equity belonging to the common stockholders in the manufacturing industry is shown to have been nearly 3 times as great at the end of 1925 as at the end of 1908. The similar equity belonging to the common stockholders in the mining industry more than doubled during the same period. In both industries, a peak, as far as aggregate values is concerned, was reached in the period shortly preceding the entrance of the United States into the World War. The decline from this peak was, however, much more marked in mining companies than in manufacturing. At the end of 1920,

all of the common stock in mining corporations could have been purchased for a value in constant dollars amounting to less than one third of what it was worth at the end of 1916. At the low point at the close of 1920, however, the common stock of manufacturing corporations still had an aggregate command over consumers' goods approximately two-thirds as great as it had at the close of the high point in 1915. In the later years of the period under consideration, factory and mining stocks each showed a large gain in aggregate market value. This gain, in the case of the concerns engaged in manufacturing, was sufficient to overtop the peak of 1915.

The period 1908 to 1925 was characterized by a marked shrinkage in the total value of the common stock of the Pullman, express, and street railway industries, that of both the Pullman and street railway stock amounting at the end of 1925 to less than half as much as in 1908. The decline in the total value of express company common stock was even more striking. The common stockholders of the electric light and power companies witnessed a great shrinkage in the value of their holdings between 1916 and 1920, but, between 1920 and the close of the period studied, the aggregate value of the common stock in this industry has quadrupled. The telephone industry also showed a shrinkage in common stock values between 1915 and 1919, but, before the end of 1925, this shrinkage had been made up with much to spare.

New Money for Funded Debt (1913 Dollars).

In Tables LXII, LXIII, and LXIV the estimated amounts of new money recorded in Tables LVI, LVII, and LVIII have been reduced to dollars of constant purchasing power by dividing the original estimates by index numbers representing the prices of direct or consumers' goods at the different dates.

The resultant data make it plain that the tendencies to invest new money in funded debt seem to be neither strikingly up nor down in the manufacturing, telephone, and electrical industries. The mining industry, including of course the extraction of petroleum and natural gas, has been drawing slightly more money from the pockets of investors in recent years than was true in the earlier years of the period. On the other hand, the funded debt of street railways formerly called for several times as much money per annum as has been secured since 1920. The largest increase in the demand upon investors has been for the funded debt of the electric light and power companies, the annual investment in this class of securities having a

TABLE LXII

VALUE, IN 1913 DOLLARS,[a] OF THE
NET NEW MONEY INVESTED BY INDIVIDUALS
IN THE FUNDED DEBT OF CORPORATIONS

(MILLIONS OF DOLLARS' WORTH OF DIRECT OR CONSUMERS' GOODS PURCHASABLE
THEREWITH AT 1913 PRICES)[b]

Year	Fac-tories	Mines, Quarries and Oil Wells	Rail-roads	Street Rail-ways	Electric Light and Power	Tele-phones	Tele-graphs
1909	$49	$23	$512	$106	$ 77	$ -86	$ -2
1910	79	28	664	103	66	52	0
1911	89	29	557	120	87	17	0
1912	-4	25	271	109	69	67	-9
1913	42	30	250	72	-79	55	0
1914	74	29	39	125	8	47	0
1915	75	28	-210	161	131	-55	[c]
1916	71	32	-93	147	118	69	0
1917	60	33	-27	121	177	-26	0
1918	36	28	-86	21	102	14	0
1919	47	30	60	16	46	82	0
1920	17	33	369	5	184	22	0
1921	0	39	61	-2	220	41	9
1922	-59	32	134	-2	132	-33	0
1923	139	53	429	28	239	73	0
1924	131	76	289	30	167	-1	0
1925	5	47	62	14	243	88	[d]

[a] "1913 Dollars" is an abbreviation for the phrase "dollars having purchasing power equivalent to that which they had in 1913."

[b] Computed from corresponding items in Table LVI by dividing by the appropriate price indices recorded in Table VII.

[c] Negative figure of less than $500,000.

[d] Positive figure of less than $500,000.

purchasing power of something like 3 times as much at the close of the period as at the beginning.

New Money for Preferred Stock (1913 Dollars).

The amount put into the preferred stock of manufacturing, mining, and street railway corporations by individuals fell off materially after 1917. The decline in street railways began at an even earlier date, becoming marked as early as 1914. Investment in the preferred stock of electric light and power corporations has shown greater stability, but there has been no such upward sweep as took place with the funded debt of the same class of corporations.

TABLE LXIII

VALUE, IN 1913 DOLLARS,[a] OF THE NET NEW MONEY INVESTED BY INDIVIDUALS IN THE PREFERRED STOCK OF CORPORATIONS

(MILLIONS OF DOLLARS' WORTH OF DIRECT OR CONSUMERS' GOODS PURCHASABLE THEREWITH AT 1913 PRICES)[b]

Year	Factories	Mines, Quarries and Oil Wells	Street Railways	Electric Light and Power	Telephones	Telegraphs
1909	$163	$19	$19	$26	$6	$0
1910	253	21	13	35	−1	0
1911	228	23	15	30	4	0
1912	172	20	25	13	1	0
1913	264	19	18	25	−1	0
1914	196	19	7	26	−2	0
1915	229	22	6	9	2	0
1916	302	20	9	19	•	0
1917	286	17	5	11	1	0
1918	153	16	3	17	1	0
1919	159	12	2	41	1	0
1920	98	19	2	42	1	3
1921	107	10	2	35	10	2
1922	161	10	2	15	11	0
1923	103	10	•	d	4	0
1924	138	9	•	d	11	0
1925	117	12	•	d	3	0

[a] "1913 Dollars" is an abbreviation for the phrase "dollars having purchasing power equivalent to hat which they had in 1913."

[b] Computed from corresponding items in Table LVII by dividing by the appropriate price indices recorded in Table VII.

[c] Negative figure of less than $500,000.

[d] Because of the extremely rapid changes occurring in the industry, reasonably dependable estimates cannot well be made until the data for the 1927 Census become available.

The preferred stock of telephone companies called for far more dollars of 1913 value between 1920 and 1925 than was true in the years before.

New Money for Common Stock (1913 Dollars).

Aggregate investments of new money in common stock, fell off sharply after 1921 in the case of manufacturing companies. The maximum for mining concerns was reached as early as 1911, and, between 1918 and 1925 there was a marked decline in investment in this class of securities. Relatively little new money was invested in street railway common stocks between 1917 and 1923, but there

TABLE LXIV

VALUE, IN 1913 DOLLARS,* OF THE NET NEW MONEY INVESTED BY INDIVIDUALS IN THE COMMON STOCK OF CORPORATIONS

(MILLIONS OF DOLLARS' WORTH OF DIRECT OR CONSUMERS' GOODS PURCHASABLE THEREWITH AT 1913 PRICES)[b]

Year	Factories	Mines, Quarries and Oil Wells	Pullman	Express	Street Railways	Electric Light and Power	Telephones	Telegraphs
1909	$1,468	$ 77	$0	$ 0	$32	$ 17	$84	$0
1910	818	348	0	17	51	195	—19	0
1911	1,680	549	0	c	32	70	43	0
1912	107	263	0	c	24	40	10	0
1913	696	69	0	c	30	85	—3	0
1914	678	89	0	c	72	115	—7	0
1915	1,305	148	0	—5	16	9	60	0
1916	100	107	0	—4	11	37	20	0
1917	842	60	0	c	10	43	34	0
1918	1,318	230	0	c	7	11	d	0
1919	975	72	0	c	1	27	—5	0
1920	232	27	0	c	c	25	—4	7
1921	1,036	6	0	0	c	76	61	2
1922	118	7	9	0	1	96	71	2
1923	—87	28	0	0	7	101	34	c
1924	—360	10	0	0	8	132	116	c
1925	188	18	0	0	9	244	27	c

* "1913 Dollars" is an abbreviation for the phrase "dollars having purchasing power equivalent to that which they had in 1913."

[b] Computed from corresponding items in Table LVIII by dividing by the appropriate price indice recorded in Table VII.

c Positive figure of less than $500,000.

d Negative figure of less than $500,000.

e No information available.

was a slight tendency to an increase in this field after 1923. Individuals put a very considerable amount of money into the common stocks of electric light and power companies in 1910, and the investments were fairly heavy until 1914. After that date, the interest of investors in this field waned until 1921, when it was again awakened. The investment of new money in the common stock of telephone corporations has followed much the same trend as that characterizing the investments in the common stock of electric light and power plants.

Reasons for Changes in the Aggregate Value of Securities.

One must not fall into the error of assuming that, because new money has failed to flow into an industry, there has been no increase in the amount of capital invested in this field. Industries grow both from within and from without. Failure of new money to appear in an industry may be due either to the fact that the industry in question is not prospering, and hence is not in a position to appeal to investors, or it may be due, on the other hand, to the fact that it is so prosperous that all the funds necessary for expansion can be extracted from the profits of the industry. The erratic nature of the fluctuations from year to year in the amount of investments in each class of securities in the given industry arises largely from the peculiar way in which these two contradictory forces interact.

What has just been said of an industry as a whole applies with equal force to each class of securities within the industry. As a young industry prospers for a time, improved conditions are likely to be manifested chiefly by an increase in the aggregate value of the funded debt, for the added prosperity makes it more probable that the bonds and mortgages will be paid, and hence the value of these securities goes up. After the bonds and mortgages reach a state in which they are fairly secure, they cease to gain much in value, and the increase moves on successively to the preferred and then to the common stock. During a period of inflation, the nominal value of the funded debt is likely to remain unchanged, but its value in terms of any constant money unit shrinks. Thus, when the various European countries inflated their currency wildly during the period of the War, the value of the funded debt, as measured in terms of consumers' goods, steadily approached, and in some cases practically reached, zero. The preferred stock behaved much like the funded debt. The common stock, however, representing a constant equity in the residual income after the claims of the funded debt and the preferred stock had been satisfied, tended to increase in value. Were it not for the fact that inflation nearly always interfered with industrial output, the common stockholders would be benefited by the process, for they would gain at the expense of the holders of the preferred stock and the funded debt.

Gain Above New Money in Value of Funded Debt (1913 Dollars).

If we subtract from the total increase in the value of any given class of securities, when measured in constant dollars, the amount of new money, also measured in constant dollars, invested during

TABLE LXV

PURCHASING POWER, IN 1913 DOLLARS,[a] OF THOSE NET[b] GAINS TO HOLDERS OF THE FUNDED DEBT ARISING FROM INCREASES IN THE MARKET VALUE OF THE SECURITIES

[(MILLIONS OF 1913 DOLLARS)]

Year	Factories	Mines, Quarries and Oil Wells	Railroads[c]	Street Railways	Electric Light and Power	Telephones	Telegraphs
1909	$ —83	$ 3	$ —533	$ —37	$ —14	$ 4	$1
1910	—54	—22	—696	—72	—26	—13	—2
1911	25	—9	—404	—5	11	—21	d
1912	—52	4	—432	—49	—23	3	—1
1913	—198	—35	—608	—34	—38	—21	—4
1914	—100	5	—416	—28	—12	11	1
1915	25	4	1,283	—89	12	13	d
1916	—221	—30	—875	—281	—125	—36	—4
1917	—633	—90	—1,912	—616	—206	—84	—6
1918	—365	—51	—671	—200	—107	—40	—5
1919	—391	—53	—1,193	—388	—166	—65	—6
1920	—196	—49	—456	—133	—117	—20	—2
1921	431	101	1,037	236	197	108	5
1922	87	37	194	235	101	—24	3
1923	—76	—29	34	—102	—62	—6	—1
1924	77	—2	—130	113	62	111	1
1925	8	—18	374	—79	—10	127	—1

[a] "1913 Dollars" is an abbreviation for the phrase "dollars having purchasing power equivalent to that which they had in 1913."

[b] Amounts over and above new money invested.

[c] Includes switching and terminal companies.

[d] Negative figure of less than $500,000.

the same period, the remainder represents the gain in the value of the class of securities arising from the activities of the industry in question. Such gains accruing to the holders of the funded debt of certain industries are shown in Table LXV.

During the period 1909 to 1925, inclusive, the bondholders lost money as often as they gained, and, in general, their losses were much heavier than their gains. The holders of the funded debt of manufacturing corporations profited in only 6 years out of the 17. The similar class of holders of the securities of mining corporations gained in exactly the same number of years. The owners of the funded debt of street railway companies were not even so fortunate, for, in only 3 years out of the 17, were they ahead of the game. Even

TABLE LXVI

NET[a] GAINS, IN TERMS OF CURRENT DOLLARS, TO HOLDERS OF THE FUNDED DEBT ARISING FROM INCREASES IN THE MARKET VALUE OF THE SECURITIES

(MILLIONS OF CURRENT DOLLARS)[d]

Year	Factories	Mines, Quarries and Oil Wells	Railroads[b]	Street Railways	Electric Light and Power	Telephones	Telegraphs
1909	$—78	$ 3	$—503	$ —35	$ —13	$ 4	$ 1
1910	—52	—21	—673	—70	—25	—13	—2
1911	24	—9	—390	—5	10	—20	•
1912	—51	3	—422	—48	—22	3	—1
1913	—198	—35	—608	—34	—38	—21	—4
1914	—100	5	—418	—28	—12	11	1
1915	25	4	1,284	—89	12	13	•
1916	—235	—32	—931	—299	—133	—39	—4
1917	—760	—109	—2,297	—741	—248	—104	—8
1918	—505	—70	—929	—277	—148	—58	—7
1919	—618	—84	—1,887	—613	—262	—109	—9
1920	—353	—88	—824	—240	—211	—37	—3
1921	721	169	1,736	396	330	186	8
1922	139	59	309	374	160	—39	4
1923	—123	—47	55	—163	—99	—11	—1
1924	123	—3	—209	181	99	181	2
1925	13	—29	613	—130	—17	213	—1

a Amounts over and above new money.
b Includes switching and terminal companies.
c Negative figure of less than $500,000.
d Computed from corresponding items in Table LXV by multiplying by the appropriate price indices recorded in Table VII.

in an industry like electric light and power, in which there has been a marked expansion of activity, the holders of the funded debt found their securities in the aggregate increasing in value in only 5 years out of 17, and the same was true of the like class of security holders in the telegraph industry. The bond and mortgage holders in the telephone industry were more fortunate than those in most of the other fields, for they lost money in only 10 years out of the 17. The figures just presented are sufficient to make it plain that the equity of the bond and mortgage holders was shrinking steadily during most of the time between 1909 and 1925.

Gain Above New Money in Value of Funded Debt (Current Dollars).

In Table LXVI, the figures just discussed have been converted into terms of gold dollars through a process of multiplying by index

TABLE LXVII

PURCHASING POWER, IN 1913 DOLLARS,[a] OF THOSE NET[b] GAINS TO HOLDERS OF THE PREFERRED STOCK ARISING FROM INCREASES IN THE MARKET VALUE OF THE STOCK

(MILLIONS OF 1913 DOLLARS)

Year	Factories	Mines, Quarries and Oil Wells	Street Railways	Electric Light and Power	Telephones	Telegraphs
1909	$ 350	$ 6	$ 5	$ —4	$ [c]	$ 3
1910	—386	—39	—24	—6	—1	—1
1911	—50	15	6	—12	—1	—3
1912	—43	5	—4	4	—1	—1
1913	—564	—35	—82	—34	—3	—2
1914	—46	—22	—14	7	2	1
1915	624	38	—33	3	[d]	—1
1916	—476	—49	—28	—23	—2	—3
1917	—1,419	—41	—65	—61	—5	—6
1918	—490	30	—13	[c]	—7	—1
1919	—416	—24	—30	—23	—5	—3
1920	—698	—34	—20	—46	1	—4
1921	529	40	17	13	—1	3
1922	546	—11	39	44	—1	5
1923	—163	—14	42	[c]	[c]	2
1924	303	—2	—5	[c]	—2	2
1925	144	—19	—2	[c]	1	[c]

[a] "1913 Dollars" is an abbreviation for the phrase "dollars having purchasing power equivalent to that which they had in 1913."

[b] Amounts over and above new money invested.

[c] Negative figure of less than $500,000.

[d] Positive figure of less than $500,000.

[e] Because of the extremely rapid changes occurring in the industry, reasonably dependable estimates cannot well be made until the data for the 1927 Census become available.

numbers of the prices of consumers' goods. The indications are, of course, approximately the same as in Table LXV, the chief difference being to increase the nominal amounts lost in years when the price index was high, and to reduce them in years when the price index was low.

Gain Above New Money in Value of Preferred Stock (1913 Dollars).

In Table LXVII the aggregate net gains arising from increases in the market value of the securities accruing to all holders of preferred stock are shown in terms of 1913 dollars. In most in-

dustries we have seen that the holders of the funded debt suffered losses which far exceeded their gains. Table LXVII shows that exactly the same situation held in the case of the preferred stock holders. In the manufacturing, mining, and telegraph industries, losses in market value exceeded gains in 11 years of the 17. In the street railway and telephone industries, the situation was even worse, for, in the former, losses outstripped gains in 12 years out of the 17, and, in the latter, in 13 years out of the 17. Reliable data are available for electric light and power companies in only 14 years, but, in 9 of the 14, the total market value of the preferred stock, when this value is expressed in dollars of constant purchasing power, was less at the end of the year than at the beginning. A study of the figures in the table also makes it clear that the situation during the period under consideration was not one in which a few prosperous years offset a large number of lean years, for, when the period is taken as a whole, the net losses of the preferred stockholders exceeded their net gains.

Gain Above New Money in Value of Preferred Stock (Current Dollars).

Table LXVIII shows the amounts presented in Table LXVII converted into terms of current or gold dollars, the conversion being effected through multiplication by suitable indices of the prices of consumers' goods.

Gain Above New Money in Value of Common Stock (1913 Dollars).

Have the common stockholders profited while the holders of bonds and preferred stocks have lost? Analysis of the figures indicates that, in both mining and manufacturing, the common stock holders did fare much better than the owners of either bonds or preferred stock. In these two industries, this class of securities was, as a whole, worth more at the end than at the beginning of the year in somewhat more than half the years 1909 to 1925, inclusive—that is, their total value would buy more direct or consumers' goods. Furthermore, it is actually true that, in both of these industries, the aggregate gains in the entire 17 years accruing to the common stockholders were larger than their aggregate losses, something which was decidedly not true in the case of either the preferred stock or the bondholders. The total market value of the common stock of the Pullman Company declined in 8 years out of the 17, and the aggregate declines were far larger than the ag-

TABLE LXVIII

NET[a] GAINS, IN TERMS OF CURRENT DOLLARS, TO HOLDERS OF THE PREFERRED STOCK ARISING FROM INCREASES IN THE MARKET VALUE OF THE STOCK

(MILLIONS OF CURRENT DOLLARS)[d]

Year	Factories	Mines, Quarries and Oil Wells	Street Railways	Electric Light and Power	Telephones	Telegraphs
1909	$ 330	$ 5	$ 5	$ −4	$ °	$ 3
1910	−373	−37	−23	−6	−1	−1
1911	−48	15	6	−11	−1	−3
1912	−42	5	−4	4	−1	−1
1913	−564	−35	−82	−34	−3	−2
1914	−46	−22	−14	8	2	1
1915	625	38	−33	3	b	−1
1916	−506	−52	−29	−25	−2	−3
1917	−1,704	−49	−79	−73	−6	−7
1918	−678	42	−19	°	−9	−1
1919	−657	−37	−48	−36	−8	−5
1920	−1,260	−61	−35	−83	2	−7
1921	886	67	29	22	−2	5
1922	870	−17	61	71	−1	8
1923	−262	−22	67	°	°	3
1924	487	−3	−8	°	−4	4
1925	236	−32	−3	°	1	−1

[a] Amounts over and above new money invested.
[b] Positive figure of less than $500,000.
[c] Negative figure of less than $500,000.
[d] Computed from corresponding items in Table LXVII by multiplying by the appropriate price indices recorded in Table VII.
[e] See note "e", Table LXVII.

gregate increases. The situation of the street railway common stockholders was still worse, for the total market value of their holdings declined in 12 years out of the 17, the net increases being sufficient to offset only a minor fraction of the large losses incurred. Common stockholders in the rapidly growing electric light and power industry lost money on the value of their stocks in 8 years out of the 17, and their aggregate losses were, if anything, a trifle larger than their gains, taking the entire period into consideration. The holders of the common stock of the telephone companies of the nation found the aggregate value of their holdings diminishing in 7 years out of the 17, and they also lost more money than they gained

TABLE LXIX

PURCHASING POWER, IN 1913 DOLLARS,[a] OF THOSE NET[b] GAINS TO HOLDERS OF THE COMMON STOCK ARISING FROM INCREASES IN THE MARKET VALUE OF THE STOCK

(MILLIONS OF 1913 DOLLARS)

Year	Factories	Mines, Quarries and Oil Wells	Pullman	Express	Street Railways	Electric Light and Power	Telephones	Telegraphs
1909	$ 1,908	$ —18	$ 16	$ 72	$ 13	$—66	$ 25	$ 5
1910	—840	—327	d	—64	—75	—22	1	—5
1911	—176	570	d	—21	—2	185	14	—3
1912	913	226	2	—30	—42	19	12	—4
1913	—1,820	—48	—17	—29	—142	—260	—68	—26
1914	460	949	e	—21	—90	7	45	—7
1915	5,346	1,244	13	27	—21	93	—11	38
1916	—911	434	—19	—2	—149	321	—69	—11
1917	—5,539	—2,616	—64	e	—420	—849	—143	—30
1918	118	—672	—12	e	—148	—256	—71	—7
1919	149	—237	—15	e	—177	—259	—51	—16
1920	—3,259	—1,614	—10	e	—67	—108	--2	—8
1921	189	922	17	e	7	115	102	12
1922	625	655	4	e	109	103	48	22
1923	—300	—408	—13	e	—51	—12	13	7
1924	4,067	1,112	15	e	97	323	43	26
1925	2,810	463	—43	—1	36	635	58	17

a "1913 Dollars" is an abbreviation for the phrase "dollars having purchasing power equivalent to that which they had in 1913."

b Amounts over and above new money invested.

c Negative figure of less than $500,000.

d Positive figure of less than $500,000.

e No information available.

when the entire 17 years are considered as a unit and the market values are expressed in terms of dollars of constant purchasing power. The common stockholders in the telegraph companies suffered a decline in the aggregate value of their stocks in 10 years out of the 17. In their case, however, the increases in the market value during the 17 years were slightly in excess of the decreases. In interpreting these findings, it should be remembered that the figures presented in these tables refer merely to losses or gains due to changes in the market value of the securities, and do not take account of either dividend or interest payments.

TABLE LXX

NET* GAINS, IN TERMS OF CURRENT DOLLARS, TO HOLDERS OF THE COMMON STOCK ARISING FROM INCREASES IN THE MARKET VALUE OF THE STOCK
(MILLIONS OF CURRENT DOLLARS)*

Year	Factories	Mines, Quarries and Oil Wells	Pullman	Express	Street Railways	Electric Light and Power	Telephones	Telegraphs
1909	$ 1,800	$ —17	$ 15	$ 68	$ 13	$ —62	$ 24	$ 4
1910	—811	—315	b	—62	—72	—21	1	—5
1911	—170	550	b	—20	—2	178	14	—2
1912	893	221	2	—30	—42	18	12	—4
1913	—1,820	—48	—17	—29	—142	—260	—68	—26
1914	462	953	c	—21	—90	7	45	—7
1915	5,350	1,245	13	27	—21	93	—11	38
1916	—970	462	—20	—2	—159	342	—75	—12
1917	—6,654	—3,143	—76	d	—505	—1,020	—177	—35
1918	164	—929	—17	d	—205	—354	—103	—9
1919	236	—375	—23	d	—279	—409	—85	—24
1920	—5,884	—2,914	—17	d	—121	—196	—3	—14
1921	317	1,543	29	d	12	193	175	20
1922	996	1,044	7	d	173	164	78	36
1923	—482	—655	—21	d	—81	—19	21	12
1924	6,525	1,784	24	d	156	519	71	41
1925	4,605	759	—70	—1	58	1,040	96	27

* Amounts over and above new money invested.
b Positive figure of less than $500,000.
c Negative figure of less than $500,000.
d No information available.
* Computed from corresponding items in Table LXIX by multiplying by the appropriate price indices recorded in Table VII.

Gain Above New Money in Value of Common Stock (Current Dollars).

Table LXX has been derived from Table LXIX merely by multiplying the amounts in Table LXIX by indices of the prices of consumers' goods. Figures in Table LXX therefore represent the gains to common stockholders expressed in terms of gold dollars, which, of course, vary in value from year to year.

Gains in 1913 Dollars Accruing to Security Holders.

It is evident that the total of gains accruing to security holders arises not merely from changes in the market value of their secur-

TABLE LXXI

PURCHASING POWER, IN 1913 DOLLARS,[a] OF NET[b] GAINS, INCLUDING INTEREST RECEIPTS, ACCRUING TO HOLDERS OF THE FUNDED DEBT

(MILLIONS OF 1913 DOLLARS)[c]

Year	Fac-tories	Mines, Quarries and Oil Wells	Rail-roads[d]	Street Rail-ways	Electric Light and Power	Tele-phones	Tele-graphs
1909	$ 89	$ 20	$ —140	$ 51	$ 18	$ 19	$ 4
1910	116	—5	—305	19	4	*	1
1911	198	9	—1	92	48	—6	3
1912	122	24	—21	53	16	19	1
1913	—25	—14	—199	75	2	—2	—2
1914	77	28	—20	87	30	33	3
1915	207	29	1,720	30	58	35	2
1916	—46	—5	—465	—167	—77	—15	—2
1917	—473	—66	—1,546	—518	—159	—64	—5
1918	—223	—27	—358	—114	—56	—22	—4
1919	—261	—31	—917	—310	—118	—47	—5
1920	—75	—27	—201	—65	—71	*	—1
1921	566	129	1,322	311	253	132	6
1922	227	70	501	318	172	2	5
1923	67	5	347	—19	20	21	1
1924	234	36	199	197	155	140	3
1925	159	23	703	—1	91	157	1

[a] "1913 Dollars" is an abbreviation for the phrase "dollars having purchasing power equivalent to that which they had in 1913."

[b] Amounts over and above new money invested.

[c] Computed from corresponding items in Table LXXIV by dividing the sub-items by the appropriate price indices recorded in Table VII.

[d] Includes switching and terminal companies.

[e] Negative figure of less than $500,000.

[f] No funded debt.

ities, but also from the interest or dividends which they receive. In bad years, the interest or dividend payments tend to offset to some extent the losses in the market value of the securities. In good years, they accentuate the gains. Tables LXV to LXX have been devoted to showing the net gains (or losses) arising from changes in the market value of the securities. Tables LXXI to LXXVI show the aggregate gains or losses accruing to the security holders when not only changes in market value but also dividends and interest payments are taken into account.

Gains Accruing to All Holders of Funded Debt Combined.

Table LXXI and Chart 34 record the net gains or losses of the holders of the funded debt of the various industries, when those in

CHART 34

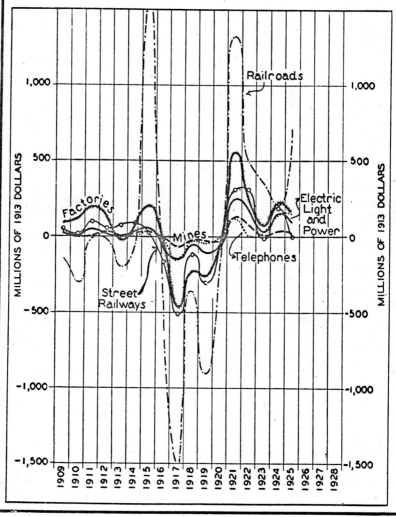

PURCHASING POWER, IN 1913 DOLLARS,
OF NET GAINS, INCLUDING INTEREST RECEIPTS,
ACCRUING TO HOLDERS OF THE FUNDED DEBT[a]

[a] For data, see Table LXXI.

a given industry are all considered as a single unit. For most industries, the period 1909 to 1915 resulted in net gains to the bond holders. During the years 1916 to 1920, however, the diminishing value of the dollar turned gains into losses, but between 1920 and 1925, the bondholders in general profited from their holdings. There are, of course, exceptions to this rule. The holders of the funded debt of telephone companies lost money in 1910, 1911, and 1913, and barely broke even in 1922. The owners of the funded debt of all manufacturing companies of the United States lost money in 1913, and the holders of the similar class of securities of street railways found their balance in the red both in 1923 and 1925. Table LXXI indicates that, in most of the fields, when interest payments are used to offset losses in capital values, the owners of the senior securities of the seven classes of corporations studied were somewhat ahead of the game if they continued in the field from 1909 to 1925.

Gains Accruing to All Holders of Preferred Stock Combined.

Table LXXII and Chart 35 indicate that the owners of preferred stock in manufacturing corporations experienced larger vicissitudes as regards gains and losses than did the owners of the funded debt, the tendency being for the net income derived from this class of securities to fluctuate vigorously from year to year. When dividends are taken into account, the preferred stockholders of all manufacturing corporations combined had a large net profit during the 17 years. The combined holders of the preferred stock of mining corporations also made gains during the period, but, when all quantities are converted into terms of dollars of constant purchasing power, these gains are seen to be extremely meager. Even when dividends are taken into account, the preferred stockholders of all street railways still suffered a deficit for the period as a whole. Satisfactory data are available for the electric light and power industry only through 1922. Up to that time, the losses still exceeded the gains. In the telephone and telegraph industries, the addition of dividends gives a net gain to the preferred stockholders.

Gains Accruing to All Holders of Common Stock Combined.

Chart 36, which is derived from Table LXXIII, is divided into two parts, the division being necessitated by the wide difference in the scales required to show the fluctuations in the large and small industries. A comparison of this chart with Chart 34, representing

TABLE LXXII

PURCHASING POWER, IN 1913 DOLLARS,[a] OF NET[b] GAINS, INCLUDING DIVIDENDS, ACCRUING TO HOLDERS OF PREFERRED STOCK
(MILLIONS OF 1913 DOLLARS)[c]

Year	Factories	Mines, Quarries and Oil Wells	Street Railways	Electric Light and Power	Telephones	Telegraphs
1909	$ 650	$ 10	$ 16	$ —2	$ 1	$ 5
1910	- 68	—33	- 13	—3	1	1
1911	279	24	17	—7	1	- 1
1912	297	14	8	10	1	1
1913	- 209	- 20	- 68	---28	—2	d
1914	302	--11	2	15	3	3
1915	993	47	- 18	11	2	1
1916	- 85	- 36	--15	—14	d	—1
1917	—1,002	—25	—55	—51	—3	—4
1918	—127	42	—7	11	--5	1
1919	—127	—13	—24	—11	—4	—2
1920	- 415	—25	--13	—33	2	—3
1921	815	49	24	29	d	4
1922	788	—2	48	63	2	6
1923	92	—5	54	•	2	3
1924	506	9	7	•	1	4
1925	394	—6	9	•	4	2

[a] "1913 Dollars" is an abbreviation for the phrase "dollars having purchasing power equivalent to that which they had in 1913."

[b] Amounts over and above new money invested.

[c] Computed from corresponding items in Table LXXV by dividing the sub-items by the appropriate price indices recorded in Table VII.

[d] Positive figure of less than $500,000.

• Because of the extremely rapid changes occurring in the industry, reasonably dependable estimates cannot well be made until the data for the 1927 Census become available.

the gains and losses of holders of the funded debt, shows that the income of the holders of the common stock was somewhat more influenced by the cyclical fluctuations in various industries and somewhat less influenced by the inflation period than were the aggregate net gains of the holders of the funded debt. The heavy losses in the street railway industry brought about by the inflation of 1916 to 1920 are quite evident. The general impression given by the charts is that, even when dividends as well as changes in capital values are taken into account, the margin of net gain is still a precarious one, depending upon the state of the industry at the moment as well as upon the monetary policy of the government. Except in

CHART 35

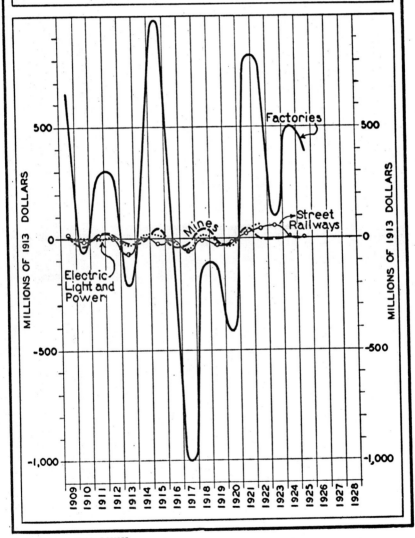

PURCHASING POWER, IN 1913 DOLLARS,
OF NET GAINS, INCLUDING DIVIDENDS,
ACCRUING TO HOLDERS OF PREFERRED STOCK[a]

[a] For data, see Table LXXII.

TABLE LXXIII

PURCHASING POWER, IN 1913 DOLLARS,[a] OF NET[b] GAINS, INCLUDING DIVIDENDS, ACCRUING TO HOLDERS OF COMMON STOCK
(MILLIONS OF 1913 DOLLARS)[c]

Year	Fac-tories	Mines, Quarries and Oil Wells	Pull-man	Ex-press	Street Rail-ways	Electric Light and Power	Tele-phones	Tele-graphs
1909	$ 2,265	$ 121	$24	$ 89	$ 60	$ —45	$ 50	$ 11
1910	—399	—175	9	—45	—22	d	27	2
1911	320	698	10	—15	53	211	41	5
1912	1,438	377	11	—27	12	46	41	3
1913	—1,246	149	—7	—26	—87	—230	—40	—19
1914	998	1,088	9	—19	—33	43	73	1
1915	5,922	1,378	22	31	34	134	19	47
1916	291	769	—10	—9	—92	362	—38	—2
1917	—4,327	—2,275	—56	*	—374	—809	—113	—20
1918	1,100	—424	—6	*	—114	—218	—45	3
1919	991	117	—9	*	—150	—223	—28	—7
1920	—2,586	—1,541	—4	*	—45	—76	19	—1
1921	829	1,023	23	*	30	155	127	19
1922	1,212	734	10	*	130	150	84	32
1923	554	—278	—7	*	—20	48	52	15
1924	4,905	1,234	20	*	124	393	89	33
1925	3,736	614	—40	1	65	724	107	24

[a] "1913 Dollars" is an abbreviation for the phrase "dollars having purchasing power equivalent to that which they had in 1913."

[b] Amounts over and above new money.

[c] Computed from corresponding items in Table LXXVI by dividing the sub-items by the appropriate price indices recorded in Table VII.

[d] Positive figure of less than $500,000.

[*] No information available.

the case of the Pullman, express, and street railway industries, the addition of dividends to the gains in the market value of the securities is sufficient to result in a net gain for the common stock holders, when all 17 years are considered. One cannot study Chart 86 however, without being convinced that, despite the smaller danger of loss in times of inflation, investment in common stocks is still a highly speculative enterprise, just as is the case with investment in bonds or preferred stock.

Gains of All Security Holders Measured in Current Dollars.

Tables LXXIV, LXXV, and LXXVI have been derived by multiplying the figures in Tables LXXI, LXXII, and LXXIII

CHART 36

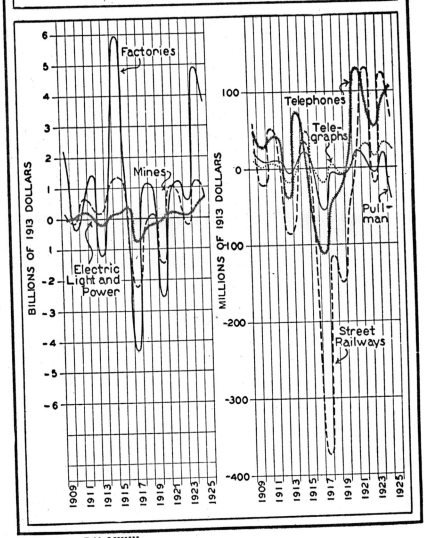

PURCHASING POWER, IN 1913 DOLLARS,
OF NET GAINS, INCLUDING DIVIDENDS,
ACCRUING TO HOLDERS OF COMMON STOCK[a]

[a] For data, see Table LXXIII.

TABLE LXXIV

TOTAL NET* GAINS, INCLUDING INTEREST RECEIPTS, ACCRUING TO HOLDERS OF THE FUNDED DEBT[b]
(MILLIONS OF CURRENT DOLLARS)

Year	Factories	Mines, Quarries and Oil Wells	Railroads[c]	Street Railways	Electric Light and Power	Telephones	Telegraphs
1909	$ 84	$ 19	$ —132	$ 48	$ 17	$ 18	$ 4
1910	112	—4	—294	19	4	d	1
1911	191	9	—1	89	47	—6	3
1912	119	23	—21	52	16	19	1
1913	—25	—14	—199	75	2	—2	—2
1914	77	28	—20	87	30	33	3
1915	207	29	1,721	30	58	36	2
1916	—49	—5	—495	—178	—82	—16	—2
1917	569	—79	—1,857	—622	—190	—79	—5
1918	—308	—38	—496	—158	—78	—31	—5
1919	—412	—48	—1,450	—490	—187	—78	—7
1920	—136	—48	—362	—117	—127	d	—1
1921	948	216	2,213	521	423	227	11
1922	362	111	799	506	274	2	8
1923	108	9	558	—30	32	34	2
1924	375	58	319	316	248	229	5
1925	261	37	1,152	—2	149	263	2

* Amount over and above new money invested.
[b] Derived from figures presented in Tables XXXVI and LXVI.
[c] Includes switching and terminal companies.
[d] Negative figure of less than $500,000.

respectively, by indices of the prices of direct or consumers' goods. The entries in Tables LXXIV, LXXV, and LXXVI represent, then, the net gains to the holders of the various classes of securities specified in each year of the period, when these net gains are expressed in terms of the gold dollars current in the various years. Because of the variations in values of these gold dollars, the figures for the different years are of course not comparable.

Current Method of Calculating Per Cent of Annual Gain.

In discussions of the profit accruing to investors in different fields, it is customary to compare the gains during any given year with some hypothetical amount of money invested. The difficulty with rates of profit arrived at by this mode of computation is that

TABLE LXXV

TOTAL NET[a] GAINS, INCLUDING DIVIDENDS, ACCRUING TO HOLDERS OF PREFERRED STOCK[b]

(MILLIONS OF CURRENT DOLLARS)

Year	Factories	Mines, Quarries and Oil Wells	Street Railways	Electric Light and Power	Telephones	Telegraphs
1909	$ 613	$ 9	$ 15	$ −1	$ 1	$ 5
1910	−65	−32	−12	−3	1	1
1911	270	23	17	−7	1	−1
1912	291	14	8	10	1	1
1913	−209	−20	−68	−28	−2	•
1914	303	−11	2	15	3	3
1915	994	47	−18	11	2	1
1916	−91	−39	−16	−15	•	−1
1917	−1,204	−30	−66	−61	−4	−5
1918	−175	59	−9	15	−8	1
1919	−201	−21	−38	−17	−6	−3
1920	−749	−45	−24	−60	4	−5
1921	1,363	82	40	49	•	7
1922	1,256	−3	77	100	2	10
1923	147	−7	87	d	4	5
1924	811	15	11	d	1	7
1925	646	−10	14	d	4	3

a Amounts over and above new money invested.

b Derived from figures presented in Tables XXXVII and LXVIII.

c Positive figure of less than $500,000.

d Because of the extremely rapid changes occurring in the industry, reasonably dependable estimates cannot well be made until the data for the 1927 Census become available.

one is never sure whether or not the base chosen has any real existence. It is of course meaningless to speak of percentages of yield on the *par* value of common stocks when their market value fluctuates wildly from year to year. Even in the case of bonds and preferred stocks, certainly a large proportion—and perhaps the vast majority—of the present holders did not obtain their securities at par; hence their profits cannot be calculated by comparing them with the face value of the securities. It appears, then, that the most legitimate way of estimating the rate of profit accruing to any investor in any given year is to use as a base the value of his investment at the beginning of the year. The net gain during the year is arrived at by adding algebraically to receipts from dividends or interest payments such changes as have occurred in the value of

TABLE LXXVI

TOTAL NET[a] GAINS, INCLUDING DIVIDENDS, ACCRUING TO HOLDERS OF COMMON STOCK[b]
(MILLIONS OF CURRENT DOLLARS)

Year	Fac-to ies	Mines, Quarries and Oil Wells	Pull-man	Ex-press	Street Rail-ways	Electric Light and Power	Tele-phones	Tele-graphs
1909	$ 2,137	$ 114	$ 23	$ 84	$ 57	$ −42	$ 47	$ 11
1910	−385	−169	9	−43	−21	c	26	2
1911	309	675	10	−14	51	204	40	5
1912	1,406	369	11	−26	12	45	40	3
1913	−1,246	149	−7	−26	−87	−230	−40	−19
1914	1,003	1,093	9	−19	−34	43	74	1
1915	5,927	1,379	22	31	34	134	20	48
1916	309	819	−11	−9	−98	386	−41	−2
1917	−5,198	−2,732	−66	d	−449	−971	−140	−24
1918	1,523	−587	−8	d	−158	−302	−65	3
1919	1,566	−186	−14	d	−237	−353	−47	−11
1920	−4,568	−2,782	−8	d	−81	−138	36	−2
1921	1,388	1,712	38	d	50	259	218	32
1922	1,932	1,170	17	d	208	239	136	52
1923	390	−446	−11	d	−31	77	85	24
1924	7,369	1,979	33	d	199	630	145	54
1925	6,123	1,007	−66	1	106	1,186	179	40

[a] Amounts over and above new money invested.
[b] Derived from figures presented in Tables XXXVIII and LXX.
[c] Positive figure of less than $500,000.
[d] No information available.

the security during the year. As has been previously noted, before such changes can be utilized for the purpose of computing profits or rates of profits, it is necessary that all nominal values be reduced to terms of money having constant purchasing power. The figures presented in Tables LXXVII, LXXVIII, LXXIX, LXXX, and LXXXI have all been computed by this method.

Percentages of Gains and Losses Accruing to Holders of Funded Debt.

It is seen from Table LXXVII that the investor in bonds and mortgages has not, as is commonly supposed, an income which is stable from year to year, but one which, in reality, is widely variable. The average loss to the bondholders of an industry has, for example, actually been more than 25% in a single year, as was the case in

TABLE LXXVII

PER CENT GAIN ON MARKET VALUE OF INVESTMENT AT BEGINNING OF YEAR ACCRUING DURING YEAR TO HOLDERS OF BONDS AND MORTGAGES[a]

(BOTH INTEREST RECEIPTS AND CAPITAL APPRECIATION INCLUDED)

Year	Factories	Mines, Quarries and Oil Wells	Railroads[b]	Street Railways	Electric Light and Power	Telephones	Telegraphs
1909	2.54	6.45	−1.42	3.09	2.85	5.36	6.36
1910	3.34	−1.36	−3.36	1.12	63.60	−.13	1.61
1911	5.64	2.78	−.01	5.23	6.68	−1.97	4.39
1912	3.37	6.62	−.23	2.81	1.96	6.33	2.23
1913	−.69	−3.59	−2.20	3.88	32.52	−.58	−4.33
1914	2.25	7.24	−.23	4.39	3.97	8.07	7.03
1915	6.11	7.08	20.73	1.46	7.84	7.53	4.94
1916	−1.32	−1.10	−4.97	−7.79	−8.71	−3.53	−4.33
1917	−14.20	−14.69	−18.39	−25.78	−18.01	−13.97	−11.09
1918	−8.07	−7.00	−5.54	−7.55	−6.61	−6.22	−10.25
1919	−10.72	−8.30	−16.07	−23.24	−13.96	−14.49	−15.67
1920	−3.60	−7.64	−4.38	−6.77	−9.71	−.01	−2.22
1921	29.66	39.08	29.47	37.33	31.83	38.81	29.75
1922	9.71	14.84	8.98	29.73	15.73	.32	13.47
1923	2.81	.99	5.88	−1.44	1.52	4.24	3.14
1924	9.62	6.37	3.12	16.02	10.28	25.30	8.84
1925	6.02	3.55	10.76	−.09	5.26	27.77	2.94
Average	2.50	3.02	1.30	1.91	7.47	4.87	2.17

[a] Derived from figures presented in Tables LIX and LXXI.
[b] Includes switching and terminal companies.

1917 with the holders of the funded debt of street railways, while the average gain in a twelve-month period may run above 63 per cent, which was true in the case of the owners of electric light and power bonds in the year 1910. If we consider the entire 17 years from 1909 to 1925 inclusive, the owners of the funded debt of street railways obtained an average annual return on their investment of 1.91 per cent. At the other extreme stand the owners of the bonds of electric light and power companies, who received on the average 7.47 per cent on their investment during the same period. Four out of the seven industries studied returned, on the average, 2½ per cent or less to investors in the funded debt, and only electric light and power, and telephone companies paid materially above 3 per cent.

CHART 37

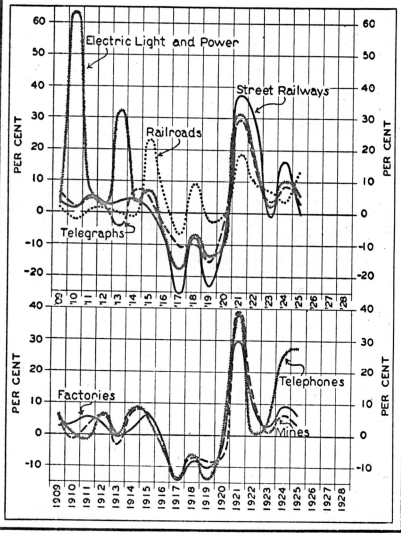

PER CENT GAIN ON MARKET VALUE OF
INVESTMENT AT BEGINNING OF YEAR ACCRUING
DURING YEAR TO HOLDERS OF BONDS
AND MORTGAGES[a]

For data see Table LXXVII.

Chart 37 indicates that, when cyclical fluctuations are eliminated, the trend of percentages of profits accruing to the holders of the funded debt was roughly horizontal between 1909 and 1915. From 1915 to 1917, there was a sharp decline in the trend. This fall was succeeded by a horizontal movement from 1917 to 1919, a sharp rise between 1919 and 1921, and an abrupt decline from 1921 to 1922, after which date the trend appears to have been horizontal in most fields.

The heavy losses to bondholders between 1915 and 1919 were, of course, occasioned, in the main, by the inflation of the currency. Similarly, the striking gains between 1920 and 1921 were due to deflation.

Percentages of Gains and Losses Accruing to Holders of Preferred Stock.

Table LXXVIII and Chart 38 indicate that the experience of the holders of preferred stock has not been materially different from that of the owners of the funded debt. Reasonably complete data are available in this case for five industries only, the figures for electric light and power companies since 1923 being too indefinite to admit of inclusion. Here, again, there are large fluctuations in percentages of gain, running from a loss of 33 per cent in electric light and power companies in 1920, to a gain of 42 per cent in mining concerns in 1915. Of the five industries for which figures are available for all years, the preferred stockholders of the telephone companies fared worst, averaging but one half of one per cent gain, while preferred stockholders in manufacturing and telegraph companies netted slightly more than 4 per cent in each case. The owners in the same class of securities of street railways received but 1.66 per cent on the average.

Chart 38 indicates that the trend of profits to investors on preferred stock was downward between 1909 and 1916, approximately horizontal between 1917 and 1920, upward from 1920 to 1922, downward from 1922 to 1923, and thereafter roughly horizontal. It will be observed that calculations for years since 1925 have not yet been made.

Apparently, the fluctuations in the profits of the preferred stockholders are slightly more violent than those in the profits of the bondholders. The different industries, while varying in year to year movements, show trends closely resembling one another.

TABLE LXXVIII

PER CENT GAIN ON MARKET VALUE OF INVESTMENT AT BEGINNING OF YEAR ACCRUING DURING YEAR TO HOLDERS OF PREFERRED STOCK[a]

(BOTH DIVIDENDS AND APPRECIATION IN VALUE OF STOCK INCLUDED)

Year	Factories	Mines, Quarries and Oil Wells	Street Railways	Electric Light and Power	Telephones	Telegraphs
1909	13.25	17.09	6.04	—2.52	6.47	14.08
1910	—1.25	—39.37	—4.29	—3.47	2.17	1.98
1911	5.30	36.23	6.09	—6.09	2.45	—3.00
1912	5.45	13.86	2.73	7.53	2.71	1.71
1913	—3.75	—15.48	—21.08	—18.96	—5.49	.73
1914	5.71	—9.53	.79	10.69	13.70	9.91
1915	18.26	42.64	—7.13	6.48	8.16	1.91
1916	—1.36	—21.29	—6.78	—7.55	.56	—2.50
1917	—16.39	—17.77	—26.53	—28.50	—12.70	—15.02
1918	—2.54	36.24	—4.46	8.28	—23.90	2.40
1919	—2.74	—8.12	—17.26	—7.52	—22.88	—7.46
1920	—9.44	—16.60	—12.04	—33.43	14.96	—14.24
1921	21.49	35.77	25.88	29.42	1.05	21.54
1922	17.81	—1.06	43.00	29.90	6.08	26.71
1923	1.79	—2.47	35.43	b	6.18	11.90
1924	9.97	5.06	3.41	b	1.30	14.50
1925	7.14	—3.09	4.49	b	7.80	4.84
Average	4.04	3.07	1.66		.51	4.12

[a] Derived from figures presented in Tables LX and LXXII.

[b] Because of the extremely rapid changes occurring in the industry, reasonably dependable estimates cannot be made until the data for the 1927 Census become available.

Percentages of Gains and Losses Accruing to Holders of Common Stock.

Fluctuations in the rates of profits of common stockholders are slightly more extreme than are the fluctuations in those accruing to the owners of either bonds or preferred stocks. In the case of the preferred stock, it will be remembered that the extremes ran from —33 per cent to 43 per cent. In the case of the common stocks, the greatest loss was 39 per cent, which was the fate of the Pullman stockholders in 1925, and the highest gain was 49½ per cent, which marked the good fortune of the owners of mining securities in 1921.

In no single industry did the experience of the owners of either

CHART 38

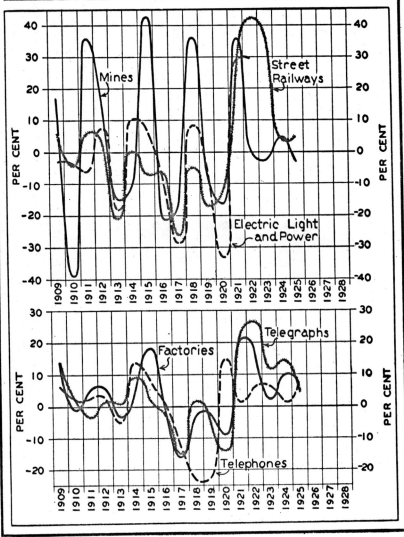

PER CENT GAIN ON MARKET VALUE OF
INVESTMENT AT BEGINNING OF YEAR ACCRUING
DURING YEAR TO HOLDERS OF PREFERRED
STOCK[a]

[a] For data see Table LXXVIII.

TABLE LXXIX

PER CENT GAIN ON MARKET VALUE OF INVESTMENT
AT BEGINNING OF YEAR ACCRUING DURING YEAR
TO HOLDERS OF COMMON STOCK[a]

(BOTH DIVIDENDS AND APPRECIATION
IN VALUE OF STOCK INCLUDED)

Year	Factories	Mines, Quarries and Oil Wells	Pullman	Express	Street Railways	Electric Light and Power	Telephones	Telegraphs
1909	28.25	5.65	13.61	65.56	4.25	−4.19	13.07	6.95
1910	−3.50	−7.99	4.93	−18.84	−1.50	4.60	5.45	1.46
1911	2.82	31.50	5.20	−5.93	3.66	17.62	8.81	3.00
1912	11.16	11.31	5.95	−15.56	.84	3.18	7.84	1.86
1913	−8.97	3.89	−3.81	−19.30	−5.98	−15.22	−7.39	−12.36
1914	7.82	28.31	5.12	−19.27	−2.50	3.24	15.78	.69
1915	42.57	28.23	12.32	51.47	2.56	9.17	3.82	39.83
1916	1.41	12.26	−5.23	13.93	−7.02	23.24	−6.83	−1.24
1917	−21.91	−33.38	−32.78	b	−31.74	−42.19	−22.36	−13.74
1918	7.31	−9.96	−5.20	b	−14.92	−19.66	−11.14	2.20
1919	6.01	−3.07	−9.61	b	−23.92	−25.78	−8.42	−6.74
1920	−14.68	−42.19	−5.36	b	−9.95	−12.01	6.88	−.95
1921	5.68	49.52	32.54	b	7.73	28.10	45.38	21.04
1922	7.67	24.53	11.85	b	33.41	22.27	18.35	30.34
1923	3.35	−7.60	−7.05	b	−3.91	5.48	8.85	11.48
1924	30.34	37.66	23.16	b	27.06	40.84	13.98	23.99
1925	13.80	13.96	−38.99	2.88	11.49	51.09	13.48	14.85
Average	7.30	8.39	.39		−.61	5.28	6.21	7.22

[a] Derived from figures presented in Tables LXI and LXXIII.
[b] No information available.

bonds or preferred stock indicate an average net loss for the entire
17 years taken as a unit. On this basis, however, the common
stockholders of the street railways actually lost 61/100 per cent
and those in the Pullman industry gained but 39/100 per cent.
Figures for the express industry are incomplete. In five out of the
seven industries for which figures are available, the common stockholders made an average gain of more than 5 per cent, which is
distinctly above the profit rate accruing to either the bondholders
or preferred stockholders in the same industry. The evidence of
Tables LXXVII to LXXIX is, then, that, during the 17 years, it
was more profitable to invest in common stocks than in bonds or
preferred stocks.

CHART 39

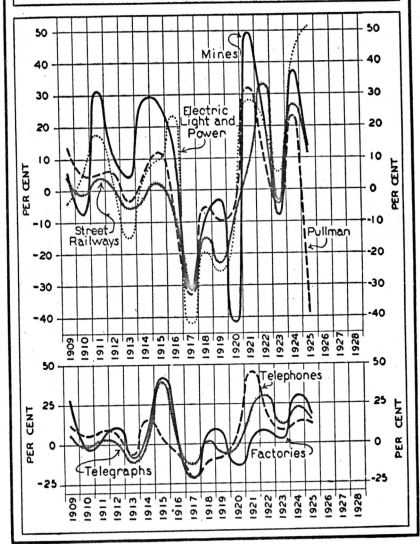

PER CENT GAIN ON MARKET VALUE OF
INVESTMENT AT BEGINNING OF YEAR ACCRUING
DURING YEAR TO HOLDERS OF COMMON STOCK[a]

[a] For data, see Table LXXIX.

TABLE LXXX

GAINS, MEASURED IN 1913 DOLLARS,[a] ACCRUING TO ALL STOCKHOLDERS OF RAILWAY, SWITCHING, AND TERMINAL COMPANIES[b]
(MILLIONS OF 1913 DOLLARS)

Year	Gain in Market Value of Stocks	New Money Invested in Stocks	Gain in Market Value Above New Money	Dividends	Total Gain to All Stockholders	Value of All Stocks Jan. 1	Per Cent Gain to Average Stockholder on Jan. 1 Investment
1909	$ 326	$—163	$ 489	$251	$ 741	$ 8,466	8.75
1910	—89	—216	128	278	406	8,792	4.61
1911	—404	—68	—336	271	—65	8,704	—.75
1912	795	114	680	258	939	8,299	11.31
1913	—1,329	84	—1,414	273	—1,140	9,094	—12.54
1914	—719	—493	—226	268	42	7,765	.54
1915	887	—311	1,198	243	1,441	7,046	20.45
1916	—1,126	154	—1,280	224	—1,056	7,933	—13.31
1917	—2,072	330	—2,402	220	—2,182	6,807	—32.06
1918	—45	—53	8	180	188	4,735	3.98
1919	—1,273	—33	—1,239	156	—1,083	4,689	—23.09
1920	—312	17	—329	125	—204	3,417	—5.97
1921	—127	—130	3	118	121	3,105	2.89
1922	836	—95	930	131	1,061	2,978	35.63
1923	1	—67	67	149	217	3,814	5.68
1924	585	6	578	165	743	3,815	19.48
1925	725	—86	811	175	986	4,400	22.41

[a] "1913 Dollars" is an abbreviation for the phrase "dollars having purchasing power equivalent to that which they had in 1913".

[b] Based upon *Statistics of Railways* published by the U. S. Interstate Commerce Commission and upon the reports of a large sample of corporations.

Percentages of Gains and Losses Accruing to Holders of Railway Stocks.

Because of the fact that, in its publication entitled *Statistics of Railways*, the Interstate Commerce Commission fails to separate data for preferred stocks from data for common stocks, it has not proved feasible, in the time available, to make estimates of the profits of stockholders of railway, switching, and terminal companies, comparable to those for other industries appearing in Tables LXXVIII and LXXIX. Tables LXXX and LXXXI have, therefore, been constructed in order to present data supplementary to

TABLE LXXXI

GAINS ACCRUING TO ALL STOCKHOLDERS OF RAILWAY, SWITCHING, AND TERMINAL COMPANIES
(MILLIONS OF CURRENT DOLLARS) [a]

Year	Gain in Market Value of Stocks	New Money Invested in Stocks	Gain in Market Value Above New Money	Dividends	Total Gain to All Stockholders	Value of All Stocks Jan. 1
1909	$ 554	$—154	$ 462	$237	$ 699	$ 7,929
1910	—38	—209	124	268	392	8,483
1911	—333	—66	—325	262	—63	8,444
1912	915	112	665	253	918	8,111
1913	—1,177	84	—1,414	273	—1,141	9,026
1914	—793	—495	—227	269	42	7,848
1915	1,064	—311	1,199	243	1,442	7,056
1916	—438	164	—1,362	239	—1,123	8,120
1917	—1,655	396	—2,885	264	—2,621	7,682
1918	987	—74	11	250	261	6,027
1919	—1,129	—53	—1,960	247	—1,713	7,014
1920	—355	31	—594	226	—368	5,885
1921	758	—218	5	197	202	5,530
1922	1,345	—151	1,482	209	1,691	4,771
1923	41	—107	108	240	348	6,116
1924	972	10	928	264	1,192	6,157
1925	1,368	—141	1,329	287	1,616	7,129

[a] Computed from corresponding items in Table LXXX by multiplying by the appropriate price indices recorded in Table VII.

the figures appearing in Table LXXIX. These figures indicate that, on the average, during the 17 years covered, all railway stockholders obtained an average return on investment amounting to 2.88 per cent per annum. This rate of return is less than that obtained by common stockholders in manufacturing, mining, electric light and power, or telephone and telegraph companies, but is materially better than the net rate of profit of the common stockholders of the Pullman company or street railways. The railway stockholders on the average fared somewhat worse than the preferred stockholders of manufacturing and mining concerns, but better than the preferred stockholders of street railway or telephone companies. For the railway stockholders, the year 1913, and the period 1916 to 1920 were anything but prosperous; but 1922 ushered in an era of marked prosperity. ·

New Money Invested in and Dividends Derived from Railway Stocks.

It will be observed that, in Tables LXXX and LXXXI, records of new money and dividends appear both in terms of 1913 dollars and current dollars. These figures are supplementary to those given for other industries in earlier tables.

Average Prices of All Units of Funded Debt (Current Dollars).

Series of index numbers showing the movements from year to year in the prices of selected groups of securities appear in many publications. It is less usual to find figures showing the changes in average value representing, in so far as it is feasible to obtain quotations, the average value of all the securities of the given class outstanding in the industry. This is the end which the figures shown in Table LXXXII are designed to attain. They are, of course, not based upon complete data, but represent the changes occurring in the average value of the bonds of a large group of corporations in each industry. The figures presented in the table are arrived at by finding the total value of all the outstanding bonds of these sample corporations, and dividing this total market value by the outstanding number of hundred dollar units of par value. The table indicates that bonds tended to decline during the period 1916 to 1920 and to rise after that date. The decline in value measured in gold dollars, was doubtless due, in the main, to the high interest rates prevailing at that period, and the recovery was similarly caused by the fall in these rates. In most industries, the average prices of bonds were not greatly different in 1925 from what they were in 1908, there being a small increase in the case of mining, electric light and power, and telephone companies, and a small decrease in the average prices of those of manufacturing and railway concerns. The bonds of street railway corporations, however, were decidedly lower at the close of 1925 than at the end of 1908, while, on the other hand, the bonds of telephone companies were much higher at the end of the period than at the beginning.

Average Prices of All Shares of Preferred Stock (Current Dollars).

Table LXXXIII shows the estimated average value per share in gold dollars of all preferred stock outstanding in the various industries. The trend between 1908 and 1925 was approximately horizontal in the case of manufacturing, telephone, and telegraph companies. The nominal value of the shares owned by the preferred

TABLE LXXXII

AVERAGE MARKET PRICE PER $100 UNIT OF FUNDED DEBT OUTSTANDING AT CLOSE OF YEAR[a]
(CURRENT DOLLARS)

December 31	Factories	Mines, Quarries and Oil Wells	Railroads	Express	Street Railways	Electric Light and Power	Telephones	Telegraphs
1908	$103.76	$ 93.41	$ 91.07	$ 91.50	$ 89.81	$ 94.86	$ 90.38	$ 92.65
1909	104.07	97.36	89.54	92.89	90.21	96.24	92.23	96.72
1910	102.86	92.16	85.69	90.29	87.06	93.71	90.16	93.91
1911	102.69	90.46	84.00	84.50	87.91	96.35	85.92	94.35
1912	102.75	92.59	82.16	81.41	87.68	95.59	89.62	91.64
1913	99.58	86.80	78.22	69.88	87.84	92.25	88.12	86.90
1914	95.68	87.54	78.16	72.36	86.19	90.01	91.52	88.02
1915	98.98	89.82	86.85	82.89	85.30	94.70	95.66	90.41
1916	102.07	92.53	89.35	83.20	83.14	91.64	97.87	89.39
1917	93.41	84.93	75.68	65.45	67.16	83.56	91.49	84.25
1918	95.44	88.11	79.79	b	68.71	88.05	97.01	82.86
1919	92.67	88.46	73.53	b	56.40	82.86	93.21	75.37
1920	86.89	80.15	69.63	b	50.36	76.63	89.66	73.33
1921	95.81	94.26	79.20	b	58.13	87.55	103.86	84.87
1922	98.13	99.33	81.70	b	71.44	96.84	108.01	91.93
1923	94.84	94.63	83.77	b	66.43	93.09	106.70	89.96
1924	98.25	97.66	84.45	b	73.07	97.04	109.89	93.50
1925	100.37	97.64	90.58	b	70.66	97.92	110.40	93.86

[a] Derived from figures presented in Tables XL and LIII.
[b] No funded debt.

stockholders of mining and street railway companies declined noticeably during the period, while, on the other hand, the preferred stock of electric light and power companies rose very materially. A very low point in preferred stock values was reached for mining companies, electric light and power, and telegraph companies in 1917, and for street railways and telephone companies in 1920 and 1919, respectively. In a general way, the average prices of preferred stocks paralleled those of the bonds of the corresponding industries, though there was more tendency for them to fluctuate from year to year.

No attempt has been made to calculate the average value per share of the common stock outstanding in the different industrial fields. The reason that this computation has been omitted is that the tendency to split up the shares of common stock and to issue

TABLE LXXXIII

AVERAGE MARKET PRICE PER $100 UNIT OF
PREFERRED STOCK OUTSTANDING AT CLOSE OF YEAR[*]

(CURRENT DOLLARS)

December 31	Factories	Mines, Quarries and Oil Wells	Street Railways	Electric Light and Power	Tele- phones	Tele- graphs
1908	$96.61	$79.93	$77.76	$74.47	$65.51	$69.56
1909	105.69	92.59	82.69	78.71	72.57	77.37
1910	98.49	59.75	77.26	80.12	69.75	75.06
1911	98.39	78.77	80.28	77.45	71.15	69.06
1912	99.18	86.08	81.73	82.57	70.66	67.50
1913	91.34	68.03	63.84	69.18	63.26	65.00
1914	89.84	58.71	60.61	75.39	65.97	67.00
1915	102.36	82.82	54.52	79.13	70.09	66.00
1916	103.80	68.71	53.78	78.52	73.05	65.75
1917	90.62	59.21	42.46	60.96	70.19	58.00
1918	96.26	89.29	45.82	74.54	60.61	64.50
1919	101.08	89.32	41.65	79.15	52.16	64.12
1920	87.88	78.83	35.87	66.04	59.17	51.95
1921	89.20	91.62	38.74	68.06	60.82	53.96
1922	101.39	87.12	52.44	94.57	65.21	65.87
1923	99.87	81.77	67.19	99.69	67.68	70.68
1924	107.53	81.66	65.76	110.35	69.00	76.22
1925	108.83	76.91	66.55	112.00	72.82	76.95

[*] Derived from Tables XLI and LIV.

stock dividends has been so marked that it does not appear that
any estimates of the average value per share of common stock
which could be presented would have any particular significance
from the standpoint of this study.

Average Values of All Units of Funded Debt (1913 Dollars).

From Table LXXXIV and Chart 40 it appears that the bond
holders of 1925 were but little more than half as well off as were the
bondholders of 1909. In practically all industries, the real value
of bonds slid slowly downward between the end of 1908 and the end
of 1915, then slipped down a steep declivity, terminating in a trough
at the end of 1920. After this there was a definite but limited
recovery to the end of 1922, and from that date up to the end of
1925, the purchasing power of the average unit of the funded debt
in most industries has remained approximately constant. Chart

TABLE LXXXIV

PURCHASING POWER, IN 1913 DOLLARS,[a] OF PRICE OF AVERAGE $100 UNIT OF FUNDED DEBT OUTSTANDING AT CLOSE OF YEAR

(REPRESENTS AMOUNT OF DIRECT OR CONSUMERS' GOODS PURCHASABLE AT PRICES PREVAILING IN 1913)[b]

December 31	Factories	Mines, Quarries and Oil Wells	Railroads	Express	Street Railways	Electric Light and Power	Telephones	Telegraphs
1908	$110.78	$ 99.73	$ 97.23	$ 97.69	$ 95.89	$101.28	$ 96.46	$ 98.15
1909	107.87	100.91	92.81	96.28	93.50	99.75	95.26	99.82
1910	106.02	94.99	88.32	93.06	89.73	96.59	92.88	96.72
1911	105.08	92.56	85.95	86.46	89.95	98.59	87.52	96.80
1912	103.53	93.29	82.78	82.03	88.34	96.31	90.43	92.29
1913	98.52	85.87	77.38	69.13	86.90	91.26	87.07	86.19
1914	95.55	87.42	78.05	72.26	86.07	89.88	90.52	87.85
1915	96.70	87.75	84.85	80.98	83.33	92.52	92.43	87.90
1916	90.44	81.99	79.17	73.72	73.67	81.20	85.33	79.96
1917	73.38	66.72	59.45	51.41	52.76	65.64	69.05	67.67
1918	63.81	58.90	53.34	c	45.94	58.86	61.36	57.46
1919	53.80	51.36	42.69	c	32.75	48.11	51.33	45.56
1920	48.79	45.01	39.10	c	28.28	43.03	48.54	42.02
1921	59.81	58.84	49.44	c	36.29	54.65	63.10	52.68
1922	61.19	61.94	50.95	c	44.55	60.39	66.14	56.75
1923	58.76	58.63	51.90	c	41.16	57.68	64.53	55.65
1924	60.64	60.27	52.12	c	45.10	59.89	66.32	57.72
1925	60.53	58.89	54.63	c	42.62	59.06	65.06	56.56

[a] "1913 Dollars" is an abbreviation for the phrase "dollars having purchasing power equivalent to that which they had in 1913."

[b] Computed from corresponding items in Table LXXXII by dividing by the appropriate price indices recorded in Table VII.

[c] No funded debt.

40 makes perfectly clear the reason why bondholders on the average received such small percentages of income during the period studied. Most of the interest received went to offset the losses in capital value occurring between 1909 and 1920, a period during which the bondholders were paying the penalty which monetary inflation always exacts from holders of fixed incomes. While the deflation of 1920 to 1922 brought a distinct recovery in the real worth of the bonds, the recovery was far from being large enough to offset the great decline which had previously occurred.

CHART 40

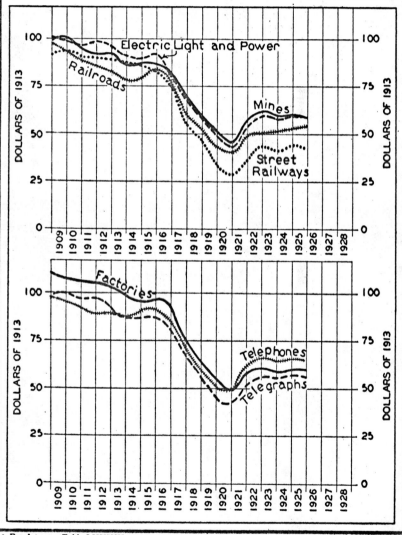

PURCHASING POWER, IN 1913 DOLLARS,
OF PRICE OF AVERAGE $100 UNIT OF
FUNDED DEBT OUTSTANDING AT END OF YEAR[a]

[a] For data, see Table LXXXIV.

TABLE LXXXV

PURCHASING POWER, IN 1913 DOLLARS,[a]
OF PRICE OF AVERAGE $100 UNIT OF
PREFERRED STOCK OUTSTANDING AT CLOSE OF YEAR
(REPRESENTS AMOUNT OF DIRECT OR CONSUMERS' GOODS PURCHASABLE
AT PRICES PREVAILING IN 1913)[b]

December 31	Factories	Mines, Quarries and Oil Wells	Street Railways	Electric Light and Power	Telephones	Telegraphs
1908	$103.15	$85.34	$83.02	$79.51	$69.91	$73.69
1909	109.55	95.97	85.71	81.58	74.95	79.85
1910	101.52	61.59	79.63	82.58	71.86	77.31
1911	100.68	80.60	82.14	79.25	72.48	70.85
1912	99.93	86.73	82.35	83.19	71.30	67.98
1913	90.36	67.30	63.16	68.44	62.50	64.47
1914	89.71	58.63	60.53	75.28	65.25	66.87
1915	100.00	80.91	53.26	77.31	67.72	64.17
1916	91.97	60.88	47.65	69.57	63.69	58.81
1917	71.19	46.51	33.35	47.89	52.97	46.59
1918	64.35	59.69	30.63	49.83	38.34	44.73
1919	58.69	51.86	24.18	45.95	28.72	38.76
1920	49.35	44.27	20.14	37.08	32.04	29.77
1921	55.68	57.19	24.18	42.48	36.95	33.50
1922	63.23	54.33	32.70	58.97	39.93	40.66
1923	61.88	50.66	41.63	61.77	40.93	43.73
1924	66.36	50.40	40.59	68.10	41.64	47.05
1925	65.64	46.38	40.14	67.55	42.92	46.37

[a] "1913 Dollars" is an abbreviation for the phrase "dollars having purchasing power equivalent to that which they had in 1913."
[b] Computed from corresponding items in Table LXXXIII by dividing by the appropriate price indices recorded in Table VII.

Average Value of All Shares of Preferred Stock (1913 Dollars).

In Table LXXXV and Chart 41, there is recorded the estimated average price in 1913 dollars of all preferred stocks outstanding in the various industries. While the prices of the preferred stocks fluctuated much more than did the values of the bonds, and while the difference between the average values of the stocks in the various industries was greater than the variations in the values of the bonds in the various industries, the trends of both preferred stocks and bonds are remarkably similar. In both cases, there is the long decline between the beginning of 1910 and the end of 1920, and the sharp recovery between the end of 1920 and the end of 1923, since which date the purchasing power represented by the

CHART 41

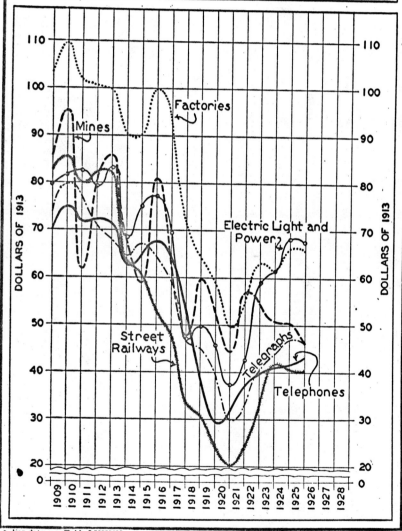

PURCHASING POWER, IN 1913 DOLLARS,
OF PRICE OF AVERAGE $100 UNIT OF
PREFERRED STOCK OUTSTANDING AT END OF YEAR[a]

[a] For data, see Table LXXXV.

value of the preferred stocks has been about stationary. Throughout the period, the prices of the preferred stocks of manufacturing corporations have tended to run higher than have those in any other field, although, from the beginning of 1924 to the end of 1925, the preferred stocks of electric light and power corporations occupied the primary place. As in the case of bonds, the preferred stock of street and electric railways have had the lowest values through most of the period.

The average share of preferred stock of street railway corporations was worth less than half as much at the close of the period as at the beginning, and the decline in the mining industry was almost as severe. In the other fields, a loss of something like one-third of the total value was typical of the period 1908 to 1925.

Theoretical Effect of Corporate Saving Upon Value of Industry.

The item of corporate surplus is hard to estimate because it depends in a measure on the respective valuations placed upon the property of the corporation at the beginning and at the end of the year, and, as we have previously seen, it is practically impossible to evaluate with accuracy the property of a corporation at any given date. When the price level is changing, it becomes doubly difficult for the accountant even to approximate the value of the corporate property. In very many cases—presumably, in fact, in the majority of instances—no scientific attempt is made to allow for changes in the value of the dollar. Under such circumstances, it, of course, follows that the relationship between reported corporate savings and actual corporate savings is likely to be an extremely indefinite one. When to this is added the fact that earnings actually reinvested do not necessarily enhance the value of the corporation to its owners by any corresponding amount, we need not be surprised if we find that little relationship exists between the amount of corporate savings reported by an industry and the changes in the total value of the corporations in this given industry.

Net Incomes Reported for Various Industries.

In Table LXXXVI, figures are recorded showing for all corporations combined and for those in a number of selected industries the reported net incomes. It is evident from this table, if we may judge by the published corporate records, that the manufacturing industry has been one in which large net income has been the rule year after year. True, in 1921, the factories of the country lost

TABLE LXXXVI

TOTAL NET INCOME OF CORPORATIONS IN VARIOUS INDUSTRIES AS ESTIMATED ON THE BASIS OF CORPORATE REPORTS

(MILLIONS OF CURRENT DOLLARS)

Year	All Indus-tries[a]	Fac-tories[b]	Mines, Quarries and Oil Wells[b]	Bank-ing[e]	Rail-roads[c]	Trans-portation by Water[b]	Street Rail-ways[d]	Electric Light and Power[d]	Tele-phones[d]
1907							$69	$ 38	$ 41
1909	$3,044	$1,277	$ 69	$ 184	$520				
1910	3 214	1,532	132	236	574				
1911	2,826	1,410	194	227	508				
1912	3,490	1,698	347	211	507		88	61	51
1913	3,905	1,878	420	177	478				
1914	2,713	1,485	261	172	381				
1915	4,272	2,349	304	168	521				
1916	8,030	3,969	742	205	746	$225			
1917	8,073	4,447	705	234	663	178	82	92	59
1918	5,079	2,613	341	281	454	101			
1919	6,795	3,684	217	403	507	96			
1920	5,000	2,577	398	329	493	61			
1921	454	—184	—202	271	375	—3			
1922	5,183	2,553	70	321	460	6	74	194	97
1923	6,697	3,457	9	342	652	10			
1924	5,913	2,684	—41	370	642	10			
1925	8,146	2,695	266	459	791	21			
1926	8,281	3,726	305	536	902				

[a] Based upon *Annual Reports* of Commissioner of Internal Revenue for years before 1916, and for years since that date, upon *Statistics of Income* published by the U. S. Bureau of Internal Revenue and upon a study of the reports of a large number of sample corporations; total includes other industries than those for which estimates are here given.

[b] Based upon *Statistics of Income*, published by the U. S. Bureau of Internal Revenue and upon a study of the reports of a large number of sample corporations.

[c] Based upon *Statistics of Railways*, published by the Interstate Commerce Commission.

[d] Based upon *Census of Electrical Industries*.

[e] Based upon *Annual Report of the Comptroller of the Currency*. Includes small amount of non-corporate income.

money, but, in no other year, did they fail to report an aggregate net income less than twice as great as their nearest rival industry. In the earlier years of the period, the net income of the railways was something like half as great as the net income of manufacturing corporations, but, in the later years, the ratio of factory to railway income was not two to one, but approximately five to one. The net income reported by banking corporations was large during the years 1916 to 1920, but fell off markedly thereafter until 1923, after which there was some recovery. The reported net income of

corporations engaged in the operation of mines, quarries, and oil wells had a decidedly upward trend between 1909 and 1917, but, from 1917 to 1921, the trend was just as decidedly downward, and net reported income remained either negative or negligible in amount until the end of 1924. Figures on the income of corporations engaged in transportation by water are not available for years preceding 1916. Their period of prosperity, as judged by their corporate reports, terminated with 1917, earnings thereafter rapidly declining until a low point was reached in 1921, when net income fell slightly below zero. Since that date, the figures reported show very meager incomes.

Corporate Savings as Actually Related to Gains in Value of Industries.

In Table LXXXVII we find figures showing the reported savings of corporations in the same industries covered by Table LXXXVI. These corporate savings represent the hypothetical amounts of income carried to surplus after the payment of all fixed charges and also of preferred and common dividends. Enormous amounts were thus transferred to the surplus account in the years 1916 to 1919, inclusive, the peak being represented by 5 billion dollars for 1916. Since the entire realized income of the nation in 1916 was only about 43 billion dollars, this would indicate a saving by corporations equivalent to approximately one-eighth of the total realized income of the nation. From Table LII it appears, however, that, despite this peak in nominal corporate saving, the purchasing power of the property used in American business fell off more in 1916 than in any other year except 1917, for which we have a record.

Now let us look at the other side of the shield. In 1921, although, according to their reports, all the corporations in the United States, after paying their dividends, had a 2½ billion dollar deficit, that year is shown by the record in Table LII to have been the one in which the gain in the purchasing power of property was the greatest. This strange relationship between the volume of corporate saving and the changes in the real value of the business property of the nation arouses one's curiosity and leads one to wonder whether or not there is any tendency for the accumulation of surpluses on the books of corporations to be reflected in increases in the market value of corporate property as reflected on the Exchanges.

Table LXXXVIII and Chart 42 set forth the facts in this regard. Chart 42 gives no clear evidence of any correlation between

TABLE LXXXVII

TOTAL SAVINGS OF CORPORATIONS IN VARIOUS INDUSTRIES AS ESTIMATED ON THE BASIS OF CORPORATE REPORTS

(MILLIONS OF CURRENT DOLLARS)

Year	All Indus- tries[a]	Fac- tories[a]	Mines, Quarries and Oil Wells[a]	Bank- ing[a]	Rail- roads[a]	Street Rail- ways[a]	Electric Light and Power[a]	Tele- phones[a]
1907						$19	$20	$22
1909	$ 1,474	$ 657	$ —66	$ 96	$257			
1910	1,375	798	—20	116	279			
1911	945	612	61	107	220			
1912	1,519	853	190	92	226	22	29	22
1913	1,718	950	209	55	175			
1914	658	595	109	61	54			
1915	2,198	1,403	160	69	185			
1916	4,694	2,274	372	124	403			
1917	4,299	2,490	276	153	276	14	31	21
1918	1,535	751	—18	194	112			
1919	3,569	1,898	10	336	169			
1920	1,889	850	250	221	159			
1921	—2,504	—1,732	—386	123	111			
1922	2,534	1,232	—69	145	190	24	90	35
1923	3,351	1,677	—214	160	361			
1924	2,404	1,016	—253	206	335			
1925	3,988	766	—3	289	468			
1926	3,517	1,586	—22	355	539			

[a] Sources of information are same as those referred to in Table LXXXVI.

these two variables, for they are similar neither as regards trends or cyclical movements. It must be remembered, however, that the period covered is one in which inflation had an important part in determining the value of securities. The graphs in Chart 42 do give some indication that, when the price level is constant, heavy corporate savings are followed a year or two later by increases in the market value of the industries making the savings. The evidence is too scanty to warrant conclusions of a very definite nature.

The comparisons recorded in Table LXXXVIII between the total corporate savings and the total value of the common stock in the same industry are based upon the assumption that, since the corporate savings are the property of the common stockholders, any increase in corporate savings should be reflected in the value of

TABLE LXXXVIII

COMPARISON FOR TWO INDUSTRIES OF
INCREASES IN THE TOTAL VALUE OF THE
COMMON STOCK AND THE CORPORATE SAVINGS
AS INDICATED BY THE REPORTS TO THE STOCKHOLDERS[a]

(MILLIONS OF DOLLARS)

| YEAR | CURRENT DOLLARS | | | | DOLLARS OF 1913[b] | | | |
| | FACTORIES | | MINES | | FACTORIES | | MINES | |
	Corporate Savings	Value Increase	Corporate Savings	Value Increase	Corporate Savings	Value Increase	Corporate Savings	Value Increase
1909	$ 657	$3,184	$ —66	$ 55	$ 697	$3,376	$ —70	$ 59
1910	798	—21	—20	20	827	—21	—20	21
1911	612	1,454	61	1,081	633	1,504	63	1,119
1912	853	998	190	478	872	1,020	195	489
1913	950	—1,124	209	22	950	—1,124	209	22
1914	595	1,143	109	1,042	593	1,137	109	1,037
1915	1,403	6,657	160	1,393	1,402	6,651	160	1,392
1916	2,274	—864	372	576	2,136	—812	349	541
1917	2,490	—5,642	276	—3,070	2,073	—4,697	230	—2,556
1918	751	1,987	—18	—611	543	1,436	—13	—442
1919	1,898	1,779	10	—262	1,200	1,125	6	—165
1920	850	—5,465	250	—2,866	471	—3,027	138	—1,587
1921	—1,732	2,052	—386	1,553	—1,035	1,226	—230	928
1922	1,232	1,184	—69	1,055	773	743	—44	662
1923	1,677	—621	—214	—610	1,044	—387	—133	—380
1924	1,016	5,948	—253	1,801	633	3,707	—158	1,122
1925	766	4,913	—3	788	467	2,998	—2	481

[a] Based upon a study of stock prices and annual reports of a large sample of corporations in these industries.

[b] Computed by dividing the various items by the appropriate price indices recorded in Table VII.

the common stock. Table LXXXIX presents a comparison of the reported corporate savings of the railways of the country and the changes in the value of preferred and common stock combined. This comparison seems to be a reasonably valid one, since many of the preferred stocks of railways have been selling well below par, and since, therefore, an increase in the corporate savings ought to increase the total value of the preferred stock as well as the total value of the common stock. An especial interest attaches to figures for the railway industry, for, in this field, all accounts are kept on forms provided by the Interstate Commerce Commission and are carefully supervised by that body. In so far, therefore, as standard

CHART 42

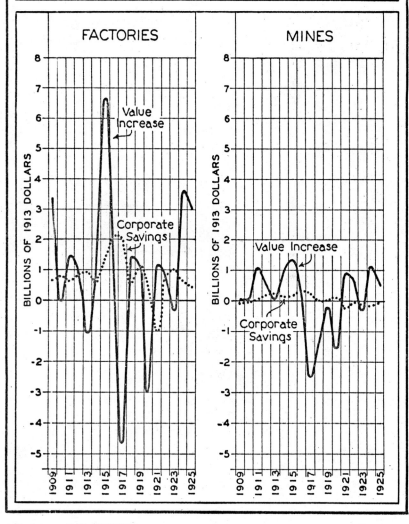

COMPARISON FOR TWO INDUSTRIES OF
INCREASES IN THE TOTAL VALUE OF THE
COMMON STOCK AND THE CORPORATE SAVINGS
AS SHOWN BY REPORTS TO STOCKHOLDERS[a]

[a] For data, see Table LXXXVIII.

TABLE LXXXIX

COMPARISON OF INCREASES IN THE TOTAL VALUE OF THE CAPITAL STOCK AND THE CORPORATE SAVINGS OF RAILWAY, SWITCHING, AND TERMINAL COMPANIES[a]

(MILLIONS OF DOLLARS)

YEAR	CURRENT DOLLARS		DOLLARS OF 1913[b]	
	Corporate Savings	Stock Value Increase	Corporate Savings	Stock Value Increase
1909	$257	$ 554	$272	$ 326
1910	279	—38	289	—89
1911	220	—333	228	—404
1912	226	915	231	795
1913	175	—1,177	175	—1,329
1914	54	—793	53	—719
1915	185	1,064	185	887
1916	403	—438	379	—1,126
1917	276	—1,655	230	—2,072
1918	112	987	81	—45
1919	169	—1,129	107	—1,273
1920	159	—355	88	—312
1921	111	758	66	—127
1922	190	1,345	119	836
1923	361	41	225	1
1924	335	972	209	585
1925	468	1,368	286	725

[a] Based upon a study of stock prices and upon *Statistics of Railways*, published by the U. S. Interstate Commerce Commission.

[b] "1913 Dollars" is an abbreviation for the phrase "dollars having purchasing power equivalent to that which they had in 1913."

accounting methods can be relied upon to show the facts, the figures for railway corporate savings should do so. A study of the figures indicates that the railways have carried to surplus a very considerable amount of their earnings in every one of the 17 years covered by the study. In poor years like 1914, 1918, 1920, and 1921, the amounts have fallen below 100 millions of dollars, expressed in dollars of 1913, but, in the 9 best years of the 17 reported, corporate savings have run well over 200 millions of dollars. If corporate savings resulted in corresponding increases in the value of railways to their owners, the logical result would be for the value of the stock in 1913 dollars to have increased steadily year by year.

What are the facts? The last column in Table LXXXIX makes it clear that, in only 6 years out of the 17, did the owners of railway

CHART 43

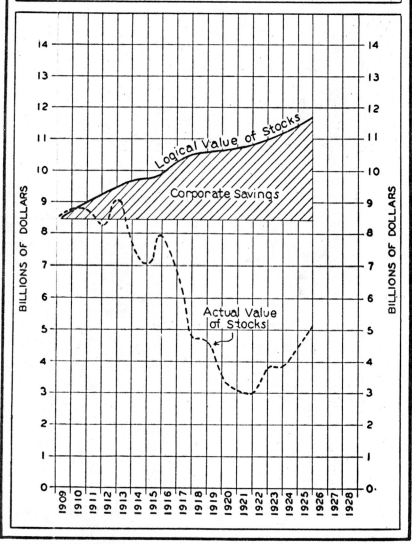

LOGICAL AND ACTUAL VALUE OF STOCKS
OF RAILWAY, SWITCHING, AND TERMINAL
COMPANIES BASED UPON CORPORATE SAVINGS
AND INCREASES IN THE TOTAL VALUE OF THE
CAPITAL STOCK[a]

[a] For data, see Table LXXXIX and figures for dollars of 1913.

TABLE XC

PER CENT OF THEIR NET INCOME[a]
SAVED BY CORPORATIONS IN VARIOUS INDUSTRIES
AS ESTIMATED ON THE BASIS OF CORPORATE REPORTS[a]

Year	All Industries	Factories	Mines, Quarries and Oil Wells	Banking	Railroads	Street Railways	Electric Light and Power	Telephones
1907						26.92	52.23	53.84
1909	48.42	51.43	—96.20	52.17	49.42			
1910	42.78	52.11	—14.86	49.15	48.64			
1911	33.44	43.41	31.60	47.14	43.37			
1912	43.52	50.23	54.82	43.60	44.60	25.28	47.32	42.09
1913	44.00	50.59	49.66	31.07	36.70			
1914	24.25	40.09	41.92	35.47	14.10			
1915	51.45	59.75	52.75	41.07	35.60			
1916	58.46	57.29	50.09	60.49	54.08			
1917	53.25	55.99	39.12	65.38	41.60	17.35	34.37	35.04
1918	30.22	28.75	—5.17	69.04	24.68			
1919	52.52	51.51	4.75	83.38	33.29			
1920	37.78	32.97	62.79	67.17	32.13			
1921	—551.54	b	b	45.39	29.61			
1922	48.89	48.23	—99.50	45.17	41.31	32.83	46.12	36.01
1923	50.04	48.50	—2,273.88	46.78	55.29			
1924	40.66	37.83	b		55.68	52.25		
1925	48.96	28.43	—1.28	62.96	59.23			
1926	42.47	42.57	—7.20	66.23	59.76			

[a] Based upon figures presented in Tables LXXXVI and LXXXVII.

[b] A deficit occurred, and the resulting negative ratio is meaningless.

[a] Available for preferred and common dividends.

stocks find the total value of their securities increasing. In one
year, the value was practically stationary, while, in the other 10
years, the total value declined. Furthermore, the losses in the bad
years were tremendous, exceeding a billion dollars in 1913, in 1916,
and in 1919, and 2 billion dollars in 1917, while in not a single year,
did the gains reach a figure as high as one billion dollars. In this
industry the actual earnings are as well authenticated as possible.
It would seem that corporate savings ought, here if anywhere, to
manifest a definite influence. Despite steady and consistent thrift
on the part of the railway corporations the values have declined
during most of the years covered by this study. The evidence
appears to be conclusive that the normal tendency for corporate
savings to add to the value of the property is very commonly nul-

CHART 44

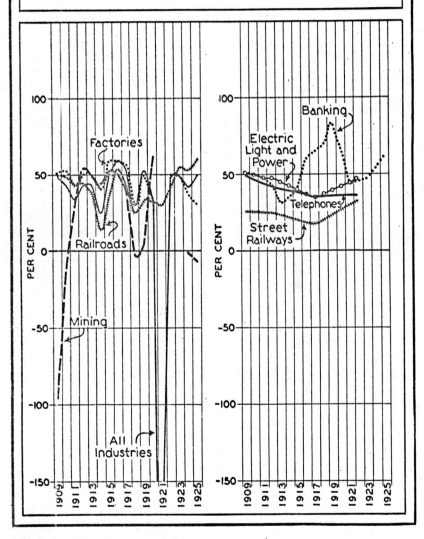

PER CENT OF THEIR NET INCOME SAVED BY
CORPORATIONS IN VARIOUS INDUSTRIES AS
ESTIMATED ON THE BASIS OF CORPORATE
REPORTS[a]

[a] For data, see Table XC.

lified and sometimes completely buried by the effects of other forces, such as inflation of the currency and rate regulation.

Chart 43 shows how far the actual total value of railway stocks has departed from the value which would have been attained had every dollar saved added a dollar to the value of the holdings of the railway stockholders. At the end of 1921, when one might have expected the total value to be *enhanced* by more than one-fourth, it had actually undergone a *shrinkage* of nearly two-thirds.[1]

Percentage of Reported Corporate Income Saved.

A famous railway president is said to have established as one of the maxims of corporate policy, "A dollar for the stockholders and a dollar for the company." Table XC and Chart 44 are devoted to showing how well this policy has been carried out by the corporations in a number of the most important industries. Three leading industries have, on the average, fallen somewhat short of the ideal indicated by the maxim just quoted, the general tendency apparently being to save approximately 40 per cent of the reported net income. The street railway industry has not succeeded in doing as well. For the period 1916 to 1920, the banking industry showed the highest degree of thrift, but the percentage of saving therein diminished rapidly between 1919 and 1922. Since then there has been an upward tendency, and, by 1924, the banks of the nation again succeeded in laying aside half of their reported income.

The enormous percentages of deficit indicated for all industries in 1921 and for mines and quarries in 1923, are not particularly significant, for they arise merely from the fact that the deficits in the instances mentioned were sizeable, while the net income was very small.

In general, Table XC and Chart 44 must lead to the conclusion that, if American industries have not brought satisfactory rates of return to investors therein, the failure to meet expectations cannot, in most cases, be ascribed to any wide-spread tendency on the part of corporation managements to pay out to the stockholders too

[1]Mr. George Soule makes the following comment:—"Dr. King seems to assume that it is normally to be expected that this percentage will not decrease, and that it was decreased only because governmental agencies were not alive to the implications of change in the price level. This language implies a judgment as to the proper theory of valuation, and therefore may not be considered impartial. It would be justified only if we approved the theory of reproduction new. If, on the other hand, the return to capital is to be limited to a return on prudent investment or the sacrifice of investors, then it would be quite normal for the percentage to decrease as prices rise."

TABLE XCI

PER CENT OF THEIR NET INCOME[c] SAVED BY GROUPS OF SAMPLE CORPORATIONS REPRESENTING THE VARIOUS BRANCHES OF MANUFACTURING AS ESTIMATED ON THE BASIS OF CORPORATE REPORTS[b]

YEAR	All Branches of Mfg.		Food		Textiles		Iron and Steel (Excluding Machinery)		Lumber		Leather		Rubber		Paper and Pulp		Printing and Publishing		Chemicals	
	No. of Corps.	Per Cent	No. of Corps.	Per Cent	No. of Corps.	Per Cent	No. of Corps.	Per Cent	No. of Corps.	Per Cent	No. of Corps.	Per Cent	No. of Corps.	Per Cent	No. of Corps.	Per Cent	No. of Corps.	Per Cent	No. of Corps.	Per Cent
1909	106	42.11	19	46.57	4	36.90	9	47.88	1	100.00	2	61.82	3	47.60	3	47.32	2	28.85	7	47.82
1910	122	42.38	21	35.72	5	36.24	11	49.34	1	100.00	2	-192.11	4	34.33	4	47.89	2	29.13	8	38.09
1911	124	30.40	23	22.39	5	14.94	10	23.11	2	75.42	3	-194.51	4	32.76	3	50.40	3	35.85	8	42.53
1912	150	37.85	26	42.14	7	37.09	13	26.51	2	60.07	4	60.21	4	42.25	3	52.24	3	30.26	7	27.79
1913	179	39.05	28	36.52	9	32.67	14	48.86	3	-10.65	4	28.25	7	33.83	5	31.57	4	30.55	13	37.48
1914	192	24.64	31	38.76	9	15.89	14	-10.08	3	1.42	5	20.23	7	49.26	5	53.55	4	22.06	13	48.15
1915	203	54.04	34	50.69	12	53.77	16	68.83	2	-20.95	5	40.96	7	67.49	5	59.23	4	45.94	14	55.25
1916	219	66.21	33	60.14	12	57.99	20	76.99	2	38.06	5	65.38	8	62.80	6	87.20	4	49.28	16	62.94
1917	221	56.95	33	64.39	12	63.12	21	56.27	2	56.02	5	40.28	9	69.07	6	81.44	4	52.28	16	58.01
1918	326	51.84	48	51.29	24	45.98	30	40.12	3	50.03	5	39.27	10	69.35	7	69.35	7	67.14	26	53.36
1919	352	55.08	52	53.42	28	57.90	32	42.95	3	78.72	5	60.18	12	68.97	7	63.58	7	73.75	26	37.84
1920	382	47.75	56	18.18	32	17.71	38	56.13	4	54.55	6	*	12	5.79	7	82.49	7	71.78	29	13.32
1921	389	-306.30	58	*	33	-13.15	38	-207.36	4	49.54	7	74.84	13	*	7	*	7	33.68	30	-287.16
1922	391	36.23	59	36.62	33	31.37	40	1.64	4	71.34	7	1.57	12	52.35	6	34.48	6	24.81	31	22.74
1923	384	44.53	57	43.55	31	43.16	38	52.38					12	36.77			6	37.38	31	36.56
1924	360	37.53	55	39.09	28	*	35	32.09	2	51.08	7	57.16	12	59.70	3	30.66	7	26.59	27	30.79
1925	375	44.96	58	28.79	32	.57	36	45.30	4	-256.35	7	59.34	13	78.95	5	41.95	7	34.41	29	39.55

[a] There was a deficit and the resulting negative ratio is meaningless.
[b] Based upon a study of the annual reports of the sample corporations indicated in the table.
[c] Available for preferred and common dividends.

TABLE XCI—Continued

PER CENT OF THEIR NET INCOME SAVED BY GROUPS OF SAMPLE CORPORATIONS REPRESENTING THE VARIOUS BRANCHES OF MANUFACTURING AS ESTIMATED ON THE BASIS OF CORPORATE REPORTS[b]

Year	Gas No. of Corps.	Gas Per Cent	Petroleum Refining No. of Corps.	Petroleum Refining Per Cent	Stone, Clay and Glass No. of Corps.	Stone, Clay and Glass Per Cent	Metal Other than Iron No. of Corps.	Metal Other than Iron Per Cent	Tobacco No. of Corps.	Tobacco Per Cent	Machinery No. of Corps.	Machinery Per Cent	Musical Instruments No. of Corps.	Musical Instruments Per Cent	Motor Vehicles No. of Corps.	Motor Vehicles Per Cent	Railway Equipment No. of Corps.	Railway Equipment Per Cent	Ship-Building No. of Corps.	Ship-Building Per Cent
1909	14	32.92	2	56.43	5	36.57	5	16.54	2	25.60	15	31.53	2	62.24			9	35.34	2	54.49
1910	17	31.32	3	60.96	7	29.45	7	16.31	2	45.77	17	47.77	2	*	1	62.00	9	41.56	2	9.22
1911	15	24.90	4	49.03	7	24.35	6	20.57	6	56.64	16	40.14	2	71.56			9	8.04	2	29.91
1912	18	22.46	5	50.15	7	22.15	6	50.75	6	30.67	22	49.71	2	63.09	3	74.89	10	45.59	2	39.36
1913	20	19.92	5	45.90	8	44.28	7	35.61	7	7.74	25	38.66	2	64.80	4	78.83	12	34.63	2	75.49
1914	22	21.95	6	26.53	9	16.26	9	30.09	6	16.47	27	17.84	2	55.58	6	81.58	12	57.13	2	100.00
1915	21	23.32	7	51.09	9	15.85	9	47.92	6	18.67	29	42.70	2	59.76	7	86.90	12	38.94	2	83.44
1916	22	24.17	7	73.01	10	54.98	11	61.01	6	29.08	30	55.38	2	66.09	10	65.97	12	62.00	2	69.33
1917	22	19.01	7	49.63	10	47.32	11	42.39	6	36.92	29	60.90	1	39.55	13	78.66	12	51.28	2	77.74
1918	23	1.01	12	70.58	12	60.11	14	37.39	11	63.70	53	50.62	1	68.11	23	46.13	13	56.84	4	56.65
1919	23	-11.70	13	70.84	16	65.90	15	42.68	11	48.98	56	52.81	1	62.29	25	67.00	16	51.32	4	58.11
1920	24	-34.48	15	77.57	16	56.01	16	36.79	12	45.30	58	47.22	1	70.86	28	28.94	16	40.14	4	44.99
1921	24	-46.90	14	-6.51	16	23.68	17	-157.44	12	38.86	57	-31.15	2	-1.27	30	*	16	-.49	4	-39.76
1922	26	52.52	15	51.33	15	45.81	15	44.82	12	41.76	59	24.60	2	59.26	29	50.00	16	21.39	4	-25.93
1923	26	31.63	13	36.99	15	60.50	16	42.55	12	33.75	59	35.77	2	65.51	29	59.33	16	52.32	4	45.09
1924	25	33.20	13	50.16	15	59.24	16	34.93	12	36.22	58	39.23	2	48.09	27	37.80	13	17.88	3	18.76
1925	24	29.16	13	62.82	16	39.84	16	46.63	12	37.13	56	44.49	2	55.55	27	47.37	15	-49.41	3	44.65

large a proportion of the net income available for dividends, for the evidence all indicates that the corporations have followed in this respect a conservative policy.

Table XCI shows the percentages of corporate income saved by sample corporations in 19 fields of manufacturing. The figures in this table are of interest in that they bring out the wide differences in policy among different industries and also the marked fluctuations from year to year in the percentages of net income carried to surplus

CHAPTER XI

FACTS BEARING ON AGRICULTURAL INCOME

Changes in the Total Physical Productivity of Agriculture.

To measure year to year changes in the total physical productivity of the agricultural industry is not easy. The records of the physical quantities of the various crops produced each year are, to be sure, reasonably complete. But a large proportion of the crops are used to feed livestock, and, to no small extent, the farmer derives his income from the sale of milk, butter, eggs, beef, and pork, rather than from the sale of hay and grain. The figures in Table XCII represent the results of an effort to overcome such statistical difficulties and to present a condensed picture of the physical productivity of the agricultural industry for the years 1909 to 1925, inclusive. The method of attack has been to calculate what the value of the various net products would have been had the price of each remained at the level measured by the average price of each product during the period 1909 to 1913, inclusive.

The question will probably be raised at this point as to why the average for a period of years has been used as a base in this particular instance, while, in previous tables in this report, it has been customary to make all comparisons on the basis of one year only, namely 1913. The reason for broadening the base in this particular instance is that crop production is notoriously variable, rising and falling greatly with the amount of rainfall, and hence agricultural prices, depending as they do very largely upon the volume of production in the given year, also vary widely from month to month and season to season. For this reason, it has seemed best to take an average for a five year period as a basis for our calculations.

Relative Importance of Different Agricultural Products.

The figures for grain and hay production appear very low in comparison with the figures for animal products. This is due to the fact that the estimates for grain and hay do not represent the total value of the amount of these products raised by the farmers, but merely the estimated value of the amounts either sold outside of the farm area, or consumed by human beings on farms or elsewhere; in other words, an attempt has been made to eliminate all grain and hay fed to livestock on the farms.

In Chart 45 it is seen that the four groups of products making up the bulk of agricultural output, are, in order of importance, animal products, grain, cotton and miscellaneous products—animal products alone accounting for nearly half of the total value. Furthermore, animal products have been increasing relatively in proportionate importance, while hay, and to a certain extent grain, show a diminution in relative importance.

A year to year comparison indicates that, when all products are combined, 1915 and 1924 are the banner years for production in the entire period covered. Although we heard much of the strenuous efforts of the farmers in 1917 and 1918, in neither of these years did physical output reach a level as high as in 1915 or even in 1916. It must be remembered, however, that, especially in 1918, the farm working force was reduced by the enlistment of a large number of the boys into the Army. The year 1918 did, however, represent a peak for that part of the period, as far as production of animal products was concerned, and the yield of potatoes was also well above normal. The net supply of grain available for human food, while larger than in 1917 and 1916, was not nearly up to the level of 1914 and 1915. The net output of grain in 1925 was lower than in any other year in the period, and the same may be said of hay, the tendency in the shipments of the latter being sharply downward owing to the diminution of the number of horses in the city. Cotton production was unusually high in 1925. The output of animal products is more stable than the output of other agricultural products, and apparently has a decided upward trend.

The net totals of grain production in Table XCII have not been arrived at by calculating and deducting from the gross production the amount of grain fed to livestock, but have been estimated on the basis of the excess of exports over imports, the amount of grain milled less the amount ground for feed, and the amount used for brewing and miscellaneous purposes. The figures for hay, in the same table, represent the estimated amounts of hay fed to livestock not on farms. As the numbers of such livestock are but roughly estimated, these figures are, of course, nothing but approximations.

Variations in Total Acreage Harvested.

The figures in Table XCII, while representing the aggregate of *net* physical production, do not show the relationships of these

TABLE XCII

ESTIMATED NET VALUE[b]
OF ALL AGRICULTURAL PRODUCTS
HAD AVERAGE PRICE OF EACH PRODUCT
IN PERIOD 1909-1913 PREVAILED THROUGHOUT*
(MILLIONS OF DOLLARS)

Year	All Products	Grain	Hay	Cotton	Potatoes	Fruit	Tobacco	Animal Products	All Other
1909	$5,629	$1,141	$144	$780	$244	$158	$ 93	$2,426	$643
1910	5,738	1,153	150	766	276	204	109	2,412	668
1911	5,934	1,149	153	881	251	222	101	2,485	692
1912	6,221	1,215	147	1,072	259	248	93	2,425	762
1913	5,953	1,223	150	887	271	203	95	2,414	710
1914	6,069	1,433	148	775	253	237	99	2,385	739
1915	6,620	1,344	146	1,074	291	305	103	2,536	820
1916	6,225	1,268	142	897	235	237	109	2,611	725
1917	5,814	1,135	133	783	279	208	117	2,493	667
1918	6,207	1,287	121	696	311	196	131	2,777	688
1919	6,340	1,207	114	892	298	197	141	2,776	715
1920	5,983	1,087	101	798	295	241	141	2,651	669
1921	6,051	1,247	97	798	314	166	161	2,568	699
1922	6,129	1,246	92	707	331	221	127	2,719	684
1923	6,346	1,107	85	677	331	242	142	3,113	649
1924	6,570	1,213	81	796	307	238	128	3,115	693
1925	6,409	924	78	1,031	288	214	133	3,026	715
1926	6,604*	1,023	73	1,050	273	298	132	3,039*	716*
1927	6,647*	1,096	73	999	313	200	143	3,114*	709*
1928	6,760*	1,113*	70*	956*	340*	249*	124*	3,191*	716*

* Based upon the *Census of Agriculture* and reports of the U. S. Department of Agriculture.

b Crops fed to livestock on farms are excluded, thus giving a total very different from the gross value of products.

* Preliminary estimate.

aggregates either to the number of farmers or to the total population. This comparison appears in Table XCIII. In the first column of this table is shown the estimated total acreage of all crops harvested. Since the figures for minor crops are not available in great detail, the probabilities are that the figures presented in Table XCIII as to acreage have an appreciable percentage of error, but there is apparently little doubt that the trend shown is approximately correct.

Acreage rose steadily from 1909 to 1919, the increase during this decade being about 16 per cent, or practically the same as the growth of population during the same 10 years. It will be observed

CHART 45

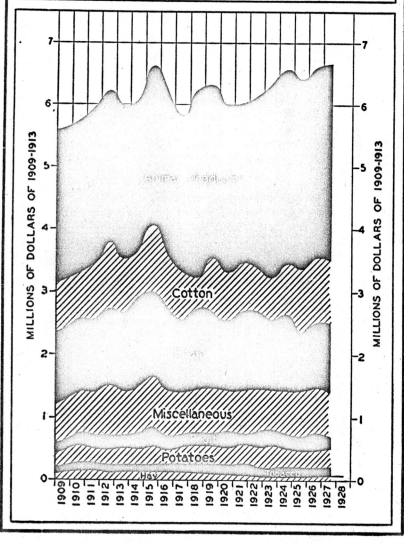

ESTIMATED NET VALUE OF ALL AGRICULTURAL
PRODUCTS HAD AVERAGE PRICE OF EACH
PRODUCT IN PERIOD 1909-1913
PREVAILED THROUGHOUT[a]

a For data, see Table XCII.

also that acreage continued to increase in 1918 despite the fact that a large number of men from the farms were called into the Army. Evidently, then, there is truth in the idea that more work per farm worker was expended on the farms of the United States during war time than in the years immediately preceding. In 1920, there was a sharp decline in acres harvested, partly due, presumably, to the fact that the demand at high wages for workers in the cities was so strong as to draw a proportion of laborers from the farm, and partly ascribable, no doubt, to the fact that, with the collapse of prices in 1920, a considerable proportion of the low-yield acreage was not worth harvesting. The decline in total acreage extended somewhat further in the next year, but, in 1922 and 1923, acreage again rose, despite the fact that the number of farmers[1] was then beginning to decrease. Between 1922 and 1927, acreage remained practically stationary, while the number of farmers declined somewhat, and the farm population fell off materially.

Effect of Tractors and Automobiles on Acreage Cultivated.

One of the factors which has enabled a diminished number of farm workers to maintain acreage undiminished has been the increasing use of the tractor on the larger farms in the Mississippi Valley and especially in the Great Plains region. The fact that most farmers now have automobiles has also helped them to economize on time in getting from place to place and doubtless has also aided in enabling a smaller number of farmers to keep up the acreage. In 1928, there was a sharp increase in acreage which finally pulled the figure above the level of 1919—and this in the face of the fact that the number of farmers declined still further.

Cultivated Acreage Per Farmer.

The number of acres per farmer in 1909 was about 50.3; in 1919, this had increased to approximately 57.4; and, in 1928, it was just above 60. It appears, therefore, that the size of the farm as measured by the area of crops cultivated has grown very materially during the 19 years, despite the fact that the number of workers per farm has diminished, and also despite the fact that a very considerable additional amount of farm land has been devoted to the intensive type of cultivation necessary for growing the vegetables and fruits required by an increasing population. Such

[1]The term "farmers" means farm operators and does not include hired employees.

increase in truck farming has evidently been more than offset by the growth in extensive farming on the Western plains.

Physical Product Per Acre Cultivated.

While each farmer has clearly been enabled by modern inventions to become more efficient as regards acreage cultivated, it is not necessarily true that the quality of each acre tilled in 1928 was as good as that of the average acre tilled in 1909, for the margin of cultivation is being pushed out upon lands that are quite arid, and these lands of course yield relatively small crops per acre. It is, therefore, of especial interest to study the value, at constant prices, of the net produce per acre harvested. These figures measure as accurately as is possible the physical net productivity per acre of all the farm land cultivated. A study of this column indicates that physical productivity per acre rose from 1909 to 1915 but fell again in 1916. Since 1916, the trend has been approximately horizontal, though there was a noticeable depression during the years 1920 to 1922 which may represent some diminution in the carefulness of cultivation in those years. In general, it appears that the effects of the intensive cultivation of part of the farm land have almost exactly offset those occasioned by the inclusion of large areas of the low yield land of the arid regions, the net result being that the physical output per acre was but slightly greater in 1928 than in 1909.

Physical Product Per Farmer.

The next column of Table XCIII shows physical output per farmer. This is the best measure that can be devised of the efficiency of the average farm as an operating unit. The evidence indicates that there was a very definite increase in the output per farmer between 1909 and 1915. During the ten years following 1915, the average output never reached as high a level as that of 1915. In both 1917 and 1920, the average output per farm was at a low ebb. Following 1920, there was a regular increase each year until 1928, with the exception of a slight decline in 1925. The deductions from Chart 46 are, in general, that the trend of the physical output per farmer has been upward ever since 1909, but that the rise was a little steeper at the beginning than at the end of the period. The year to year fluctuations due to changes in the weather are so large that it is impossible to state with precision the exact nature of the trend. It appears, nevertheless, that, despite the reduction in the number

TABLE XCIII

NET VALUE AT AVERAGE PRICES OF 1909-1913 OF TOTAL FARM PRODUCTS PER ACRE, PER FARMER AND PER CAPITA

YEAR	ACRES OF CROP HARVESTED[a] (THOUS.)	NUMBER OF FARM- ERS[a] (THOUS.)	POPULA- TION OF THE CONTINEN- TAL UNITED STATES[b] (THOUS.)	VALUE OF NET PRODUCE AT AVERAGE PRICES OF 1909-1913			
				Total[c] (Mil- lions)	Per Acre Harvested	Per Farmer	Per Capita
1909	316,028	6,289	90,508	$5,629	$17.81	$ 895.05	$62.19
1910	328,655	6,307	92,422	5,738	17.46	909.78	62.08
1911	334,993	6,322	93,837	5,934	17.71	938.63	63.24
1912	332,085	6,336	95,249	6,221	18.73	981.85	65.31
1913	336,755	6,346	97,111	5,953	17.68	938.07	61.30
1914	337,160	6,353	98,974	6,069	18.00	955.30	61.32
1915	346,698	6,359	100,390	6,620	19.09	1,041.04	65.94
1916	346,411	6,365	101,787	6,225	17.97	978.00	61.16
1917	354,309	6,369	103,234	5,814	16.41	912.86	56.32
1918	363,346	6,374	104,377	6,207	17.08	973.80	59.47
1919	366,063	6,378	105,007	6,340	17.32	994.04	60.38
1920	361,136	6,381	106,422	5,983	16.57	937.63	56.22
1921	360,176	6,387	108,370	6,051	16.80	947.39	55.84
1922	363,515	6,271	109,742	6,129	16.86	977.36	55.85
1923	364,265	6,297	111,478	6,346	17.42	1,007.78	56.93
1924	358,530	6,344	113,466	6,570	18.32	1,035.62	57.90
1925	363,515	6,317	115,004	6,409	17.63	1,014.56	55.73
1926	364,690	6,200*	116,442*	6,604*	18.11*	1,065.22*	56.71*
1927	363,598	6,124*	117,980*	6,647*	18.28*	1,085.34*	56.34*
1928	367,469	6,102*	119,440*	6,760*	18.40*	1,107.83*	56.60*

   [a] Based upon *Census of Agriculture* and reports of the U. S. Department of Agriculture.
   [b] See Table I.
   [c] See Table XCII.
   * Preliminary estimate.

of workers per farm, and also despite the relatively low prices of farm products prevailing in years since the close of the World War, the average farmer has succeeded in maintaining the same standard of physical output prevailing prior to 1920, but that he has not been able materially to raise the level.

Agricultural Output per Inhabitant of the United States.

The last column of Table XCIII shows the physical output of agricultural produce per inhabitant of the Continental United

CHART 46

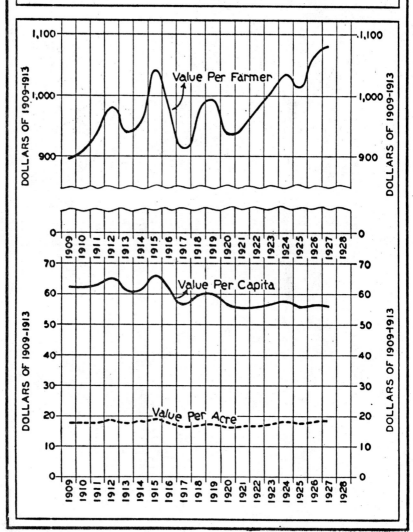

NET VALUE AT AVERAGE PRICES OF 1909-1913
OF TOTAL FARM PRODUCTS
PER ACRE, PER FARMER, AND PER CAPITA[*]

* For data, see Table XCIII.

States. The population of the United States has, of course, been growing rapidly. Since 1915, agricultural output has not been keeping pace with population. Between 1909 and 1916, production per capita apparently ran on approximately a level trend, but after 1915, a marked decline became apparent, and, from 1917 to 1928, the output of agriculture per inhabitant remained on a level materially lower than that characterizing the years 1909 to 1916. The average output for the years 1917 to 1925, was, in fact, only about 91 per cent as great as the output during the years 1909 to 1916. This decline in per capita production of agricultural products resulted in some curtailment of exports and in some shift of consumption from meat to vegetable products. Every shift in this direction makes it possible for a fixed number of acres to supply food for a number of persons relatively much larger than could be fed from meat grown on the same acreage.

Value of Business Property Devoted to Agriculture.

Table XCIV records in terms of current dollars the value of various kinds of business property devoted to agriculture. The figures in this table are either taken directly from the reports of the Federal Bureau of Agricultural Economics or are estimated from the reports of that Bureau or from the *Census of Agriculture*. An interesting column in this table shows the nominal value of farm land in the various years. We see portrayed here the steady rise in its aggregate value between 1909 and 1915 and the very rapid ascent between 1915 and 1920. It was, of course, this steep upward incline which led farmers and others to believe that agricultural land was an extremely profitable investment, and, because of this belief, many thousands of persons bought farms on relatively small payments. The disastrous results of this practice, with its aftermath of wholesale foreclosures of farm mortgages and failures of numerous banks, are too well known to need emphasis at this point. It is, indeed, true that the increase in nominal value between 1915 and 1920 would disappear if reduced to terms of dollars of constant purchasing power, but the fact must be kept in mind that people interested in buying farm land did not realize that the upward movements in values were merely reflections of currency inflation and that the upward trend would therefore cease when currency inflation stopped.

It is interesting to observe how long the effects of the exorbitant valuations due to currency inflation persisted after that

TABLE XCIV

VALUE OF BUSINESS PROPERTY
DEVOTED TO AGRICULTURE[a]
(MILLIONS OF CURRENT DOLLARS)

Jan. 1	A Land	B Build-ings	C Live-stock	D Auto-mo-biles[b]	E Tools and Im-ple-ments	F Crops on Hand	G Mis-cella-neous Prop-erty	H Total Value of Property Devoted to Agri-culture A+B+C+D+E+F+G	I Value of Farms Leased from Non-Farmers	J Non-Farmer Cred-itors' Equity in Owned Farms	K Prop-erty of Farmers Devoted to Agri-culture H-(I+J)
1909	$27,973	$2,350	$4,569	$ 11	$1,198	$1,944	$ 677	$38,721	$ 9,094	$1,817	$27,810
1910	28,437	2,527	4,925	16	1,265	2,190	700	40,060	9,482	1,894	28,684
1911	28,712	2,619	5,256	28	1,392	2,079	713	40,798	9,770	1,948	29,080
1912	29,393	2,691	4,955	35	1,420	2,107	722	41,323	10,161	2,024	29,138
1913	31,090	2,801	5,407	47	1,676	2,201	769	43,989	10,877	2,172	30,940
1914	32,012	2,833	5,749	54	1,773	2,284	795	45,500	11,328	2,276	31,896
1915	33,145	2,954	5,785	64	1,634	2,341	817	46,741	11,915	2,426	32,400
1916	37,020	3,121	5,795	78	1,764	2,735	898	51,411	13,365	2,799	35,247
1917	40,153	3,278	6,438	114	1,993	3,254	982	56,211	14,620	3,188	38,403
1918	44,577	3,349	7,862	153	2,548	5,164	1,132	64,785	16,235	3,650	44,900
1919	50,379	3,808	8,319	236	3,289	5,273	1,268	72,573	18,619	4,268	49,686
1920	54,815	4,595	8,015	304	3,595	6,087	1,377	78,787	20,892	4,989	52,906
1921	52,877	5,139	5,784	403	3,500	3,822	1,272	72,798	20,493	5,382	46,923
1922	43,053	4,925	4,684	304	3,088	2,489	1,041	59,583	17,083	5,544	36,956
1923	39,774	4,751	5,092	285	2,746	3,364	996	57,007	15,769	5,599	35,639
1924	38,876	4,738	4,837	363	2,817	3,598	982	56,211	15,316	5,619	35,276
1925	37,779	4,707	4,858	361	2,692	3,824	964	55,186	14,799	5,606	34,781
1926	36,836	4,719	5,239	350	2,649	3,603	950	54,345	14,549	5,629	34,167
1927	35,056*	4,731*	5,269*	349	2,460	3,167	908*	51,938*	14,004*	5,655	32,279*
1928	34,217*	4,750*	5,770*	344	2,242	3,426	903*	51,652*	13,767*	5,724*	32,161*

[a] Based upon *Census of Agriculture* and reports of U. S. Department of Agriculture.
[b] Fractional value of automobiles assumed to be devoted to business purposes is 0.3.
* Preliminary estimate.

phenomenon had passed into history. The total value of farm land in the United States was still declining in 1928, even though the worst of the price inflation was over before 1921 had ended.

The estimates in Table XCIV of the total value of buildings, tools and implements, crops on hand, and miscellaneous property, are not sufficiently accurate to be worthy of much consideration,

even though they have been computed as carefully as the data on hand permit. The figures on livestock, however, are reasonably dependable. It will be observed that the nominal value of livestock increased tremendously between 1912 and 1919, when the peak was reached. The precipitous decline beginning in 1920 brought the total value in 1922 almost back to the level of 1909. While the aggregate value of livestock increased somewhat between 1923 and 1928, the total nominal value in 1928 was still no greater than in 1914.

The reader's attention is called to the fact that the estimated value of automobiles, as here given, refers not to the total value of automobiles on farms, but merely to that fraction of the total value estimated to represent the percentage of automobile use devoted to business purposes. Examination of the next to the last column in the table shows that, while the total value of farm property rose between 1909 and 1920 and then declined sharply until 1922, after which it tended slightly downward, the equity of non-agricultural creditors in the owned farms steadily rose, this type of partial ownership being three times as extensive in 1928 as in 1909. It appears, then, that the burden of debt owed by farmers to non-farmers has, in recent years, been growing larger, while values of farm property have been shrinking. Column K indicates that, as a net result, that part of the property of farmers devoted to agriculture had a value in gold dollars approximately the same in 1928 as in 1912, despite the fact that the gold dollar would buy so much less of everything in the later years.

Sources of Agricultural Income.

Table XCV and Chart 47 deal with the net receipts in terms of gold dollars, of the agricultural industry derived from each of a number of sources. For this reason, year to year comparisons are not particularly significant. Receipts from crops constitute slightly more than half of the total value of farm produce, and this proportion has changed but little during the period covered by this study. The value of dairy products makes up slightly more than one-eighth of the net value of all farm produce, while meat animals account for something more than one-fifth, and eggs and poultry for another one-eleventh. These proportions did not change radically between 1909 and 1928.

The graphs in Chart 47 bring out clearly the enormous growth

TABLE XCV

NET[b] RECEIPTS OF AGRICULTURE FROM VARIOUS SOURCES[a]
(MILLIONS OF CURRENT DOLLARS)

YEAR	Total Net Receipts	Crops Not Fed to Livestock	Dairy Products	Eggs	Poultry	Other Meat Products	Wool and Mohair	Honey and Wax	Sold for Urban Use	
									Horses, Mules and Dairy Cows	Land
1909	$ 6,049	$3,354	$ 771	$292	$192	$1,291	$66	$ 6	$38	$38
1910	6,341	3,488	830	319	210	1,347	61	6	42	38
1911	5,946	3,313	792	293	193	1,224	51	7	43	31
1912	6,479	3,693	850	316	198	1,283	52	7	42	38
1913	6,388	3,431	853	298	214	1,450	45	7	42	47
1914	6,393	3,407	848	303	219	1,451	45	7	72	42
1915	6,804	3,789	864	338	209	1,394	56	7	112	36
1916	8,046	4,553	960	367	238	1,715	45	7	116	46
1917	11,026	6,564	1,282	310	272	2,354	110	9	80	44
1918	13,473	7,501	1,633	516	337	3,262	140	12	41	30
1919	14,889	8,544	1,889	635	392	3,221	124	14	31	38
1920	14,042	8,215	1,968	632	409	2,618	90	22	21	67
1921	9,098	5,151	1,350	487	349	1,598	39	13	13	98
1922	9,264	5,262	1,276	457	331	1,784	63	11	13	67
1923	10,350	5,749	1,555	566	395	1,858	89	11	12	115
1924	10,527	5,894	1,545	539	426	1,914	93	12	11	94
1925	11,280	6,039	1,667	605	432	2,335	104	12	11	75
1926	10,498*	5,077*	1,681	563*	488	2,497	95	12*	10	75*
1927	10,642*	5,491*	1,700*	527*	424*	2,332	92	12*	11	53*
1928	10,519*	5,124*	1,753*	563*	455*	2,438*	114	12*	13	48*

a Based upon *Census of Agriculture* and reports of U. S. Department of Agriculture.
b Crops fed to livestock are excluded, thus giving a total very different from the gross value of products.
* Preliminary estimate.

occurring between 1914 and 1919, in the nominal agricultural income. When we see how striking this increase was, we can readily understand how it happened that, during the period mentioned, most farmers had visions of a constantly accelerating demand for their products, and also why it was that farm land skyrocketed in value during these five years. The terrific debâcle of 1920 and 1921 is also vividly portrayed.

CHART 47

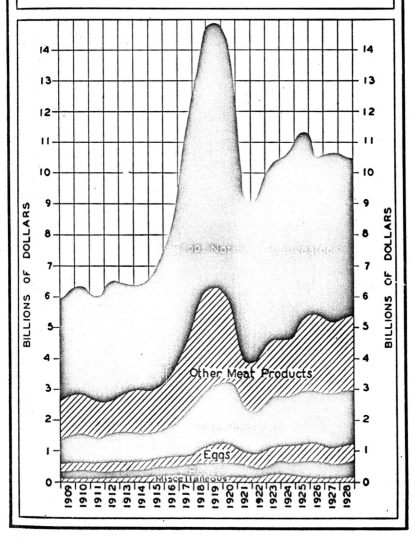

NET RECEIPTS OF AGRICULTURE
FROM VARIOUS SOURCES[a]

* For data, see Table XCV.

Payments by Agriculture to Other Industries.

Table XCVI[1] indicates the approximate amounts of business-expense money paid out by agriculture to other industries. In this table, as in the one preceding, all amounts are entered in terms of dollars current in the given year, and hence the comparisons of one date with another are not of prime significance. It will be observed that the owners of leased farms and the holders of mortgages on farms are treated as investors in the agricultural industry, the result being that payments to these classes are not counted in the list of business expenses appearing in Table XCVI. Similarly, amounts paid in the form of wages and salaries to employees engaged in agriculture are not listed in this table, for payments to employees are not deductions from the income of the industry.

None of the quantities appearing in Table XCVI can be computed with any high degree of precision. In general, however, it appears that, at the close of the period, out of the 11 billions of dollars, representing the total net receipts of farmers, landlords, and mortgage holders combined, between 2 and $2\frac{1}{2}$ billions had to be paid out to other industries for their contributions to agriculture.

Total Realized Income of Agriculture.

When total payments to other industries have been subtracted from the net receipts accruing to the agricultural industry, the figures entered in Column C of Table XCVII are obtained. These figures show the realized income of agriculture in terms of gold dollars. By subtracting from the items in this column the amount paid to employees in wages and salaries, we arrive at the figures in Column E which represent the aggregate income of landlords, holders of farm mortgages, and farmers and their families. The figures in the last two columns show that the combined nominal income of agricultural employees and of the entrepreneurs and investors in the industry reached a peak in either 1919 or 1920, declined until 1921, and, since then, has moved upward.

Realized Income of Entrepreneurs and Other Property Owners.

Table XCVIII pictures the total realized income of mortgage holders, landlords, and agricultural entrepreneurs after it has been

---

[1] The reader who is interested in a more detailed discussion of the way in which the figures in Tables XCV and XCVI have been derived is referred to *Income in the United States*, Volume II, Chapter III, and *Income in the Various States*, Chapters VII, VIII, and IX. Both of these books are publications of the National Bureau of Economic Research.

TABLE XCVI

PAYMENTS FOR BUSINESS PURPOSES
MADE BY AGRICULTURE TO OTHER INDUSTRIES*
(MILLIONS OF CURRENT DOLLARS)

Year	Total Payments	Tools and Implements	Fertilizer	Business Use of Automobiles	Binder Twine	Harness and Saddles	Business Buildings Including Insurance	Feed	Interest Payments to Banks and Merchants	Taxes	Cotton Ginning	Spraying	Horseshoeing
1909	$1,147	$177	$115	$ 24	$17	$58	$107	$307	$166	$ 74	$46	$26	$32
1910	1,214	223	135	31	16	56	120	282	180	77	36	26	32
1911	1,225	196	160	37	13	56	126	269	185	80	41	30	33
1912	1,281	184	147	55	17	57	135	312	174	83	53	31	34
1913	1,354	229	161	68	23	57	143	283	195	85	46	28	36
1914	1,411	198	188	73	21	57	146	333	196	87	50	27	35
1915	1,419	173	160	93	28	57	150	346	196	90	62	29	36
1916	1,524	219	162	145	25	59	159	318	214	93	55	35	39
1917	1,951	287	221	187	44	76	171	442	256	99	62	56	50
1918	2,384	363	293	201	63	82	172	581	340	109	68	50	61
1919	2,837	456	326	298	49	95	210	633	430	133	82	58	67
1920	3,143	527	379	431	42	73	233	568	503	166	87	58	77
1921	2,307	255	206	330	27	34	276	341	479	194	74	43	47
1922	2,133	251	198	355	29	42	240	367	321	184	62	37	46
1923	2,485	378	230	428	25	49	236	462	355	175	61	36	50
1924	2,364	337	231	316	30	41	236	499	357	175	63	30	49
1925	2,352	403	257	383	30	35	120	461	327	172	85	30	48
1926	2,446*	443	282	379	31	33	140*	452*	327*	171*	104		
1927	2,432*	479	206	362	27	32	125*	570*	278*	171*	101		
1928	2,572*	487*		403	29	37*	115*	615*					

* Based upon *Census of Agriculture* and reports of U. S. Department of Agriculture. Payments to landlords and mortgage holders are not included here, for these payments are considered part of income of the agricultural industry.

* Preliminary estimate.

divided into three shares: namely, the interest paid to mortgage holders, the rent paid to landlords, and the amount remaining, which is the realized income of farmers and their families. It should be kept in mind that the figures in Column B, representing as they do realized income, take no cognizance of the sweeping changes in the value of farm property which have occurred during this period.

The share of the owners of leased farms has grown much less rapidly than has the share of the mortgage holders. When both amounts are expressed in terms of the dollars current at the various

TABLE XCVII

REALIZED INCOME OF THE AGRICULTURAL INDUSTRY[a]
(MILLIONS OF CURRENT DOLLARS)

Year	A Receipts[b]	B Payments to Other Industries[c]	C Realized Agricultural Income A-B	D Wages and Salaries[d]	E Income of Entrepreneurs and of Property[e] C-D
1909	$6,049	$1,147	$4,902	$ 717	$4,185
1910	6,341	1,214	5,127	715	4,413
1911	5,946	1,225	4,722	751	3,971
1912	6,479	1,281	5,198	754	4,444
1913	6,388	1,354	5,034	776	4,258
1914	6,393	1,411	4,982	756	4,226
1915	6,804	1,419	5,385	773	4,612
1916	8,046	1,524	6,523	828	5,694
1917	11,026	1,951	9,074	1,029	8,045
1918	13,473	2,384	11,089	1,213	9,876
1919	14,889	2,837	12,051	1,491	10,561
1920	14,042	3,143	10,899	1,663	9,236
1921	9,098	2,307	6,791	1,405	5,386
1922	9,264	2,133	7,132	1,203	5,928
1923	10,350	2,485	7,864	1,231	6,633
1924	10,527	2,364	8,163	1,232	6,931
1925	11,280	2,352	8,929	1,253	7,676
1926	10,498*	2,446*	8,052*	1,272*	6,779*
1927	10,642*	2,432*	8,210*	1,252*	6,958*
1928	10,519*	2,572*	7,947*	1,279*	6,668*

[a] Includes interest received by mortgage holders and rent received by landlords.
[b] See Table XCV.
[c] See Table XCVI.
[d] See Table XIX.
[e] Exclusive of imputed rent on owned homes.
* Preliminary estimate.

dates, we see that the rent of leased farms increased by about 60 per cent between 1909 and 1927, while, during the same period, payments of interest to non-farm mortgage holders practically trebled. The realized income of farmers, also expressed in gold dollars, rose by about 65 per cent, a fraction slightly greater than the increase in rent accruing to landlords. Apparently farmers tend to receive something less than 6 per cent of their entire realized income from sources other than agriculture. This percentage has

not changed radically between 1909 and 1927 except during the ups
and downs of inflation and deflation, when it oscillated decidedly.

Entire Realized Income of Farmers (1913 Dollars).

The figures in Column F of Table XCVIII have been divided
by indices of the prices of the direct or consumers' goods used by
farmers and the results are shown in Column H. The fact should be
carefully noted that the index appearing in Column G represents
the price of consumers' goods only, and hence is very different from
the index compiled by the United States Bureau of Agricultural
Economics showing the prices of all goods bought by farmers.
The index in Table XCVIII includes the prices of goods produced on
the farm and also consumed there, as well as the prices of goods purchased by the farmer for the direct use of himself or his family,
but not the prices of goods bought for business purposes.

When all quantities are expressed in dollars of constant purchasing power, the income of all farmers was roughly stationary between
1909 and 1915, then rose sharply until 1918, declined somewhat in
1919, fell off rapidly in 1920, and tumbled precipitously in 1921.
The much heralded prosperity of the farmer in 1918 and his poverty
in 1921, were, then, no mere figments of the imagination, for the
total income of all farmers in 1921 would buy but slightly more
than half as many direct goods as would their income in 1918.
The purchasing power of the income of all farmers taken as a unit
increased regularly each year from 1921 until 1927 with a slight
decline in 1926. By 1923, it approximately equalled the figure for
1915 which was considered a good year for agriculture. The income
in 1925 was about half way between the income of 1915 and that of
1916, in both of which years the farmers were sharing in the prosperity brought on by European war orders.

Realized Income per Farmer (1913 Dollars).

Column J represents an estimate of the average realized income, in terms of 1913 dollars, per farm family. The figures in this
column show that the income per farm family remained between
the limits of $550 and $625 during the entire period 1909 to 1914,
then rose steadily to a sum of $876 in 1918, after which it fell
abruptly to $451 in 1921. The recovery after 1921 was steady until
$658 was attained in 1927 except for a slight decline in 1926. This
average was materially higher than the average for 1915, the year
which, up to that time, was the best in the period recorded. Only

TABLE XCVIII

REALIZED INCOME OF FARMERS*
(MILLIONS OF DOLLARS)

	A	B	C	D	E	F	G	H	I	J
YEAR	REALIZED ENTREPRENEURIAL AND PROPERTY INCOME FROM AGRICULTURE[a]	PAYMENTS TO NON-FARMERS[b]		REALIZED INCOME OF FARMERS		ENTIRE REALIZED INCOME OF FARMERS	INDEX OF PRICES OF GOODS USED BY FARMERS[d]	ENTIRE REALIZED INCOME IN 1913 DOLLARS	NUMBER OF FARMERS (THOUS.)	REALIZED INCOME OF FARMER AND FAMILY IN 1913 DOLLARS
		Interest	Rent	From Agriculture A-(B+C)	Other[c]	D+E		F÷G		H÷I
1909	$4,185	$ 76	$ 628	$3,481	$232	$3,714	.968	$3,838	6,289	$610
1910	4,413	79	671	3,663	241	3,904	.995	3,925	6,307	622
1911	3,971	84	720	3,167	246	3,413	.973	3,509	6,322	555
1912	4,444	88	700	3,656	249	3,905	.987	3,958	6,336	625
1913	4,258	93	721	3,444	255	3,699	1.000	3,699	6,346	583
1914	4,226	101	734	3,391	256	3,647	1.008	3,617	6,353	569
1915	4,612	110	751	3,752	264	4,015	.985	4,078	6,359	641
1916	5,694	125	812	4,757	274	5,030	1.108	4,540	6,365	713
1917	8,045	144	916	6,986	289	7,275	1.409	5,165	6,369	811
1918	9,876	160	1,023	8,692	310	9,002	1.613	5,581	6,374	876
1919	10,561	200	1,173	9,187	359	9,546	1.845	5,175	6,378	811
1920	9,236	238	1,193	7,805	430	8,234	2.001	4,114	6,381	645
1921	5,386	247	1,136	4,002	484	4,486	1.557	2,881	6,387	451
1922	5,928	240	1,016	4,671	477	5,148	1.481	3,475	6,271	554
1923	6,633	238	1,009	5,387	461	5,848	1.452	4,029	6,297	640
1924	6,931	234	1,049	5,647	449	6,096	1.466	4,157	6,344	655
1925	7,676	235	1,073	6,367	431	6,801	1.588	4,283	6,317	678
1926	6,779*	236*	1,055	5,488*	424	5,912*	1.621	3,647*	6,200*	588*
1927	6,958*	238*	989*	5,730*	428*	6,158*	1.529	4,028*	6,124*	658*

　　[a] See Table XCVII. Excludes imputed rent on owned homes.
　　[b] Based upon *Census of Agriculture* and reports from U. S. Department of Agriculture.
　　[c] Derived after study of L. C. Gray's article on "Accumulation of Wealth by Farmers"—American Economic Review, March 1923. Includes imputed rent of owned homes.
　　[d] See Table VII.
　　[e] Includes income of farmers and members of their families, but excludes income of hired employees.
　　* Preliminary estimate.

in the four years 1916 to 1919, which were obviously years of abnormal prosperity for the farmers, was this level ever reached before. The available evidence indicates that the condition of the farmer during the period following 1923 was better than it had been before

the World War. Farm incomes in terms of dollars were still very low as compared to those in the city, but this was true in pre-war as well as in post-war days. There seems, then, to be no ground for the frequently repeated assertion that, in recent years, the condition of the farmer has been absolutely worse than it was before 1914, but it is true that he has failed to obtain his proportion of the remarkable increase in income characterizing the period beginning with 1923.

Changes in the Real Value of Farm Property.

As previously stated, the figures in Table XCVIII fail to make allowance for the changes in property value which have occurred during the period in question. These variations in the value of the farmer's wealth have been so tremendous that, when they are taken into consideration, a very different picture is given of the year-to-year changes which have taken place in the income of the farmers of the nation. As in the other studies of property values previously noted in this report, all quantities at all dates have been expressed in terms of command over consumers' goods—that is, the changes in value of property, when measured in terms of 1913 dollars, represent the changes in the amount of direct goods which could have been obtained for the amount of money represented by the value of the property at the various dates.

Column B of Table XCIX shows the tremendous amplitude of the fluctuations in the value of farm property. In 1915, the increase in value amounted to 3 ¾ billions, while, in 1916, the total value of farm property fell off by nearly 5 billions. The value of farm property declined in 10 years and increased in only 7 of the years in this period. Furthermore, in the 17 years covered, the gains aggregated only about 13 billions and the losses about 21 billions. The farmer, therefore, had to deduct from his realized income approximately 8 billions of dollars in order to arrive at his actual total income. When the deductions for the years of heavy losses are made, we find that, in 1916, the farmers actually had a negative total income, for, while the value of farm property was increasing, it was increasing so much more slowly than the value of consumers' goods that the loss in purchasing power exceeded realized income. Column G of Table XCIX shows that, when changes in property values are taken into account, the average income of the farmer and his family varied from a $60 deficit in 1916 to a net income of $1,230 in 1915. On this basis, both 1921

TABLE XCIX

TOTAL INCOME OF FARMERS[d]

	A	B	C	D	E	F	G	H
Year	Entire Realized Income in 1913 Dollars[a] (Millions)	Property Gains in 1913 Dollars[b] (Millions)	Total Income of Farmers in 1913 Dollars (Millions)	Index of Prices of Goods Used by Farmers[c]	Total Income of Farmers in Current Dollars (Millions)	Number of Farmers[a] (Thous.)	Income of Farmer and His Family	
			A+B		C×D		1913 Dollars C+F	Current Dollars E+F
1909	$3,838	$—1,827	$2,011	.968	$1,946	6,289	$ 320	$ 309
1910	3,925	1,206	5,130	.995	5,103	6,307	813	809
1911	3,509	1,012	4,521	.973	4,397	6,322	715	696
1912	3,958	3,027	6,985	.987	6,892	6,336	1,102	1,088
1913	3,699	—708	2,991	1.000	2,991	6,346	471	471
1914	3,617	2,795	6,411	1.008	6,465	6,353	1,009	1,018
1915	4,078	3,743	7,821	.985	7,701	6,359	1,230	1,211
1916	4,540	—4,922	—381	1.108	—423	6,365	—60	—66
1917	5,165	—2,998	2,167	1.409	3,052	6,369	340	479
1918	5,581	—1,710	3,871	1.613	6,244	6,374	607	980
1919	5,175	—930	4,245	1.845	7,831	6,378	666	1,228
1920	4,114	1,097	5,211	2.001	10,429	6,381	817	1,634
1921	2,881	—2,396	485	1.557	755	6,387	76	118
1922	3,475	170	3,646	1.481	5,400	6,271	581	861
1923	4,029	—645	3,383	1.452	4,911	6,297	537	780
1924	4,157	—2,013	2,144	1.466	3,144	6,344	338	496
1925	4,283	—3,243	1,040	1.588	1,651	6,317	165	261
1926	3,647*	218*	3,865*	1.621	6,265*	6,200*	623*	1,010*
1927	4,028*	1,081*	5,108*	1.529	7,810*	6,124*	834*	1,275*

[a] See Table XCVIII.
[b] See Table LI.
[c] See Table VII.
[d] Includes income of farmers and members of their families, but excludes income of hired employees.
* Preliminary estimate.

and 1925 appear to have been very bad years for the farmers, the average farm family in 1921 netting only $76 and in 1925 only $165. Next to 1915, the years 1914 and 1912 were, for the farmer, the two best of the 17 years covered by this investigation.

Comparison of Realized and Total Income of Farmers.

In Chart 48, we find pictured the fluctuations which have occurred in the realized income and also in the total income of

farmers. The fact that the last mentioned quantity is much more irregular than the former is brought out vividly by this chart. Those interested in knowing more of the details of the calculations of the income of farmers will do well to refer to Chapter IX of the publication of the National Bureau of Economic Research entitled *Income in the Various States*.

Entrepreneurial Return of Farm Families.

It has been the custom in the past for many students of agricultural income to estimate what is commonly referred to as the "labor income" of the farmer. In calculating this quantity, the procedure normally followed is to subtract from the total income of the farmer an allowance for interest on his investment. The results of a computation of a somewhat similar nature appear in Table C. In this table, an allowance of 5½ per cent of the value at the beginning of the year of the property owned by farmers has been deducted from the total income derived by farmers from agriculture. It may be contended that, logically, the interest rate used should have been varied from time to time. There is good ground for so doing, but it was felt that, since the interest rate on farm mortgages is the one which seems most logical for use in this particular computation, and since the rate on farm mortgages is so inelastic and comes so near to remaining constant year after year, it was scarcely worth while to use different rates for different periods. Column D shows us that, when the deduction calculated in Column B has been made, the remaining income, namely that which is supposed to compensate the farmer for his entrepreneurial services, and also to compensate both the farmer and the members of his family for their physical labor, is an extremely variable quantity ranging from $384 loss in 1916 to $1,161 of positive income in 1920. The variability of this figure is indicated in Chart 48. After eliminating the cyclical fluctuations, the trend is seen to have been distinctly upward during the early part of the period after which it dropped precipitously in 1916, and thereafter remained on a lower level. The years in which the farmer and his family were most adequately rewarded for their services were 1912, 1915, 1919, 1920, and 1927, and the years in which their net reward fell below zero were 1916, 1921 and 1925. In both 1909 and 1917, the incomes did not actually go below the zero mark, but were only $50 and $136 respectively.

TABLE C

TWO HYPOTHETICAL APPORTIONMENTS
OF THE AGRICULTURAL INCOME OF FARMERS

YEAR	A TOTAL INCOME OF FARMERS FROM AGRICULTURE[a] (MILLIONS)	B 5½% OF PROPERTY INVESTMENT OF FARMERS[b] (MILLIONS)	C INCOME ASCRIBABLE TO EFFORTS OF FARMERS AND MEMBERS OF FAMILY Total (Millions) A-B	D Per Farm Family[c]	E WAGE ALLOWANCE FOR FARMERS AND FAMILIES[d] (MILLIONS)	F INCOME ASCRIBABLE TO PROPERTY (MILLIONS) A-E	G PER CENT OF VALUE OF BUSINESS PROPERTY[e]
1909	$1,714	$1,399	$ 314	$ 50	$3,011	$—1,298	—5.10
1910	4,862	1,442	3,419	542	2,929	1,932	7.37
1911	4,152	1,461	2,691	426	3,072	1,079	4.06
1912	6,643	1,459	5,184	818	3,165	3,477	13.11
1913	2,736	1,548	1,188	187	3,249	—513	—1.82
1914	6,209	1,594	4,615	726	3,206	3,003	10.36
1915	7,437	1,613	5,824	916	3,238	4,199	14.32
1916	—696	1,747	—2,443	—384	3,529	—4,226	—13.30
1917	2,763	1,899	864	136	4,349	—1,586	—4.59
1918	5,935	2,230	3,705	581	5,067	867	2.14
1919	7,472	2,456	5,015	786	6,064	1,408	3.15
1920	10,000	2,593	7,407	1,161	6,950	3,050	6.47
1921	271	2,258	—1,986	—311	5,949	—5,677	—13.83
1922	4,924	1,731	3,193	509	5,594	—670	—2.13
1923	4,450	1,665	2,785	442	5,805	—1,355	—4.48
1924	2,695	1,646	1,049	165	5,959	—3,264	—10.90
1925	1,217	1,619	—402	—64	5,967	—4,750	—16.14
1926	5,841*	1,586*	4,255*	686*	5,958*	—117*	—.41*
1927	7,382*	1,486*	5,896*	963*	5,861*	1,521*	5.63*

[a] Column D of Table XCVIII + (Column B × Column D of Table XCIX).
[b] 5½ × Column K of Table XCIV.
[c] Column C ÷ number of farmers.
[d] Number of farmers × 1½ × average wage of hired men.
[e] Column F ÷ Column K of Table XCIV.
* Preliminary estimate.

Percentage Return on Farmers' Investments.

Farm income may also, with equal logic, be viewed from an entirely different angle. If, instead of allowing interest on the farmer's investment as a primary charge, we calculate instead a minimum wage allowance for the services of the farmer and his family, and deduct this allowance from the total income of the

CHART 48

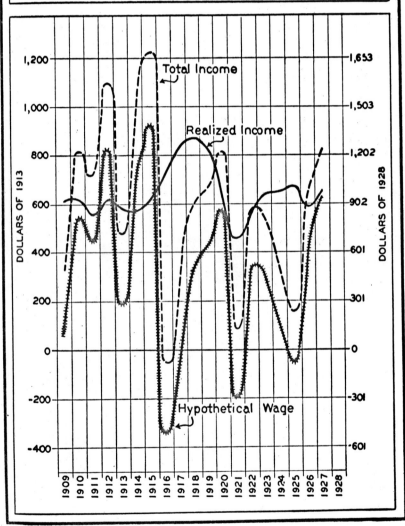

REALIZED INCOME, TOTAL INCOME,
AND HYPOTHETICAL WAGE
PER FARMER AND HIS FAMILY[a]

* For data, see Tables XCVIII, XCIX and C.

farmers, we shall have an estimate of the amount of income ascribable to farm property. By dividing this remaining income by the value of the property at the beginning of the year, we can ascertain the farmer's rate of return on his investment. In Column E of Table C, we have calculated the wage allowance for the farmers by assuming that the services of the farmer and his family together should be worth 1½ times the wage of a hired man, an allowance which certainly seems low enough. On this basis, it appears from the figures in Column G that, in 9 years out of the 17, the return on the farmer's investment was less than nothing, the highest net loss being more than 16 per cent in 1925, with losses of 13 per cent in both 1916 and 1921, and 11 per cent in 1924. The maximum gain, which occurred in 1915, amounted to 14 per cent. Gains of 10 per cent in 1914, and 13 per cent in 1912, were also recorded. When the percentages for the 19 years are added algebraically, we find that the aggregate of losses exceeds the aggregate of gains, the sum showing an average annual net loss on the farmers' investment of about 0.3 per cent.

CHAPTER XII

FACTORS RELATING TO INCOME FROM MINES, QUARRIES, AND OIL WELLS

The industry dealt with in this book under the general title "Mining" is composed of four parts:

1. Metal mines.
2. Coal mines.
3. Petroleum and gas wells.
4. Other non-metal mines and quarries.

The conditions prevailing in these four divisions are often quite diverse; hence, in the following pages, certain facts have been presented for some of the individual fields. In addition, a study has been made of the concentration of ownership in this industry.

Ratio of Interest Payments on Funded Debt to its Par Value.

Table CI shows the ratio of the total interest actually paid to the amount of funded debt outstanding, as shown by the records of a number of sample companies in three of the four branches of the industry. The figures indicate that, in the coal industry, a slow but steady increase in this ratio persisted during the entire period between 1911 and 1925. Records for oil and gas producers are not complete enough to have significance before 1918. From that date until 1921, the ratio of interest payments to principal tended to increase, but, after 1922, there was a marked decline. In the case of corporations operating metal mines, reports are available from the larger companies only. The rate of interest payments on the funded debt of these larger companies increased steadily from 1909 to 1922. After that date, a diminution in the rate of payment is apparent. It appears to be true that the changes in these ratios of interest to par value of the funded debt accord fairly well with the movements of interest rates in general, giving but relatively little indication of any changes which may have occurred in the stability of this particular industry.

Ratio of Dividend Payments on Preferred Stock to its Par Value.

The ratio of dividends actually paid to the par value of preferred stock outstanding is given in Table CII. In the earlier years

TABLE CI

RATIO OF THE TOTAL INTEREST ACTUALLY PAID ON THE FUNDED DEBT TO THE TOTAL FUNDED DEBT OUTSTANDING IN A SAMPLE GROUP OF CORPORATIONS IN EACH OF THE SPECIFIED BRANCHES OF MINING*

Year	All Mines, Quarries and Oil Wells		Coal		Oil and Gas		Metals	
	Number of Corporations	Interest Rate Paid	Number of Corporations	Interest Rate Paid	Number of Corporations	Interest Rate Paid	Number of Corporations	Interest Rate Paid
1909	12	.049	7	.049	b	b	5	.051
1910	12	.049	7	.049	b	b	5	.054
1911	14	.049	7	.048	b	b	7	.054
1912	17	.049	7	.048	b	b	9	055
1913	21	.050	10	.048	2	.060	9	.055
1914	21	.050	9	.049	2	.060	10	.056
1915	25	.051	11	.050	2	.060	12	.056
1916	20	.052	12	.050	1	.060	7	.055
1917	20	.052	12	.050	1	.060	7	.056
1918	26	.053	13	.050	7	.057	6	.060
1919	30	.055	13	.050	9	.055	8	.061
1920	32	.058	14	.050	10	.061	8	.062
1921	37	.061	14	.050	15	.067	8	.064
1922	39	.062	15	.050	15	.067	9	.065
1923	39	.061	15	.050	15	.063	9	.064
1924	35	.059	13	.051	15	.060	7	.062
1925	36	.059	14	.051	15	.060	7	.062

* Based upon a study of the annual reports of specified numbers of sample corporations in this field.
b No information given in corporation reports available.

of the period covered, the records for coal mining corporations reveal enormous fluctuations in the rates paid, varying from less than 2 per cent in 1909 to more than 23 per cent in 1913. These fluctuations were caused, not by changes in the nominal rates on preferred stock, but by the fact that, in some years, no dividends on preferred were paid by some of the companies having issues of that type, while, in other years, large amounts of back dividends were disbursed to the holders of preferred stock. Since 1918, the preferred stock of coal mining corporations seems to have attained an investment status, and the amplitude of the fluctuations has diminished.

TABLE CII

RATIO OF THE TOTAL DIVIDENDS
ACTUALLY PAID ON THE PREFERRED STOCK
TO THE TOTAL PAR VALUE OF THAT CLASS OF STOCK
OUTSTANDING IN A SAMPLE GROUP OF CORPORATIONS
IN EACH OF THE SPECIFIED BRANCHES OF MINING[a]

YEAR	All Mines, Quarries and Oil Wells		COAL		OIL AND GAS		METALS	
	Number of Corporations	Dividend Rate Paid	Number of Corporations	Dividend Rate Paid	Number of Corporations	Dividend Rate Paid	Number of Corporations	Dividend Rate Paid
1909	4	.055	3	.019	b	b	1	.070
1910	5	.056	3	.019	b	b	2	.069
1911	6	.070c	4	.080c	b	b	2	.067
1912	7	.067c	4	.100c	b	b	3	.055
1913	9	.093c	5	.232c	1	.070	3	.055
1914	10	.061	6	.069c	1	.070	3	.048
1915	10	.046	6	.057	1	.047	3	.038
1916	11	.061	7	.094c	1	.040	3	.042
1917	11	.078c	7	.119c	1	.040	3	.065
1918	17	.063	9	.056	5	.072	3	.067
1919	20	.058	10	.055	7	.067	3	.042
1920	22	.060	11	.056	8	.070	3	.042
1921	22	.058	11	.054	8	.067	3	.038
1922	22	.048	11	.055	8	.046	3	.034
1923	22	.053	11	.050	8	.059	3	.033
1924	20	.054	10	.054	7	.058	3	.033
1925	19	.048	11	.045	6	.051	2	.047

[a] Based upon a study of the annual reports of the specified numbers of sample corporations in this field.
[b] No information given in corporation reports available.
[c] Large dividend rates due to payments of back dividends by various companies and to nominal par value of $1 per share for the preferred stock of the Island Creek Coal Company.

In the case of corporations producing oil and gas, information for years earlier than 1918 is too scanty to be significant. In general, preferred dividends in this field have tended downward since 1918. The drop in 1922 represents the effect of the passing of dividends by some of the companies.

Data have been secured from too few metal mining concerns to assure us that the figures are indicative of conditions in that industry as a whole. What data there are show that the ratio of dividends actually paid on preferred stock to the par value of the same has, in general, been low, though, in this regard, the years 1909 to 1911 and 1917 and 1918 were well above normal. In these years, the mining concerns studied came nearer to meeting their obligations on preferred stock than they did in any other years of the period.

Output and Earnings of Coal Mine Employees.

Estimates of the average annual earnings per employee attached to the bituminous and anthracite coal industries and the average output per employee are presented in Table CIII and in Chart 49.

These figures make it clear that the output of bituminous coal per employee had a distinct upward trend between 1909 and 1918, then fell off until 1922, and thereafter increased steadily, the figure for 1926 being the highest recorded for this industry. It should be clearly understood that the figures on production, as here given, show the output per employee attached to the industry and not the output per employee actually at work. In times of industrial depression, the demand for coal slackens, but most of the employees do not leave the industry, hence the output per employee falls greatly in such periods.

Changes in the output per employee in the anthracite field paralleled rather closely the changes in the output per employee in the bituminous industry during the period 1909 to 1923 inclusive. There was the same upward trend between 1909 and 1918, the same decline between 1918 and 1922, and a similar recovery in 1923. Since 1923, anthracite per capita output has been declining while the output per employee in bituminous fields has been rising.

The output per employee is, of course, affected by the amount of surplus labor attached to the industry, the average hours worked per year per laborer, the relative size of the office force, the introduction of new machinery, the existence of strikes, and changes in the difficulty of mining coal caused by increases in the average depth of mines and the exhaustion of the most easily mined beds.

Earnings per employee likewise represent the average earnings for all employees attached to the industry, whether actually at work or not. As might be expected, the average calculated on this basis rises in years of prosperity and falls in periods of depression. The trend of earnings per employee in the bituminous industry was upward between 1909 and 1923. Thereafter the evidence indicates

TABLE CIII

PRODUCTION AND EARNINGS PER EMPLOYEE IN THE COAL INDUSTRY

| YEAR | BITUMINOUS MINES | | | | | ANTHRACITE MINES | | | | |
	Total Pay[a] (Millions)	Short Tons Mined[b] (Millions)	Employees Attached to Industry[a] (Thousands)	Average Annual Earnings Per Employee	Tons Per Employee	Total Pay[a] (Millions)	Short Tons Mined[b] (Millions)	Employees Attached to Industry[a] (Thousands)	Average Annual Earnings Per Employee	Tons Per Employee
1909	$ 291	380	557	$ 522	682	$ 92	81	179	$ 515	452
1910	335	417	577	581	723	98	84	174	560	485
1911	332	406	574	578	707	104	90	178	584	508
1912	365	450	567	644	794	102	84	186	550	453
1913	406	478	589	690	812	109	92	182	598	502
1914	362	423	599	604	706	107	91	187	570	486
1915	352	443	596	590	742	114	89	184	619	484
1916	429	503	573	749	877	131	88	167	785	524
1917	572	552	613	933	900	141	100	156	900	638
1918	755	579	629	1,201	921	188	99	151	1,241	653
1919	723	466	641	1,129	727	212	88	161	1,319	548
1920	1,042	569	658	1,585	865	241	90	154	1,565	582
1921	757	416	681	1,111	610	288	90	177	1,626	511
1922	737	422	707	1,042	597	160	55	173	927	317
1923	1,055	565	714	1,476	790	281	93	172	1,639	544
1924	711	484	633	1,124	765	303	88	173	1,754	508
1925	748	520	602	1,243	864	217	62	169	1,288	366
1926	779	573	604	1,290	949	297*	84	178	1,672*	475
1927	716*	520*	607*	1,180*	856*	300*	81*	179	1,674*	450*

a Based upon *Census of Mines and Quarries* and upon reports of the U. S. Bureau of Mines, the U.S. Geological Survey and the Pennsylvania Department of Internal Affairs.

b Taken from various Statistical Abstracts.

* Preliminary Estimate.

that the trend in that field was slightly downward, the cyclical peak in 1926 being much lower than that of 1923.

Average earnings per employee in the anthracite mines have had an upward trend somewhat steeper than that of earnings in the bituminous field. Just as in the case of the bituminous mines, the earnings of anthracite miners show some tendency to decline after 1923 but the evidence of any downward inclination of the trend in this field is much less conclusive than in the bituminous industry. The figures in Table CIII for average annual earnings

CHART 49

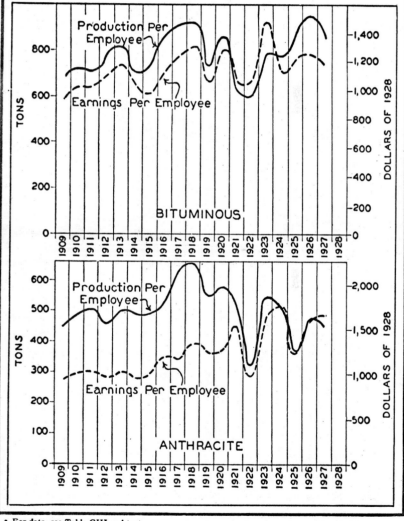

PRODUCTION AND EARNINGS
PER EMPLOYEE IN THE COAL INDUSTRY[a]

* For data, see Table CIII and text.

per employee are expressed in terms of current dollars and cannot legitimately be compared for different years. The figures plotted in Chart 49 have all been reduced to dollars having purchasing power equal to that which they possessed in 1928, and thus show the respective abilities of the persons attached to the coal mining industry to buy direct or consumers' goods at the various dates. The averages for the various years are as follows:

Calendar Year	Average Earnings in 1928 Dollars of Employees Attached to the Industry	
	Bituminous Mines	Anthracite Mines
1909	943	930
1910	1,023	986
1911	1,017	1,028
1912	1,118	955
1913	1,177	1,020
1914	1,013	956
1915	973	1,020
1916	1,145	1,200
1917	1,221	1,178
1918	1,303	1,347
1919	1,052	1,229
1920	1,295	1,279
1921	1,053	1,542
1922	1,061	944
1923	1,475	1,638
1924	1,124	1,754
1925	1,216	1,260
1926	1,254	1,625
1927	1,169	1,659

Tendency Toward Centralized Ownership of Mineral Properties.

Is the control of the mining industry drifting into the hands of a few giant corporations? To throw light on this question, a study has been made of the net income available for dividends, the amount of dividends paid, and the amount of interest paid on the funded debt by the 20 mining corporations which, in each particular year, were the largest for which reports could be secured. These

TABLE CIV

BOND INTEREST, DIVIDEND PAYMENTS, AND REPORTED NET INCOME OF 20 GIANT MINING CORPORATIONS[a]
(THOUSANDS OF DOLLARS)

Year	Reported Income Available for Dividends	Dividends Paid	Interest Paid on Funded Debt	Total Interest and Dividends Paid
1909	$ 18,430	$ 14,906	$ 3,699	$ 18,605
1910	24,732	22,074	4,878	26,952
1911	31,994	25,443	6,021	31,464
1912	43,685	23,521	6,073	29,594
1913	59,018	35,928	6,539	42,467
1914	32,811	26,790	6,777	33,567
1915	55,542	27,208	7,913	35,121
1916	161,177	75,193	7,227	82,420
1917	133,739	88,092	6,763	94,855
1918	118,326	77,727	11,361	89,088
1919	105,312	59,749	12,631	72,380
1920	151,770	58,393	18,198	76,591
1921	30,185	47,237	24,629	71,866
1922	107,178	57,077	24,178	81,255
1923	138,380	110,348	34,375	144,723
1924	140,098	98,683	33,792	132,475
1925	227,638	109,744	32,363	142,107
1926	218,711	111,190	29,925	141,115

[a] Based upon the annual reports of the 20 corporations in this field which, in each year, had the largest market value of all the sample corporations for which reports were secured.

basic figures appear in Table CIV. All three items were very much larger in the latter half of the period than they were at the beginning of the period. The net income reported available for dividends was more than 10 times as great in 1926 as in 1909. The aggregate of dividends paid was 7 times as large in 1926 as in 1909, while, during the same period, payments of interest on funded debt were multiplied by 8. A study of the corresponding items for the mining industry as a whole will show no such remarkable increase.

Table CV and the left hand section of Chart 50 serve to bring out the relationship between these items for the 20 giant corporations and the industry as a whole. The percentage of the total interest on the funded debt of the entire mining industry which was paid out by the 20 leading corporations had a somewhat hori-

TABLE CV

PERCENTAGES OF THE NET INCOME AND DISBURSEMENTS TO CAPITAL FOR ALL MINING CORPORATIONS COMPRISED IN THE CORRESPONDING ITEMS REPRESENTING 20 GIANT CORPORATIONS[a]

Year	Reported Income Available for Dividends[b]	Dividends Paid[c]	Interest Paid on Funded Debt[d]	Total Interest and Dividends Paid
1909	31.14	9.05	23.57	10.32
1910	20.52	11.89	29.12	13.32
1911	17.79	15.66	32.99	17.41
1912	13.10	12.14	30.77	13.86
1913	14.53	13.50	30.51	14.76
1914	13.44	13.73	29.15	15.38
1915	19.35	14.14	31.26	16.13
1916	22.14	14.57	26.58	15.17
1917	15.12	14.19	23.05	14.59
1918	23.84	14.32	35.23	15.49
1919	41.85	18.55	35.58	20.24
1920	28.88	24.66	44.92	27.62
1921	[e]	15.66	52.31	20.61
1922	1,791.97[f]	25.59	46.62	29.56
1923	[e]	36.71	61.87	40.64
1924	[e]	38.65	56.12	41.99
1925	93.43	32.75	48.85	35.40

[a] The percentages in this table are obtained by dividing each sum for the 20 corporations which had the largest market value of all the sample corporations for which reports were secured, by the corresponding total for all mining corporations, and multiplying the quotient by 100.

[b] Derived from figures presented in Tables LXXXVI and CIV.

[c] Derived from figures presented in Tables XXXIV, XXXV, and CIV.

[d] Derived from figures presented in Tables XXXVI and CIV.

[e] Deficit for year, hence ratio, if computed, would be meaningless.

[f] This unusually high percentage is due to the fact that the 20 giant corporations had an income of $107,178,000 as compared with a figure of $5,981,000 for the entire industry.

zontal trend between 1909 and 1917, but, since that date, has risen very rapidly. The tendency at the beginning of the period appears to have been for the 20 leading corporations to pay about one-fourth of the aggregate interest, while, at the close of the period, they were paying approximately one-half.

There has been an upward trend in dividends paid by the 20 leading corporations throughout the entire period, but, just as in the case of interest payments, the upward slope of the trend in-

CHART 50

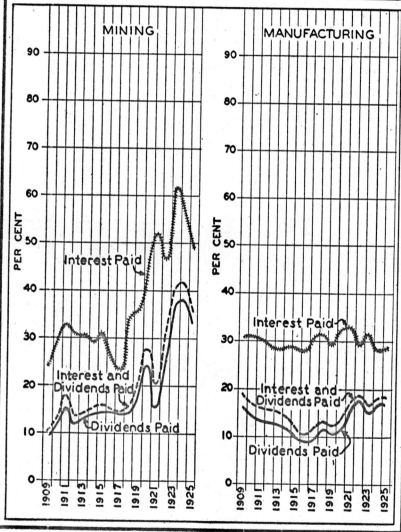

PERCENTAGES OF THE NET INCOME AND
DISBURSEMENTS TO CAPITAL FOR
ALL MINING CORPORATIONS COMPRISED IN THE
CORRESPONDING ITEMS REPRESENTING
20 GIANT CORPORATIONS[a]

[a] For data, see Tables CV and CVII.

creased greatly after the close of the World War. As a matter of fact, the relative increase in the volume of dividends has been even greater than in the case of interest payments, for, in 1909, the 20 leading corporations were paying but one-tenth of the entire dividend bill of the mining industry, while, after 1923, the tendency has been for them to pay more than one-third of the total. The percentages representing ratios of the net income of the 20 giant corporations to the net income of the mining industry as a whole fluctuate so much that it is difficult to draw conclusions therefrom, but there appears to be a trend which is perhaps even more steeply upward than in interest and dividend payments.

All the available evidence points to the conclusion that the mining industry is rapidly drifting toward domination by a few great corporations.

CHAPTER XIII

FACTORS RELATING TO THE INCOME DERIVED FROM MANUFACTURING

Centralized Ownership in Manufacturing.

A study has been made of the development of those 20 manufacturing corporations which were largest in each of the years specified as compared to the development of this industry as a whole. It should be understood that the 20 corporations making up this group are not the same in each year, for, in some years, one corporation fell among the largest 20 and in another year another corporation would take its place.

The figures in Table CVI indicate that the net income reported available for dividends was not quite 5 times as great in 1926 as in 1909, while the amount of dividends paid quadrupled and the amount of interest paid on the funded debt increased by only about 50 per cent during this period. It should be understood that all the figures given in Table CVI are expressed in terms of the dollars current in each of the respective years. Evidently, then, the amount of interest paid on the funded debt, if converted to dollars of constant purchasing power, would show no increase during the period. On the other hand, the respective volumes of income available for dividends and of dividends paid did show a marked growth in the case of the 20 largest corporations.

Table CVII and the right hand section of Chart 50 give, for the manufacturing industry comparisons similar to those for the mining industry in the left hand section of Chart 50. Inspection of the chart indicates that, throughout the period, about the same proportion of the total interest on the funded debt paid by all corporations in manufacturing has been paid by the 20 largest corporations, this percentage being about 30 per cent. The ratio of the total amount of dividends paid by the 20 leading corporations to the total of dividend payments made by all corporations in the manufacturing industry shows a decided decline between 1909 and 1916 and a decided increase after that. It appears, however, that the percentage of total dividend disbursements by all corporations paid out by the 20 leading corporations was but a trifle greater in 1925 than in 1909. In so far, then, as interest on funded debt and

TABLE CVI

BOND INTEREST, DIVIDEND PAYMENTS, AND REPORTED NET INCOME OF 20 GIANT MANUFACTURING CORPORATIONS[*]

(THOUSANDS OF DOLLARS)

Year	Reported Income Available for Dividends	Dividends Paid	Interest Paid on Funded Debt	Total Interest and Dividends Paid
1909	$185,095	$114,881	$50,082	$164,963
1910	213,443	124,845	50,957	175,802
1911	167,121	121,676	50,973	172,649
1912	177,249	126,493	50,408	176,901
1913	203,889	136,157	49,462	185,619
1914	132,793	120,460	51,809	172,269
1915	246,270	108,448	51,848	160,296
1916	533,290	171,402	52,404	223,806
1917	502,548	219,965	59,785	279,750
1918	521,805	252,059	62,500	314,559
1919	508,480	219,113	60,992	280,105
1920	612,792	235,762	71,750	307,512
1921	146,656	271,626	75,749	347,375
1922	410,483	269,949	65,506	335,455
1923	554,652	308,610	73,658	382,268
1924	557,608	328,104	71,056	399,160
1925	728,337	386,078	71,334	457,412
1926	875,341	489,651	77,609	567,260

[*] Based upon the annual reports of the 20 corporations in this field which, in each year, had the largest market value of all the sample corporations for which reports were secured.

dividends are concerned, there is no evidence that the concentration observable in mining has extended to the manufacturing industry.[1] The figures in Table CVIII representing the reported net income available for dividend payments indicate that, in both 1924 and 1925, the percentage representing the 20 giant corporations was materially larger than at the beginning of the period and was approximately twice as great as the corresponding percentage in the

[1] In this connection, Col. M. C. Rorty says: "The fact, that the twenty largest manufacturing corporations do not show a definite increase in the ratio of their interest and dividend disbursements to total similar disbursements for all manufacturing establishments, does not necessarily indicate that there is not a tendency for a concentration of manufacturing interests to take place. A more correct study might be of the disbursements of the largest 5% or 10% of the total *number* of manufacturing establishments. Still another study might be of the proportion of total disbursements made by establishments showing less and more than the average annual output. A complete study of this trend would involve the plotting of distribution curves."

TABLE CVII

PERCENTAGES OF THE NET INCOME AND DISBURSEMENTS TO CAPITAL FOR ALL MANUFACTURING CORPORATIONS COMPRISED IN THE CORRESPONDING ITEMS REPRESENTING 20 GIANT CORPORATIONS[a]

Year	Reported Income Available for Dividends[b]	Dividends Paid[c]	Interest Paid on Funded Debt[d]	Total Interest and Dividends Paid
1909	15.46	16.75	30.87	19.45
1910	14.72	15.29	30.93	17.92
1911	12.67	13.66	30.43	16.31
1912	11.03	13.39	29.56	15.86
1913	11.42	13.10	28.47	15.30
1914	9.62	12.11	29.19	14.70
1915	10.96	10.26	28.53	12.94
1916	13.67	8.82	28.14	10.51
1917	8.95	9.82	31.26	11.51
1918	11.46	11.86	31.77	13.55
1919	10.46	10.72	29.68	12.45
1920	18.58	12.01	32.98	14.10
1921	[e]	15.46	33.44	17.52
1922	15.39	17.75	29.34	19.23
1923	15.37	15.22	31.92	16.93
1924	19.92	17.24	28.21	18.52
1925	19.00	17.18	28.76	18.33

[a] The percentages in this table are obtained by dividing each sum for the 20 corporations which had the largest market value of all the sample corporations for which reports were secured, by the corresponding total for all manufacturing corporations, and multiplying the quotient by 100.

[b] Derived from figures presented in Tables LXXXVI and CVI.

[c] Derived from figures presented in Tables XXXIV, XXXV, and CVI.

[d] Derived from figures presented in Tables XXXVI and CVI.

[e] There was a deficit, hence a percentage, if calculated, would be meaningless.

period 1914 to 1919, inclusive. As we have previously seen, one is not justified in placing too much dependence upon the figures reported as representing the net income of corporations, but, in so far as these figures do have any significance, it would seem that a considerable degree of concentration of control was also developing in the manufacturing industry, but that the giant corporations were saving, or in other words carrying to surplus, a proportion of their income much larger than that saved by the smaller corporations.

Ratio for Funded Debt of Interest Payments to Par Value.

Table CVIII shows for sample corporations in each of 19 important branches of the manufacturing industry the ratio of the total amount of interest actually paid to the par value of the funded debt outstanding. It will be seen that the movements in these rates are strikingly similar in the different fields.

Ratio for Preferred Stock of Dividend Payments to Par Value.

The entries in Table CIX show for sample corporations in the 19 sections of manufacturing the actual volume of dividends on preferred stock compared to the total par value of preferred stock outstanding. From these figures it is clear that the variation in the different branches of the industry as regards rates paid has been much greater in the case of preferred stock than in the case of the funded debt. For a considerable period of years following 1919, the sample corporations in the paper and pulp industry, for example, never paid over 3 per cent on their outstanding preferred stock, while, during the same years in the petroleum refining industry, the sample corporations were paying between 5 and 8 per cent. The variations from prosperity to depression are shown clearly to have had much more effect on dividends of preferred stock than upon interest on the funded debt.

TABLE CVIII

RATIO OF THE TOTAL INTEREST ACTUALLY PAID ON THE FUNDED DEBT TO THE TOTAL FUNDED DEBT OUTSTANDING IN A SAMPLE GROUP OF CORPORATIONS IN EACH OF THE SPECIFIED BRANCHES OF MANUFACTURING[a]

Year	All Branches of Mfg.		Food		Textiles		Iron and Steel (Excluding Machinery)		Lumber		Leather		Rubber		Paper and Pulp		Printing and Publishing		Chemicals	
	No. of Corps.	Int. Rate	No. of Corps.	Int. Rate	No. of Corps.	Int. Rate	No. of Corps.	Int. Rate	No. of Corps.	Int. Rate	No. of Corps.	Int. Rate	No. of Corps.	Int. Rate	No. of Corps.	Int. Rate	No. of Corps.	Int. Rate	No. of Corps.	Int. Rate
1909	98	.051	17	.053	2	.040	14	.050	2	.062	2	.052	3	.059	4	.054	2	.054	5	.050
1910	99	.051	15	.051	2	.040	13	.051	2	.060	2	.052	3	.057	4	.054	2	.054	5	.050
1911	110	.049	18	.052	2	.040	14	.050	2	.060	2	.052	3	.057	4	.054	1	.057	5	.051
1912	121	.049	21	.052	2	.040	16	.050	2	.060	2	.052	3	.057	3	.054	2	.060	6	.051
1913	127	.051	21	.053	3	.044	14	.050	2	.060	2	.052	3	.042	3	.053	3	.059	8	.052
1914	135	.050	22	.053	4	.048	17	.050	2	.060	2	.051	3	.026	4	.054	3	.058	8	.053
1915	135	.051	23	.053	3	.049	16	.050	2	.059	2	.051	3	.040	4	.054	3	.058	5	.052
1916	134	.051	21	.052	4	.049	17	.050	2	.059	2	.051	3	.055	5	.054	3	.057	5	.051
1917	129	.051	20	.052	5	.050	16	.050	2	.059	2	.051	3	.054	5	.053	3	.054	6	.052
1918	169	.052	24	.054	7	.054	21	.051	2	.064	2	.051	3	.053	5	.051	4	.056	12	.052
1919	177	.053	23	.055	8	.059	24	.052	3	.067	2	.051	2	.053	5	.052	3	.059	13	.053
1920	198	.055	28	.058	11	.063	26	.052	3	.065	1	.050	4	.056	6	.055	2	.060	18	.056
1921	227	.058	30	.062	12	.066	32	.053	3	.064	2	.051	6	.062	5	.056	3	.064	20	.064
1922	226	.058	32	.061	15	.068	33	.054	3	.065	2	.052	7	.058	6	.056	3	.067	20	.070
1923	223	.058	33	.059	15	.067	30	.054	4	.064	3	.052	8	.057	6	.056	3	.064	17	.070
1924	205	.057	32	.058	13	.068	30	.054	4	.063	3	.052	8	.062	6	.056	2	.061	12	.069
1925	205	.057	35	.058	14	.068	32	.054	4	.063	3	.057	7	.062	6	.057	4	.060	11	.066

[a] Based upon a study of the annual reports of the specified numbers of corporations in the various fields.

[b] Sample reports could not be located for this field.

TABLE CVIII—Continued

RATIO OF THE TOTAL INTEREST ACTUALLY PAID ON THE FUNDED DEBT TO THE TOTAL FUNDED DEBT OUTSTANDING IN A SAMPLE GROUP OF CORPORATIONS IN EACH OF THE SPECIFIED BRANCHES OF MANUFACTURING[a]

Year	Gas		Petroleum Refining		Stone, Clay and Glass		Metals other than Iron		Tobacco		Machinery		Musical Instruments		Motor Vehicles		Railway Equipment		Ship-Building	
	No. of Corps.	Int. Rate	No. of Corps.	Int. Rate	No. of Corps.	Int. Rate	No. of Corps.	Int. Rate	No. of Corps.	Int. Rate	No. of Corps.	Int. Rate	No. of Corps.	Int. Rate	No. of Corps.	Int. Rate	No. of Corps.	Int. Rate	No. of Corps.	Int. Rate
1909	22	.049	1	.053	4	.054	2	.052	1	.050	8	.049	1	.058	b	b	7	.051	1	.050
1910	22	.049	2	.051	4	.054	3	.054	1	.050	9	.050	1	.059	b	b	8	.052	1	.050
1911	22	.049	3	.053	5	.054	3	.053	2	.051	11	.050	1	.060		.057	9	.051	1	.050
1912	22	.049	2	.053	8	.055	3	.053	2	.056	13	.052	1	.060	3		8	.051	2	.051
1913	22	.049	2	.053	7	.056	4	.052	2	.059	15	.053	2	.060	4	.055	9	.051	2	.052
1914	21	.049	3	.053	8	.056	4	.050	2	.059	15	.053	2	.060	4	.055	9	.051	2	.051
1915	24	.050	3	.054	8	.056	4	.050	2	.059	15	.054	2	.060	5	.055	9	.051	2	.050
1916	23	.050	3	.054	8	.057	5	.050	2	.059	15	.053	2	.060	4	.055	9	.051	1	.050
1917	21	.050	3	.054	8	.057	5	.050	2	.059	15	.054	1	.060	3	.055	8	.051	1	.050
1918	23	.050	5	.056	10	.056	7	.051	2	.061	23	.056	1	.060	8	.056	8	.052	2	.050
1919	23	.052	5	.060	11	.056	9	.053	3	.062	22	.056	1	.060	9	.059	8	.053	3	.050
1920	24	.053	8	.064	10	.060	10	.054	3	.062	24	.059	2	.064	7	.061	8	.056	3	.050
1921	25	.054	12	.068	9	.065	10	.054	5	.063	27	.063	2	.067	10	.065	6	.059	3	.051
1922	24	.054	11	.067	8	.066	10	.054	4	.063	25	.064	2	.066	12	.068	6	.058	3	.051
1923	24	.053	11	.066	7	.065	11	.054	4	.061	25	.065	2	.063	11	.066	6	.056	3	.050
1924	22	.053	10	.063	6	.061	11	.055	4	.060	22	.063	2	.060	10	.064	5	.056	3	.051
1925	22	.053	7	.059	6	.058	10	.055	5	.060	20	.063	2	.060	8	.062	6	.056	3	.052

TABLE CIX

RATIO OF THE TOTAL DIVIDENDS ACTUALLY PAID ON THE PREFERRED STOCK TO THE TOTAL PAR VALUE OF THAT CLASS OF STOCK OUTSTANDING IN A SAMPLE GROUP OF CORPORATIONS IN EACH OF THE SPECIFIED BRANCHES OF MANUFACTURING[a]

Year	All Branches of Manufacturing		Food		Textiles		Iron and Steel (Excluding Machinery)		Lumber		Leather		Rubber		Paper and Pulp		Printing and Publishing		Chemicals	
	No. of Corps.	Div. Rate	No. of Corps.	Div. Rate	No. of Corps.	Div. Rate	No. of Corps.	Div. Rate	No. of Corps.	Div. Rate	No. of Corps.	Div. Rate	No. of Corps.	Div. Rate	No. of Corps.	Div. Rate	No. of Corps.	Div. Rate	No. of Corps.	Div. Rate
1909	91	.059	18	.053	3	.060	11	.064	1	.080	2	.048	6	.069	3	.022	[b]	[b]	5	.050
1910	106	.061	19	.054	4	.059	12	.066	1	.040	2	.050	7	.085[c]	3	.026	1	.060	6	.050
1911	117	.060	21	.050	4	.057	12	.066	2	.056	3	.052	8	.073	3	.027	2	.062	6	.055
1912	139	.060	22	.055	6	.063	16	.066	2	.076	4	.054	9	.072	3	.027	2	.062	7	.053
1913	161	.062	25	.058	10	.057	16	.068	2	.077	5	.057	10	.074	5	.024	3	.064	9	.050
1914	169	.058	26	.057	12	.057	17	.065	2	.076	5	.056	9	.077	5	.018	3	.064	10	.038
1915	176	.059	28	.054	12	.066	19	.065	2	.077	5	.056	9	.075	4	.018	3	.059	11	.053
1916	183	.064	28	.068	12	.060	19	.073[c]	2	.077	5	.056	10	.071	6	.029	3	.054	12	.052
1917	179	.072	27	.080[c]	12	.072[c]	18	.081[c]	1	.070	5	.070	10	.074	6	.043	3	.061	12	.054
1918	252	.070	36	.071[a]	21	.074[a]	26	.069	2	.052	5	.065	10	.073	6	.045	5	.032	19	.064
1919	269	.061	39	.069	24	.068	30	.065	2	.050	7	.071	11	.072	6	.045	6	.031	20	.065
1920	285	.067	41	.073[c]	25	.075[c]	35	.067	3	.043	8	.075	11	.080	5	.045	6	.041	21	.058
1921	294	.061	44	.056	25	.064	35	.067	3	.043	9	.038	11	.066	6	.047	6	.084[c]	21	.053
1922	300	.057	46	.048	26	.058	37	.060	3	.087[c]	9	.033	11	.066	6	.041	6	.069	22	.044
1923	294	.061	44	.057	24	.068	34	.068	3	.037	9	.040	11	.069	6	.040	6	.068	22	.047
1924	263	.062	30	.058	21	.055	33	.071	2	.114[c]	9	.039	9	.062	4	.042	6	.083[c]	21	.053
1925	275	.061	40	.051	22	.056	32	.066	2	.070	9	.037	9	.066	6	.068	7	.085[c]	23	.056

[a] Based upon a study of the annual reports of the specified numbers of corporations in the various fields.

[b] Sample reports could not be located for this field.

[c] High rates for this year due to payment of back dividends.

TABLE CIX—Continued

RATIO OF THE TOTAL DIVIDENDS ACTUALLY PAID ON THE PREFERRED STOCK TO THE TOTAL PAR VALUE OF THAT CLASS OF STOCK OUTSTANDING IN A SAMPLE GROUP OF CORPORATIONS IN EACH OF THE SPECIFIED BRANCHES OF MANUFACTURING[a]

YEAR	GAS		PETROLEUM REFINING		STONE, CLAY AND GLASS		METALS OTHER THAN IRON		TOBACCO		MACHINERY		MUSICAL INSTRUMENTS		MOTOR VEHICLES		RAILWAY EQUIPMENT		SHIP-BUILDING	
	No. of Corps.	Div. Rate	No. of Corps.	Div. Rate	No. of Corps.	Div. Rate	No. of Corps.	Div. Rate	No. of Corps.	Div. Rate	No. of Corps.	Div. Rate	No. of Corps.	Div. Rate	No. of Corps.	Div. Rate	No. of Corps.	Div. Rate	No. of Corps.	Div. Rate
1909	6	.043	1	.081	8	.042	4	.059	2	.061	10	.068	3	.052	b	b	7	.068	1	.070
1910	8	.048	2	.085	8	.051	5	.058	2	.061	12	.072[c]	3	.046	1	.070	9	.067	1	.070
1911	8	.050	3	.078	8	.047	5	.058	2	.061	15	.070	3	.046	2	.058	9	.069	1	.070
1912	8	.050	3	.066	9	.047	4	.063	5	.055	21	.064	3	.061	3	.071	11	.068	1	.070
1913	9	.050	3	.052	9	.040	6	.073	5	.063	23	.069	3	.071	6	.041	11	.068	1	.035
1914	9	.051	3	.009	10	.063	7	.069	5	.063	24	.053	3	.069	7	.042	11	.068	1	.000
1915	9	.051	3	.009	10	.076[c]	7	.069	6	.065	24	.048	3	.031	7	.050	11	.067	1	.035
1916	10	.050	3	.066	10	.050	9	.071	6	.064	25	.058	1	.031	9	.059	11	.067	1	.105[c]
1917	10	.050	3	.143[c]	10	.042	9	.116[c]	6	.063	25	.058	3	.060		.067	11	.072	2	.070[c]
1918	10	.048	2	.065	10	.043	11	.071	6	.065	43	.064	3	.039	19	.065	12	.071	2	.071
1919	10	.048	4	.031	10	.046	11	.073	10	.064	43	.072[c]	3	.054	20	.060	12	.074	1	.070
1920	11	.045	4	.070	9	.054	11	.073	11	.067	43	.064	3	.067	24	.066	12	.070	1	.070
1921	14	.050	5	.070	10	.046	11	.066	11	.065	45	.059	2	.071	24	.054	12	.069	1	.101[c]
1922	11	.057	5	.069	10	.045	9	.066	11	.064	46	.053	3	.051	23	.065	14	.068	2	.111[c]
1923	13	.047	5	.070	11	.059	10	.065	11	.065	47	.057	3	.054	20	.065	13	.069	2	.086[c]
1924	13	.058	5	.070	11	.064	10	.065	10	.063	44	.055	3	.076[c]	19	.060	12	.069	1	.125[c]
1925	13	.060	6	.067	11	.066	10	.065	9	.058	42	.060	3	.068	17	.066	13	.069	1	.059

CHAPTER XIV

FACTORS RELATED TO THE INCOME OF THE CONSTRUCTION INDUSTRY

Trend of the Total Value of Construction.

It is widely held that one of the most significant indicators of the degree of prosperity prevailing in our nation is the total value of construction undertaken during a given period. It is not feasible to estimate with any high degree of precision the actual extent of the construction completed in the United States in the various years, but it is possible to approximate the trends at the various dates. The figures in Table CX showing the value in current dollars of the urban construction in the United States for the years 1909 to 1918 are based primarily upon the volume of building permits reported for leading cities. Since 1919, the F. W. Dodge Company has compiled records of construction contracts[1] for a considerable proportion of the area of the United States. This proportion has been growing from year to year, and hence it has been necessary to make supplementary estimates for a constantly smaller fraction of the urban area. The building permit records for the years 1909 to 1918 have been converted to relatives, and, by aid of this series of relatives applied to the F. W. Dodge reports for 1919, estimates in terms of absolute value have been made for the earlier years.

The estimates of the total extent of building construction on the farms of the United States have been based in a general way on the reports of the United States Census of Agriculture, but the data in this field are so scanty that no reliance should be placed upon the approximations here given. Although a considerable but unknown amount of work on repairs and minor additions has been carried on both in country and city during the entire period, it is impossible to make satisfactory estimates of its volume.

Trend of the Physical Volume of Construction.

The index of construction costs given in Table CX is that prepared by the American Telephone and Telegraph Company and presumably represents the changes in cost per unit of construction

---

[1] These figures purport to include public works, railway construction, etc. as well as building.

TABLE CX

ESTIMATED TOTAL VALUE OF CONSTRUCTION

YEAR	VALUE IN CURRENT DOLLARS (Millions)			INDEX OF CONSTRUC- TION COSTS[e]	VALUE IN 1913 DOLLARS[d] (Millions)
	Urban[a]	On Farms[b]	Total		
1909	$2,830	$373	$3,202	.934	$3,428
1910	2,675	420	3,095	.964	3,211
1911	2,583	442	3,025	.970	3,119
1912	2,735	477	3,211	.981	3,274
1913	2,512	503	3,015	1.000	3,015
1914	2,305	514	2,819	.968	2,912
1915	2,344	529	2,873	.984	2,919
1916	2,950	559	3,509	1.168	3,004
1917	2,394	605	2,999	1.440	2,083
1918	2,271	608	2,880	1.604	1,795
1919	3,433	752	4,185	1.896	2,207
1920	3,297	823	4,120	2.430	1,695
1921	2,976	899	3,876	1.749	2,216
1922	4,177	800	4,978	1.704	2,921
1923	4,567	760	5,327	1.890	2,819
1924	5,141	758	5,899	1.867	3,159
1925	6,592	458	7,050	1.884	3,742
1926	6,972*	312*	7,284*	1.908	3,752*
1927	6,924*	402*	7,326*	1.864	3,929*
1928	7,426*	363*	7,789*	1.869*	4,167*

[a] Based upon records of building permits and the F. W. Dodge Co. figures on building contracts.
[b] Based upon *Census of Agriculture.*
[e] From American Telephone and Telegraph Co. *Summary of Business Conditions.*
[d] Figures in fourth column divided by those in fifth column.
* Preliminary estimate.

which have occurred in the various years. Division by this index gives, then, a rough approximation to the total value which the actual volume of construction would have had if the price level had remained constantly on the 1913 basis.

The physical volume of construction, which was on a high level in 1909 apparently declined steadily until 1915, rose slightly in 1916, then fell off abruptly during the next two years, recovered somewhat in 1919, but fell again in 1920. Thereafter a long upward movement began which was still continuing in 1927. The total volume of construction in 1927 was noticeably larger than in 1909, but the volume for 1909 was not exceeded until 1925.

TABLE CXI

TOTAL VALUE OF CONSTRUCTION
IN DOLLARS OF 1913 PURCHASING POWER

Year	Total Value[a] (Millions)	Population of the Continental United States July 1st[b] (Thousands)	Value Per Capita	Increase in Population During Year[c] (Thousands)	Value Per Additional Inhabitant[d]
1909	$3,428	90,508	$37.88	2,173	$1,578
1910	3,211	92,422	34.74	1,635	1,964
1911	3,119	93,837	33.23	1,293	2,412
1912	3,274	95,249	34.37	1,686	1,942
1913	3,015	97,111	31.05	2,069	1,457
1914	2,912	98,974	29.42	1,497	1,945
1915	2,919	100,390	29.08	1,345	2,170
1916	3,004	101,787	29.52	1,535	1,957
1917	2,083	103,234	20.18	1,262	1,650
1918	1,795	104,377	17.20	672	2,672
1919	2,207	105,007	21.02	1,187	1,860
1920	1,695	106,422	15.93	1,701	997
1921	2,216	108,370	20.45	1,723	1,286
1922	2,921	109,742	26.62	1,553	1,881
1923	2,819	111,478	25.28	1,978	1,425
1924	3,159	113,466	27.84	1,627	1,942
1925	3,742	115,004	32.54	1,531	2,444
1926	3,752*	116,442*	32.22*	1,473*	2,547*
1927	3,929*	117,980*	33.30*	1,513*	2,597*
1928	4,167*	119,440*	34.88*		

[a] See Table CX.
[b] See Table I.
[c] Derived from figures presented in Table I.
* Preliminary estimate.

Relationship of Construction to Population.

It has been customary to compare the physical volume of construction with the population of the United States in order to ascertain the quantity of construction per capita. This form of comparison is legitimate in so far as repairs are concerned and also in so far as one is interested in the improvements in and additions to building demanded by the population as a whole. With increasing prosperity, people call for better residences, better schools and other public structures, better office buildings, better mercantile establishments, better factories, and better railways; hence there is a tendency for the physical volume of construction per capita to be increased by prosperity.

CHART 51

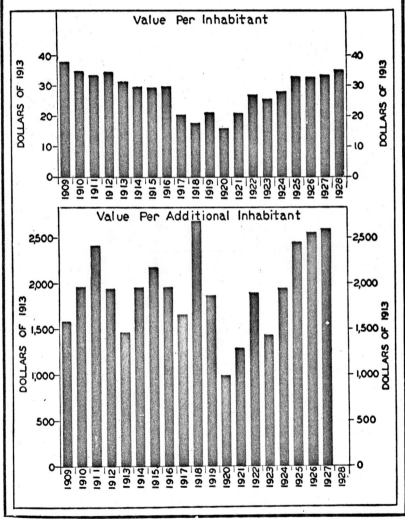

TOTAL VALUE OF CONSTRUCTION
IN DOLLARS OF 1913 PURCHASING POWER[a]

ᵃ For data, see Table CXI.

The fact should be noted that all figures in Table CXI are expressed in terms of dollars of constant purchasing power. These figures have been plotted in Chart 51. The upper graph in this chart shows that the value of construction per inhabitant, measured in 1913 dollars declined almost continuously between 1909 and 1920, but has increased with considerable regularity since. The great depression in building during the war was brought about largely by public restrictions on building. In the years immediately following the World War, high construction costs, indicated by the index in Table CX, postponed the immediate resumption of construction activities to make up for the construction deficit incurred during war time. With the return of construction costs to a more moderate level, it will be observed that the volume of building soon began to increase.

Relationship of Construction to Population Growth.

It is of interest to compare the physical volume of construction not only with the total population of the country but also with the increase in the population during each year. Such a comparison appears in the last column of Table CXI and in the lower section of Chart 51.

When the comparison is made on this basis, we see that the trend shown is very different from that indicated by the value of construction per inhabitant. In general, the value per *additional* inhabitant, expressed in dollars of constant purchasing power, shows a trend approximately horizontal between 1909 and 1919. There was a marked depression in 1920 and 1921, just as was the case when the comparison was made with the entire population. The growth in the volume compared with the *additions* to our population is seen to have been materially steeper between 1920 and 1927 than is the growth when compared with the population as a whole. Since 1924, also, the volume of construction per new inhabitant has been on a higher level than was normally the case during the pre-war period. It appears, therefore, that, in recent years, we have been providing building accomodations for our increased population at a rate somewhat larger than was formerly the case, but these figures may indicate primarily that the existing population is demanding a better grade of building accomodations to accord with its increased income.

CHAPTER XV

FACTORS RELATED TO INCOME IN TRANSPORTATION

Trends of Railway Freight and Passenger Traffic.

The bulk of long distance freight movement and a large part of the long distance passenger transportation in the United States is done by the railways of the country. In recent years much has been said of the competition of motor cars with the railroads. The facts brought out in Table CXII and Chart 52 are of unusual interest in this connection.

The volume of freight traffic is probably best measured by the number of ton-miles. The fairest year-to-year comparison of the service rendered to the public in the transportation of goods is probably given by the number of ton-miles per capita. The upper part of Chart 52 shows that, while the course of the trend is somewhat obscured by cyclical movements, the indications are that it was sharply upward between 1909 and 1918. On the other hand, between 1918 and 1926, it was approximately horizontal. Whether this change in the slope of the trend has been occasioned by the use of the motor truck instead of the freight car for short hauls, or whether it represents a tendency to move fewer bulky goods per person, it is not possible to ascertain from the available data. It seems probable, however, that the competition of the motor truck has been at least partially responsible for the failure of the curve, representing ton-miles per capita, to rise above the 1918 level in any of the years from 1918 to 1926.

The graph in the lower part of the same chart illustrates the changes which have occurred in the number of passenger-miles per capita. This curve shows a trend which was nearly horizontal between 1909 and 1915, rose sharply from 1915 to 1919, and thereafter declined steadily until the end of the period recorded, the number of passenger miles per capita being less in 1926 than in 1909. There can be little doubt but that the decline since 1920 has been occasioned primarily by the use of the automobile for passenger transportation. It is, however, interesting to observe that, in spite of the universal use of automobiles, the number of passenger miles per capita was more than 90 per cent as large in 1926 as in 1909.

TABLE CXII

VOLUME OF RAILWAY SERVICE
PER EMPLOYEE AND PER CAPITA

Year	Revenue Freight Carried[a] (Billions of Ton Miles)	Passenger Traffic[a] (Billions of Passenger Miles)	Employees Attached to Industry[b] (Thousands)	Ton Miles of Freight Per Employee	Passenger Miles Per Employee	Population of the Continental United States[c] (Thousands)	Ton Miles of Freight Per Capita	Passenger Miles Per Capita
1909	237	31	1,620	146,257	18,967	90,508	2,618	339
1910	254	33	1,758	144,744	18,645	92,422	2,753	355
1911	259	33	1,763	146,908	18,818	93,837	2,759	353
1912	284	34	1,774	159,947	19,209	95,249	2,979	358
1913	297	35	1,895	156,585	18,675	97,111	3,055	364
1914	283	34	1,899	148,946	17,894	98,974	2,857	343
1915	309	33	1,883	164,033	17,620	100,390	3,076	330
1916	365	35	1,844	197,801	18,999	101,787	3,583	344
1917	397	40	1,852	214,391	21,596	103,234	3,847	387
1918	409	43	1,969	207,625	21,948	104,377	3,916	414
1919	367	47	2,075	176,962	22,575	105,007	3,497	446
1920	414	47	2,163	191,259	21,900	106,422	3,887	445
1921	310	38	2,122	145,896	17,772	108,370	2,856	348
1922	342	36	2,097	163,073	17,080	109,742	3,115	326
1923	416	38	2,080	200,153	18,413	111,478	3,734	344
1924	391	36	2,040	191,863	17,823	113,466	3,450	321
1925	417	36	1,891	220,797	19,130	115,004	3,630	314
1926	447	36	1,902	235,016	18,927	116,442*	3,839*	309*
1927	432*	34*	1,856*	232,759*	18,319.*	117,980*	3,664*	287*
1928	436*	32*				119,440*	3,652*	265*

[a] Taken from *Statistics of Railways* issued by the Interstate Commerce Commission.
[b] Derived from Tables IV and VI.
[c] See Table I.
* Preliminary estimate.

Transportation Output Per Railway Employee.

The upper part of Chart 52 presents the line showing the changes which occurred during the period 1909 to 1926 in the ton-miles of freight per employee. This graph indicates that the freight output per railway employee was fairly constant between 1909 and 1914, then rose sharply until 1917, declined until 1921, and rose again until 1926. It is of interest to observe that the 1926 figure is decidedly higher than the 1917 peak. If, then, we take into consideration the entire period 1909 to 1926, it is apparent that em-

CHART 52

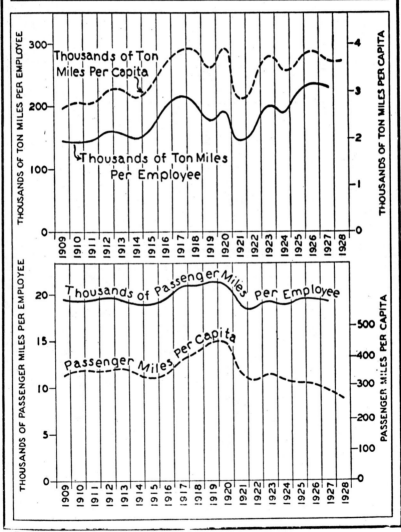

VOLUME OF RAILWAY SERVICE
PER EMPLOYEE AND PER CAPITA*

* For data, see Table CXII.

TABLE CXIII

PHYSICAL SERVICE RENDERED PER EMPLOYEE ATTACHED TO THE PULLMAN BUSINESS

Year	Number of Car Days[a]	Number of Employees Attached to Industry[b]	Car Days per Employee Attached to Industry
1909	[c]		[c]
1910	[c]		[c]
1911	1,614,843	18,422	87.7
1912	1,888,515	18,481	102.2
1913	2,162,321	21,104	102.5
1914	2,153,147	21,104	102.0
1915	2,150,990	20,402	105.4
1916	2,181,166	20,174	108.1
1917	2,374,029	19,655	120.8
1918	2,187,735	19,247	113.7
1919	2,427,418	19,904	122.0
1920	2,500,120	22,647	110.4
1921	2,465,399	22,718	108.5
1922	2,499,041	21,069	118.6
1923	2,652,525	21,622	122.7
1924	2,781,417	25,235	110.2
1925	3,007,022	26,221	114.7
1926	3,153,181	26,777	117.8
1927	3,171,330	27,151	116.8

[a] Taken from *Preliminary Abstracts of Statistics of Common Carriers*, published by the Interstate Commerce Commission.
[b] Derived from Tables IV and V.
[c] Data not available.

ployees have, on the average, become more efficient. The graph in the lower chart shows that the upward trend from 1909 to 1917 in the number of ton-miles of freight carried per employee, occurred also in the number of passenger-miles per employee. The decline in the passenger traffic per employee did not begin, however, until a year later than was the case with freight traffic. In passenger traffic, as in freight traffic, the low point was reached in 1921, after which date the trend was distinctly upward. While more freight was hauled per average employee in 1926 than in 1917, the volume of passenger traffic per employee did not change materially between 1918 and 1926.

TABLE CXIV

PULLMAN CAR MILEAGE PER CAPITA

Year	Number of Car Miles[a] (Thousands)	Population of the Continental United States[b] (Thousands)	Car Miles Per Capita
1909	•		•
1910	○		•
1911	641,723	93,837	6.84
1912	674,375	95,249	7.08
1913	704,341	97,111	7.25
1914	700,623	98,974	7.08
1915	708,323	100,390	7.06
1916	714,916	101,787	7.02
1917	775,407	103,234	7.51
1918	697,213	104,377	6.68
1919	773,251	105,007	7.36
1920	811,214	106,422	7.62
1921	799,572	108,370	7.38
1922	820,827	109,742	7.48
1923	890,719	111,478	7.99
1924	943,334	113,466	8.31
1925	1,043,663	115,004	9.08
1926	1,112,967	116,442*	9.56*
1927	1,140,476	117,980*	9.67*

[a] Taken from *Preliminary Abstract of Statistics of Common Carriers*, published by the Interstate Commerce Commission.
[b] See Table I.
• Data not available.
* Preliminary estimate.

Output of Pullman Service per Employee and per Inhabitant.

Table CXIII and Chart 53 portray the changes in the efficiency of employees in the Pullman industry. The graph in the upper part of the chart shows that the number of car days per employee ran up rapidly between 1911 and 1917. Since the last mentioned date, the trend appears to have been approximately horizontal. It appears, then, that the average Pullman employee was turning out in 1927 approximately the same amount of service as in 1917.

The lower part of the chart shows the changes that have occurred in the number of Pullman car-miles per capita. This graph indicates that the Pullman riding habits of the average American remained unchanged between 1911 and 1918, but, since the World War, there has been a marked tendency for more people to ride on

CHART 53

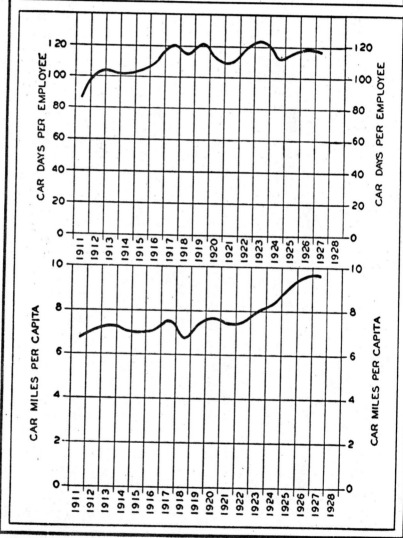

VOLUME OF PULLMAN SERVICE
PER EMPLOYEE AND PER CAPITA[a]

[a] For data, see Tables CXIII and CXIV.

TABLE CXV

ESTIMATED REVENUE CAR MILEAGE
PER EMPLOYEE AND PER CAPITA
FOR STREET AND INTERURBAN RAILWAYS

Year	Revenue Car Miles[a] (Thousands)	Number of Employees Attached to Industry[b]	Revenue Car Miles Per Employee Attached to Industry	Population of Continental United States[c] (Thousands)	Revenue Car Miles Per Inhabitant
1909	1,725,000	249,791	6,906	90,508	19.06
1910	1,785,000	264,936	6,737	92,422	19.31
1911	1,845,000	278,947	6,614	93,837	19.66
1912	1,921,620	287,804	6,677	95,249	20.17
1913	2,000,000	292,563	6,836	97,111	20.59
1914	2,068,000	295,632	6,995	98,974	20.89
1915	2,022,000	298,159	6,782	100,390	20.14
1916	2,110,000	299,926	7,035	101,787	20.73
1917	2,139,802	301,483	7,098	103,234	20.73
1918	2,051,356	303,457	6,760	104,377	19.65
1919	2,086,282	306,181	6,814	105,007	19.87
1920	2,141,891	307,290	6,970	106,422	20.13
1921	2,109,493	307,937	6,850	108,370	19.47
1922	2,124,523	307,540	6,908	109,742	19.36
1923	2,201,417	319,238	6,896	111,478	19.75
1924	2,216,952	318,154	6,968	113,466	19.54
1925	2,209,686	317,801	6,953	115,004	19.21
1926	2,229,481	318,836	6,993	116,442*	19.15*
1927	2,213,793*	321,642	6,883*	117,980*	18.76*

[a] Based upon the *Census of Electric Railways* and data presented in the magazine, *Aera.*
[b] Derived from Tables IV and V.
[c] See Table I.
* Preliminary estimate.

Pullman cars. In 1926, the average person in the United States required 45 per cent more Pullman car service than he did in 1918. Losses in railway passenger traffic are evidently confined to day coaches. Pullman car mileage has grown at the expense of day coach travel mainly because of the increased income of the average inhabitant.

Service of Street Railways per Employee and per Inhabitant.

Table CXV and Chart 54 illustrate the changes that have occurred in street railway service. The term street railways is here used to include not only surface lines but also elevated railways and

CHART 54

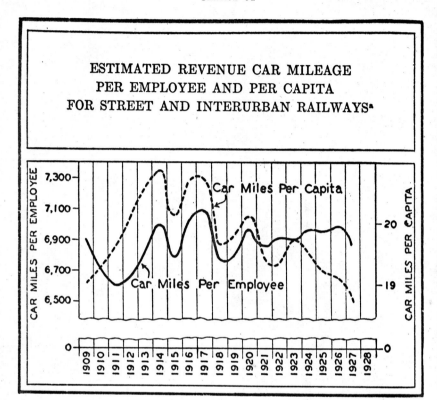

ESTIMATED REVENUE CAR MILEAGE
PER EMPLOYEE AND PER CAPITA
FOR STREET AND INTERURBAN RAILWAYS*

* For data, see Table CXV.

subways. Records for interurban electric lines of the older type are also, in many instances, included in these figures. The records for the railways carrying the heavy commutation traffic out of the great cities are included in the statistics for steam railways.

The solid graph in Chart 54 shows that the number of car-miles per employee had an approximately horizontal trend during the entire period 1909 to 1927. Available evidence indicates that any gains arising from the substitution of one-man for two-man cars have been offset by the addition of employees in other branches of the service. The dotted graph in Chart 54 shows clearly the rising trend in car-miles per capita characterizing the period 1909 to 1914. From 1914 to 1917, the trend became stationary, and, since 1917, has been drifting steadily downward. The use of the street car as

TABLE CXVI

NUMBER OF KILOWATT HOURS
PER EMPLOYEE AND PER CAPITA
PRODUCED BY PRIVATE AND MUNICIPAL
ELECTRIC LIGHT AND POWER PLANTS

Year	Kilowatt Hours Generated[a] (Millions)	Number of Employees Attached to Industry[b]	Kilowatt Hours Generated Per Employee	Population of Continental United States[c] (Thousands)	Kilowatt Hours Per Inhabitant
1907	5,862	48,770	120,197	87,198	67
1912	11,569	80,208	144,237	95,249	121
1917	25,438	107,167	237,368	103,234	246
1922	40,292	153,918	261,776	109,742	367
1923	47,433*			111,478	425*
1924	50,440*			113,466	445*
1925	56,617*			115,004	492*
1926	63,281*			116,442*	543*
1927	68,771*			117,980*	583*
1928	69,339*			119,440*	581*

[a] Based upon *Census of Electric Light and Power* and *Survey of Current Business*.
[b] Derived from *Census of Electric Light and Power*.
[c] See Table I.
* Preliminary estimate.

a means of transportation has been on the decline for a decade. When one observes the extensive substitution of motor busses for street cars, the surprising thing is that the decline in car miles per capita has been so slight, being less than 10 per cent between 1917 and 1927. Apparently, the heavy traffic on elevated railways and subways in the great cities has, to no small extent, offset the shrinkage caused by the closing down of many unprofitable street railway lines.

Electric Output per Employee and per Inhabitant.

Table CXVI and Chart 55 show something of the progress of the electric light and power industry. As we have seen, in both steam and electric railways, the respective amounts of traffic per inhabitant have been changing slowly during the period of this study. The reverse is the case in the production of electricity. Production per capita, measured in kilowatt hours, has risen at a surprisingly rapid rate of speed throughout the period. Similarly,

CHART 55

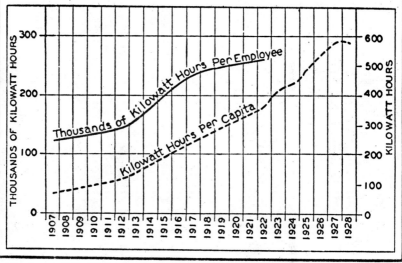

NUMBER OF KILOWATT HOURS
PER EMPLOYEE AND PER CAPITA
PRODUCED BY PRIVATE AND MUNICIPAL
ELECTRIC LIGHT AND POWER PLANTS[a]

a For data, see Table CXVI.

the number of kilowatt hours per employee has increased very
markedly. Chart 55 makes it plain that, not only are Americans
coming to use electricity to an extent scarcely dreamed of in the
earlier years of the century, but the generating plants are becoming
more efficient and hence are able to turn out more electricity per
person attached to the industry. This increase in efficiency is
presumably due to the fact that existing capacity is becoming more
freely utilized, that the average size of plants has been increasing
and that the larger plants require in their operation fewer persons
per unit of output than do the smaller plants.

Telephone Service per Employee and per Inhabitant.

The difficulty of measuring changes in physical output is greater
in the case of the telephone industry than in any of the industries

TABLE CXVII

ESTIMATES OF CHANGES IN THE
PHYSICAL OUTPUT PER EMPLOYEE
ATTACHED TO THE TELEPHONE INDUSTRY

	A	B	C	D	E	F
Year	Miles of Wire per Telephone[a]	Estimated Total Messages Sent[a] (Millions)	Index of Total Message Distance $\dfrac{AxB}{100,000,000}$	Number of Employees Attached to Industry[b] (Thousands)	Messages per Employee $B \div D$	Index of Message Distance per Employee $\dfrac{100,000 \times C}{D}$
1907	2.12	12,500	265	147	85,150	180
1909	2.23	13,360	298	150	89,365	199
1910	2.26	14,330	324	165	86,848	196
1911	2.28	15,430	352	185	83,270	190
1912	2.32	16,753	389	204	81,922	191
1913	2.34	17,410	407	218	79,680	187
1914	2.38	18,100	431	226	80,230	191
1915	2.36	17,120	404	230	74,435	176
1916	2.32	19,820	460	244	81,230	188
1917	2.46	21,846	537	268	81,424	201
1918	2.45	22,010	539	282	77,994	191
1919	2.40	20,452	491	297	68,862	165
1920	2.38	21,714	517	311	69,820	166
1921	2.46	22,759	560	318	71,569	176
1922	2.60	24,739	643	322	76,782	200
1923	2.75	26,375	725	350	75,435	207
1924	3.00	27,500	825	370	74,425	223
1925	3.26	29,000	945	377	76,943	251
1926	3.48	30,500	1,061	381	80,052	278
1927	3.72	31,500	1,172	385	81,818	304

[a] Based upon *Census of Telephones* and reports of the Bell Telephone Company.
[b] See Tables IV and V.

heretofore discussed. As the size of an exchange is increased, more service is given to each subscriber, because of the fact that he is thus put in contact with a larger number of other persons. Furthermore, the increase in the size of a telephone exchange usually means that it covers a larger geographical area, hence more service is also rendered to the subscriber because the average distance between him and the person he talks to is greater than was previously the case. Under these circumstances, it is manifestly unsatisfactory

TABLE CXVIII

ESTIMATED VOLUME OF
TELEPHONE SERVICE PER INHABITANT

Year	A Estimated Total Messages Sent[a] (Millions)	B Index of Total Message Distance[a]	C Population of the Continental United States[b] (Thousands)	D Messages Per Capita A÷C	E Index of Message Distance per Capita 100,000,000B÷C
1907	12,500	265	87,198	143	304
1909	13,360	298	90,508	148	329
1910	14,330	324	92,422	155	350
1911	15,430	352	93,837	164	375
1912	16,753	389	95,249	176	408
1913	17,410	407	97,111	179	420
1914	18,100	431	98,974	183	435
1915	17,120	404	100,390	171	402
1916	19,820	460	101,787	195	452
1917	21,846	537	103,234	212	521
1918	22,010	539	104,377	211	517
1919	20,452	491	105,007	195	467
1920	21,714	517	106,422	204	486
1921	22,759	560	108,370	210	517
1922	24,739	643	109,742	225	586
1923	26,375	725	111,478	237	651
1924	27,500	825	113,466	242	727
1925	29,000	945	115,004	252	822
1926	30,500	1,061	116,442*	262*	911*
1927	31,500	1,172	117,980*	267*	993*

[a] See Table CXVII.
[b] See Table I.
* Preliminary estimate.

to gauge the volume of telephone traffic by the number of messages sent. Tables CXVII and CXVIII and Chart 56 are used to present the results of an attempt to approximate roughly the volume of telephone service as compared to the number of employees and also as compared to the population of the country. The upper graph in Chart 56 shows that the number of messages per employee declined between 1907 and 1927. At the same time the number of messages per inhabitant has been rising rapidly, the average number in 1927 being nearly twice as great as in 1907.

CHART 56

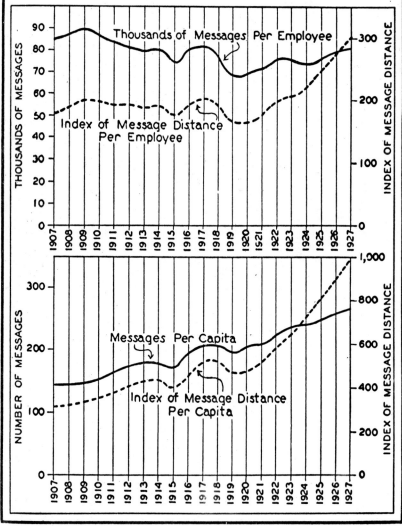

ESTIMATED VOLUME OF TELEPHONE SERVICE
PER EMPLOYEE AND PER CAPITA*

* For data, see Tables CXVII and CXVIII.

TABLE CXIX

THE TONNAGE OF THE AMERICAN MERCHANT MARINE AS COMPARED TO THE POPULATION OF THE CONTINENTAL UNITED STATES

July 1	Tonnage Afloat[a]	Population[b] (Thousands)	Tonnage Per Capita
1909	7,388,755	90,508	.0816
1910	7,508,082	92,422	.0812
1911	7,638,790	93,837	.0814
1912	7,714,183	95,249	.0810
1913	7,886,551	97,111	.0812
1914	7,928,688	98,974	.0801
1915	8,389,429	100,390	.0836
1916	8,469,649	101,787	.0832
1917	8,871,037	103,234	.0859
1918	9,924,518	104,377	.0951
1919	12,907,300	105,007	.1229
1920	16,324,024	106,422	.1534
1921	18,282,136	108,370	.1687
1922	18,462,967	109,742	.1682
1923	18,284,734	111,478	.1640
1924	17,740,557	113,466	.1564
1925	17,405,902	115,004	.1514
1926	17,311,147	116,442*	.1487*
1927	16,887,501	117,980*	.1431*
1928	16,683,061	119,440*	.1397*

[a] Taken from reports of the U. S. Commissioner of Navigation and from *Merchant Marine Statistics.*
[b] See Table I.
* Preliminary estimate.

The procedure used here in estimating the volume of service rendered by the telephone industry is based not only upon the number of messages but also upon the number of miles of wire per telephone, it being assumed that the changes in this mileage are accompanied by roughly proportional changes in the average distance which messages travel.[1] Column C of Table CXVII indicates,

[1]Col. M. C. Rorty says in this connection: "The message mile index is very inexact and perhaps should not be used. A large fraction of the wire mileage is in the leads from central offices to subscribers' premises. This wire mileage is very inefficiently used, i. e., it is busy not more than 10% to 12% of the time even during the busier portions of the day. On the other hand the inter-office and long distance trunks are used at as closely as possible 100% efficiency during busy hours. The ratio of subscribers' loop to trunk mileage is constantly varying and is affected by technical factors which have no relation to the actual message miles of traffic. For example, the introduction of cheaper, very small gauge cables has tended to reduce the number of central offices and to increase the average length of subscribers' lines."

CHART 57

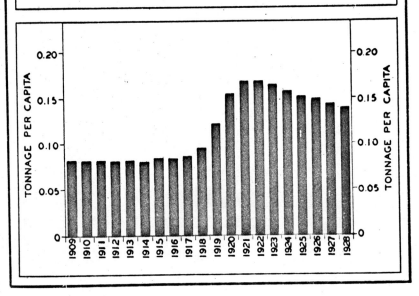

THE TONNAGE OF THE AMERICAN MERCHANT
MARINE AS COMPARED TO THE POPULATION OF
THE CONTINENTAL UNITED STATES*

* For data, see Table CXIX.

then, that actual telephone service more than quadrupled between
1907 and 1927. The volume of service per employee remained
approximately constant between 1907 and 1919. After 1920, a
rapid upward movement began which was still continuing in 1927.
Apparently the average employee in 1927 rendered something like
70 per cent more service to the public than he did in 1907, while the
average inhabitant in the United States received more than three
times as much telephone service in 1927 as in 1907.

Size of Merchant Marine Compared to Population.

Table CXIX and Chart 57 include comparisons between the
size of the American merchant marine and the population of the

United States. Between 1909 and 1914, per capita tonnage remained practically unchanged, but, from 1915 to 1917, it rose slightly. Only after 1917, was there any evidence of marked growth. Between 1917 and 1921, the tonnage per capita increased over 95 per cent. This remarkable growth, however, was destined to be short lived. In 1922, the per capita figure declined very slightly, and this decline proceeded with increased rapidity until 1927, the last year recorded. While the tonnage per capita has been constantly declining, the total drop to date has been but about 15 per cent of the figure attained at the peak, and the tonnage of the American merchant marine per inhabitant of the United States is still 75 per cent greater than it was in 1909.

CHAPTER XVI

BANKING TRANSACTIONS AS RELATED TO INCOME

In the United States, payments of any size are usually made by check, hence the volume of banking transactions is one of the most accurate criteria of the activity of business in the country. When business is active, there is, of course, a tendency for production, and therefore realized income, to be large. *A priori*, therefore, one would expect some rather definite mathematical relationship to exist between the volume of banking transactions and that of the realized income of the people of the United States. Table CXX and Chart 58 are devoted to an analysis of such relationships. The first comparison is made between the sum of loans and private deposits and the total realized income of the inhabitants of the nation; the second comparison between the volume of bank clearings and total realized income; and the third, which covers only the years since 1919, between the total volume of debits to private accounts and realized income.

Bank Credit and Realized Income.

The sum of loans and private deposits measures in ... ly the extent of credit issued by banks. The graph in Chart 58 indicates that the ratio of combined loans and private deposits to realized income has pursued a somewhat upward trend, marked, however, by a definite depression during the war period. It appears, therefore, that the percentage of the business of the nation done by banks is tending slightly to increase, but that this general tendency was interrupted during the period of the World War. In times of depression, such as 1914 and 1921, the ratio of loans and private deposits to total realized income is abnormally high, while, in years of relative prosperity such as 1909, 1913, and 1923, the ratio tended to be somewhat below the trend.

In considering bank clearings as a measure of business activity, one should keep in mind the fact that the area covered by banks reporting to clearing houses is gradually being extended, and that this fact is likely to affect the trend of the ratio of bank clearings to entire realized income.

The graphs in Chart 58 show that the trend of this ratio has

TABLE CXX

BANK ACTIVITY COMPARED WITH THE REALIZED INCOME OF THE PEOPLE OF THE CONTINENTAL UNITED STATES

YEAR	SUM OF LOANS AND PRIVATE DEPOSITS[a] JULY 1 (MILLIONS)	BANK CLEARINGS[b] (MILLIONS)	DEBITS TO PRIVATE ACCOUNTS[c] (MILLIONS)	REALIZED INCOME OF THE PEOPLE OF THE CONTINENTAL UNITED STATES[d] (MILLIONS)	RATIO TO ENTIRE REALIZED INCOME OF		
					Sum of Loans and Private Deposits	Bank Clearings	Debits to Private Accounts
1909	25,338	$165,780	•	$29,605	.856	5.60	
1910	27,742	164,020	•	31,430	.883	5.22	
1911	28,889	160,210	•	31,858	.907	5.03	
1912	30,916	174,020	•	33,977	.910	5.12	
1913	32,044	169,950	•	35,723	.897	4.76	
1914	33,806	155,240	•	35,647	.948	4.35	
1915	34,857	187,820	•	37,205	.937	5.05	
1916	40,585	261,430	•	43,288	.938	6.04	
1917	46,884	306,920	•	51,331	.913	5.98	
1918	50,332	332,280	•	60,408	.833	5.50	
1919	57,947	417,770	566,000	65,949	.879	6.33	8.58
1920	68,803	452,110	611,000	73,999	.930	6.11	8.26
1921	64,256	356,210	500,000	63,371	1.014	5.62	7.89
1922	64,922	382,820	545,000	65,925	.985	5.81	8.27
1923	70,302	413,490	582,000	74,337	.946	5.56	7.83
1924	74,221	455,420	612,000	77,135	.962	5.90	7.93
1925	80,513	512,070	704,000	81,931	.983	6.25	8.59
1926	84,968	523,840	750,000	85,548*	.993*	6.12*	8.77*
1927	88,263	554,990	823,000	88,205*	1.001*	6.29*	9.33*
1928	92,630			89,419*	1.036*		

[a] Taken from *Annual Reports* of the U. S. Comptroller of the Currency.
[b] Taken from *Statistical Bulletins* of Standard Statistics Co.
[c] See *Journal of the American Statistical Association*, Sept. 1928, p. 303.
[d] See Table VIII.
• Data not available.
* Preliminary estimate.

roughly paralleled that of the ratio of loans and private deposits to realized income; but the first mentioned trend, though in general upward, was broken by a large depression from 1910 to 1915, the deepest part of the trough being in 1914. The graph gives no indication that there is any definite relationship between the size of this ratio and the prosperity of the country.

CHART 58

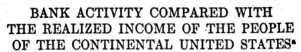

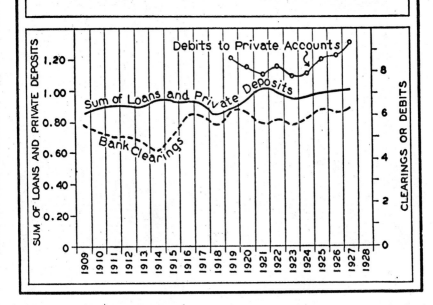

* For data, see Table CXX.

Ratio to Total Realized Income of Debits to Private Accounts.

Bank clearings obviously represent but a fraction of the total banking business of the area tributary to clearing houses, for only those checks cashed at a bank other than that on which they are drawn pass through the clearing house. Under these circumstances, it is evident that, for any specified area, the volume of debits to private accounts represents much more completely than does the volume of bank clearings the aggregate amount of business carried on by aid of bank facilities. Chart 58 indicates that the movements of the ratio of such *debits* to aggregate realized income paralleled closely the movements of the ratio of *bank clearings* to aggregate

TABLE CXXI

BANK ACTIVITY COMPARED WITH THE TOTAL INCOME OF THE PEOPLE OF THE CONTINENTAL UNITED STATES

Year	Sum of Loans and Private Deposits[a] July 1 (Millions)	Bank Clearings[a] (Millions)	Debits to Private Accounts[a] (Millions)	Total Income of the People of the Continental United States[b] (Millions)	Ratio to Total Income of		
					Sum of Loans and Private Deposits	Bank Clearings	Debits to Private Accounts
1909	$25,338	$ 165,780	[c]	$31,158	.813	5.32	
1910	27,742	164,020	[c]	32,496	.854	5.05	
1911	28,889	160,210	[c]	34,020	.849	4.71	
1912	30,916	174,020	[c]	39,182	.789	4.44	
1913	32,044	169,950	[c]	30,145	1.063	5.64	
1914	33,806	155,240	[c]	41,798	.809	3.71	
1915	34,857	187,820	[c]	52,877	.659	3.55	
1916	40,585	261,430	[c]	28,506	1.424	9.17	
1917	46,884	306,920	[c]	18,196	2.577	16.87	
1918	50,322	332,280	[c]	43,380	1.160	7.66	
1919	57,947	417,770	566,000	54,071	1.072	7.73	10.47
1920	68,803	452,110	611,000	72,681	.947	6.22	8.41
1921	64,256	356,210	500,000	88,262	.728	4.04	5.67
1922	64,922	382,820	545,000	75,377	.861	5.08	7.23
1923	70,302	413,490	582,000	72,819	.965	5.68	7.99
1924	74,221	455,420	612,000	90,191	.823	5.05	6.79
1925	80,513	512,070	704,000	85,369	.943	6.00	8.25
1926	84,968	523,840	750,000				
1927	88,263	554,990	823,000				

[a] For sources of information see Table CXX.
[b] See Table LII.
[c] Data not available.

realized income. The fact that the former ratio seems to fluctuate more widely is due merely to the fact that it is a larger ratio. If plotted logarithmically, it would be readily seen that the amplitude of the vibrations is proportionally about the same as that of the vibrations of bank clearings. Records of the total volume of debits to private accounts are not available for years prior to 1919.

While the three sets of ratios all move about their respective trend lines, their oscillations are so much larger than those in the

curve representing income that it is evident that none of them can safely be used to forecast the realized income of the nation.

In Table CXXI, the sum of loans and deposits, bank clearings and debits to individual accounts have been compared with the estimated *total* income in contradistinction to the *realized* income. None of the ratios show any definite upward or downward trend.

CHAPTER XVII

GOVERNMENT AS A FACTOR IN NATIONAL INCOME

The Number of Persons Employed by Government.

Estimates of the total number of persons working for each of the various divisions of government service within the limits of the United States appear in Table CXXII. The number of men in the Army, Navy, and Marine Corps moved upward slowly but steadily between 1909 and 1915, advanced with an accelerated pace in 1916, and then rose abruptly to a peak after the United States entered the war. The war closed in 1918, but the period of Army reduction extended to 1923, at which date the number of men found in the armed forces of the United States was smaller than at any time since 1916. By 1924, the number had increased slightly. Since then it appears to have remained stationary on a level some 80 per cent higher than that prevailing during the period 1909 to 1911.

Between 1909 and 1927, the number of men in the armed forces grew at a rate distinctly more rapid than the proportional increase in the population of the nation.

The number of employees in the postal service was kept almost constant between 1909 and 1918. Thereafter, the number of workers in this branch of the service tended to increase. Even so, the increase did not keep pace with the growth of the population of the country, for the working force of the Post Office Department increased by but 23 per cent between 1909 and 1927, while the population of the United States grew by over 30 per cent.

The number of employees engaged in other activities of the Federal Government showed a steady expansion between 1909 and 1915, a sharp rise during 1917 and 1918 to a marked peak in 1919, and then a decline, at first rapid and later slow,—this decline apparently continuing until 1927. At the peak of the war and after-war demand for civil assistance by the government, the number of such employees was more than three times as great as it was in 1909. By 1927, however, the number had diminished to such an extent that it was only about 70 per cent larger than in 1909.

Since States and Counties showed no marked tendency to take on additional employees during the war period, the trend of numbers employed in that field has been much more regular than in the

TABLE CXXII

ESTIMATED NUMBERS OF PERSONS ATTACHED TO THE VARIOUS BRANCHES OF GOVERNMENT IN THE CONTINENTAL UNITED STATES

| | | THOUSANDS OF EMPLOYEES ATTACHED TO VA... BRANCHES OF GOVERNMENT | | | | | | | |
| | | UNITED STATES | | | | CITIES AND VILLAGES | | | |
YEAR	All Branches	Army, Navy and Marines[a]	Postal Service[b]	General Government[c]	STATES AND COUNTIES[d]	Police and Fire Departments[e]	Municipal Utilities[f]	General Government[f]	SCHOOL DISTRICTS[g]
1909	1,643	137	282	143	169	98	29	211	573
1910	1,709	134	286	145	182	102	30	238	591
1911	1,765	139	286	149	194	105	31	255	607
1912	1,821	147	289	149	206	107	32	264	626
1913	1,879	150	294	151	217	111	33	280	644
1914	1,947	161	296	162	213	114	35	297	669
1915	2,013	169	299	176	205	117	35	319	694
1916	2,085	202	301	192	197	120	36	319	717
1917	2,744	790	300	232	192	123	38	321	748
1918	5,210	3,023	290	433	214	126	39	305	779
1919	4,042	1,699	319	511	241	128	38	305	800
1920	2,719	374	326	468	268	131	45	283	826
1921	2,689	334	330	365	294	135	53	326	852
1922	2,618	260	321	301	305	138	50	366	877
1923	2,633	237	337	265	301	142	58	390	903
1924	2,674	250	338	261	301	146	57	386	934
1925	2,736	247	342	263	309	150	60	401	966
1926	2,785*	246*	345*	255*	316*	153*	62*	408*	999*
1927	2,819*	249*	347*	243*	321*	157*	64*	419*	1,018*

a Based upon reports of the War Dept. and the Navy Dept.
b Based upon reports of the Postmaster General.
c Based upon the *Official Register* and the reports of the U. S. Civil Service Commission.
d Based upon *The Census of Wealth, Debt, and Taxation, The Financial Statistics of States* issued by the U. S. Bureau of the Census, and upon numerous State reports.
e Based upon reports of Fire and Police Departments in various cities and upon the U. S. *Census of Population.*
f Based upon *The Financial Statistics of Cities*, issued by the U. S. Bureau of the Census, and upon numerous State reports.
g Based upon reports of the U. S. Commissioner of Education.
* Preliminary estimate.

Federal civil service. The estimates presented indicate, however, that when the entire period is taken into consideration, the increase in employment in the State and County civil service is found to be relatively much larger than the growth in the Federal civil service, the increase between 1909 and 1927 being approximately 90 per cent as contrasted to the 70 per cent growth for the national government.

Between 1909 and 1927, the number of policemen and firemen rose by 60 per cent. At the same time, the number of employees engaged in operating municipal utilities increased 120 per cent and the number of those employed in the other branches of the government of cities and villages grew by approximately 98 per cent. The school districts of the country employed about 78 per cent more people in 1927 than in 1909.

All the evidence, therefore, indicates that, in each type of governmental agency except the postal service, the fraction of the population employed therein grew,—in other words, the proportion of the activities of the nation carried on by government was steadily enlarged.

The graphs representing the percentages of the gainfully occupied population employed in each non-military division of government are found in Chart 59. This chart also brings out the fact that, as regards numbers, the school employees form the largest class of those working for government in the United States. The percentages are as follows:

Percentage of Gainfully Occupied Population Employed by

Calendar Year	Federal Government	State and County Governments	Municipal Governments	School Districts
1909	1.24	.49	.99	1.67
1910	1.22	.52	1.06	1.68
1911	1.22	.54	1.09	1.70
1912	1.21	.57	1.12	1.73
1913	1.20	.59	1.15	1.74
1914	1.21	.56	1.18	1.77
1915	1.25	.54	1.24	1.83
1916	1.28	.51	1.23	1.86
1917	1.35	.49	1.23	1.90
1918	1.79	.53	1.17	1.93
1919	2.06	.60	1.17	1.99
1920	1.98	.67	1.15	2.06
1921	1.70	.72	1.26	2.09
1922	1.51	.74	1.34	2.12
1923	1.43	.71	1.41	2.14
1924	1.39	.70	1.37	2.17
1925	1.38	.70	1.39	2.20
1926	1.34	.71	1.40	2.24
1927	1.30	.71	1.41	2.24

CHART 59

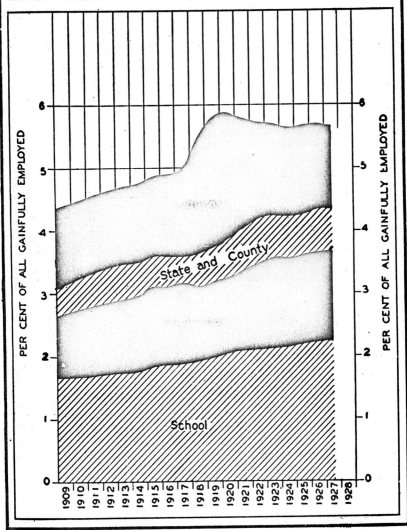

PERCENTAGES OF ALL GAINFULLY OCCUPIED,
EMPLOYED IN NON-MILITARY SERVICE
BY THE VARIOUS BRANCHES OF GOVERNMENT*

* For data, see text.

TABLE CXXIII

ESTIMATED TOTAL AMOUNTS DISBURSED BY THE VARIOUS BRANCHES OF GOVERNMENT IN DIRECT PAYMENT FOR THE SERVICES OF EMPLOYEES

Year	All Branches of Government	MILLIONS OF DOLLARS PAID BY							
		FEDERAL GOVERNMENT			States and Counties[a]	CITIES AND VILLAGES			Schools[a]
		Army, Navy and Marine Corps[a]	Post Office Department[a]	Miscellaneous Civil Departments[a]		Police and Fire Departments[a]	Municipal Utilities[a]	Miscellaneous Civil Departments[a]	
1909	$1,226	$113	$153	$148	$151	$117	$24	$223	$296
1910	1,314	110	160	157	166	126	26	254	316
1911	1,384	112	166	156	181	131	26	275	337
1912	1,465	119	174	156	199	138	27	290	362
1913	1,558	123	187	163	217	142	30	308	387
1914	1,656	128	199	177	219	151	33	334	414
1915	1,734	134	206	194	215	152	33	358	441
1916	1,821	149	214	212	212	157	35	365	477
1917	2,464	668	220	271	211	162	37	369	525
1918	5,272	3,023	243	563	245	179	40	388	591
1919	4,489	1,861	295	665	290	204	48	424	703
1920	3,519	527	346	644	351	238	61	482	870
1921	3,751	472	372	541	416	266	78	587	1,019
1922	3,775	397	383	458	441	262	79	647	1,109
1923	3,898	342	396	465	447	282	94	695	1,177
1924	4,053	334	426	450	459	297	99	739	1,249
1925	4,338	342	474	471	487	324	104	817	1,320
1926	4,750*			500					
1927	4,992*								

[a] Sources of information are same as those referred to in Table CXXII.

* Preliminary estimate.

Salaries of Employees of Various Branches of Government.

It is, of course, obvious that this increase in the proportion of gainfully occupied persons employed by government tends to increase the ratio of tax levies to national income.

Table CXXIII shows the amounts disbursed in the form of wages and salaries by the various branches of government. As these totals are all expressed in dollars current in the various years, those for different dates are not comparable.

In Table CXXIV, we find the results obtained by dividing the

TABLE CXXIV

ESTIMATED AVERAGE ANNUAL PAY* OF EMPLOYEES
IN VARIOUS BRANCHES OF GOVERNMENT SERVICE
IN THE CONTINENTAL UNITED STATES

| YEAR | All Branches of Government | FEDERAL GOVERNMENT | | | STATES AND COUNTIES | CITIES AND VILLAGES | | | SCHOOLS |
		Army, Navy and Marine Corps	Post Office Department	Miscellaneous Civil Departments		Police and Fire Departments	Municipal Utilities	Miscellaneous Civil Departments	
1909	$ 746	$ 829	$ 541	$1,030	$ 893	$1,187	$ 847	$1,058	$ 517
1910	769	822	560	1,080	909	1,238	845	1,066	535
1911	784	810	579	1,050	931	1,251	852	1,080	556
1912	805	810	602	1,045	967	1,285	855	1,096	578
1913	829	822	638	1,077	1,001	1,279	911	1,102	601
1914	850	799	671	1,097	1,028	1,321	960	1,122	619
1915	861	792	689	1,106	1,053	1,294	965	1,123	635
1916	874	738	711	1,106	1,074	1,303	972	1,143	666
1917	898	845	736	1,165	1,100	1,313	983	1,149	703
1918	1,012	1,000	839	1,301	1,143	1,422	1,016	1,269	758
1919	1,111	1,096	924	1,300	1,203	1,592	1,264	1,388	878
1920	1,294	1,411	1,062	1,377	1,309	1,817	1,361	1,704	1,053
1921	1,395	1,413	1,128	1,483	1,416	1,968	1,479	1,802	1,195
1922	1,442	1,525	1,192	1,522	1,446	1,895	1,586	1,766	1,264
1923	1,480	1,441	1,176	1,752	1,486	1,985	1,620	1,784	1,303
1924	1,516	1,335	1,261	1,721	1,529	2,030	1,733	1,916	1,336
1925	1,585	1,385	1,386	1,792	1,575	2,164	1,744	2,037	1,367
1926									
1927									

* Derived from figures presented in Tables CXXII and CXXIII.
* Preliminary estimate.

quantities in Table CXXIII by the numbers of employees recorded
in Table CXXII. The figures in Table CXXIV represent, therefore,
the average pay per employee in each branch of the government
service, this average pay being measured in terms of the dollars
current in each year. In order to permit of year to year comparisons,
the figures appearing in Table CXXIV have been deflated by dividing them by index numbers representing the average prices, at
the various dates, of consumers' goods used by urban employees.
The figures thus derived, which appear in Table CXXV, illustrate
the changes from year to year in the ability of government employees to buy consumable commodities. The facts are brought out

TABLE CXXV

PURCHASING POWER, IN 1913 DOLLARS,[a] OF THE AVERAGE ANNUAL PAY OF EMPLOYEES IN VARIOUS BRANCHES OF GOVERNMENT SERVICE IN THE CONTINENTAL UNITED STATES

| | | PURCHASING POWER[b] OF ANNUAL EARNINGS OF EMPLOYEES OF | | | | | | | |
| | | FEDERAL GOVERNMENT | | | | CITIES AND VILLAGES | | | |
YEAR	All Branches of Government	Army, Navy and Marine Corps	Post Office Department	Miscellaneous Civil Departments	STATES AND COUNTIES	Police and Fire Departments	Municipal Utilities	Miscellaneous Civil Departments	SCHOOLS
1909	$790	$878	$573	$1,090	$945	$1,257	$897	$1,120	$547
1910	794	848	578	1,115	938	1,278	872	1,100	552
1911	809	836	597	1,083	961	1,291	879	1,114	574
1912	819	825	613	1,064	984	1,308	870	1,116	588
1913	829	822	638	1,077	1,001	1,279	911	1,102	601
1914	836	785	660	1,078	1,011	1,299	944	1,103	608
1915	832	765	666	1,069	1,017	1,250	932	1,085	614
1916	783	661	637	991	962	1,167	871	1,024	597
1917	689	648	564	893	844	1,007	754	881	539
1918	644	636	534	828	727	905	646	807	482
1919	606	598	505	710	657	869	690	758	479
1920	620	676	509	659	627	870	652	816	504
1921	775	785	627	824	787	1,094	822	1,001	664
1922	860	910	711	908	863	1,131	946	1,054	754
1923	867	844	689	1,026	871	1,163	949	1,045	763
1924	889	783	739	1,009	896	1,190	1,016	1,123	783
1925	909	794	795	1,028	903	1,241	1,000	1,168	784

[a] "1913 Dollars" is an abbreviation for the phrase "dollars having purchasing power equivalent to that which they had in 1913."

[b] Computed from the corresponding items in Table CXXIV by dividing by the appropriate price indices recorded in Table VII.

[c] Preliminary estimate.

by the graphs in Chart 60. On the right-hand side of this chart, a scale has been appended showing the average pay of each class when converted to dollars having the average purchasing power which they possessed in 1928.

Chart 60 brings out forcefully the striking effect of inflation on various classes of government employees. The amount of direct or consumers' goods which the average employee could buy with me salary fell off very sharply in the case of policemen and firemen,

CHART 60

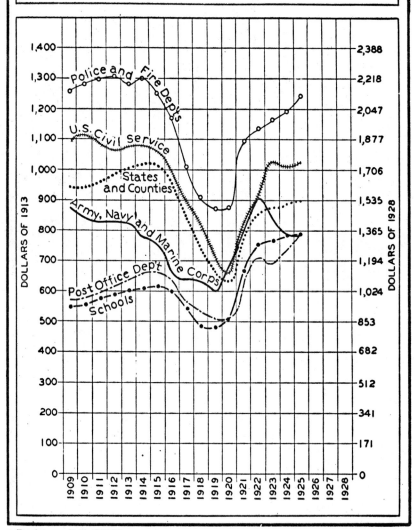

PURCHASING POWER, IN 1913 DOLLARS,
OF THE AVERAGE ANNUAL PAY OF EMPLOYEES
IN VARIOUS BRANCHES OF GOVERNMENTAL
SERVICE IN THE CONTINENTAL
UNITED STATES[a]

[a] For data, see Table CXXV.

soldiers, sailors and marines, and miscellaneous civil employees of the Federal, State and County governments. Between 1915 and 1919, a somewhat less startling but still very marked, decline in the incomes of both post office and school employees also occurred. After 1920, the purchasing power of the average income increased greatly in the case of every class of governmental employee, but in 1925, the rise was still not sufficient to bring the average pay of policemen, firemen, Federal civil service employees, State and County employees, or members of the military and naval forces of the United States to the level prevailing during the period 1909 to 1912. By 1925, however, the postal and school employees had secured advances sufficient not only to offset losses occurring during the period of inflation but to give them substantially better incomes than they had in pre-war days.

Pensions and Gratuities Paid by Various Branches of Government.

Table CXXVI reveals the substantial increases in public expenditure arising out of payments for pensions, bounties, and gratuities. Between 1909 and 1927, the total sum represented by payments of this class was quintupled. Since the figures in Table CXXVI are expressed in terms of dollars current in various years, this increase of 400 per cent is partially accounted for by the rise in the price-level, but even when this factor is allowed for, the increase is startling. It might be inferred that practically all of the increase was ascribable to the large payments made by the Federal government to soldiers of the World War. The truth is, however, that, such expenditures of County and State governments increased at a rate proportionally more rapid than did the amount of the pensions and gratuities expended by the Federal government. In 1925, the cities and villages were paying nearly 10 times as much as in 1909, the counties 8½ times as much, and the States nearly 9 times as much, while the Federal government was paying out only 3½ times as much. In recent years, the total of governmental pensions, gratuities, and the like, has amounted to something more than 1 per cent of the entire realized income of the nation.

Interest Paid by Branches of Government.

In Table CXXVII there is recorded the total amount of interest paid out by various branches of government. Everyone is, of course, familiar with the enormous increase in the debt of the Federal government accompanying the World War, and hence no

TABLE CXXVI

APPROXIMATE AMOUNTS OF PENSIONS AND GRATUITIES PAID OUT BY THE VARIOUS BRANCHES OF GOVERNMENT IN THE CONTINENTAL UNITED STATES

YEAR	THOUSANDS OF DOLLARS				
	All Branches of Government	City and Village[a]	County[b]	State[b]	Federal[c]
1909	$186,520	$ 5,900	$ 9,246	$10,400	$160,974
1910	185,458	6,062	9,746	11,000	158,650
1911	185,491	8,398	10,287	11,650	155,156
1912	196,503	9,300	10,854	12,320	163,579
1913	207,965	10,125	11,475	13,070	173,295
1914	205,951	10,845	12,198	13,940	168,968
1915	201,918	11,705	12,993	14,883	162,337
1916	203,831	13,750	13,992	16,064	160,025
1917	219,276	17,039	14,810	17,062	170,365
1918	469,182	18,522	16,087	18,576	415,997
1919	582,790	21,998	17,633	20,432	522,727
1920	713,713	22,000	26,233	30,503	634,977
1921	813,249	22,097	34,812	40,574	715,766
1922	887,678	40,286	61,528	71,962	713,902
1923	801,063	45,330	48,159	56,525	651,049
1924	869,902	52,330	107,516	126,490	583,566
1925	812,798	58,026	78,364	92,519	583,889
1926	889,849*				
1927	935,152*				

[a] Based upon *The Financial Statistics of Cities*, published by the U. S. Bureau of the Census.
[b] Based upon *The Financial Statistics of States*, published by the U. S. Bureau of the Census.
[c] Based upon reports of the U. S. Commissioner of Pensions and of the U. S. Veterans' Bureau.
* Preliminary estimate.

one will be surprised at the increase from 18 millions to 780 millions in the amount of interest paid to individuals. Since 1919, the date when the maximum figure was reached, the Federal government has each year cut down its total of interest payments. By 1925, the aggregate had been reduced to 560 millions.

Between 1909 and 1918, State and local governments doubled their volume of interest payments. Furthermore, there has been no tendency in these other branches of government to imitate the Federal government by reducing in recent years the volume of interest payments, for the interest total for State and local governments continued to rise between 1918 and 1925, the figure for the latter year being two-thirds greater than that for 1918. The figures

TABLE CXXVII

ESTIMATED INTEREST PAYMENTS
MADE BY ALL BRANCHES OF GOVERNMENT
IN THE CONTINENTAL UNITED STATES

(MILLIONS OF DOLLARS)

YEAR	TOTAL INTEREST PAYMENTS	INTEREST PAID TO BANKS BY ALL BRANCHES OF GOVERNMENT[a]	INTEREST PAID TO CORPORATIONS OTHER THAN BANKS[b]	INTEREST PAID TO INDIVIDUALS		
				Total	By Federal Government[c]	By State and Local Governments[d]
1909	$ 209	$ 67		$142	$ 15	$127
1910	253	74		178	15	163
1911	269	72		197	16	181
1912	278	77		201	16	185
1913	291	75		216	17	199
1914	312	80		232	17	215
1915	343	86		257	17	239
1916	356	85		272	18	254
1917	454	93		361	88	273
1918	766	170	$ 59	537	285	252
1919	1,412	285	62	1,064	780	284
1920	1,413	267	68	1,078	771	307
1921	1,427	288	74	1,065	741	324
1922	1,524	309	85	1,130	758	372
1923	1,540	334	123	1,083	702	381
1924	1,490	349	168	973	594	379
1925	1,499	379	141	979	560	419

[a] Based upon reports of the U. S. Comptroller of the Currency.
[b] Based upon *Statistics of Income*, published by the U. S. Bureau of Internal Revenue. Figures before 1918 believed to be small.
[c] Based upon the *Annual Reports* of the Secretary of the Treasury.
[d] Based upon *The Financial Statistics of States* and upon *The Financial Statistics of Cities*, published by the U. S. Bureau of the Census.

just mentioned refer to the payments of interest to individuals. In addition, the various branches of government have been increasing the volumes of interest payments to banks and other corporations, the banks receiving more than five times as much income from this source in 1925 as in 1909. Figures for other corporations for years prior to 1918 are not available, but, since 1918, these payments have also been expanding at a rapid rate.

TABLE CXXVIII

AMOUNTS AND PERCENTAGES OF THE ENTIRE REALIZED
INCOME OF INDIVIDUALS RECEIVED FROM
EACH BRANCH OF GOVERNMENT

	INCOME IN MILLIONS OF DOLLARS RECEIVED FROM				PER CENT OF REALIZED INCOME[a] RECEIVED FROM			
YEAR	All Branches of Government	Federal Government	State and County Government	Municipal Government and Schools	All Branches of Government	Federal Government	State and County Government	Municipal Government and Schools
1909	$1,554	$ 590	$187	$ 777	5.25	1.99	.63	2.62
1910	1,678	601	205	872	5.34	1.91	.65	2.77
1911	1,767	606	223	938	5.55	1.90	.70	2.94
1912	1,862	630	243	989	5.48	1.85	.72	2.91
1913	1,981	664	265	1,053	5.55	1.86	.74	2.95
1914	2,093	691	271	1,132	5.87	1.94	.76	3.18
1915	2,192	714	271	1,207	5.89	1.92	.73	3.24
1916	2,297	753	272	1,272	5.31	1.74	.63	2.94
1917	3,044	1,418	276	1,350	5.93	2.76	.54	2.63
1918	6,278	4,531	311	1,437	10.39	7.50	51	2.38
1919	6,136	4,123	362	1,651	9.30	6.25	.55	2.50
1920	5,311	2,923	447	1,940	7.18	3.95	.60	2.62
1921	5,629	2,842	535	2,252	8.88	4.48	.84	3.55
1922	5,792	2,709	624	2,459	8.79	4.11	.95	3.73
1923	5,783	2,555	604	2,623	7.78	3.44	.81	3.53
1924	5,896	2,387	746	2,762	7.64	3.09	.97	3.58
1925	6,130	2,430	719	2,981	7.48	2.97	.88	3.64

[a] For figures showing entire realized income, see Table XIV.

Income Drawn by Individuals from Various Branches of Government.

Of the realized income of all the individuals of the nation, the percentage derived from all branches of government increased from 5.25 in 1909 to 7.48 in 1925. The changes in percentages for three subdivisions of government are set forth in Table CXXVIII.

Relative to national income the greatest increase in percentages has occurred in the case of the municipal government and schools, the rise between 1909 and 1925 being 1.02 per cent. The least increase in percentages is found in the State and County governments, the percentage of the entire realized income rising in this field from 0.63 to 0.88 in the years between 1909 and 1925.

CHAPTER XVIII

MERCHANDISING AS RELATED TO ENTIRE REALIZED INCOME

Estimating the Volume of Sales at Wholesale and Retail.

Of the processes of estimation giving rise to the figures presented in this volume, one of the most difficult and laborious was that of approximating the total values of goods sold respectively by wholesalers and by retailers. Since the Federal government has never taken a census of trade, these estimates must rest upon highly scattered sources. The chief sources from which the information concerning the various items have been gleaned are indicated in the footnotes to Tables CXXIX and CXXX.

A large proportion of the value of all goods sold is included in the broad category designated as "manufactured articles." The method used in estimating the total value of sales falling in this category is as follows: The detailed list of articles reported upon by the United States *Census of Manufactures* has been checked over item by item, and those items have been set aside which appear to represent articles in such a form as to be ready for use by the consumer. To the sum of the values of such articles, has been added another sum representing the aggregate of fractional estimates of the values of other classes of items, part of which were presumably in form suitable for consumption and part of which were not in this form. To the figures thus obtained, a margin has been added to allow for the wholesalers' profit and for freight and other expenses required for moving the goods from the manufacturer to the retailer.

In the case of practically all the items entered in the various columns of Table CXXIX, it has been necessary to make numerous guesses concerning fractions of total products actually passing into the hands of retailers and also concerning margins obtained by various classes of dealers other than retailers. In most cases, the data so derived represent merely rough approximations. It is believed that the final figures show much more accurately the relative changes from year to year than they do the absolute total values of goods sold. Since all figures are expressed in terms of dollars current in the various years, the absolute changes are not

TABLE CXXIX

ESTIMATED TOTAL VALUE[a] OF
THE VARIOUS CLASSES OF COMMODITIES
SOLD BY WHOLESALERS TO RETAILERS

(MILLIONS OF DOLLARS)

Year	All Classes of Commodities	CLASS OF COMMODITY											
		Eggs[b]	Natural Ice	Poultry[b]	Fish	Flowers and Shrubs	Fruits and Vegetables[b]	Dairy Products[b]	Wood for Fuel	Anthracite Coal[c]	Bituminous Coal[c]	Kerosene, Gasoline, Lubricating Oil[c]	Manufactured Articles[d]
1909	$ 7,960	$146	$115	$ 83	$ 51	$45	$263	$ 533	$14	$129	$157	$ 110	$6,315
1910	8,747	160	140	88	54	43	278	557	16	135	176	120	6,980
1911	8,655	157	139	76	52	37	331	541	16	146	169	134	6,858
1912	9,270	166	158	78	52	43	249	589	17	142	191	163	7,322
1913	9,417	162	181	86	51	41	333	610	18	156	201	251	7,328
1914	9,273	164	128	83	57	36	330	613	17	154	187	267	7,235
1915	8,622	182	78	76	69	42	356	653	17	151	187	290	6,521
1916	9,549	203	118	92	81	50	440	756	21	156	274	482	6,875
1917	13,397	257	191	97	99	67	729	993	34	190	488	677	9,573
1918	16,831	301	228	128	102	77	679	1,253	32	221	423	959	12,428
1919	18,454	369	118	132	150	87	799	1,555	30	243	362	1,111	13,498
1920	25,302	353	246	132	174	107	980	1,538	37	269	473	1,644	19,348
1921	18,395	285	135	74	132	83	664	1,121	34	303	387	1,437	13,740
1922	19,306	258	143	107	122	102	703	1,160	33	189	474	1,635	14,380
1923	22,105	272	121	118	118	112	687	1,390	43	328	539	1,689	16,688
1924	20,983	261	68	138	108	107	642	1,359	34	334	351	1,840	15,740
1925	23,416	309	93	140	113	118	764	1,492	31	235	391	2,220	17,510
1926	22,721*												
1927	21,371*												
1928	21,193*												

[a] Estimated on the basis of published material found in hundreds of books and documents and from nterviews with numerous individuals.

[b] Based mainly upon various reports of the U. S. Department of Agriculture and from the *Census of Agriculture.*

[c] Based upon reports of the U. S. Geological Survey and the U. S. Bureau of Mines.

[d] Based in Census years upon the U. S. *Census of Manufactures.*

* Preliminary estimate.

particularly significant, but it is possible to compare the trend of the sales in one group of commodities with the trend of sales in another.

Table CXXX has been derived from Table CXXIX by multiplying the amounts in Table CXXIX by ratios believed to represent the relationship between the retail price and the wholesale price. Much effort has been expended in collecting data concerning

TABLE CXXX

ESTIMATED TOTAL VALUE[a] OF THE VARIOUS CLASSES OF COMMODITIES SOLD BY RETAIL MERCHANTS TO THEIR CUSTOMERS

(MILLIONS OF DOLLARS)

Year	All Classes of Commodities	Class of Commodity							
		Fresh Meat[c]	Canned Meat[b]	Fruits and Vegetables[c]	Dairy Products[b]	Eggs[c]	Natural Ice	Flowers and Shrubs	Poultry[c]
1909	$18,300	$1,112	$ 522	$ 523	$ 994	$253	$161	$ 99	$132
1910	20,039	1,296	522	579	1,077	272	198	95	134
1911	20,124	1,423	648	714	1,107	269	197	81	126
1912	21,266	1,511	573	708	1,118	283	226	95	127
1913	22,135	1,626	697	690	1,146	295	259	89	135
1914	21,790	1,659	705	689	1,188	295	183	80	131
1915	21,501	1,609	613	754	1,254	317	110	93	123
1916	23,714	1,724	799	896	1,385	344	164	111	141
1917	37,871	2,407	992	1,679	2,097	511	318	181	183
1918	40,703	2,891	1,258	1,312	2,289	522	328	181	209
1919	43,233	2,902	1,268	1,462	2,655	582	156	191	200
1920	45,031	2,224	1,317	1,393	2,160	456	252	186	159
1921	41,048	2,806	1,043	1,381	2,019	468	172	181	118
1922	43,878	2,629	1,077	1,500	2,350	426	204	227	180
1923	51,240	2,780	1,285	1,420	2,459	456	172	250	196
1924	48,540	2,854	1,228	1,334	2,460	431	96	236	215
1925	53,487	3,073	1,372	1,472	2,627	463	131	258	221
1926	54,925*								
1927	56,888*								
1928	57,867*								

[a] Estimated on the basis of material published in hundreds of books and documents and upon interviews with numerous individuals.

[b] Based upon the *Census of Agriculture*, the *Census of Manufactures*, and upon various reports of the U. S. Department of Agriculture.

[c] Based upon the *Census of Agriculture* and various reports of the U. S. Dept. of Agriculture.

[d] Based upon reports of the U. S. Geological Survey and the U. S. Bureau of Mines.

[e] Based largely upon the *Census of Manufactures*, and upon the reports of the U. S. Bureau of Forestry.

[f] Based upon the *Census of Manufactures*, and upon the reports of the National Automobile Chamber of Commerce.

[g] Based mainly upon the reports of the U. S. Bureau of Internal Revenue and prices of tobacco collected from various sources.

[h] Based primarily upon data from *Census of Manufactures* and ratios of retail to wholesale prices collected from numerous sources.

[i] The totals here presented are materially larger than the estimates made by Dr. Paul H. Nystrom. The primary reasons for the discrepancy is that our estimates include a large number of items which he apparently did not take into account, as, for example, ice, flowers and plants, coal, building materials, and farm machinery.

* Preliminary estimate.

such ratios. For the years since 1915, it is believed that the ratios are not widely in error, but, for the earlier years of the period, information is so scanty that the ratios represent nothing but con-

TABLE CXXX—Continued

ESTIMATED TOTAL VALUE* OF THE VARIOUS CLASSES OF COMMODITIES SOLD BY RETAIL MERCHANTS TO THEIR CUSTOMERS

(MILLIONS OF DOLLARS)

YEAR		CLASS OF COMMODITY								
	Fish	Wood for Fuel[e]	Anthracite Coal[d]	Bituminous Coal[d]	Natural Gas[d]	Kerosene, Gasoline, Lubricating Oil[d]	Lumber[e]	Automobiles and Trucks[f]	Tobacco[g]	Other Manufactured Goods[h]
1909	$ 69	$33	$429	$225	$ 37	$ 125	$ 859	$ 212	$1,042	$11,474
1910	74	35	453	254	41	137	757	285	977	12,852
1911	70	37	487	245	44	154	667	325	774	12,756
1912	70	37	461	272	51	186	765	471	785	13,528
1913	70	40	525	280	51	277	722	551	926	13,754
1914	77	40	519	275	57	297	770	569	935	13,321
1915	109	39	507	271	62	325	942	812	901	12,660
1916	117	42	515	316	67	525	890	1,315	992	13,372
1917	147	68	813	540	97	892	1,382	1,894	1,484	22,185
1918	144	66	776	553	91	1,106	1,091	1,608	1,568	24,710
1919	197	60	784	416	88	1,192	1,606	2,279	1,787	25,408
1920	178	60	754	441	86	1,385	2,931	2,001	1,591	27,456
1921	201	73	976	489	110	1,538	994	1,572	1,731	25,177
1922	197	58	606	553	128	1,769	1,870	2,300	1,778	26,026
1923	182	87	1,050	692	144	1,851	2,631	3,384	1,905	30,295
1924	163	76	1,001	521	154	1,997	1,751	2,967	1,942	29,114
1925	169	63	698	562	151	2,379	2,371	3,628	2,013	31,838

sidered guesses. In Table CXXX, a number of items appear which are not included in Table CXXIX. These items consist of articles which, in the main, are sold directly by manufacturers or producers to retailers.

Values of Goods Sold at Wholesale and Retail.

It is believed that the estimates recorded in the various columns of Table CXXX represent general tendencies in the sales of different groups of commodities at retail, and that the aggregate of all retail sales is not very widely in error. For recent years, our preliminary estimates of total sales have been compared with the index numbers of total wholesale and total retail sales prepared by the Federal

TABLE CXXXI

ROUGH ESTIMATES OF THE PERCENTAGES OF ENTIRE REALIZED INCOME PAID TO RETAILERS AND OF REAL VALUE OF SALES PER CAPITA

Year	Value of Retail Sales Current Dollars[a] (Millions)	Entire Realized Income[b] (Millions)	Per Cent of Realized Income Paid to Retailers	Index of Prices of Direct Goods[c] (All Classes)	Real Value of Sales (Millions)	Population of United States[d] (Thousands)	Real Value of Sales per Capita
1909	$18,300	$29,605	61.81	.95255	$19,212	90,508	$212
1910	20,039	31,430	63.76	.97643	20,523	92,422	222
1911	20,124	31,858	63.17	.96973	20,752	93,837	221
1912	21,266	33,977	62.59	.98097	21,679	95,249	228
1913	22,135	35,723	61.96	1.0000	22,135	97,111	228
1914	21,790	35,647	61.13	1.0077	21,623	98,974	218
1915	21,501	37,205	57.79	1.0070	21,352	100,390	213
1916	23,714	43,288	54.78	1.0913	21,730	101,787	213
1917	37,871	51,331	73.78	1.2858	29,453	103,234	285
1918	40,703	60,408	67.38	1.5175	26,822	104,377	257
1919	43,233	65,949	65.56	1.7571	24,605	105,007	234
1920	45,031	73,999	60.85	1.9801	22,742	106,422	214
1921	41,048	63,371	64.77	1.6926	24,251	108,370	224
1922	43,878	65,925	66.56	1.5829	27,720	109,742	253
1923	51,240	74,337	67.58	1.5977	32,071	111,478	288
1924	48,540	77,135	62.93	1.6024	30,292	113,466	267
1925	53,487	81,931	65.28	1.6517	32,383	115,004	282
1926	54,925*	85,548*	64.20*	1.6617	33,053*	116,442*	284*
1927	56,888*	88,205*	64.50*	1.6195*	35,127*	117,980*	298*
1928	57,867*	89,419*	64.71*			119,440*	

[a] See Table CXXX.
[b] See Table VIII.
[c] Derived from figures presented in Table VII.
[d] See Table I.
* Preliminary estimate.

Reserve Board, and the trends have been adjusted to accord with the indices prepared by this agency.

Relation of Retail Sales to Entire Realized Income.

Table CXXXI is devoted to showing the relation between the estimated value of retail sales and the entire realized income of all inhabitants. The fourth column of this table indicates that the percentage of the entire realized income of the people of the United States which they pay out to retailers has fluctuated from year to

year but has shown no very marked trend in either an upward or downward direction. These estimates indicate that the percentage of realized income so expended was relatively low in 1915 and 1916, unusually high in 1917, 1918, and 1923, and moderately low in 1920. It appears that, as a rule, between three-fifths and two-thirds of the realized income of the people of the nation is paid over the counter to retailers.

Per Capita Sales in Dollars of 1913.

The sixth column of Table CXXXI shows the estimated total value of retail sales, when all figures are reduced to terms of 1913 dollars. Sales measured on this basis, increased more than 80 per cent between 1909 and 1927, most of the increase taking place after 1916. Sales per capita, similarly measured, are seen to have remained practically stationary between 1909 and 1916, to have risen to a very high peak in 1917, and to have fallen back to the old level in 1920. After that date, they advanced sharply, and thereafter remained on a level much higher than that characterizing the pre-war period—the per capita figure for 1927 being approximately 40 per cent greater than the per capita figure for 1909.

CHAPTER XIX

GENERAL FACTS RELATED TO INCOME

Place of Residence and Value of Residential Property.

Table CXXXII contains figures representing very rough estimates of the classification of the population of the United States on the basis of whether they do or do not reside on farms, and whether or not they live in their own homes. In this table, there are also estimates of the value of residential property, including

TABLE CXXXII

ESTIMATED POPULATION RESIDING IN
OWNED AND LEASED HOMES
AND THE VALUE OF SUCH HOMES

Year	Population of United States Not Residing on Farms[a]	Population of Cities and Villages Residing in Owned Homes[a]	Value on January 1, of Residential Property, Including ....nd, Occupied by[b]	
	(Thousands)	(Thousands)	Owners (Millions)	Tenants (Millions)
1920	74,848	22,088	$22,642	$32,675
1921	76,778	22,496	26,709	39,212
1922	78,772	22,765	28,178	42,087
1923	81,057	23,182	28,559	42,546
1924	84,077	23,794	28,978	44,805
1925	86,216	24,140	29,380	46,278
1926	88,295	24,458	29,599	47,416
1927	90,209	24,717	29,339	47,874

[a] Derived from figures presented in Table I.
[b] Based upon F. W. Dodge Co. figures of residential construction values.

land, occupied by owners and tenants respectively. The figures in the second column of the table show the rapid growth of the urban population which has taken place since 1920. Although, during these 7 years, the urban population increased 20 per cent, these rough estimates indicate that the proportion living in owned homes increased only 10 per cent. It appears, therefore, that tenancy is on the increase in the cities of the United States. Unfortunately,

TABLE CXXXIII

A SUMMARY OF THE ESTIMATES OF
INCOME FROM MISCELLANEOUS SOURCES
(MILLIONS OF DOLLARS)

Year	Total Miscellaneous Income	Income from Urban Poultry and Gardens	Rental Value of Owned Urban Homes	Interest on Investments in Other Durable Goods	Profits from Urban Cow-Keeping	Net Income from Foreign Investments	Rent Paid to Individuals for Leased Homes Not on Farms
1909	$2,747	$ 70	$ 886	$ 850	$ 52	$ —74	$ 963
1910	2,955	75	935	932	56	—78	1,035
1911	3,020	72	946	966	54	—82	1,064
1912	3,152	80	971	1,018	59	—86	1,110
1913	3,316	78	1,017	1,070	61	—90	1,180
1914	3,468	82	1,052	1,116	61	—85	1,241
1915	3,605	85	1,064	1,187	62	—68	1,275
1916	3,874	100	1,092	1,334	66	—46	1,328
1917	4,330	211	1,100	1,625	86	—51	1,358
1918	5,242	281	1,144	2,302	109	—26	1,433
1919	5,882	197	1,249	2,740	126	—17	1,588
1920	7,415	187	1,465	3,717	135	—8	1,919
1921	7,104	117	1,663	3,015	100	—7	2,216
1922	7,132	120	1,687	2,596	85	354	2,289
1923	7,505	128	1,713	2,834	97	369	2,364
1924	7,764	132	1,757	2,923	95	390	2,467
1925	7,940	147	1,760	3,000	96	419	2,517
1926	8,020 *	144*	1,768	3,023*	102	410	2,572
1927	8,040*	136*	1,746	3,051*	109*	410*	2,587

* For mode of estimation, see the report of this Bureau, entitled *Income in the Various States*, pp. 243-247.

however, the validity of these estimates is open to serious question, especially as regards the number of tenants. The estimates concerning the value of residential property are also based upon very scanty evidence.

Miscellaneous Items of Income.

The items in Table CXXXIII are measures of the magnitude of certain miscellaneous items which enter : to the totals of realized income as presented in the earlier tables in this volume. All of the estimates in this table are extremely rough. There can, however, be no question but that, in the aggregate, these categories do constitute a large and significant part of the entire realized income of the people of the United States. There is some reason for believing that the totals entered in the second column of Table CXXXIII show, in a very general way, the trend that has occurred in the aggregate of these particular types of income.

Magnitude of Errors in Estimates.

The facts and figures presented in the preceding tables and charts are intended to give a picture of the income of the people of the United States and the sources from which this income is derived —a picture as accurate as it is possible to obtain with the amount of time and effort available for this investigation. The reader should, however, understand that practically all of the items here presented are subject to considerable margins of error. Rough guesses concerning the sizes of the errors in different industries appear in Table G, page 33, of *Income in the Various States*. Since these estimates represent nothing but carefully weighed opinions, it does not seem necessary to repeat them here. For more recent years, it is believed that the magnitude of errors has been somewhat reduced. For earlier years, the errors may be greater than those indicated.

The End.

INDEX

INDEX